From VPI to State University

T. Marshall Hahn Jr.

From VPI to State University

President T. Marshall Hahn Jr. and the Transformation of Virginia Tech, 1962–1974

Warren H. Strother and Peter Wallenstein

MERCER UNIVERSITY PRESS I MACON, GEORGIA I 2004

ISBN 0-86554-787-4
MUP/H594

© 2004 Mercer University Press
1400 Coleman Avenue
Macon, Georgia 31207

First Edition.

Book design by Burt & Burt Studio

∞The paper used in this publication meets the minimum requirements
of American National Standard for Information Sciences—Permanence of Paper
for Printed Library Materials, ANSI Z39.48-1992.

Library of Congress Cataloging-in-Publication Data

Strother, Warren H., 1925-

From VPI to state university : President T. Marshall Hahn, Jr. and the transformation
of Virginia Tech, 1962-1974 / Warren H. Strother and Peter Wallenstein.— 1st ed.

p. cm.

Includes bibliographical references (p.   ) and index.

ISBN 0-86554-787-4 (alk. paper)

1. Virginia Polytechnic Institute and State University—History.
2. Hahn, T. Marshall (Thomas Marshall), 1926- I. Wallenstein, Peter. II. Title.

T171.V89S77 2004

378.755'785—dc22

2004009088

For the students, faculty, staff, and alumni of Virginia Tech,

especially from the years of Marshall Hahn's presidency,
July 1, 1962, through December 31, 1974,

and

for our lunchtime companions on Tuesdays at Bogen's:
Lyle Kinnear, Charlie Engel, Al Payne, J. B. Jones, and Jim Montgomery.

Contents

Preface

Warren H. Strother, a former newspaperman, came to Virginia Tech to work with T. Marshall Hahn Jr. in 1964. He stayed more than a quarter century, until his retirement at the beginning of 1991. Before he retired, he began the huge task of researching and writing the history of Virginia Tech during the years of Marshall Hahn's presidency. The foreword to this book, drafted by Warren Strother as he worked on other parts of the book in the early 1990s, recounts the origins of his involvement with the institution and the task of writing its history.

Warren Strother and the University shared a commitment to the task of producing a history of the Hahn years. The school supplied him resources (in particular, time); the office of the provost was committed to the completion of the project. Strother retired from the University, however, and technical and other support became less readily available. Moreover, he ran into serious health problems that, on top of the magnitude of the project, left him more than a bit discouraged. Thus—although he had done an enormous amount of archival work and interviewing, had an insider's knowledge of the people in his story and of many of the events he recounted, and had even drafted numerous sections—the book remained some considerable distance from completion.

Entirely independently, Peter Wallenstein embarked in early 1997 on a short history of the school's first 125 years, an anniversary celebrated later that year. Then, having himself become a historian of the institution, he met Warren Strother, whose unfinished book he came to know about.

He also met a number of other retired Tech people, chief among them J. B. Jones, Charlie Engel, Al Payne, Jim Montgomery, and Lyle Kinnear. The group had long met twice a month for lunch at Bogen's restaurant in downtown Blacksburg, and Wallenstein—though hardly retired—was welcomed into the group.

During summer 2000, Warren Strother and Peter Wallenstein began discussing the feasibility of collaborating on Strother's project to bring it to completion. Wallenstein already had extensive research commitments, however, that left his research time fully taken; and having already deferred some projects to write the 1997 history, he was unwilling to defer his other work again. The most promising way to find time for the Tech project, then, seemed to be to reduce his involvement in teaching for a while—in a manner not so different from how Tech's centennial history was written thirty years earlier. That meant buying Wallenstein out of teaching for a number of courses, and that is where Ray Smoot and the Virginia Tech Foundation came in. The Foundation supplied a grant that made it possible for a great deal of time—time that would otherwise have gone to teaching eight classes beginning in 2001—to be made available instead for working on the book on Marshall Hahn and Virginia Tech. Funds were transferred from the Foundation to the history department to hire a temporary faculty member to teach some of Wallenstein's courses.

In addition to the Virginia Tech Foundation, University archivist Tamara Kennelly helped the project with her knowledge of the sources in her keep, and staff writer Clara Cox shared some of her research into the Hahn years. Rick Griffiths, Jane Wills, and graduate student Mercedes Meeks supplied vital assistance in obtaining the photos. Most of the photographs are from VT Imagebase, Digital Library and Archives, University Archives, Virginia Polytechnic Institute and State University. Several are in hard copy at Special Collections, Newman Library. Still others are from Marshall Hahn's personal collection.

Many of Wallenstein's students in various undergraduate courses—particularly on the history of Virginia Tech in 1997 and 1998—contributed to the finished project, and their essays are cited wherever appropriate. The inclusion of their work also highlights the significance of undergraduate research at a research university—a marker of the kind of institution Hahn brought about and also of Wallenstein's convictions as a history teacher. To be singled out for their contributions are four Virginia

Tech undergraduates—Cordel Faulk, Christopher Johnston, and William "Joel" Charbonneau, each of whom worked with Wallenstein as an undergraduate research assistant in the late 1990s, and Erin Mooney, who, again on this book, did a great deal of the work on the index.

Finally, we could not have written this book without the availability of a great collection of interviews, most of them done by Strother in the late 1980s and early 1990s, and we wish to express our deep appreciation to dozens of people, particularly those cited throughout the book, for their willingness to speak at length of their recollections.

We have sought to address many dimensions of change during the Marshall Hahn years at Virginia Tech—research, teaching, funding, construction, athletics, student policy, faculty governance, alumni relations, and so on. Accompanying each chapter's narrative are various boxes and an occasional illustration. Most features supply flavor and texture to the broader account; they highlight particular individuals, events, or perspectives. Some boxes provide broader context or historical background for the material in the narrative. With limited space, we determined to emphasize the early years when the greatest changes were set in motion. We tried not to neglect the later developments, but it would take a different team of authors of another book to recount them in similar detail.

From VPI to State University embodies multiple voices. To begin with, the authors share a commitment to telling the history of the Marshall Hahn years—in large part—through the voices of the people who experienced that time in the institution's development. In addition, Strother's drafts of many portions of the story have made their way into the final product. Wallenstein's reading of the past—not as a participant in the events under review, but rather as a member of the faculty who came to the school some years after President Hahn left—reflects his training as an academic historian as well as his work on the school's history, and has also done much to shape the final product. In short, Wallenstein edited Strother's work, but he did more than that, for he took the book in directions that it would not otherwise have gone. Yet, in the end, he and Strother agreed to leave each voice with its integrity intact.

The book is a joint product of two writers' work. The journalist/participant did the interviews and much of the archival work, and he drafted much of the book, but he could not complete it. The historian—who could not possibly have started this project from scratch—came in later, added new material, wrestled the story into book format, gave it structure, and reworked the text. The original writer went through the new draft of the entire manuscript, caught some errors, urged the addition of stories, and cheerfully watched it all come together. Neither of us could have done the job alone, but together we have brought it to completion.

We have multiple audiences in mind for our work. Close to home, many people might well like to see written down a coherent view of changes that they remember being a part of, whether as students, alumni, faculty, staff, or administrators. Many might wish to read accounts of notable people and events from those times. A younger crop of readers can find in these pages an account of the origins of many of the dominant features of the modern Virginia Tech. To the substantial degree that a knowledge of history can offer guidance in the present, providing this history of the Hahn years—the foundational years of the modern institution—might assist the twenty-first century's faculty and administrators to make viable decisions as they navigate their own times.

In addition, we have written with more distant audiences in mind. Virginia Tech was hardly the only public institution of higher education to experience extraordinary change in the 1960s, so this project is something of a case study of an important era in American higher education. Developments at VPI had their counterparts elsewhere. To some degree, moreover, this book might offer guidance as something of a manual for academic administrators—by deed, Hahn showed how it could be done. Far from Blacksburg, then, this book is designed for students of higher education. It is meant for practitioners of the craft of writing the history of higher education, and it is meant for practitioners of the craft of managing institutions of higher education—as faculty, as administrators, and as members of boards of visitors, trustees, or directors.

To administrators and would-be administrators alike, however, we offer a warning about human agency, individual capabilities, and the larger social, political, and fiscal context. The people whose creativity and energy emerge in this book, though they were certainly fallible, set out to accomplish much, and they did so. The individual at the center of the book, the prime mover in the enterprise of transforming VPI into Virginia Polytechnic Institute and State University, was an extraordinary specimen among academic administrators. He set upon his work at a time that seemed propitious, when much was needed and much could be accomplished. Indeed, he moved mountains, as he promoted change at a school and throughout a state.

The two people listed as authors of this book wish to acknowledge an additional co-author. Duncan Lyle Kinnear (1904-2001) died in June 2001 while we were pushing ahead to complete this book. Kinnear authored the centennial history of Virginia Tech—which itself was brought to completion in 1972, before the Hahn years came to an end—and he concluded his book with a hefty chapter, "The Hahn Administration." That chapter greatly lightened our load as we sought to reconstruct the dozen years of transformation whose history is recounted in these pages. As one of us said to the other on the day of the Deacon's funeral, "The grand old man is gone." But we enjoyed him when he was here, and his work lives on in ours.

Warren H. Strother
Peter Wallenstein

Foreword

Warren H. Strother

Thomas Marshall Hahn Jr., the eleventh president of Virginia Polytechnic Institute (1962-1974), is an unusual person, perhaps the most unusual man I have had the opportunity to know. The first time I really saw him in action was in spring 1963, when I was among several newspaper reporters accompanying Governor Albertis S. Harrison Jr. and his Budget Advisory Board on a tour of each state institution in Virginia, reviewing their budget requests for 1964-1966. I was then a reporter for the *Richmond Times-Dispatch*. We came up from Roanoke aboard a big chartered bus, and President Hahn greeted the visitors and took them into his office in Burruss Hall on the VPI campus. The governor and his budget advisors sat around the conference table then in Dr. Hahn's office while the president outlined VPI's funding requests for the next two years.

Dr. Hahn was terribly young looking, not at all like the reserved and dignified Dr. Walter Newman he had succeeded in 1962 as president of VPI. The young president was cheerful, friendly, and relaxed—or certainly appeared to be so—in welcoming the governor and a group of high-ranking legislators and state officials to the campus. As he was to do many times later, he urged the governor and the budget planners—so they wouldn't have to spend so much on the multitude of problems that result when young people are not educated—to allocate more money to the education of Virginia's young people.

Hahn's close-cropped hair emphasized his unusually youthful appearance; he wore a short crew cut, left over from his brief Navy career at the end of World War II. A tall man, he was only thirty-six years old at the time and anything but a stiffly starched shirt. There was a twinkle in his eyes, and he obviously had a well-developed sense of humor. His presentation to Governor Harrison and the budget group was effective—brief, full of facts and figures, well organized, and persuasive. The man knew how to speak effectively. Beyond that, everyone present was struck by the fact that Hahn used no notes or text. All of it seemed to come off the top of his head; but he had handed out copies of the material he was using, and it came out verbatim. I have never, before or since, seen anyone else with so true a photographic memory, and it made for an impressive performance.

I've been impressed ever since. It is well to say here, up front, that I have been a great admirer of Marshall Hahn over the years since I first came to know him. Undoubtedly, Hahn and his colleagues, myself included, sometimes made mistakes, misjudged some things, and generally proved very human. But I do not think I have ever met anyone with greater ability or quicker wit. He had a marvelous ability to think ahead, to look down the road and figure out what should happen in the weeks and months and years ahead. Often, being so keenly aware of the possibilities, he could significantly influence what actually happened. His ability to relate to people, to talk to them in their own terms without making them feel he was talking down to them, has always been impressive and effective.

But to return to the early 1960s: I had known something of Marshall Hahn since the Board of Visitors selected him in early December 1961 to succeed Dr. Walter Newman as president of Virginia Polytechnic Institute. By sheer coincidence, I had written the story for the *Richmond Times-Dispatch*. There was no news conference and no advance speculation—just a phone call from Paul Saunders as I sat at my desk in the *T-D* newsroom: "Come on over, we've got a little news story for you." Paul, then the editor of the *Southern Planter*, was a member of the VPI Board of Visitors, and he and Guy L. Furr, then rector of the Board, were at the John Marshall Hotel a block away. If I remember correctly, Stuart Cassell was with them, too. The Board had met for much of that wintry afternoon and indeed had named T. Marshall Hahn Jr. the VPI president-elect. They gave me a biographical sketch and a photograph of Hahn and responded to a few questions. The story and accompanying photograph appeared in the next day's editions of the paper, as well as in other papers around the state distributed by the Associated Press. Never in my wildest dreams did I imagine that VPI's new president, the man about whom I wrote in the dusk of that wintry day, would so profoundly affect my professional and personal life.

I had the opportunity to see Dr. Hahn several times in the early 1960s, each in connection with my work for the newspaper. Every year, the *Times-Dispatch* published a special Virginia economic development section, and I wrote regularly for it. I visited the campus at Blacksburg once or twice to interview Hahn for articles about economic development and the growing Virginia economy. He was outspoken about the need for more rapid economic growth in Virginia and the role of education in sustaining and expanding economic growth, especially since finding ways and means to strengthen the state's economy was a major theme of Governor Harrison's administration. Marshall Hahn and Stuart Cassell, Hahn's right-hand man in dealing with the General Assembly, were also very much in evidence at the 1964 General Assembly session, working the halls and committee rooms. My primary General Assembly assignment for the newspaper was the developing 1964-1966 state budget. Hahn knew the value of the media in his quest for state funding, and I got to know him pretty well.

Then, in autumn 1964, I came to Blacksburg to work for Dr. Hahn and Virginia Polytechnic Institute, and it changed the focus of my professional life. Working closely with Marshall Hahn, I came to admire and respect him all the more, as well as Stuart Cassell. They turned out to be fine people. As university administrators and as human beings, they were sensitive, intelligent men of character and integrity. I suppose I worked as closely with Dr. Hahn, day in and day out, for the ten years we were together as anyone on the campus, with the exception of Lon Savage, his executive assistant, and other members of Hahn's immediate office staff.

Marshall Hahn is a strong man, intellectually and emotionally, and once he makes a decision and determines a course of action, he is awesomely tenacious in achieving what he sets out to do. The VPI president was a demanding, hard-driving leader, with enormous energy, who worked extremely hard himself. But the work environment was not unpleasant or burdened with hostility. At least among the Burruss Hall staff, most people maintained their sense of humor, Hahn included. He was fun to work for; his inspiration and vision were infectious; and everyone around him worked hard.

I also came to know and love many other people at VPI in those early years. They were full of bright, bold ideas and worked hard at transforming VPI into a major state university, to better serve Virginia and its citizens. Perhaps the best part of all was living and working among so many young people, the VPI students. It has been a joy, year after year, to see the transformation of newly arrived freshmen through the early years of adulthood and to anticipate, even see, the impact of all those bright youngsters when they began their careers. I know of no other professional activities in which one has better opportunities to meet and know so many young people than those associated with a university campus. There are hundreds of one-time VPI students whom I remember fondly and for whom I have great respect and affection. Now in retirement I can only salute them and wish them well.

Another large part of one's affection for an institution such as Virginia Tech has to be the great admiration one has for its graduates, the alumni. Many VPI alumni whom I knew well had graduated long before I came to work on the campus. I do not think VPI has produced a more impressive group of former students, individually and collectively, than those who were students in the decades of the 1920s, 1930s, and 1940s—and who, in the 1960s and 1970s, were active alumni and in many cases members of the faculty, the administration, or the Board of Visitors. Almost all were of the first generation in their families to have a chance at formal education beyond high school, and they obviously made the most of it. Perhaps VPI, as it operated in those decades, was the kind of institution best suited in the context of that era to accommodate those particular young people and provide the kind of education they needed most.

In the following pages, I attempt to recount some of the major concerns of Marshall Hahn and his colleagues as well as to recall a few less serious matters during his twelve-and-a-half-year administration. Having been so much a part of the Hahn years at VPI, in no way could I have been an unbiased observer, although I attempt to be as objective as possible. I have written in third person (other than in this foreword), hoping that it would help me be more objective. Others less personally and emotionally involved in that era at VPI may wish to reexamine VPI's development and Dr. Hahn's impact upon higher education in Virginia during the years he was president.

Perhaps the larger part of the source material for this book came from Dr. Hahn's VPI files, which have since been transferred to the archives in Special Collections in Newman Library. Some of it came from various other VPI documents, publications, and papers, including personal files. Other material came from external publications of various types, including my old newspaper, the *Times-Dispatch*. Most of the remainder came from personal interviews with many people—former governors and other state officials, active and retired VPI faculty and administrators, and others. I have talked with Dr. Hahn himself at great length concerning his work at VPI and in Virginia. Ultimately, some of the material had to come from my personal memories, which I have rendered as faithfully as possible.

Prologue

In late October 1966, as Virginia Polytechnic Institute was undergoing a periodic accrediting review, the Visiting Committee of the Southern Association of Colleges and Schools (SACS) spent a week on the campus in Blacksburg. Under the direction of Dr. Herman E. Spivey, vice president of the University of Tennessee, the twenty-five-member group surveyed the state of the school before reporting on its findings. The group reviewed self-study materials; conducted extensive interviews with VPI administrators, faculty, staff, and students; and sent representatives to look at the VPI branch at Danville.

Among the materials that had been supplied to the visitors was a two-volume report that had been prepared on the campus during a yearlong self-study. The self-study had produced "a vast body" of material, as the Visiting Committee observed, "for subsequent evaluation and action by VPI leaders." In fact, the visitors called the institution's report "a remarkably uninhibited compendium of VPI faculty and student opinion about everything pertaining to VPI as it is thought to be and as it is hoped it may become."[1]

On the scene, as it was, in the transition between what VPI was "thought to be" in 1966 and what it was "hoped it [might] become" in the years ahead, the Visiting Committee displayed some amazement at what it discovered. As it stated in its own report,

VPI for the past several years seems to have undergone more change than in the preceding quarter century, and it is hard to imagine a more dynamic institution. This dynamic activity...happened so fast and so recently that many of the campus leaders are not quite clear yet what the score is right now, although they think they like it, whatever it is. No doubt in the near future VPI will need to slacken the pace a little...to allow all to become clear as to what the changes in organization, mission, and direction imply. ...None of this comment is intended to be negative (quite the contrary), but only indicative of the tempo and dynamism of VPI. ...There is no doubt that VPI is a better institution than ever, and is headed upward, steeply and rapidly.[2]

In those few sentences, the twenty-five members of the Visiting Committee, all outsiders to Virginia Tech, summed up their assessment of the tremendous changes underway at the school. A fuller investigation of those "past several years"—and the next several as well—will clarify the nature and origins of the changes that so struck the visitors. How did the school undertake and accomplish a transformation that, within the first five years of T. Marshall Hahn's presidency, had it "headed upward, steeply and rapidly"? Regardless of whether the reinvention of the school did, in fact, "slacken the pace a little" over the next few years, what new image and institution emerged?

How, in short—by what means and in what ways—did Virginia Polytechnic Institute change between 1962 and 1975? What was the role of the dynamic new president of the institution? How did the school relate to broader trends in society, politics, and higher education—in Virginia, in particular, and across America in general—during the 1960s?

By 1962, when Hahn became president of VPI, the school was ninety years old, and it had always been one of the nation's land-grant schools— "agricultural and mechanical" (A&M) institutions that traced their origins to the Morrill Act passed by Congress in 1862 during the Civil War. Before assuming the presidency at VPI, Hahn earned his undergraduate degree in physics at the University of Kentucky, earned a doctorate in physics at the Massachusetts Institute of Technology, taught in the physics department at the University of Kentucky, chaired the physics department for five years at VPI, and served for three years as dean of the college of arts and sciences at Kansas State University.

All four of those schools—Kentucky, MIT, VPI, and Kansas State—were (and are) members of the land-grant fraternity, so they shared certain characteristics that eased a person's transition, whether as faculty member or academic administrator, from one to another. Only two of the four were in the South, however, and VPI was more typical of the land-grant schools in the South than of those outside the region.

Many of the greatest changes of the Hahn years at VPI are best understood in the context of its being first and foremost a Southern public land-grant institution. A technical school, it had built only a rudimentary base in the liberal arts, but it had developed considerable strengths in agriculture, engineering, and business administration. Originally a teaching school, its research strengths had shown considerable growth in recent years, but they continued to emphasize agriculture and the sciences, and most departments had limited graduate programs, if any at all. VPI was largely a technical institution, an undergraduate school, a teaching college.

In other ways, too, VPI revealed its land-grant origins, but in ways that pointed to the regional peculiarities of the Southern variant. A school restricted to male students during its first half century, it had never enrolled many women, and it had recruited few women to the faculty. Before the 1950s, the state of Virginia maintained a rigid system of racial segregation in public education, from first grade through graduate school, so VPI never enrolled an African American student until 1953—and never more than four at a time before 1962. When President Hahn took the helm in 1962, most male freshmen and sophomores were required to live in barracks and participate fully as members of the Corps of Cadets. It was an overwhelmingly white, male, military environment.

None of these various dominant characteristics survived the 1960s without considerable dilution. Significant change in any one of them would have made for a different school. Significant change in several of those features—in fact, in all of them—combined to make the school such a different place in 1974 (or even by 1966) than it had been in 1962 as to amaze people who, based on what the school had long been, thought they knew what to expect. Captain Hahn steered the ship in new directions and propelled it to new realms of excellence.

From the perspective of a twenty-first-century observer of the events of the 1960s, Virginia Polytechnic Institute's first eight or nine decades provide a baseline from which to measure the transformation that took place in its tenth decade, on the watch of—and driven by the energy and vision of—President T. Marshall Hahn Jr. By 1974, Hahn's last year at the helm, Virginia Tech was taking its place among the nation's comprehensive public universities, open to a multiracial and coeducational constituency. It offered undergraduate degrees and master's degrees in such disciplines as history and political science. It had doctoral programs in a wide range of studies, and it had—or soon would have—top-notch undergraduate programs in such areas as theater arts and music. Across the curriculum, its faculty members were recruited, nurtured, and evaluated as researchers as well as teachers. VPI had become a university—Virginia Polytechnic Institute and State University.

By the time Marshall Hahn decided to relinquish the VPI presidency, his footprints were all over the school and all over the state. He anticipated, articulated, and spurred changes in Virginia's social, political, and economic spheres. From the time of his appointment as president, he spoke to multifarious groups across the Commonwealth, networked with political leaders, and proselytized the gospel of enhanced public support for higher education. Such support, he said, would pay rich dividends for Virginia and its citizens. Across the 1960s, Hahn left his stamp on successive blueprints for an upgraded system of higher education. He pushed hard with the governor's office and in the legislature to secure the funding and policy changes he needed for Blacksburg and desired for the entire system. Especially given Hahn's wider view, by no means was the transformation of higher education in Virginia restricted to the Blacksburg campus.

This book's publication year marks the fiftieth anniversary of Dr. Hahn's arrival at VPI in 1954 to head the physics department. It marks the thirtieth anniversary of his stepping down in 1974 after twelve and a half extraordinary years as president of Virginia Tech.

[1] Southern Association of Colleges and Schools, Visiting Committee, *Report on Virginia Polytechnic Institute, October 23-26, 1966*, 1.

[2] Ibid., 1-2.

1: Convergence—A Man and a School

Dr. T. Marshall Hahn Jr. first came to Blacksburg and the Virginia Polytechnic Institute in June 1954. Only twenty-seven years old at the time, the precocious physicist was recruited from the University of Kentucky to replace Professor Frank L. "Scribe" Robeson ('02), a VPI faculty member for some fifty years who had asked to be relieved of the headship of the physics department. If Hahn's appointment as a full professor and head of the department while still so young surprised some of his new colleagues, his energetic development of physics at VPI in the next five years no doubt surprised them even more.

Marshall Hahn to 1954

Thomas Marshall Hahn Jr. was born December 2, 1926, in Lexington, Kentucky. There his photographic memory and high IQ began to show up early, and there he grew into a young man. His father, Thomas Marshall Hahn Sr., taught physics at the University of Kentucky.

Hahn and his two siblings—David and Elizabeth, both younger than he—grew up in Lexington during the Great Depression, so there wasn't much money. Their father did his Ph.D. work at Chicago during the summers when he wasn't teaching. By the time Marshall Jr. was old enough to begin school, his father took a year off to complete his Ph.D. under Arthur Compton at Chicago, and his oldest son began first grade in a public school near the university on Chicago's South Side. His teacher, soon recognizing that Marshall was well beyond the beginner level, moved him up to second grade, which he completed before the family returned to Lexington.

More than a half-century later, Hahn still vividly recalled the Depression days in Lexington—his newspaper route, the part-time job in the florist shop to earn money, and his chores in the family garden, growing vegetables. He disliked green beans forever afterward because he often had to fill up on them as a teenager and would become hungry again within a couple of hours. Always an outstanding student, Hahn was permitted to skip the ninth and twelfth grades—he did not complete high school before going to college.

Having skipped three years of school, Hahn Jr. was but fifteen years old when he enrolled at the University of Kentucky shortly before the United States entered World War II. While attending the university, he saved money by living at home with his parents and earned enough at the florist shop for books and tuition. He also gained more time. Attending UK on an accelerated wartime schedule, he graduated in two-and-a-half years, at age eighteen, in 1945.

Then he went into the Navy. He spent a year teaching physics at the Naval Academy Preparatory School at Bainbridge, Maryland, where his students were sailors who, having been selected to go to the Naval

Academy at Annapolis, were returned from active duty in the fleet. Hahn himself declined an opportunity to enter the Naval Academy. He had had enough of undergraduate education, and life in the Navy did not appeal to him.

After his brief naval service, he took a job for a year as a civilian scientist at the Naval Ordnance Laboratory at White Oak, Maryland. By that time he was weighing career choices, which he had narrowed to medicine and physics. He opted for physics, applied to several universities, and accepted a graduate assistantship at the Massachusetts Institute of Technology (MIT).

The year at the Naval Ordinance Lab in suburban Washington also brought together Marshall Hahn and Margaret Louise "Peggy" Lee of Dinwiddie County, Virginia. Seeking female companionship, Hahn visited the Methodist Church in Hyattsville, Maryland, one Sunday morning. The situation looked promising, so he returned in the evening for a Christmas program that the Methodist Youth Fellowship presented to residents of the Methodist Home for the Aged there in Hyattsville.

Hahn recalls that the young ladies of the church were having trouble serving ice cream, which was frozen solid. Displaying what proved to be characteristic imagination and force of will, Marshall solved the problem by chopping the dessert with a meat cleaver. In the process, he met Peggy Lee, a graduate of Madison College (now James Madison University) who was teaching school in Hyattsville. In the months that followed, a romance developed. Much of their courtship, however, took place through the US mail, for Marshall soon went off to MIT.

The assistantship at MIT, together with two years' GI Bill benefits, was enough to see him through graduate school, which he dispatched at his characteristic fast pace, completing the degree in 1950 at the age of twenty-three. At MIT, however, perhaps for the first time in his life, he found himself in truly fast company. Working with his MIT classmates, he perceived several of them to be potential Nobel Prize winners who might well outshine him. Instead of pure research, therefore, he turned his mind toward university teaching—and academic administration.

Marshall Hahn and Peggy Lee married in 1948. By the time they arrived at VPI in 1954, they were the parents of two children, William, born in Massachusetts in 1949, and Elizabeth, born in 1953 at Lexington. Their youngest child, Anne, was born in Blacksburg.

From Kentucky to VPI

Armed with a brand-new doctorate from MIT, Marshall Hahn accepted an appointment in 1950 as associate professor in the physics department at the University of Kentucky. For Hahn, going to Lexington, Kentucky, meant returning home. He spent four years at UK. Midway through that time, he became a full professor, director of graduate studies in physics, and director of Kentucky's nuclear accelerator laboratories. By his own account, he also learned a great deal about how to get along well with people in general and colleagues in particular, as mentors took him aside and counseled him on tactics and demeanor.

Meanwhile, in Blacksburg, Virginia, Dr. Louis A. Pardue was President Walter Newman's vice president (then VPI's chief academic officer). Pardue had known the Hahn family in Kentucky. Indeed, Pardue had been a friend and colleague of Marshall Hahn Sr., who for many years was a member of the physics faculty at Kentucky. Pardue left Kentucky in 1950, about the same time Marshall Hahn Jr. arrived there as a new associate professor.

Four years later, Pardue had a role in Hahn's move to VPI as head of the physics department. Pardue was in Lexington on a visit, Hahn recalled years later, "and mentioned to me, I don't know whether he did this with any intention or not, that the department head would be retiring" at VPI. Hahn was going gangbusters at Kentucky, but he realized that VPI promised a significant opportunity. For one thing, "I was sort of capped out at Kentucky"—he had gone about as far as he could in department administration—since the department head there was a fairly young man himself.[1] As for VPI, unlike Kentucky it had no real graduate program or research program, so Hahn would be in a position to build those activities. After applying for the job and accepting an offer, build them he did.

During his five years in the VPI physics department, Hahn often traveled throughout the state, seeking sources of funding and equipment for his physics laboratories, recruiting physics students, or speaking at alumni meetings. His efforts to find support for physics soon brought him into close contact with Dr. John Redd "Jack" Hutcheson, who introduced him to the realities of Virginia politics and the Byrd Organization, the long-dominant political group headed by US Senator Harry F. Byrd Sr. of Berryville. Hahn found Jack Hutcheson well informed and immensely helpful, and the young professor, a newcomer to Virginia, developed a growing familiarity with the Old Dominion—its society, its geography, and its politics, including its political leaders.

1.2 Dr. John Redd Hutcheson (1886-1962; class of '07) served nearly a quarter of a century as director of VPI's Agricultural Extension Service, and then he served for a time (1945-1947) as president of VPI. As the multitude of World War II veterans flooded the campus on the GI Bill, however, Hutcheson fell ill, and Dr. Walter Newman (Hutcheson's vice president) and Stuart Cassell (business manager) had to take over running the school. Hutcheson recovered, but meanwhile the VPI Board of Visitors had reassigned him as chancellor and appointed Dr. Newman to succeed him as president. In effect, Hutcheson was on special assignment for the Board. In this capacity, in 1948 he was principal organizer and became the first president of the VPI Educational Foundation (now the Virginia Tech Foundation). Retiring as chancellor in 1956 to devote all of his energies to the Foundation, Hutcheson remained active on its behalf until his death in January 1962. A campus building, Hutcheson Hall, commemorates "Dr. Jack" and his older brother, Thomas Barksdale Hutcheson ('06), who was dean of Agriculture from 1946 until his death in 1950. A plaque inside the building recognizes each for having given a lifetime of service "to agriculture, Virginia, and alma mater."

It soon became apparent to Hahn that an enormous window of opportunity was opening for higher education in Virginia, and especially for VPI. As he saw with increasing clarity, higher education in Virginia would have to grow rapidly in the decades immediately ahead. As Virginia was located across the Potomac River from Washington, DC, and not far from the populous Northeast, the state's economics and demographics were changing rapidly. The changing technology undergirding the economy required larger numbers of college graduates. At the same time, a combination of high birthrates after World War II, significant migration into Virginia, and strong economic growth would soon produce large numbers of students seeking college admissions. VPI, especially with its scientific and technical orientation, should be in the forefront of an expanding state system of colleges and universities. Already it was the largest institution of higher education in Virginia, even though enrollment was largely restricted to white male students and the school had a compulsory military system for most freshmen and sophomores.

Indeed, President Walter Newman had already, despite a host of obstacles, done much to build the foundation of a university in Blacksburg. The greatest obstacle, perhaps, was Virginia's extremely conservative political structure, maintained by a scheme of legislative apportionment that left most power in rural hands and a highly restricted electorate that gave virtually all power to whites. With the help of the poll tax and control of the county courthouses, the organization reduced the likelihood that many unreliable would-be voters, especially black Virginians, would cast ballots. Senator Byrd's dominant organization of conservative Democrats grew out of an alliance of Virginia business and agricultural interests. The General Assembly, heavily dominated by rural senators and delegates, was not generous in its appropriations for public higher education—or for most other state functions.

Another problem was the weight of history and tradition at the Blacksburg school itself. As to curriculum and clientele, all state institutions of higher education in Virginia were limited as to who could attend them and what they could study there. VPI was a technical school, focused on practical, world-of-work professions and occupations, especially those related to engineering and agriculture. Such an understanding was rooted in the state's post-Civil War history, in its political leadership, and in the mindset of its higher education establishment, including many of the faculty and staff of VPI. Nothing in the Virginia statutes made it so, although that concept had been reinforced over the years by various state study commissions, by the VPI Board of Visitors, and even by Walter Newman himself in his inaugural address. The University of Virginia was the nearest thing to a genuine university in Virginia—the only school with a broad liberal arts curriculum and a wide array of graduate programs. Virginia's other institutions of higher education were structured much more narrowly.

At least some of the changes Professor Hahn saw occurring in Virginia convinced President Newman that VPI, if it was to continue serving the state effectively, had no choice but to break out of its traditional curricular limitations. The state was changing, and the school must too. Newman spoke of the evolution of various other land-grant institutions in the nation into "true public universities" designed to meet the needs of an

1.3 VPI's first ninety years—The Virginia General Assembly established VPI in 1872 to take advantage of the benefits of the Morrill Land-Grant College Act, which had been passed during the Civil War. For each vote a state had in the electoral college—that is, for each of its members of the US Senate or the US House of Representatives—Congress had allocated 30,000 acres of federal land in the western territories to be sold. The proceeds would be used to support at least one agricultural and mechanical college. The income from the investment of the proceeds was to be used primarily for operating costs—none of it for land and no more than 10 percent for buildings.

In many cases, then, a state—once its people accepted the opportunity and sought to put the funds to work—looked for local contributions of some sort to provide a place to establish the college. That became available to Virginia when a small Methodist boys' school near Blacksburg—the Preston and Olin Institute, chartered in 1854 but by 1872 unable to continue operations on its own—signed over its real property (one building on five acres) to be converted into a land-grant institution, and Montgomery County pledged $20,000 in cash. The question might never have arisen, except that in the early 1870s both Virginia Military Institute and the University of Virginia (as well as a host of other schools) badly wanted the money; each had substantial support in its quest, and, in effect, each blocked the other's success.

The same act that authorized Virginia Agricultural and Mechanical College, as it was called, near the little town of Blacksburg also designated a new school for black Virginians, Hampton Normal and Agricultural Institute, as a place where black Virginians could benefit from the Morrill Act. Black students would not be admitted to the Blacksburg school. At that time, black Virginians made up a bit more than 40 percent of the state population, whites something less than 60 percent. Hampton would get one-third of the federal funds, and VAMC would get two-thirds.

In the years to come, Congress added to the land-grant institutions' funds. One example was the Hatch Act of 1887, which propelled the schools into supporting experiment stations and conducting significant research so as to enhance agricultural productivity. Another was the Second Morrill Act, passed in 1890, which increased the funds available to the schools. Yet another was the Smith-Lever Act of 1914, which added extension work to the schools' opportunities and obligations, with the intent that the work of the land-grant schools would be brought more directly to the attention of rural people across the state. By the time Walter S. Newman or T. Marshall Hahn became president of the Blacksburg school, it had grown significantly in size, in funds, and in operations, and it had been renamed Virginia Polytechnic Institute.

In some cases, a land-grant school is also the flagship campus of the state university. Examples are the University of Kentucky, West Virginia University, the University of Tennessee, the University of Florida, and the University of Maryland. In other states, such is not the case. Thus, there developed both VPI and the University of Virginia; North Carolina State in Raleigh and the University of North Carolina in Chapel Hill; Clemson and the University of South Carolina; Texas A&M and Texas; Auburn and Alabama; Mississippi State and Mississippi; Kansas State and Kansas.

entire state rather than "any specific clientele." He characterized such "true public universities" as having "no choice" but, rather, a "responsibility…to serve all the young people of the state who can benefit from higher education and who wish to attend."[2]

By the early 1960s, Dr. Newman was saying in official reports that VPI, "although chartered as an agricultural and mechanical college," was already "functioning as a public university in her educational contributions to the welfare of the state and the nation."[3] Few people paid attention. But President Newman's goal for VPI was to break out of its traditional limitations and become a comprehensive land-grant university. In fact, he achieved significant growth in terms of physical plant development, enrollment, and academics, especially in the latter part of his fifteen-year administration. The foundations were in place on which Marshall Hahn would eventually build a university along the lines of which Walter Newman had dreamed.

Interlude in Kansas

The Hahns bonded with Blacksburg, but Marshall had his sights set on further advancement in academic administration. In 1959, he accepted an appointment as dean of the College of Arts and Sciences at Kansas State University. When he left VPI that summer, he could be proud of what he had accomplished during his five years in Blacksburg. Physics enrollments had tripled, and he had developed a new master's program in nuclear engineering as well as a Ph.D. program in physics. In fact, Hahn had begun recruiting graduate candidates for the Ph.D. in physics even before he had a Ph.D. program in place, but the program was there when the first candidates were ready to receive their degrees.[4]

In Hahn's five years at VPI, he was able to obtain more than $635,000 in research grants, largely from the Atomic Energy Commission and the National Science Foundation. One of them paid for a nuclear reactor simulator for teaching purposes, the first in the nation. Hahn also helped Dr. Newman persuade the General Assembly to appropriate almost a million dollars for a new physics building, subsequently named Robeson Hall. The building was completed after Hahn went to Kansas State, but the $350,000 UTR-10 teaching and research reactor built into it was paid for from one of Hahn's AEC grants. He returned from Kansas State in 1960 to make the dedicatory address for the new reactor.[5]

1.4   Lyle Kinnear on Walter Newman and Marshall Hahn—Lyle Kinnear offered an informed, perceptive assessment of Newman and Hahn and how the accomplishments of one related to those of the other. Newman, he said, "laid the foundation for the expansion into the university. That is just as clear cut. There is no question about it. You can go back and read his reports to the Board of Visitors, and you can see him pushing at the Board, preparing the Board to expand." Kinnear went on:

> I'm not going to say he had the vision to expand like Dr. Hahn did. When Dr. Hahn came in, he didn't know these things couldn't be done. See, Newman came to VPI from the State Board of Education. He was a native Virginian, and he knew the resentment every time VPI tried to get outside of Agriculture, Engineering, and Business. So, he didn't want to precipitate any fight, but he simply saw that we had to move. And then when Hahn came in, he didn't realize that we couldn't do these things, so he would go ahead and do them. Now, we would sit back in amazement and wait for the heavens to fall in. When Dr. Hahn would propose certain things, we'd say to ourselves, "Why, the state will be on us like a chicken on a June bug." But they didn't. Of course, the whole condition had changed by that time too. Even the legislature could see the need for expansion…. Dr. Hahn could be a very persuasive and a very eloquent speaker and could point out the need for it.

Kinnear came back to the point. "Newman left Hahn with an institution ready to move ahead, to become a university. He left the institution with the best rapport with the state we've ever had in the history of VPI. If anybody tries to say that Newman didn't lay the foundation," he began, and then he qualified the thought. "Maybe he wasn't [fully] aware that he was going towards it, but he laid it. And he paved the way for the acceptance of it. No question about that in my mind." Newman's credentials as an authentic Virginian, together with his long experience throughout the state, in his many capacities in public education at all levels, gave him advantages that proved important. As Kinnear explained, "everybody knew him. He could get up with [any] group, and he could relate to the group…. And he would tell the VPI story anywhere he went. And he was always telling people 'VPI.' He left Hahn two things that anybody would want—an institution ready to expand, maybe not too sure of the direction to expand, but they wanted to expand in the direction of increasing its offerings. And he left the institution with a fantastic amount of good will." (Dunn interview with Kinnear, 15, 22-23)

When Hahn was leaving VPI to go to Kansas State, the possibility of returning as president occurred to him, but he made no commitments to himself or to anyone else. Walter Newman, trying hard to convince him to stay, discussed the possibility of splitting off Vice-President Pardue's responsibilities as director of graduate studies and reassigning them to Hahn if he would remain at VPI. But Hahn declined; he was too far along to turn back. Disappointed, Newman suggested that they stay in touch; he wanted Hahn to come back one day, he said. "He didn't say for what," Hahn later recalled.[6]

Marshall and Peggy Hahn both left Blacksburg for Kansas with some reluctance. Prospects in Virginia and at VPI clearly were something to consider. Moreover, they had made friends, built a new house for their growing family, and were busy making it a home. Still, Marshall felt that the Kansas State opportunity was too good to turn down. Yet Peggy would have stayed if she could. As they began the long drive to Manhattan, Kansas, she recalled years later, "I cried and cried and cried until we got to the West Virginia line, and then I decided I was being very foolish. I would put all of this behind me, and look forward to whatever was coming."[7]

Dr. Hahn's governing consideration was that the opportunity at Kansas State, as dean of the college of arts and sciences at a large Midwestern university, would be invaluable to him were he to move at some point into academic administration at a level higher than the head of a single department or even a dean. VPI had graduate programs but was focused principally on undergraduate education, and it did not even have a college of arts and sciences. Hahn obviously had larger goals in mind. Sensing this, James McCain, president of Kansas State, had asked for and received a commitment from Hahn to stay at Kansas State at least three years, preferably five.[8] Hahn stayed three years. But in that third year, he was prepared to consider new opportunities.

Kansas State, VPI, or the University of South Carolina?

Whatever he may have been thinking in 1959 when he mentioned the prospect that Hahn might someday return to VPI, Walter Newman became specific in autumn 1961. Newman had had a serious heart attack the previous March, and by autumn he decided to retire and so informed the Board of Visitors. He had indeed stayed in touch with Marshall Hahn, and, yes, Hahn would be interested in the VPI presidency. Newman had seen Hahn's extraordinary abilities up close. The retiring president figured they would be sorely needed on the next watch at VPI, and he urged the Executive Committee of the VPI Board of Visitors to appoint Hahn to succeed him. Thus it was that, at a meeting in November of the executive committee, Guy L. "Fuzzy" Furr ('16) of Roanoke, the Appalachian Power Company executive who then was rector of the VPI Board, discussed Hahn's possible interest in returning as president. During the meeting, he picked up the phone and called Hahn in Kansas.[9]

It was almost too late, for Hahn had just returned from an interview regarding the presidency of the University of South Carolina. He had gone to Columbia, South Carolina, to spend a weekend with Gov. Ernest F. "Fritz" Hollings (who also served as chairman of the Board of Trustees of the University of South Carolina). Hollings—he all but offered the USC presidency to Hahn—indicated he would make a formal offer shortly, after talking with two additional candidates. During the time of those final interviews, Furr called Hahn, who accepted the rector's invitation to travel to Richmond to discuss the VPI presidency. Hahn (who three decades later recalled the incident with some amusement) got back in touch with Governor Hollings, who immediately offered him the South Carolina position, but Hahn, instead of accepting, went to meet with the VPI Board of Visitors and President Newman.

Dr. Newman's enthusiasm in his advocacy of Dr. Hahn as his successor seemed perhaps excessive to some of the Board members.[10] Hahn easily lived up to Newman's billing, though, and the Board offered him the VPI presidency. He accepted forthwith, and called Governor Hollings back to reconfirm his unavailability. At a second special meeting of the Board in Richmond on December 4, 1961—two days after he turned thirty-five—Hahn was formally appointed president of Virginia Polytechnic Institute, effective July 1, 1962. For some years, he would be the youngest land-grant college president in the entire nation.

Hahn took the job at VPI, not the one at South Carolina. Leaving the deanship at Kansas State, he returned to the South. After three years away, he and Peggy returned to Virginia, to Blacksburg, to VPI. He stayed within the land-grant orbit.

1.5 Marshall Hahn, VPI, and South Carolina—Regarding the two schools' recruitment of Marshall Hahn to be their next president, one published version—based in part on an interview with Fritz Hollings—has it that Hahn actually accepted the USC job ("in early 1962") but then, while still in Columbia, heard that he had also been offered the VPI position and ended up going to Blacksburg instead (Lesesne, *University of South Carolina*, 156, 381).

Hahn gives a very different account, according to which he had gone to Columbia for his interview, and Hollings made it clear afterwards that two men remained to be interviewed but the job would then be Hahn's if he wanted it. Hahn, for his part, said he would have to consult with Peggy. They kept in touch, but in the course of events Hahn phoned to let Hollings know that he would not be accepting the USC position. Disappointed, Hollings mused that, after seeing Hahn, he did not want to offer the position to either of the other two candidates. Might Hahn, Hollings urged, recommend an alternative candidate?

Hahn, acquainted with the merits of the people he had known at MIT, suggested Thomas F. Jones Jr. A native of Tennessee, Jones had earned his degrees at Mississippi State and MIT, had been on the electrical engineering faculty at MIT when Hahn was there, and since 1958 had been dean of the School of Electrical Engineering at Purdue University. Governor Hollings succeeded in tapping Dr. Jones to take the South Carolina presidency that Dr. Hahn had turned down. Jones took office in Columbia the same day Hahn did in Blacksburg, and he served twelve years, almost as long as Hahn did. During the 1960s at USC, President Jones encountered many of the challenges and attempted many of the changes that President Hahn did at VPI (Lesesne, *University of South Carolina*, ch.4).

Politics and Preparation

No doubt, the VPI president-elect needed all of his considerable energy in winter and spring 1962. He continued his responsibilities at Kansas State and at the same time prepared as well as he could to become chief executive of the institution he had left almost three years earlier. At the same time, he had to work with state officials in Richmond as a new governor took office and the legislature worked on educational policy and the state budget.

In early January 1962, the Virginia General Assembly convened for its biennial session, and Albertis S. Harrison Jr. was inaugurated to succeed Governor J. Lindsay Almond Jr. Quite aside from the biennial budget bill, which contained recommended agency and institutional appropriations for the two years ending in mid-1964, several matters during that Assembly session were of considerable interest to VPI. For example, the school had supported distant branch colleges since the 1930s—a statewide system of community colleges did not develop until the mid-1960s—and legislation was proposed in 1962 that would authorize two additional two-year branch colleges, one at Wytheville and the other in the Clifton Forge-Covington area. Both communities were anxious to obtain VPI branches; steering committees had worked hard in both areas to win approval. The Assembly authorized both branches, for there was little opposition.

Another bill of considerable interest to VPI proposed the creation of a Virginia Associated Research Center (VARC) to manage and operate a space radiation effects laboratory that the National Aeronautics and Space Administration (NASA) wanted to build at Newport News. The laboratory, housing a high-energy particle accelerator, would be used by NASA to investigate the effects of radiation in space, as well as for basic research and associated graduate programs. A cooperative effort of the University of Virginia, Virginia Polytechnic Institute, and the College of William and Mary, it grew out of an existing cooperative graduate program provided by the three institutions for the young engineers and scientists at NASA's Langley Laboratory. NASA-Langley strongly encouraged the proposed legislation, and Governor Harrison was excited about its potential. The VARC proposal occasioned some controversy in the legislature, especially since it would involve three separate state institutions, plus NASA.

The soft-spoken Walter Newman was popular and active in Richmond; he worked closely with the Governor's Office and the General Assembly in his quiet and reserved way and no doubt was in close touch with these developments. In mid-January 1962, President Newman and Rector Furr visited the capitol along with Marshall Hahn, the president-elect, to introduce Hahn to the governor, members of the Assembly, and other key state officials. They paid a courtesy call on Governor Harrison, an introduction that both the governor and the VPI president-elect would long remember. Governor Harrison was a distinguished-looking man, much like one might expect a governor to look—tall, at ease in a dignified way, with a shock of white hair neatly combed and parted. The energetic, youthful-looking Marshall Hahn, with his close-cropped crew cut, projected a different image than had the genial and dignified Walter Newman.

The next day, Dr. Hahn and Dr. Newman attended a conference on the proposed VARC legislation, along with Dr. Floyd Thompson of NASA-Langley; University of Virginia president Dr. Edgar Shannon; and president of William and Mary Dr. Davis Y. Paschall. Also among the conferees were Alvin Duke Chandler, the chancellor of William and Mary, and Dr. William H. McFarlane, the staff director of the State Council of Higher Education. The latter two were strong supporters of the VARC proposed legislation, and of course Floyd Thompson was anxious to see the plan come to fruition.[11] Marshall Hahn, who had been fully informed about the VARC proposal, had reservations about a high-profile research program in high-energy physics in Newport News, but at that point he was mainly listening. The VARC legislation was approved, with the research center set up to operate under a governing board composed of the presidents of the University of Virginia, Virginia Polytechnic Institute, and William and Mary.

Dr. Hahn traveled to Virginia with some frequency in winter and spring 1962; he accepted a number of speaking engagements to talk about the need to strengthen the state's higher educational system. Newspaper profiles of the new VPI president and news accounts of his talks began to appear in the press. Hahn also visited the capitol several times to get to know the legislators. He was not able to be in Virginia, however, when Governor Harrison and the entire General Assembly visited the Roanoke area aboard a special train during the first weekend of February. The trip included a buffet luncheon at VPI, along with a campus tour.

The legislators and others who made the trip to Blacksburg were impressed, for it was a pretty campus, far larger than most of them had imagined. Perhaps their biggest surprise was the huge coliseum then under construction. A Norfolk and Western Railway official later wrote from Richmond that he himself had found the campus development of recent years "astonishing."[12]

Transition

Later in the spring, Hahn arranged with the VPI alumni office to mail a "Dear Friend" letter to the school's 25,000 alumni, written under a letterhead that said, "T. Marshall Hahn, Jr., Manhattan, Kansas." The letter was full of Hahn's enthusiasm for his new job back at VPI. "I know what I'm getting into, and I'm delighted," he said. He also made a strong pitch for financial support from alumni.

Meanwhile, Dr. Newman had obtained Governor Harrison's approval for the president-elect to go to Harvard University to attend a ten-day Institute for New Presidents in the final two weeks of June 1962. VPI would pay the $300 fee, and Hahn would use his own leave time from Kansas State.

First, Hahn had Virginia commitments in early June. On June 6, he spoke to about 1,000 members of the National Holstein-Frisian Association, who came up from their convention in Roanoke to visit the VPI campus. The next day, he made the commencement address at Radford College, where, emphasizing "excellence and intellectual growth," he urged the young women graduates to make strong individual commitments.

The Blacksburg campus itself ended its school year with commencement on Sunday, June 10, when 1,164 candidates received their degrees. Former Governor Colgate Darden was the commencement speaker. Walter Newman received several impressive gifts from the students and faculty at the last VPI commencement over which he presided.

After the festivities in Blacksburg ended, the Hahns left town for a while. They took vacation time in Williamsburg. Then they visited Peggy's family, who operated a dairy farm in Dinwiddie County (see box 4.4). Dr. and Mrs. Hahn left the children there and went on to the Institute at Harvard, where they made new friends and found discussions of the problems and opportunities for college presidents stimulating and pleasant. They looked forward to the great adventure—the opportunities and challenges—that awaited them in Blacksburg.

A New Home in Blacksburg

Back in Blacksburg, Dr. Newman had a problem, and therefore Dr. Hahn had a problem. The Newmans were building a new house in Blacksburg in which to relocate after they left the Grove, the president's home on the campus. It was doubtful, however, that the new house would be finished before July 1, when Newman would no longer be president. Averting an awkward situation, Marshall Hahn simply told Walter Newman not to worry; he would use other accommodations until the

Newmans' new home was completed and they could move into it. The Hahns' furniture was in storage anyway.

Dr. Hahn had planned to stay in a motel until the Newmans could move, but it was unnecessary. He and his family stayed in the home of Professor H. L. "Herb" Manning for the month or more that it took for the new home to be completed. Dr. Manning, head of the industrial engineering department, was on temporary assignment at the US Naval Missile Center at Point Mugu, California.

Writing in late July to thank Manning for the use of the house, Hahn said, "It helps immensely to have a place in which to relax.... Living in a motel this first month would have greatly aggravated things."[13] Shortly after that, former president Walter Newman and his wife moved out of the Grove, and President T. Marshall Hahn Jr., Peggy Hahn, and their three children moved in.

T. Marshall Hahn Jr., President of VPI

Marshall Hahn returned to Virginia Polytechnic Institute in summer 1962 without any illusions as to the challenges he faced as president. But he was keenly aware of real opportunities, and he was confident of his ability to take advantage of them. This was the reason he had turned down Governor Hollings's offer of the presidency of the University of South Carolina. Hahn felt there was a better opportunity to build a nationally prominent university in Virginia than in South Carolina.[14] At age thirty-five, he was brash and energetic enough to tackle one of the more challenging assignments in American higher education. He did so with an enthusiasm that must have been astonishing. When he left Virginia Tech twelve-and-a-half years later, he had succeeded beyond many people's wildest dreams.

By 1974, VPI had developed into a rapidly growing comprehensive university, very different from the institution to which Hahn returned in 1962. It was the "public university" Walter had talked about, a nationally distinguished land-grant university with a thriving liberal arts college, strong professional schools, and an increasingly prestigious graduate school—all (certainly in Hahn's view) with a reasonable balance of teaching and research supplemented by statewide extension work.

Looking back almost three decades later, Hahn recalled that he had accepted the VPI presidency "deliberately, with the idea that with engineering and agriculture, both of which had some national prominence, that you could develop a nationally prominent institution...that you could really build." Growing numbers of would-be students seeking college admission, together with the national concern for education in the wake of the Soviet Union's launching of the Sputnik satellite, had suggested to him that institutions of higher education in general—and VPI in particular—would be able to grow rapidly. Such growth would make it possible to bring in large numbers of new faculty and staff.[15]

"There was real opportunity to stir things up," Hahn explained. "The state needed to be awakened, the institution needed to be vitalized, and the opportunity was just hitting you over the head every morning."

Dr. and Mrs. Hahn, together with their children—Anne, Bill, and Betty—at home at the Grove early in Hahn's presidency. Courtesy of T. Marshall Hahn Jr.

1 Hahn interviews, 27 May 1989, 1 July 1989.

2 Kinnear, *The First 100 Years*, 403.

3 Ibid.

4 Andrew Robeson interview, 15 February 1989.

5 Kinnear, *The First 100 Years*, 294-95; Jeff Spaeth, "The Secret in Robeson Hall: Nuclear Power in Blacksburg," in Wallenstein, *Essays, Fall 1997*.

6 Hahn interview, 1 July 1989.

7 Mrs. Hahn interview.

8 Hahn interview, 1 July 1989.

9 E. H. Lane, letter to Frank O. Moseley, 25 May 1967.

10 Mrs. Jane Wilhelm, who was a BOV member at that time, later recalled how determined she was that Dr. Newman should not be permitted to select his successor without ample demonstration of Dr. Hahn's abilities. She said, however, that as adamant as she was on the point prior to Hahn's coming to Richmond to meet with the Board, once he entered the meeting room she changed her mind even before he said a word. His self-assured presence alone, she said, convinced her.

11 Hahn papers, 1962; Paschall interview.

12 Martin Burkes, N&W general counsel, writing to Walter Newman, 19 February 1962.

13 Hahn letter to Dr. Manning, 26 July 1962.

14 Hahn interview, 1 July 1989.

15 Ibid.

2: Launching a Presidency

Marshall Hahn's official tenure as president of Virginia Polytechnic Institute and chancellor of Radford College had been set for July 1, 1962. That turned out to be a Sunday, so Monday, July 2, was the new chief executive's first day in the president's office in Burruss Hall.

The day became a kind of welcome home in reverse, for Dr. Hahn had an open house for the VPI faculty and staff. Many of those who came by, offering congratulations and good wishes, were colleagues and friends from his earlier years as professor and department head of physics at VPI. A clutch of newsmen and photographers from local and regional newspapers and radio and television stations showed up to record the occasion and interview the new president. Dr. Hahn talked about continuing the "tremendous progress" Dr. Newman had made and about land-grant universities as "institutions of the people." VPI's mission, he said, was "to provide educational opportunities for young people of Virginia and the nation."[1]

Professor Lyle Kinnear, then a member of the faculty, wrote in his centennial history of the school that the news reports of interviews in Burruss Hall reassured the faculty that the new president was already "familiar with the overall teaching, research, and extension activities of the institution." People also observed that, in referring to VPI, President Hahn kept using the term "university."[2] Even old-timers grew increasingly accustomed to the term—and to the concept behind it.

Year 100, Day 1

President Hahn's first day on the job turned out to be the 100th anniversary of President Abraham Lincoln's signing into law the Morrill Land-Grant College Act, which made possible the development of the land-grant college system. The anniversary was observed with some ceremony in the nation's capital. There, Senator George Aiken of Vermont—Congressman Justin S. Morrill's home state—made an anniversary speech in the Senate, as did a number of other senators.

Virginia's congressional delegation paid simultaneous tribute to the land-grant system's 100th anniversary and the change of administration at VPI. Senators Harry F. Byrd Sr. and A. Willis Robertson of Virginia recognized Dr. Newman's accomplishments as he left the VPI presidency and congratulated Dr. Hahn upon his appointment. They and other members of the Virginia delegation—especially Congressmen Richard H. Poff of Radford, W. Pat Jennings of Marion, and J. Vaughn Gary of Richmond—entered statements in the *Congressional Record* and sent congratulatory telegrams. All through that first day, similar messages from other prominent people arrived at the president's office.[3]

Tragedy

The festive atmosphere generated by the beginning of a new administration did not last long in Burruss Hall. It was dissipated the next evening—Tuesday, July 3—in high tragedy, as an unexpected event jeopardized the effective launching of the Hahn administration. Dr. Lou Pardue, who as vice-president was VPI's chief academic officer, was critically injured in an automobile accident on US Route 460 on Christiansburg Mountain. Returning from a long, tiring day in Richmond, he encountered a blinding rainstorm, and his car collided head-on with another vehicle. Several people were seriously hurt.

Pardue himself sustained multiple fractures, internal injuries, and head injuries, and for a time he was near death. At first he was taken to nearby New Altamount Hospital at Christiansburg, and President Hahn persuaded Dr. Edgar N. Weaver, a neurosurgeon, to come up from Roanoke to provide emergency assistance. Later in the night, Pardue was moved to Roanoke Memorial Hospital, where he stayed for some time. Dr. Hahn subsequently acknowledged to Dr. Weaver "a debt beyond repayment" for his help that terrible first night.[4]

Even after a lengthy hospital stay and convalescence at home, Pardue proved unable to resume his customary activities. In March 1963, he requested of the Board that he be "relieved of his present position and assigned to less arduous duties," a request that was quickly granted.[5] Some weeks later, however, he shocked the entire community when, in the Pardues' Blacksburg home, he took his own life.

The long months of Dr. Pardue's incapacity left the new president and his staff with a particularly heavy load. Pardue's sudden disability—followed by his slow convalescence and then his unexpected death—obviously complicated Marshall Hahn's early months as president. Had Pardue stayed healthy and available to advise Hahn and help carry out his initiatives, the new president's first year might have brought even greater change than it actually did.

Writing to Dr. Warren Brandt at Kansas State University in spring 1963, Hahn said about Pardue that he sustained "permanent injury in his accident, and then several months ago he suffered what probably should be identified as a nervous collapse. It is an obvious tragedy."[6] And yet the accident on Christiansburg Mountain opened the way for Brandt to move to Virginia Tech. Between them, as we will see, Hahn and Brandt worked to move mountains and transform VPI.

Inauguration

In the waning months of the Newman administration, the Board of Visitors had approved appointment of a committee chaired by Vice President Lou Pardue to plan the inauguration of President Hahn. Later, following Dr. Pardue's accident, Dr. Wilson Bell was asked to take the chairmanship. The inauguration took place April 4, 1963, in the coliseum. It was a great success—deftly done and enjoyed by everyone. Above all, Marshall Hahn had a most appropriate platform, at the outset of his tenure as president, from which to speak of his views on higher education in general and the challenges facing VPI in particular.

The audience was appropriate and auspicious. It included many members of the General Assembly and other state officials, members of the faculty and staff, and people from the surrounding community. Also present were representatives of leading institutions of higher education in Virginia and indeed across the nation.

Tom Rice, the rector, presided with "dignity and aplomb," according to Dr. Kinnear, who was present. Mr. Rice summarized the personal history of the new president—"his vocation and avocation are the development of this center of learning"—and then formally installed Dr. T. Marshall Hahn Jr. as president. The major address was by Luther H. Hodges, US secretary of commerce. Virginia Governor Albertis S. Harrison Jr., in extending greetings from the Commonwealth, paid glowing tribute to President-emeritus Walter Newman and to the VPI that he had guided for so long. As for Marshall Hahn, Governor Harrison said, "his qualifications befit his opportunities."[7]

Dr. George Oliver, president of Richmond Professional Institute, represented the Virginia Association of Colleges. Dr. Russell I. Thackrey brought greetings and best wishes from the members of the National Association of State Universities and Land Grant Colleges. C. Eugene Rowe, president of the Alumni Association, extended the well-wishes of 25,000 alumni, and Dr. S. A. Wingard, head of plant pathology and physiology, expressed similar sentiments on behalf of the faculty. Senior class president David E. Lowe conveyed the students' good wishes.

Mr. Hodges spoke from the national perspective of an urgent need for greater numbers of scientists and engineers and for research and development to strengthen America's economy and its ability to compete in growing world markets. He said at least fifty additional top-quality graduate education centers were needed in the years immediately ahead. VPI, he said, should be one of those centers; "your aim should be to develop an educational center second to none in the nation."

President Hahn had something like that in mind, and his elaboration on the same basic theme constituted much of his inaugural address. Good as the school was in 1962, he said, it must become far better—in teaching, in research, and in outreach. Moreover, it must grow prodigiously. Great growth in size, he noted, had to come at the same time as all concerned worked not only to "retain" but to "upgrade the excellence of programs."

Hahn characterized VPI's first ninety years as having displayed "amazing growth." Yet he urged his audience to consider how the school must, at minimum, double its facilities by 1975. By that time, the number of students enrolled on the Blacksburg campus "must more than double." Also, he warned that this—a "most conservative projection," itself having a "frightening impact"—assumed a constant "percentage of college age seeking a higher education, and in fact we recognize this proportion will actually increase." Even at a mere doubling, he observed, "as much physical plant must be added at VPI as has been developed in the entire previous history of the institution."

All in all, Hahn said, "it is almost impossible to comprehend the growth and development which must be achieved in the years to come." Huge sums would be required to "attract and retain a distinguished faculty," to put in place "the buildings, laboratories, and complex scientific equipment necessary for educational excellence in today's technology,"

2.1 Professor Kinnear on President Hahn's inaugural address—A decade later, Professor Kinnear, who observed the ceremonies with something of a historian's eye, summed up portions of Dr. Hahn's address:

In retrospect the speech is a summary of many of the challenges and problems through which Hahn led the institution for the next decade. Displaying a familiarity with the rapidly changing characteristics of society, which in turn were making increasingly insistent demands for a more sophisticated quality program in higher education, Hahn...noted the complexities of the changing Virginia scene. The effects these changing conditions would have upon VPI as the state's land-grant university were noted. At the mention of the word "university" in connection with VPI, a number of people in the audience were seen to smile, but Hahn continued...unperturbed. One of the significant effects, he suggested, would be the increasing necessity to improve the instructional, research, and extension programs of the institution. "We must respond in our instructional programs," he said, "to the thought-provoking challenge of educating today's youth for careers in tomorrow's world in fields that do not yet exist." Continuing, he said, "We must devise and strengthen educational curricula which will generate maximum effort on the part of each student, with emphasis on excellence."

The pressures for greater emphasis on excellence, he warned, were even more critical when viewed from the perspective of the increasing number of college age youth in the years to come. "These greater numbers of young people," he said, "must be viewed not as problems but as our most precious assets, as investments which will yield the richest dividends." (Kinnear, *The First 100 Years*, 421) and "to acquire" the "outstanding library which must be the center of a distinguished university." Whatever the cost, he warned, "we know that we cannot afford the wasteful ineffectiveness of educational mediocrity. Nor can we fail to provide the necessary educational preparation for the increasing numbers of young persons entering our labor force, our greatest asset, if Virginia is rapidly to move forward with its economy."

In conclusion, the new president called on "every public official, every citizen, every faculty member, every student, and every alumnus" to lend support to these multiple transformations of the school he would be leading.[8]

Hahn had written the speech himself, he later confided in a letter to a former colleague at Kansas State. Commerce secretary Luther Hodges returned the honorarium he was paid, and Hahn, writing to thank him, said he would put it in the president's discretionary fund and to good use "to further the progress toward the objectives we both have expressed." To his mother in California, the newly inaugurated president reported that everything had gone "smoothly and successfully.... The children greatly enjoyed the day and were very much in evidence.... Governor Harrison took them for a ride...in his limousine [and] they were beside themselves with excitement."[9]

The president's follow-up correspondence after the inauguration was voluminous. He wrote to virtually everyone who came, especially all of the media people, the public officials, the student and alumni leaders, and everyone on campus who had any kind of role in planning and executing the program, plus friends from Kentucky and Kansas. To Warren and Esther Brandt in Kansas he wrote, "We are very hopeful you will share with us our enthusiasm for the potential and future of VPI."

Recruiting a Vice-President: Warren W. Brandt

As the new VPI president's letter to Warren Brandt revealed, Hahn was working hard on Brandt. Following Lou Pardue's death, Hahn moved quickly to recruit a new vice president. He had one or two other names on a short list, but he probably never seriously considered anyone but Brandt.

Dr. Warren W. Brandt was head of the chemistry department at Kansas State, and following Hahn's departure he was also serving as associate dean of arts and sciences. The president invited Dr. and Mrs. Brandt to visit in late April, when the dogwoods and the redbuds bloomed across the landscape and the unfolding spring in the mountains was at its loveli-est. The two-day visit was busy; the deans and central administrative staff all found an opportunity to talk with the candidate, who was almost an alter ego of Marshall Hahn, even down to the close-cropped, GI-style haircut (Hahn's dated from his time in the Navy, Brandt's from his time in the Army). Brandt recalled much later that, at one point during the visit when he went to meet with a group of deans, Dr. Laura Jane Harper greet-ed him and said, "He told us you were the one he wanted, so come on in [so] we can look at you."

Brandt had just built a new home in Manhattan, Kansas, and was reluctant to move. But Hahn was persuasive, and VPI presented an excit-ing opportunity. In late April, Hahn wrote to his deans and directors to say that Dr. Brandt had accepted and would come aboard July 1. General announcement of the appointment was delayed, however, until late May to further distance it from Dr. Pardue's death. Meanwhile, Hahn soon began forwarding memos, letters, and other material to Brandt in Kansas. "I have many little items into which you can get your teeth immediately," he wrote.[10]

Warren Brandt—like Hahn, someone who had circulated through the land-grant system—was a 1944 graduate of Michigan State University (and valedictorian of his class) and had taken his Ph.D. in chemistry in 1949 at the University of Illinois. He taught at Purdue University for a dozen years and was chairman of the chemistry department's analytical division before going to Kansas State. He was a Guggenheim Fellow at Oxford University in England in 1958-1959, had published in technical chemistry journals, and had held national office in the American Chemical Society.

Warren Brandt arrived on schedule, dug in quickly, remained at VPI for six years, and profoundly affected the institution's development in the 1960s. The files reflect his concern with position allocation and faculty recruitment, salaries, the quality of graduate students, visiting scholar suggestions, registration and scheduling matters, student affairs—the whole gamut of academic activity. As Professor Kinnear observed, Brandt proved "an efficient, tough-minded leader far more concerned with build-ing VPI into his concept of a university than in following precedent and Tech traditions."[11]

Thinking about it more than a quarter century later, Brandt recalled most of all how green and inexperienced he was, coming in as vice president. His administrative experience did not go much beyond having been a department head and, for a couple of years, an associate dean. Nonetheless he had Marshall Hahn's complete confidence. The physicist and the chemist communicated easily, for they thought alike, and their responses to almost any situation were virtually identical. Hahn, Brandt & Co. had a difficult job to do in reshaping the institution, and Warren Brandt became important to Marshall Hahn in getting it done.

Commencement 1963

Before Brandt arrived at Blacksburg, Hahn's first academic year as president at VPI concluded with the 1963 commencement. There had been unsuccessful efforts to obtain prominent national figures to give the commencement address—the deans had recommended John Gardner, President Miller of West Virginia University, President Atwood of Emory University, and President Harrar of the Rockefeller Foundation, in that order, but all declined because of prior commitments. Dr. Hahn had also asked Senator Harry F. Byrd Sr. to speak, but the senator, too, had a conflict on that date. The note conveying his regrets did, however, invite Hahn to call him concerning Byrd's funding of additional scholarships.[12]

When commencement weekend came, Walter T. Skallerup Jr., deputy assistant secretary of defense for security policy, was the speaker for the commissioning ceremonies for the ROTC graduates in the Corps. For the commencement exercises, on Sunday, June 9—held for the first time in

2.2 VPI's first Rhodes Scholar, William Walker Lewis Jr.—Word came during Hahn's first year as VPI president that William Walker Lewis Jr. ('63), son of a VPI alumnus ('35) and agronomy professor, had been named the school's first Rhodes Scholar. Excelling alike at athletics and academics, the younger Lewis majored in physics with a perfect grade point average, and he captained the tennis team, quite aside from his many other activities. Hahn had worked hard during his first tour at VPI to build up the physics department and recruit undergraduates of Lewis's caliber. Surely such excellence, and recognition of it, was what Hahn was looking for as president—and was entirely consistent with Lt. Gov. Godwin's call at Lewis's commencement exercises the next June to cultivate the quality of excellence.

the new coliseum, the basketball arena—Lieutenant Governor Mills E. Godwin Jr. was the speaker. Godwin's exhortations undoubtedly made the coliseum ring for the graduating seniors and the recipients of advanced degrees. Speaking of the life ahead of them in uncertain times, he urged them to cultivate the quality of excellence. "Average," he declared, "will not be adequate for the new age."[13]

It was the first of a dozen commencements over which Marshall Hahn would preside at VPI, and as soon as the great growth kicked in, each was considerably larger than any before it.

Winning Friends and Influencing People

Perhaps the core characteristic that made Marshall Hahn a natural politician was his keen sensitivity for effective interpersonal relationships and his great capacity for winning friends and influencing people. Among the new people on the VPI Board of Visitors early in Hahn's presidency, for example, were Wyatt A. Williams ('36) and John W. "Jack" Hancock Jr. ('25), and Hahn came to rely on them. VPI's Board of Visitors, as we shall see, was vital to Hahn's objectives in achieving institutional change. And, as would become clear again and again, Hahn worked well with his Board.

Marshall Hahn was a naturally friendly, outgoing person who enjoyed meeting people and getting to know them. He did it with an enthusiasm that tended to generate friendly relationships quickly. His almost instinctive alliance with Jack Hancock, which developed almost as soon as he assumed the presidency, is an excellent example.

Hahn intuitively was interested in building public support for whatever purpose. His office paid close attention to all major newspapers in Virginia, and almost anyone who did anything to warrant attention in the public prints received an appropriate note from Marshall Hahn. This was especially true for VPI alumni or for newspaper or other media people who had occasion to write or broadcast about VPI or its president; each promptly received a brief thank-you note. Hahn visited the General Assembly in Richmond in January 1962, for example, and *Roanoke Times* reporter Ben Beagle wrote of the president-elect and Walter Newman at the legislative session; Beagle shortly thereafter got a note from Hahn, who was back in Manhattan, Kansas: "I sincerely appreciate your generous remarks and your clear presentation of my views. Such support is invaluable as I assume the tremendously challenging responsibility at VPI."[14]

Lon Savage, then education writer for the *Richmond Times-Dispatch*, wrote a similar report for the paper's February 22 edition and received a similar note from Dr. Hahn. This type of apparent personal attention by Marshall Hahn continued throughout his administration. Savage, who later joined Hahn's staff as his executive assistant, became the individual responsible for generating such letters from the VPI president.

In much the way that Hahn did not wait until assuming the presidency before getting involved in legislative affairs, he did not wait until he was back at VPI to begin his public speaking in Virginia; he made a series of Virginia talks while commuting from Kansas.

Once he became president, he took to the stump as often as possible; he spoke to almost any group that invited him. His message was closely tied with Governor Harrison's economic development theme. Hahn later echoed these ideas in his inaugural address—the need for Virginia to strengthen and broaden its educational system to meet the demands of the 1960s and 1970s, when so many young people would be seeking educational opportunities, and when the nation's underlying technology would be changing so rapidly. Hahn's fall 1962 speaking schedule included such groups as the Virginia Academy of Science, the Roanoke Junior League, the Richmond Kiwanis Club, the Virginia Poultry Federation, the Peninsula Engineers' Club, the General Electric Management Association in Salem, the Pulaski Chamber of Commerce, a dozen or more alumni chapters, the Virginia Association of Soil Conservation Districts, and the Wytheville Lions Club. As he commented much later, it was a good thing he was young and blessed with abundant energy; he needed it, for his days were long.

These efforts paid off. Charles G. Hammon Jr. of Suffolk, a new friend from Tidewater, noted their impact when he wrote Hahn in October 1963 to thank the president for his hospitality at the Oyster Bowl football game. Hammon, vice president and general manager of the Norfolk, Franklin, & Danville Railway Co., wrote that Hahn's speeches were attracting attention. "Such people as Shirley Holland and Lewis Rawls [influential members of the Virginia legislature] are now aware of the challenges of the future as pertains to higher education and to VPI in particular," wrote Hammon. "I am sure your visits to this area…have been one of the main factors in awakening the people to the needs."

2.3 President Hahn and Senator Byrd—Among the key people with whom Hahn became good personal and political friends was US Senator Harry F. Byrd Sr. (1887–1966), whose Democratic Organization dominated Virginia politics into the 1960s. Byrd's relationship with VPI went back many years, after a term as governor of Virginia in 1926–1930, he had served on the VPI Board of Visitors until 1944. On occasion, Hahn stopped by the senator's office in Washington, D.C., to exchange greetings and perspectives; he hesitated not at all to cultivate the relationship.

In the late summer of 1962, just after Hahn returned to VPI as its president, he encouraged Senator Byrd to set up a scholarship fund "for rural boys with college potential." The senator agreed to do so and pledged $50,000, payable at $10,000 a year. Byrd asked that no publicity be generated about the gift, other than listing the scholarship in the VPI catalog along with other special scholarships for which students might apply. In late 1964, after Hahn wrote to Byrd to acknowledge a $10,000 installment, Byrd wrote that he wanted to increase the total commitment to $100,000, and he suggested that, if Hahn thought it advisable, the scholarship competition be opened to all students, rather than restricted to farm youths, an offer that Hahn readily accepted.

Meanwhile, in 1963, Hahn attended the traditional late summer picnic at Byrd's home in Berryville. In view of its being an overtly political event, he thought it unwise to pay for the expenses for the trip to Berryville from state funds; so in early September he asked Mark Oliver in the Alumni Office to reimburse the $41.75 cost from the president's discretionary fund, which the Alumni Association Board had set up for just such purposes. Hahn always tried to be scrupulous in spending state money.

Soon afterwards, Senator Byrd shocked Virginia's political community by announcing he would decline to run for reelection (primarily because of his wife's poor health), and the State Chamber of Commerce solicited letters from prominent Virginians to submit as a collection to him as part of the recognition and honors to be bestowed upon him at retirement. President Hahn's letter, which was included in the collection, expressed deep appreciation, not only for Senator Byrd's assistance for VPI but also for "the sound and sane leadership you have given in your service to the state and nation," which Hahn characterized as "one of the most vital influences in helping to preserve the opportunities for individual achievement so vital to the continued forward progress of our economy." Byrd later wrote to Hahn that he was "deeply touched…. I will treasure your wonderful letter as long as I live." (The senator did run again after all, and he was easily reelected in November 1964 one last time.)

In an interview many years later, Wyatt Williams recalled that it took only about a year after Marshall Hahn became president for him to know just about everyone in the General Assembly on a first-name basis. Hahn was "very persuasive," Williams said; "he did his homework, and got to the right people...and put his facts out. He was pretty darn smart, and his facts were pretty convincing."

One of the first politicians with whom Hahn quickly developed a close friendship was Lieutenant Governor Mills E. Godwin Jr., an Organization lieutenant in the Virginia Senate who was Albertis Harrison's running mate in the 1961 state elections. Godwin and Hahn initially were thrown together by chance on several occasions, as when the lieutenant governor visited VPI to participate in a 4-H conference. The Hahns and the Godwins began to know each other as they met at various other functions. And when Mills Godwin and his wife Katherine came out to VPI for commencement in June 1963—the lieutenant governor was the commencement speaker—the two families already were good friends. The Godwins were among the guests in the president's home for commence-ment weekend, and the lieutenant governor later said in his thank-you note that he and Katherine "felt like members of the family before we left."

Much later, Godwin was to remember those days: "Marshall was an entirely different personality, and he came on the scene at a time when change was taking place. He was prepared to play a very special role in what was to occur." It was clear that Peggy Hahn played very special—crit-ically important—roles as well (see box 4.4). Godwin and Governor Harrison had both developed "some closeness to the Hahn family," Godwin recalled, "I guess because of Peggy and the fact that she was from Dinwiddie County...a part of the Southside. My wife and Peggy struck it off from the very first...and were real close. We saw quite a bit of them in the early years he was there, and really until he left."

To some it must have seemed a strange alliance—the traditional, Byrd Organization stalwart from Chuckatuck who had done yeoman duty in both the House and Senate for some two decades, and the youthful-look-ing college president with the crew-cut. Mills Godwin was among the Organization leaders who had savaged Governor Lindsay Almond's pro-posed sales tax program in the 1960 General Assembly after Almond abandoned "Massive Resistance" to school integration. But Godwin and Hahn became close friends, as did their families.

Political Power and Academic Administration

Marshall Hahn—himself in many respects a political conservative—was very much at home in Virginia's dominant Democratic party of the 1960s. However, he acknowledged parting company with the Byrd Democrats on some issues, even significant issues—especially school desegregation.

Regardless of how Hahn regarded the stance the Organization took on one matter or another, he recognized how crucial it was to get along. VPI was Hahn's first priority as president of the school in Blacksburg. Whatever might have come in second hardly mattered. Much later, asked about his early alliance with Senator Byrd, Governor Godwin, and many other Organization types, Hahn suggested it was like asking Willie Sutton why he robbed banks—for Sutton, that's where the money was, and for Hahn, that's where the power was. In the first half of the 1960s, he pointed out years later, Virginia still had "a powerful monolithic political organization."[15]

As for Mills Godwin, Hahn observed, "I liked Mills and saw in him the potential to move the state forward. The state needed to move forward in education and economic development. It was almost a sleeping giant in terms of [its] potential.... I wouldn't have seized on the opportunity if I hadn't had the conviction both about what the state needed to do and did do, and what the man could and would do."[16]

Dr. Hahn readily acknowledges his political machinations. As he later observed, good university presidents have to be good politicians. "A president of a state university, and even I think more so of a land-grant university, takes a big risk if he ever forgets that appropriations are political decisions made by elected officials.... You are an educational leader, that's your first responsibility. But to be an effective educational leader, you have got to maintain that political base, generate the political support, and you can't expect the merits of the case alone will persuade or govern."[17] Much of the story of Marshall Hahn and his time as president of VPI is the story of how he put those convictions into everyday practice.

2.4 J. Ambler Johnston ('04) and VPI, from McBryde to Hahn—James Markham Ambler Johnston (1885–1974) made his way to VPI in 1900 as a fifteen-year-old, graduated, and became a successful architect. Johnston's career, and his account of it, point up several salient things about VPI. Across the twentieth century, the school—whatever its limitations—had a profound influence on many students, and they in turn had a profound influence on it. When President Hahn went to work to transform the institution, he was trying to remake a school that had often been very good at what it did, but he wanted it to do a broader range of things, and on a grander scale, and he wanted to push excellence in research as well as in teaching. In his quest, he was able to tap the extraordinary loyalty of a number of alumni, many of them from the 1930s and 1940s, some of them from the very first years of the twentieth century.

Early on, Ambler Johnston had joined forces with VMI graduate William L. Carneal to form the architectural firm Carneal and Johnston. From the 1910s through the Hahn years, that firm designed a host of buildings on the VPI campus (see Pezzoni, "Our Native Stone"), including the residence hall that, named after Johnston in 1969, is known to Virginia Tech students as AJ. From 1928 on, "Uncle Ambler" served on the VPI Alumni Association Board of Directors, for a time as its president. In 1961 the school awarded him its highest honor, the Distinguished Alumni Citation. When he died at the age of eighty-eight on 7 February 1974, Warren Strother wrote of him (*Techgram,* March 1974) that he was "the elder statesman among VPI alumni."

Johnston developed a passionate interest in, and became an authority on, the Civil War. He teamed with Robert E. Lee biographer Douglas Southall Freeman to identify and preserve Civil War battlefields, especially in the Richmond area, and to see that historical markers be placed near them to make them known to other people. A director of the Richmond Civil War Round Table, he became well acquainted with a young historian, James I. Robertson Jr., who from 1961 to 1965 led the work of the Centennial Commission on the Civil War. Johnston later helped recruit Robertson for VPI's new history department (see box 4.7), and he originated what became the Johnston-Lucinian Fund, a source of support in that department for endeavors in Virginia history.

Toward the end of his long life, Ambler Johnston recorded a memoir for Robertson, who published it in the fall 1970 *Context*. In it Johnston traced something of both the significance and the transformation of VPI across the twentieth century. He began by telling of his first trip from Salem to Blacksburg, "by horse and buggy." It took an entire day, as he and his father "left Salem after breakfast, drove up what is now US Route 11, stopped at Elliston at the Big Spring for lunch." The next day they met with President John M. McBryde, and the senior Johnston decided to let his young son begin school at VPI that fall.

"It is utterly impossible to explain to anyone today what a crude institution VPI was at the time," Johnston asserted in 1970. Yet he also pointed out the limited background that he and his classmates brought to the campus. "Looking back now on those days, one must realize that the Civil War was then but thirty-five years behind us. Every cadet had been born and raised in the era of poverty pervading the South." Moreover, "many boys (and I was one of them) had never lived in a house with electric lights or central heating" (not to mention indoor plumbing). All were in the Corps of Cadets, and "all of this made us susceptible to discipline of a type unthinkable today."

Ambler Johnston described the few buildings in the old Upper Quad back when he enrolled, but he also enumerated the extraordinary faculty then. Among the star faculty whom President McBryde had brought with him to VPI from the University of South Carolina were "E. A. Smyth, R. J. Davidson, S. R. Pritchard, and T. P. Campbell—all of whom enabled their students at poverty stricken VPI to take their place in the world by sheer ability," and all of whom have buildings named after them. Other men Johnston named were the commandant, J .S. A. Johnson (for whom Johnson Hall is named); L. S. Randolph, a "truly outstanding professor" (Randolph Hall); math professor John E. Williams, "later a dean, and one of the most beloved men" (Williams Hall); William Patton, "a natural-born engineer and teacher" (Patton Hall); Hugh Worthington, "not so well known [in later times], but equally beloved"; and "Carol M. Newman, for whom the Newman Library is named."

"People used to walk in those days," Johnston reminded his readers. "On Sundays we had little to do but go walking. You could find VPI boys over all of the country anywhere within ten miles of Blacksburg. We walked to the top of Brush Mountain; we walked over to Roanoke Valley; and one time about four of us actually walked to Mountain Lake. On many an occasion we walked to Radford to attend a dance!" Johnston said he would "never forget one incident" when, "one Sunday, while out walking with a group of cadets, we came to Smithfield and found the doors open, papers scattered all over the floor—in short, [the place was] utterly abandoned." Among "some papers on the floor of the first room on the left as you enter the front door, I picked up and read a letter [from the 1840s] from someone in the US Army in Mexico [who] told of having met a charming and interesting gentleman from Virginia by the name of Robert E. Lee. I put the paper back in the pile. It was probably swept up later as trash."

Johnston also recalled his more memorable fellow students, many of whom had made their mark on the world and also upon their alma mater. "Being too young and ill-prepared, I came near flunking out the first year and had to attend summer school in order to enter the sophomore class." Two classes ahead of him was "another cadet who also was obliged to attend summer school" that year, F. Donaldson Brown, and the experience they shared that summer brought them closer together. "We were both so impecunious that we had but one pair of white trousers between us good enough to go to Saturday night dances at the Yellow Sulphur Spring (to which, of course, we walked). One Saturday, Don would sport the white trousers, and the next Saturday I did so. He later became vice president of finance of the General Motors Co. For him the Continuing Education Center is named. His brother Thompson became vice president and general manager of DuPont Co."—and also rector of the VPI Board of Visitors.

Johnston explained how he came to survive, even thrive, at VPI: "During that summer I was coached in mathematics with the result that in my sophomore year I was no longer the dumbbell of the 1904 class." And again that next year, "Purviance Tams ['02—see box 14.4] coached me in descriptive geometry and mechanics." They maintained a close lifelong friendship.

A big adventure had brought a fifteen-year-old the forty miles to Blacksburg. By the time he left VPI he had traveled much farther from home. At the end of his "Rat" year, "the Corps made a train trip to the Pan American Exposition in Buffalo, New York, where we put on a right big show. We were well-dressed, well-drilled, lived in tents, paraded every day on the great square, and got some good write-ups in the Buffalo papers." Another year passed, and "we went to an exposition in Charleston, South Carolina. We had a good time and passed in review before President Theodore Roosevelt with our band playing 'Dixie.' This was the first time I saw Fort Sumter,…and I think I got a good idea of Charleston harbor to help in later years when I read in earnest about the Civil War." At the end of his senior year, "the Corps went to an exposition in St. Louis."

Entering Johnston's class his sophomore year were "two outstanding men," Frank L. "Scribe" Robeson and William E. "Bill" Wine. After one of them (Hahn took his place as physics department head in 1954), Robeson Hall is named. As for the other, Johnston suggested, "The Wine Award is the only thing that present-day Techmen have to remember him by," but he had tremendous influence in shaping VPI. So of course did Ambler Johnston.

[1] Kinnear, *The First 100 Years*, 416.

[2] Ibid.

[3] Hahn letter to Senators Byrd and Robertson and Congressmen Poff, Jennings, and Gary, in Hahn papers, 1962.

[4] *Techgram*, 15 July 1962; Hahn letter, 7 July 1962.

[5] Kinnear, *The First 100 Years*, 418.

[6] Hahn letter to Brandt, 4 May 1963.

[7] Kinnear, *The First 100 Years*, 421.

[8] Ibid., 421-22.

[9] Hahn papers, 1963.

[10] Letters to Brandt, 15 April, 11 June 1963.

[11] Kinnear, *The First 100 Years*, 423.

[12] Hahn papers, 1963.

[13] *Techgram*, 15 June 1963.

[14] Letter to Ben Beagle, 25 February 1962.

[15] Hahn interview, 31 August 1989.

[16] Ibid.

[17] Hahn interview, 24 March 1990.

Dr. Louis A. Pardue, vice president and director of Graduate Studies under President Walter Newman, came to VPI in 1950 and died in 1963.

Dr. Warren W. Brandt worked side by side with President Hahn from 1963 to 1969 to make VPI into a university. He succeeded Lou Pardue as VPI vice president and director of Graduate Studies (1963-1965); then the two positions were separated, and he continued as vice president until that position was divided in 1966, when he became vice president for academic affairs. The photo dates from 1968.

Three chief executives: President T. Marshall Hahn Jr., together with Lieutenant Governor (and future governor) Mills E. Godwin Jr. and former president Walter S. Newman. Courtesy of T. Marshall Hahn Jr.

J. Ambler Johnston ('04), architect, had a huge presence at VPI through much of the twentieth century and certainly in the Hahn years. By the beginning of Hahn's presidency, "Uncle Ambler" was in his late seventies. This is an earlier photo.

3: Let There Be a University

In Marshall Hahn's first year as president, he moved decisively to transform VPI into a university. He began with what he had, and he set out to make what he wanted. He went to work on the structure of the school, the leadership of the units, and a host of other matters. On campus, the major units were the five schools, each with a dean with whom Hahn would be working. With Lou Pardue hurt so seriously, President Hahn worked directly with the deans, all of whom he knew well from his days as department head. Other groups, other individuals, had more authority over the institution as a whole.

The puzzle had many pieces—many kinds of pieces—and they all needed close attention and vigorous leadership. On few of them could a school president act directly. To obtain approval of major changes in policy and structure, he set out to work with the VPI Board of Visitors and the State Council of Higher Education.

President Hahn and the Board of Visitors

The VPI governing board or board of trustees, like those at other public institutions of higher education in Virginia, is known as the Board of Visitors. Its members are appointed by the governor for four-year terms, and they may not serve more than two consecutive terms (although, as sometimes happens, it is possible to serve more years by appointment to an unexpired term plus full terms and/or with nonconsecutive appointments). It is the institution's policy-making board, setting the basic policies under which VPI operates, subject to its corporate charter as spelled out in the statutes. Its members are unpaid trustees, reimbursed only for their expenses. The chairman of the Board of Visitors—called the

3.1 Marshall Hahn's first Board of Visitors—Four of the thirteen members' terms came to an end in 1962. Governor Albertis Harrison reappointed Edward H. Lane ('12), who ran the Lane Co. (at that time most famous for its cedar chests), and Erwin H. Will ('22), CEO of Virginia Electric and Power Company. Neither the rector, G. L. Furr ('16) of Roanoke, nor Oscar F. Smith III ('26) of Norfolk was eligible to succeed himself. In late June 1962, just before Hahn took the reins in Blacksburg, the governor appointed Harry C. Wyatt ('24) of Roanoke, vice president and general manager of the Norfolk and Western Railway, and Wyatt A. Williams ('36), a prominent Orange County gentleman farmer and cattleman, to succeed them.

Harry Wyatt—who previously had served a four-year term on the State Council of Higher Education, the coordinating agency for Virginia's public colleges and universities—was a natural, public-spirited, hard-headed businessman. Wyatt Williams, equally public-spirited, had gotten on Governor Harrison's list with the help of a good friend, Parke Brinkley ('38), who then was state commissioner of agriculture. Wyatt Williams was the son-in-law of Professor Ralph E. Hunt, who for many years was professor and head of animal husbandry at VPI. In the years that followed, both appointments proved fortunate for Marshall Hahn.

At its August 1962 meeting, the Board elected W. Thomas Rice ('34) of Richmond (see box 8.4), president of the Atlantic Coast Line Railroad (and also outgoing president of the VPI Alumni Association), as the new rector. Rice had initially been appointed to the VPI Board by Governor Lindsay Almond in February 1961 to fill the unexpired term of John Tyssowski of Delaplane, who had recently died (VPI *Catalog*, 1962-1963; statement from Mr. Rice, 11 September 1991). The Board reelected Mrs. Elva D. Redding, the president's secretary, as clerk.

A new executive committee was appointed, composed of Rector Rice, Granville M. Read, Edward H. Lane, Erwin H. Will, and William J. Erwin. G. M. Read ('14), of Forest, was a retired chief engineer for DuPont; Bill Erwin was president of Dan River Mills. The other Board members, aside from Harry Wyatt and Wyatt Williams, were Mrs. English Showalter of Roanoke; Paul D. Sanders of Richmond, editor of the *Southern Planter*; Mrs. E. Floyd Yates of Powhatan County; George M. Cochran, a Staunton attorney; Mrs. Henderson P. Graham, of Marion; and Mrs. Donald (Jane) Wilhelm, of Arlington. The ex-officio members at that time were Dr. Woodrow W.

rector, elected from the membership by majority vote—usually is one of the senior members.

Wilkerson of Richmond, state superintendent of public instruction, and Roderick G. Cowherd of Gordonsville, president of the state Board of Agriculture and Immigration.

A standing committee of the Alumni Association Board periodically recommended to the governor individuals for possible appointment to the VPI Board. Chairing the committee was J. Ambler Johnston Jr. ('04), one of the founders of Carneal & Johnston, a Richmond architectural and engineering firm. Johnston was no longer actively managing the firm by the time Dr. Hahn got to know him (then in his eighties, he was listed on the company letterhead as a consultant), but Carneal & Johnston had for years worked closely with VPI in building design and construction.

Marshall Hahn and Ambler Johnston were good friends almost from the start; the young man and the elder man obviously had great mutual admiration. In December 1962, Dr. Hahn wrote to Ambler Johnston forwarding three recommendations for possible future openings on the Board of Visitors. They were John W. "Jack" Hancock Jr. ('25) and M. W. Armistead III, both of Roanoke, and Stuart Shumate of Richmond. Jack Hancock was a Roanoke business executive (Roanoke Electric Steel) who soon became one of Marshall Hahn's closest friends. Bill Armstead was publisher of the Roanoke newspapers, and Stuart Shumate was president of the RF&P Railroad.

When two new vacancies occurred on the Board the following summer, Governor Harrison appointed Jack Hancock to fill one of them. For the other, he chose Mrs. Mavis M. Gibbs of Richmond, women's editor of the *Southern Planter*. In addition, the governor appointed William E. Blewett Jr. of Newport News, president of the Newport News Shipbuilding and Drydock Co., to fill the unexpired term of Granville Read, who had died the previous winter.

All three served effectively, but it is doubtful that the appointment of any individual to the Board could have pleased Marshall Hahn more than that of Jack Hancock, one of the leading citizens of Roanoke. Earlier, in April, Hancock had been elected to the Board of the VPI Educational Foundation, and Hahn had written him to express his appreciation for Hancock's willingness to serve in that capacity. Hancock was also on the Advisory Board of the Roanoke Technical Institute. (So was Frank Clement, board chairman of the Shenandoah Life Insurance Company, who also would later serve on the Board of Visitors and was eventually designated an honorary VPI alumnus.)

The Board of Visitors was crucial to President Hahn's aspirations to transform the school and create a university. Who was on the Board—and how the members related to each other, to the school, and to the new president—was of vital importance. Hahn generally had reason to think he had a good Board, and in any case it was his job to work with its members. They had the best interests of the institution at heart, though they did not all necessarily agree on what was best for the school. Fortunately for Hahn, one new member appointed in December 1962 was John W. Hancock Jr., who together with some other members had ties to VPI that ran back many years.

W. Thomas Rice ('34), elected rector at the BOV's August 1962 meeting, provided excellent leadership as rector at the beginning of Hahn's presidency. Rice stayed on the Board beyond that time, but not as rector. The election in August 1964 of his successor, Harry C. Wyatt ('24), as rector turned out to be most fortunate, certainly from Marshall Hahn's point of view.

Wyatt also was a tough-minded businessman, pragmatic and results-oriented. Once he knew where Marshall Hahn was going in the business of building a university, he was strongly supportive. Like Hahn, Wyatt was persistent; once he set out on a given course, he was not easily deflected from it. His BOV leadership—he was rector from 1964 to 1970—proved valuable to the president and the institution in the 1960s. With Wyatt in charge at the Board, President Hahn did not run into serious opposition on his initiatives to transform VPI into his image of what it could and should be. After the divisive decision in 1964 (see chapter 8) to end mandatory enrollment as cadets (most underclassmen had previously been required to be in the Corps), the BOV and President Hahn usually were on the same page. Tom Rice, however, opposed that decision.

By 1966, with Ambler Johnston's alumni committee coming up with excellent nominations and Hahn's good friend and strong ally Governor Mills Godwin making excellent appointments, President Hahn had a strong—and loyal—governing board with which to work. When Walter Newman left the presidency in 1962, the Board of Visitors worked largely though a committee system—the group was divided into several committees, each with responsibility for a different area of policy concerns: academics, student life, and so on. That system disappeared in the early years of the Hahn administration. Then the only real standing committee

3.2 Harry C. Wyatt ('24)—In Hahn's days as department head, he and Jack Hutcheson sought corporate support for Hahn's physics program. A warm friendship with Harry C. Wyatt grew out of an effort to build a nuclear accelerator for research in nuclear physics. Such an accelerator, Hahn recounted many years later, had to be enclosed in a very large, high-pressure tank, "which made me think of a railroad steam locomotive." Hahn approached Harry Wyatt about having the Norfolk and Western "build such a tank in its Roanoke shops as a contribution," and the venture "was successful and led to a lasting and close friendship."

Harry Wyatt had a round face, wire-rimmed glasses, and a ruddy complexion. His personal history was very different from that of the president, but the two shared some important characteristics, and each had a great deal of respect for the other. Wyatt was a largely self-made man, making his way up the Norfolk & Western hierarchy with determination and hard work. A native of Ivanhoe, deep in southwest Virginia, he left home early. In 1916, at age fourteen, he took a job as a mail clerk with the Norfolk & Western Railway Co. Later, he became a shop apprentice and began his long climb up through the ranks. The route led through Greenbrier Military Academy, from which he graduated in 1920, and VPI, where he had to cope with both the Corps of Cadets and electrical engineering. By the early 1940s, Wyatt had become the railroad's assistant general superintendent for motive power. In 1964, when he became rector of the VPI Board, he was N&W's senior vice president. (Marquis *World Who's Who in Commerce and Industry*, 15th ed.)

was the executive committee, empowered to meet on short notice and make quickly needed decisions, subject to full-board confirmation at a regular meeting.

Thinking about it all much later, Hahn said he felt it essential to work with the Board as a whole rather than breaking it down into committees. "There is a lot you do with a board that is both educational and persuasive, and you almost have to do it yourself," he said. As Hahn explained, he "felt that you could be more persuasive with a board if you keep [it] working pretty much as a committee of the whole," plus "keep them informed…. The more a board understands, the more likely it is that a capable board will think exactly like you do.[1]

Marshall Hahn is a persuasive person, for he "lays out his facts so well," in Wyatt Williams's phrase. Hahn went to great lengths to be sure his Board members were fully aware of the context of what he talked about and the ramifications of specific policy decisions. Hahn's educational

3.3 Changing of the guard at BOV—1964 and 1966—The BOV had several changes in 1964. Not only did Harry Wyatt replace Tom Rice as rector, but Erwin Will was chosen as vice-rector, a new position. Mrs. Wilhelm was reappointed, but Mrs. Graham rotated off the VPI Board (actually, she moved over to the new board of Radford College after its separation from VPI in 1964) and was replaced by Adger S. Johnson (see box 12.3). Three more changes took place in 1966, and by that time it was a different Board than the one in place in July 1962.

By 1966, Ed Lane and Erwin Will were senior members of VPI's Board of Visitors—both had served the maximum eight consecutive years, and they would indeed be missed. Ed Lane physically was a large man; his normal temperament seemed a bit on the sour side, and his facial expression seemed always on the verge of a scowl. Politically, he might be best described as a rightwing conservative. He was chairman and CEO of the Lane Co. and a strong admirer of Marshall Hahn; at one point he attempted to interest Hahn (who then was a member of the Lane Company board) in leaving VPI to become a Lane Company executive. A strong supporter of VPI athletics, his personal and corporate gifts for the construction of the new stadium that opened in 1965 were sufficient to warrant its being named E. H. Lane Stadium.

Erwin Will, chairman and CEO of Virginia Electric & Power Co., Inc., was of smaller physical stature; he was energetic, tough, and a politically astute man, much at ease in the behind-the-scenes rough and tumble of Virginia politics and in big-business lobbying at the capitol. He thought briefly of trying to bring Marshall Hahn into the corporate leadership of Virginia Electric & Power Co., but abandoned the idea. Hahn was important for Virginia to have at VPI, Will concluded, and he probably could do more good there than at VEPCO (Will interview).

Bill Blewett, president of the Newport News shipyard, died in October 1965, and Edward H. Lane and Erwin H. Will, both ineligible for reappointment, left the Board at the end of June 1966. Governor Godwin appointed three able men to fill the vacancies on the VPI Board: Waldo G. Miles of Bristol, a Ninth District Democratic leader who had been Godwin's campaign manager the previous year; John W. Landis, a vice president at Babcock & Wilcox, Inc., the Lynchburg engineering firm that became prominent because of its nuclear power work; and Clifford A. Cutchins III, of Norfolk. Dr. Hahn had written Ambler Johnston in 1965 suggesting that he add Cutchins's name to the list of desirable candidates submitted periodically to the governor by Johnson's Alumni Association committee. Cutchins ('44), a good friend of Mills Godwin, likely would be the next president of the Virginia

National Bank, Hahn noted (Hahn letter, 1 June 1965). Cutchins was appointed to fill Blewett's term, which would expire June 30, 1968.

As Lane and Will were about to complete their service on the Board, President Hahn made a point of especially honoring the two men. The occasion was a big dinner Wednesday evening, June 29, 1966, the next-to-last day of their tenure on the Board. Faculty, administration, student leaders, and members of the official boards (Student Aid, the Foundation, alumni, and the Board of Visitors) were all invited with spouses or dates. The festivities were in the Yellow Room of Owens Dining Hall. Many members and former members of the Board of Visitors were able to attend. The food, fellowship, and appropriate exchanges of thanks and best wishes made for quite an evening.

Ambler Johnston was moved two days later to write Dr. Hahn to say how thoughtful it had been to have the farewell ceremony for Lane and Will. "It may be the beginning of the creation of an unorganized organization of the future, 'The Society of Former Members of the Board of Visitors of VPI,'" Johnston said. It turned out to be so, although the organization of the William Preston Society did not come into being until well into President William E. Lavery's administration. By then, Ambler Johnston's little vision of the future was perhaps long forgotten.

process for his Board members was not limited to actual board meetings. When the BOV was to consider a policy question, Hahn later said, "I had already been through the issues with every individual, and I knew exactly how" they would vote. "Where some people go astray is in getting to the point there is a knowledge gap or data gap between them and the board," Hahn pointed out. "Capable, logical people," he said—"if they have the same knowledge base"—"are generally going to arrive at the same conclusion."[2]

VPI and SCHEV

A few years before Marshall Hahn assumed the presidency at VPI, the Virginia General Assembly recognized the need for expansion of opportunities for public higher education. In 1954 it directed the Virginia Legislative Advisory Council to explore the extension divisions of such state schools as Virginia Polytechnic Institute, the University of Virginia, and William and Mary. The council responded with a report titled "The Crisis in Higher Education in Virginia and a Solution." It highlighted an emerging crunch between the rising numbers of college-age Virginians and the shortage of facilities to accommodate them. To handle the additional students, it proposed only an increase in two-year extension divisions of the existing schools. Nothing suggested a transformation—in size or mission—of VPI's operations in Blacksburg.

In 1956 the legislature created the State Council of Higher Education of Virginia (SCHEV), a new agency responsible for coordinating the expansion of higher education in the Commonwealth. Whatever else SCHEV did, it was assigned the task of gatekeeping requests by existing institutions to plant new branches or divisions of the sort that William and Mary, the University of Virginia, and VPI had been developing during the preceding thirty years. Legislators decided that Virginia's institutions of higher education must increasingly "constitute a coordinated system." SCHEV also undertook to approve or disapprove the expansion of programs on those institutions' home campuses.

Like the VPI Board of Visitors, SCHEV was of crucial importance to VPI's new president. It had the power to facilitate or obstruct Hahn's initiatives. Closer to home, he had five deans to work with on matters like appointments and curricula.

Five Schools, Five Deans

The major academic divisions of VPI when Hahn became president in 1962 were the schools: Agriculture, Business, Engineering and Architecture, Home Economics, and Science and General Studies. Business had recently become a separate school, and Architecture was anxious to do the same. Another unit, the Graduate School, was presided over by the vice president, assisted by the Graduate Committee, although graduate as well as undergraduate programs in each of the schools were generally the responsibility of the respective deans.

The School of Business grew out of the School of Applied Science and Business Administration, where the business administration department had grown into the largest at VPI. The Board of Visitors approved a new School of Business Administration in 1960, and in that same year Dr. Newman brought in Dr. H. H. "Bill" Mitchell from Mississippi State University to develop it. Dr. Mitchell, delighted with the changes Marshall Hahn's coming seemed to signal, was already at work building his School of Business (the "administration" part was dropped early on) when Hahn arrived. The new school began operations in September 1961 with three departments—economics, accounting, and business administration.[3] A big bulldog of a man, Dean Mitchell sometimes seemed a bit gruff, but he had a keen sense of humor, too, and a big, deep-throated laugh. He enjoyed his leadership role.

Dean G. Burke Johnston, who had presided over the School of Applied Science and Business Administration, continued as dean of Science and General Studies, which included most of the sciences—among them biology, chemistry, and physics—as well as mathematics. Johnston, the epitome of a Southern gentleman, was steeped in classical English literature; he loved learning for the joy of learning and often infected his students with the same enthusiasm. He had strongly influenced the development of a core curriculum of basic courses in the humanities and sciences for all students in the various degree programs in Science and General Studies. His school also offered baccalaureate and some graduate programs in such areas as distributive education, industrial arts education, statistics, and general science. In addition to major programs, Dean Johnston's faculty taught the service courses backing up a variety of engineering, agriculture, and business curricula—English, history, foreign languages, political science, philosophy, religion, and so on—intended to provide a broader background for students in the technical fields.

The two larger schools—Agriculture, and Engineering and Architecture—were better known than the other schools, for their curricula undergirded the institution's mystique as a technical school. In the School of Agriculture, Dean L. B. "Deet" Dietrick was tall and serious but blessed with a more droll sense of humor than that of his colleagues. Industrious and even-tempered, he seemed as much a part of Agriculture as Hutcheson Hall. But he had been on the campus a long time, was soon to retire, and seemed a bit unhappy.

Deet Dietrick was both dean of the School of Agriculture (which he had been since 1952) and director of the statewide Agricultural Extension Service (since 1945). The latter organization, operating in conjunction with local governments and the Federal Extension Service of the US Department of Agriculture, was the primary off-campus educational arm of VPI. Its responsibilities extended "to all people of Virginia having an interest in subjects related to agriculture and home economics."[4] Dr. Harold N. Young was director of the Agricultural Experiment Station, which conducted agricultural research at Blacksburg and at two fruit research laboratories and a dozen regional research stations scattered throughout Virginia.

John W. Whittemore headed the School of Engineering and Architecture, where he had served in the dean's office since 1943 and as dean since 1952. Like agriculture, the engineering school had an extension component, the Engineering Extension Division, which operated two-year extension branches at Richmond Professional Institute, at the Norfolk branch of William and Mary, at VPI's two-year branch college at Danville, and also in conjunction with Bluefield College at Bluefield, Virginia. The engineering dean was responsible for the Engineering Experiment Station, a statutory agency designed to assist industry in the solution of technical problems. Dean Whittemore was cooperative and friendly, a good faculty leader full of innovative ideas. But he was slowing down, also expecting soon to retire, and he died in April 1963.[5]

The School of Home Economics, where Dr. Laura Jane Harper served as dean, emerged after the home economics programs were reorganized in 1960 following a series of internal and external studies on how best to organize home economics at Radford College and VPI. The curriculum for the first two years of study was the same on both campuses. Beyond that, the larger part of the home economics work was on the VPI campus, including its extension and research components, but home economics education—the training of home economics teachers—was retained at Radford.

Dean Harper commuted back and forth to work with the home economics faculties at the two campuses. Even as Dr. Hahn prepared to leave Kansas State and assume the VPI presidency, Dr. Harper had initiated work aimed at reorganizing the school's curriculum and developing more adequate facilities for home economics at VPI.[6] Full of high-tension energy and not at all hesitant to speak out, she provided strong leadership for home economics at both VPI and Radford. Her keen mind rarely overlooked an opportunity, and an acerbic wit made life interesting for colleagues. There was much mutual respect in the relationship of the youthful president and the deans, and Dean Harper was no exception.

The organizational structure was still evolving when President Hahn arrived. For one thing, the architecture group, increasingly unhappy in the engineering school, was anxious to secede and form a separate school.

3.4 Laura Jane Harper—Shortly after completing a master's degree at the University of Tennessee, Laura Jane Harper, a native of Mississippi, arrived at VPI in 1949 as associate professor of foods and nutrition. Although she went on leave during 1952-1955 to do Ph.D. work at Michigan State University in human nutrition, she remained on the VPI faculty for the next three decades. During much of the period when Radford and Tech were joined, she directed the home economics programs at both places. She would have preferred to remain full-time in teaching and research, but in 1960 she agreed, with some reluctance, to become dean of the new School of Home Economics, a position in which she served until she retired in 1980.

Dr. Harper's research specialty was child nutrition. Throughout much of the 1950s and 1960s, she directed a regional research project (on the nutrient needs of preadolescent girls) involving research teams from land-grant schools in Georgia, Louisiana, Tennessee, Texas, and Virginia. Active in research, teaching, outreach, and administration, she exemplified Virginia Tech's tripartite mission of research, teaching, and service as the school emerged as a major university. Moreover, she played crucial roles in fostering the personal and professional development of young women, white and black alike, at a historically white-male institution. Dean Harper gave the Founders Day address in 1980, "Against the Odds: Women at VPI." Harper Hall, a beautiful new campus residence hall near where she had done much of her work in home economics, was dedicated in her honor in October 1999. (Miles, "A Fighter to the End")

Architectural engineering had been for many years an option in engineering, but starting in 1956 students could earn degrees in architecture, and the architecture faculty and department head wanted to obtain independence as well as enhanced facilities. Walter Newman and Marshall Hahn alike encouraged the change, and, in summer 1962, the Board of Visitors approved the creation of a new School of Architecture. But by then, Professor Leonard J. Currie, who had directed the program since the mid-1950s, had grown weary of waiting. Before Hahn became president, Currie resigned to move to the new University of Illinois campus at Chicago Circle; but, before he left, he suggested several people qualified to take on the leadership of the new school. And one of them was eventually selected (see chapter 4).

President Hahn had five experienced deans to work with. It remained to be seen how they would work together, but one thing he knew. He would soon have three new deans to select. Agriculture, Engineering, and Architecture would all soon be headed by new people, whether they were appointed from within or recruited from elsewhere. Chances were they'd be new recruits, and one of their key jobs would be to go out and, in turn, recruit the best new faculty they could find.

3.5 Geological sciences—Geological sciences, a component of the School of Engineering and Architecture, also was in transition. The department offered two courses of study in Engineering. Geology was designed primarily as the foundation for graduate work, whereas geophysics was intended to prepare its graduates to go directly into the field of petroleum exploration or some phases of mining geology. In 1962, the department began offering a third option in the School of Science and General Studies with "a broader base of science, mathematics, and language needed in advanced graduate work" (VPI *Catalog*, 1963-1964). In the following year, all of the geological sciences were offered through the College of Arts and Sciences. Dr. Byron N. Cooper, who headed the department, had been at VPI since 1946 and was steadily building what would become a nationally recognized program. In not many years it became one of the centers of excellence in the developing university (see box 4.9).

Moreover, the curriculum in at least some of the five schools would undergo renovation. To achieve such further changes would require the active cooperation of the deans, the Board of Visitors, and the State Council. Marshall Hahn would take all the help he could get.

The Quest for a Broader Curriculum

The new president was deeply concerned with the traditional limitations on VPI's academic programs. A year before Hahn took over as president, the Board of Visitors had agreed—after considerable discussion—to request State Council authorization of baccalaureate programs in English, history, and political science, beginning in September 1962. President Newman had long wanted to broaden the curriculum into the humanities and social sciences. He believed major programs in those fields would strengthen all of VPI's academic programs. The Board's approval in August 1961 was historic. As Professor Kinnear noted in his centennial history, "It represented a distinct break with the long-held practice of offering humanities and the social sciences only as service courses for work in agriculture, engineering, and applied sciences."[7]

Just before Christmas that year, William H. McFarlane, director of the State Council of Higher Education, wrote to Dr. Newman that "a majority of the [Council] members still regard the proposal as implying a shift from primary emphasis on technological education to a more diversified university-type program." McFarlane inquired if VPI would be interested in advanced undergraduate work in the humanities and social sciences— to broaden the content of the degree programs in the applied sciences, engineering, and agriculture. President Newman was "keenly disappointed," convinced that such an outcome was not satisfactory, and he so wrote McFarlane in early January 1962. He also expressed the hope that the question could be raised again following further study.

The issue—still unresolved that summer after Marshall Hahn became president—was on the agenda when the State Council held a previously scheduled meeting at Radford College on July 16. Actually, the Council had decided to put off a decision on the matter until the new president was on board. At any rate, Dr. Hahn and Dean Burke Johnston attended the Radford meeting to plead the case again. President Charles Martin of Radford had preceded them to express his concern about women students enrolled in VPI classes at Blacksburg. McFarlane's minutes of the meeting noted that the staff was directed to prepare a formal recommendation for consideration in a special meeting August 27, and that "the sense of the Council's directive [was] that any recommendation proposing favorable action should place appropriate limitation on the contemplated programs, so as to emphasize the training of male public school teachers."[8]

Prior to the July meeting at Radford College, however, Howard C. Gilmer Jr., a member of the Council and a prominent Pulaski lawyer who had a summer home on Claytor Lake, had invited the other members of the Council and their wives to his place at the lake for a Sunday get-together on the day before the meeting. Marshall and Peggy Hahn also were invited, and they attended. The new VPI president was delighted with the opportunity, and he no doubt used all of his considerable skills in winning friends and influencing people at the informal dinner at the Gilmers' lake cottage. This was Hahn's get-acquainted opportunity. VPI in those days was all agriculture and engineering in the perception of most

Virginians, and Hahn was intent upon changing that perception. The membership of the State Council of Higher Education was a good place to start.

At the SCHEV meeting at Radford College itself, Burke Johnston said little; the president had cautioned him that too much argument might be counterproductive. But nearly thirty years later Dr. Johnston recalled how one of the SCHEV members kept insisting that VPI was trying to become a university, when instead it should emulate "Boston Tech" (meaning MIT). Johnston said he pointed out that MIT offered a Ph.D. in foreign languages, and VPI should at least be able to offer an undergraduate major in English. The Council member, he recalled, turned quickly to Dr. McFarlane and asked if that were true. McFarlane had to admit that it was, and, in Burke Johnston's recollection at least, the tone of the discussion thereafter became somewhat less intense.[9] Rather than restrict its curriculum to that of MIT, as had been urged, it turned out that VPI merely asked for half a loaf, if that.

The minutes of the July 16 meeting did not go into the substance of Hahn's arguments, but in August the president summarized them in a letter to Dr. Harold Miller at Woodstock, a Council member who had been unable to get to the Radford meeting. Hahn stressed that the request for baccalaureate programs in history, political science, and English did not involve a change in VPI's mission. The principal objective, he wrote, was to provide the conditions necessary to attract and retain the quality of faculty necessary for a strong service program in general education for students in the technical fields.

But, as Hahn explained to Miller, "We have found, as has been the experience at other institutions of our type across the country, that the quality of faculty we need for such efforts can be attracted only when there is also opportunity to teach a few students majoring in those areas.... These students, by virtue of their presence in such classes, would in fact help raise the level of excellence in daily recitations. In other words, no additional resources are required, and we are simply asking for approval for awarding the baccalaureate degree."[10]

Hahn also argued that the opportunity to go into such programs would be desirable for students in engineering or other technical fields who discover they would prefer something in the social sciences or humanities. "Such students now leave the institution, and frequently the state, or else complete their major in a field of secondary interest. Thus we are losing an excellent source of male teachers for secondary schools.... We expect to emphasize the preparation of secondary school teachers, but it would not be appropriate that we offer the bachelor of education degree."

The efforts of President Hahn and Dean Johnston were successful, for the Council on August 27 approved the VPI request to inaugurate major programs in English, history, and political science leading to the Bachelor of Science degree, effective with the opening of the 1962-1963 session. If, as Kinnear indicated, BOV approval of the curricular change was historic, the SCHEV approval was even more so.

Yet the August 27 resolution of approval limited the new programs to male undergraduates, aside from special exceptions as permitted by law. The qualification reflected the Radford College complication—women students, with few exceptions, could not enroll at VPI if the course of study they sought was offered at Radford. If Radford College offered such courses and majors as the Blacksburg campus would soon offer in English, history, or political science, most female students would be excluded from them. VPI's curriculum could expand to include more course offerings as well as majors in some new disciplines, but its constituency would not, at the same time, be redefined unless the restrictions on female students were relaxed.

The August 27 resolution also stipulated that it was based "on the need to maintain the quality of the undergraduate general education program for the Institute's male students in technological and other specialized disciplines."[11] Yet the new curricular possibilities became clear when commencement came at the end of President Hahn's first year. In 1963, for the first time, VPI awarded diplomas to undergraduates with majors in the newly-authorized fields in the humanities and social sciences—among them Fred H. Armstrong Jr. in English; Ronald W. McCubbins in political science; and John M. Katon, Edwin C. Stanley, Carey T. Sweeny, and Joseph H. Umbarger in history.

Jousting with SCHEV—"Schools" or "Colleges"?

Early in 1963, President Hahn moved to change the names of the various divisions of VPI from "schools" to "colleges," thus deliberately emphasizing VPI's evolution as a university. At the Board's February meeting, he recommended that the name of the School of Science and General Studies be redesignated the College of Arts and Sciences. In fact, all of the schools on the campus should be designated colleges, he said, except the graduate division, which would be called the Graduate School. The Board of Visitors readily approved the changes Hahn proposed. Then, carrying through on his commitment to the State Council to emphasize opportunities for the education of male public school teachers, Hahn asked and received Board authorization that the teacher education courses necessary for certification to teach in secondary schools be made available on an elective basis for students in all approved major programs.

The State Council of Higher Education was not happy with the Board action with respect to the redesignation of schools as colleges. In late March, the Council discussed the matter and adopted a motion that, because no change in VPI's mission had been authorized, it "declines to approve" the redesignations. Dr. Hahn was so informed in a letter dated April 4, 1963.

Hahn and the Board of Visitors agreed with each other, however, that it was an internal matter, and they ignored the State Council's concerns. Bill McFarlane was still unhappy about the situation in June 1964 when he told the Council that—even though both VPI and the State Budget Office had received copies of the Council resolution disapproving the name change—recent VPI budget activity reflected the change.

VPI had also, McFarlane complained, instituted a new activity—coordination of community colleges and general extension programs. This had given budgetary identity and approval to general extension programs without Council approval, he noted. Such actions indicated "lack of understanding, communication, and cooperation between the Budget Office and the Council," asserted McFarlane, who added that program coordination would be impossible to achieve unless Council authority was reflected in the state budget for higher education. The Council concurred, and all agreed that its chairman should discuss the issue with Governor Harrison.

By that time, it was far too late. McFarlane, the Council staff director, had bitterly opposed any effort to broaden VPI's mission. The redesignation of the schools as colleges and the identification of a college of arts and sciences clearly pointed the way to the development of a true university. McFarlane himself was to remain the Council's staff director for only a short time longer, and with his departure SCHEV's skepticism about the transformation of VPI proved much reduced.

3.6 Moving Dr. McFarlane out of SCHEV—The development of the Virginia Associated Research Center (VARC) was just getting under way when Dr. Hahn became president of VPI in summer 1962. Governor Albertis Harrison was strongly supportive of the project, partly at least because Dr. William H. McFarlane, then director of the State Council of Higher Education, was excited about it and saw it as the beginnings of a major graduate center. A joint agreement among the University of Virginia, William and Mary, and VPI was signed in July 1962. In the early years of the Hahn administration, several new faculty positions in high-energy physics were authorized for VPI's participation in the VARC project.

But VARC got off to a slow start; if the truth be known, none of the three participating institutions were happy with the arrangement. Joe Blackburn, who served for a time as a member and chairman of the State Council, recalled years later that William and Mary "was bound and determined that [VARC] was not going to work...that they were not going to have [VPI and the University of Virginia] in their back yard. We figured it was doomed from the start" (Blackburn interview). Meanwhile, the University of Virginia wanted to make sure that VPI did not gain some advantage with the VARC undertaking, and vice versa, Blackburn said. A University of Virginia professor, Dr. Klaus Ziock, was appointed acting director of VARC in January 1963 and served in that capacity until August 1, 1964. Late in 1963, VARC's Graduate Study Advisory Board, chaired at that time by Warren Brandt, recommended instituting a graduate program in physics at VARC.

In summer 1964, William and Mary president Davis Y. "Pat" Paschall and Marshall Hahn put their heads together and decided that Bill McFarlane would be much less of a problem for them as director of VARC than at the State Council. Many years later, Dr. Paschall, then president emeritus of William and Mary, recalled how he and Marshall Hahn compared notes and agreed that McFarlane was the major roadblock in their efforts to win approval of the State Council for key program changes at their respective institutions. Hahn was reticent about sharing details of how that particular problem was resolved—when he was told in summer 2000 about Paschall's account of events, he responded with what appeared to be a mixture of disapproval and merriment: "He shouldn't have told you that"—but the former president of William and Mary was much less reticent.

Dr. Paschall said that he and President Hahn, having found it difficult to learn what had happened to several requests for Council approval of certain academic programs, found upon investigation that McFarlane had sent them to President Shannon at the University of Virginia for his staff to review and offer recommendations. Dr. McFarlane, a graduate of the University of Virginia, turned out to be reluctant to recommend proposed program changes at either institution to the Council, especially at the graduate level, Dr. Paschall recalled.

"We must have had lunch together one day, and decided that this director of VARC was a powerful responsibility, and we three presidents couldn't run the minutiae of that thing," Paschall said. Hahn agreed, Paschall noted, and asked where someone could be found capable of running the research center. Paschall recalled, "I said the only man I know in Virginia who has got his whole soul wrapped up in it is McFarlane, and I don't believe you could find an abler man, a graduate of the University of Virginia, majored in philosophy." Hahn, Paschall remembered, was enthusiastic; "he said that's 'capital thinking.'"

Hahn later brought up the subject at a meeting of the governing committee, Paschall said. Shannon had no objections, but they all agreed that they would need to talk to Governor Harrison about it. The governor, Paschall recalled, though agreeing that McFarlane would be fine for the director's job at VARC, was reluctant to have him leave the State Council directorship, but he finally gave the two presidents leave to talk to McFarlane about the VARC position. The governor's words were, as Paschall recalled them: "If he's interested in doing it, you can tell him informally and confidentially that it would have my blessing…but I am no part of persuading him to leave" (Paschall interview). Hahn and Paschall had their way. McFarlane left SCHEV to accept the directorship of VARC.

The Graduate School

President Hahn was intent upon changing the basic character of the institution, and a university has a flourishing graduate program. When Dr. Brandt came to VPI in 1963, he was also dean of the Graduate School, and he took a great deal of interest in strengthening the graduate programs. It was a much more difficult task than strengthening and broadening VPI's undergraduate curricula, but Brandt did not hesitate. With the full support of President Hahn, he began making VPI's Graduate School into something very different from what it had been. The academic standards became much more demanding. For a time, Brandt screened every application for admission to the Graduate School, and he eliminated from further consideration applicants whom he judged unqualified. He focused his attention on graduate students partly because their numbers were more manageable and partly in view of their importance to the research mission of the new VPI.

The Graduate Committee, the senior faculty group that was the main policy-making body for graduate studies, was reorganized to encourage greater faculty participation and direction. In addition to tightening admissions requirements, the new regime altered the graduate curricula of the various departments. In the context of the overall reorientation of VPI—through the broadening of its curriculum, a dramatic expansion of highly qualified faculty, and an emphasis on research as well as teaching excellence—the rising prominence of the Graduate School was soon readily apparent. With the help of the deans and department heads, potential new areas where strong graduate programs could be developed were identified and staffed.

In 1964 the Board of Visitors approved an associate dean position for the Graduate School, and Dr. Howard Massey, professor of horticulture, took on the task on a part-time basis. In summer 1965, after Massey was appointed associate director of the Agricultural Experiment Station, Brandt appointed Dr. Fred W. Bull dean of the Graduate School.

A few months later, Dr. Bull reflected on all this in an interview reported in the October 1965 *Techgram*. "VPI has been a good undergraduate institution a long time, but it had never achieved much recognition for graduate work," Bull noted. "There were some graduate programs, but the institution wasn't research oriented; there didn't seem to be much real interest in building graduate programs. Well, in the past few years there has been a complete reversal. We've been encouraged to develop good graduate programs, and the Graduate School is one of the most rapidly growing schools on the campus."

3.7 Dean Fred W. Bull and graduate education at VPI—No one could have been more delighted with the changes apparent on the campus in those years than Fred Bull. Few were more committed to excellence and academic integrity. He was blunt, plain-spoken, and to the point, calling the shots as he saw them. He was very like Stuart Cassell, in that he loved VPI with a passion, and worked very hard at any assignment at the school. Bull had grown up in Victoria, Virginia, the son of a boilermaker for the old Virginian Railroad. He had earned a string of degrees from VPI, from a B.S. in chemical engineering in 1933 to a Ph.D. in 1953. He had worked some years in industry as well, and knew the practical, everyday problems of engineers, perhaps one reason he proved so successful as head of the chemical engineering department, and worked so hard on behalf of graduate education at VPI.

Dean Bull labored diligently in the administration of the Graduate School, though it was a difficult task. The dean of the Graduate School had no real leverage, for the control of budgets, faculties, the rewards system, and almost everything else that begets power on a university campus lay elsewhere—with the vice president, the college deans, the department heads. (Warren Brandt, when he also was dean of the Graduate School, had had, and used, that control.) But Dr. Bull continued to control the admission of advanced degree candidates, and with his Graduate Committee, he managed to influence significantly the continuing development of VPI's Graduate School until his death in 1979.

Budgeting for a Budding University

Marshall Hahn had moved with some dispatch to begin the transformation of VPI into a university. To push the double transformation along—the increased size and the changing mission—he needed more than approval of organizational and curricular changes. He needed funds.

In those days, the governor and his budget advisors, including the senior members of the House Appropriations and Senate Finance committees, spent two weeks on a bus trip prior to each legislative session, visiting each state institution of Virginia. Thus, in March 1963, Governor Harrison and his Budget Advisory Board visited the VPI campus for a quick tour and a discussion of the institution's funding proposals for the next biennium. The 1964 General Assembly, when it convened in January, would, working with the governor, produce a state budget for the fiscal years 1964–1966.

When the governor and his colleagues arrived on the VPI campus, they were warmly welcomed and much impressed by the vigorous young president. On March 16, President Hahn outlined the institution's funding request for Governor Harrison; L. M. Kuhn, his budget director; and the members of the governor's Budget Advisory Board. If there were any doubts about Hahn's commitment to broaden higher educational opportunities in the Commonwealth, his proposals for VPI's rapid growth dispelled them. He outlined a proposed two-year budget that would permit VPI to increase its enrollments in each of the two years by about 1,000 full-time equivalent (FTE) students for each regular session and 200 FTE students for each summer session. Many of the additional students would be housed in residence halls then under construction (Miles and Newman); the remainder would have to be accommodated in the community.

Hahn stressed the value to Virginians that the state's political leaders could expect from his initiatives. He reminded everyone that out-of-state enrollments at VPI could not exceed 20 percent of the total—some out-of-state students were essential for educational purposes, he said, to insure a diverse student group—and also that every effort was being made to keep fees as low as possible: "Such large numbers of boys of limited means attend VPI and then make such major contributions to our economy that we feel that it is very important that the cost be held down so that as many boys as possible can attend." Many young people, especially from rural areas, still were unable to attend, he pointed out. Hahn found the time opportune to report that Senator Harry F. Byrd had recently pledged a gift of $50,000 to provide $500 four-year scholarships to rural youth of limited means. Hahn also stressed that he would welcome careful review of the proposed budget: "Our philosophy and practice has long been and continues to be to get the maximum mileage from each dollar invested in VPI."

For VPI's instructional programs, Hahn's initial two-year budget proposal contemplated an increase of at least $2 million over 1962–1964—$705,180 of it from state taxpayer funds, the remainder from student fees and other special revenues. He proposed the funding of an additional 64 instructional positions, a modest number in view of the anticipated enrollment increases. Hahn also requested $1.3 million for increased faculty salaries—still leaving them, he noted, about 25 percent below the national average for similar land-grant institutions—and he sought authorization for a new faculty salary system (see chapter 4).

For building construction, the new president asked for $8.6 million, including funds to complete existing construction projects and match the $850,000 available in private funds for a continuing education center. He requested appropriations for a new home economics building; the renovation of McBryde Hall; facilities for the new College of Architecture; a vocational and technical education building; half the cost of two new residence halls; and various other projects, including a proposed television production facility. Some $200,000 was requested for library books and periodicals, and a similar amount for laboratory equipment. Other funding requests included significant increases for the Agricultural Experiment Station and the Agricultural Extension Service. Operating appropriations were requested for the new branch colleges at Wytheville and at Clifton Forge-Covington, as well as for the Roanoke Technical Institute and the Danville branch.[12]

Hahn outlined the budget requests for the visiting tour group on March 16 and again in Richmond on April 12. In doing so, he became something of an instant celebrity—the governor, legislators, and others present were amazed at the tall, youthful-looking physicist's presentations. Hahn distributed to each member of the group a carefully prepared statement containing all of the funding proposals, but he did not keep a copy for himself. Then, from memory, he went through the complex document, discussing the details without so much as looking at a note. Many years later, several of those present for their initial meeting with him still recalled the performance with some astonishment.

"A Quality University Education"

The Board of Visitors, which had approved Hahn's initial budget proposal, a little more than a year later formally adopted a broad policy statement that VPI would seek to develop the facilities to accommodate Virginia high school graduates who had "the ability to complete successfully a quality university education." Nor was it assumed that only male students would fit that description. The Board spoke of "a growing demand for women educated in the programs of VPI, and this will be taken into consideration in the future development of the institution."[13] The institutional mission of VPI was indeed changing.

[1] Hahn interview, 24 March 1990.

[2] Ibid.; Wyatt Williams interview.

[3] VPI *Catalog*, 1961-1962; Kinnear, *The First 100 Years*, 390.

[4] VPI *Catalog*, 1962–1963.

[5] *Techgram*, 1 May 1963.

[6] Ibid.; Miles, "A Fighter to the End"; Harper and Howery, "History of Home Economics at V.P.I."

[7] Kinnear, *The First 100 Years*, 404.

[8] SCHEV minutes, 15 December 1962, 27 August 1962.

[9] Burke Johnston interview, 23 August 1990.

[10] Hahn letter, 11 August 1962.

[11] SCHEV minutes, 27 August 1962.

[12] For Roanoke Technical Institute, the VPI president proposed that the City of Roanoke be relieved of its part of the operating costs, so that RTI's funding would be entirely from student fees and state appropriations. Also included in the capital funding proposals were the purchase of several homes adjacent to the campus; some property owned by the Montgomery County school system; and a tract of farmland for the Agricultural Experiment Station.

[13] Kinnear, *The First 100 Years*, 435.

The Board of Visitors, 1962-1963: Mrs. Henderson P. (Jouette) Graham, Mrs. E. Floyd (Mary) Yates, Mrs. English (Jean) Showalter, Mrs. Donald (Jane) Wilhelm Jr., Roderic G. Cowherd (ex officio), Wyatt A. Williams, Mrs. H. R. (Elva) Redding (secretary), Granville M. Read, Edward H. Lane Sr., Harry C. Wyatt, Erwin H. Will, and George M. Cochran. Not pictured: W. Thomas Rice (rector), Paul D. Sanders, and Woodrow W. Wilkerson (ex officio). Photo from the 1963 *Bugle*.

The Board of Visitors, 1966-1967: Mrs. Donald (Jane) Wilhelm Jr., John W. Landis, Adger S. Johnson, John W. Hancock Jr., William J. Erwin Sr., Mrs. English (Jean) Showalter, Mrs. H. R. (Elva) Redding (clerk), Harry C. Wyatt (rector), Waldo G. Miles, Cliford A. Cutchins III, Charles W. Wampler Jr. (ex officio), George M. Cochran, Mrs. Mavis M. Gibbs, and Wyatt A. Williams (vice rector). Not pictured: W. Thomas Rice. Photo from the 1967 *Bugle*.

Clifford A. Cutchins III ('44) and John W. Hancock ('25)—many years after the Hahn presidency—in the atrium of Hahn Hall, September 1989. Photograph by Bob Veltri.

Dr. Fred W. Bull (B.S. '33, Ph.D. '53), department head of chemical engineering when Hahn arrived, served as dean of the Graduate School from 1965 until well after the end of Hahn's presidency. The photo dates from 1969.

4: Three Rs of a University Faculty

Marshall Hahn's first year as president was an extremely busy time, immersed as he was in both internal and external concerns, and without Lou Pardue to work directly with the deans of the five schools. Hahn knew that to build the university he envisioned, he had to compete nationally for top-flight faculty. To do so, he would have to be able to pay competitive salaries, and he began working on the salary problem almost from the beginning. He also took considerable time to talk personally with prospects—new deans, department heads, and individual faculty members—whom he and Warren Brandt were trying to recruit to VPI.

Faculty retiring from VPI had to be replaced; replacing them offered opportunities to alter the institution. Moreover, to meet anticipated enrollment increases in the years immediately ahead, more new faculty and staff would be needed, regardless of who retired. The structure of rewards—both starting salaries and pay raises—could be used, perhaps, to attract new people and, beyond that, to channel current faculty toward greater emphasis on research. The three Rs of acquiring a first-rate university faculty—recruitment, research, and rewards—were deployed in the quest of the new VPI.

Faculty salaries had been one of Walter Newman's most difficult problems as president. Faculty members were paid according to a salary scale with specific steps for each faculty rank—instructor, assistant professor, associate professor, and professor. Annual salary increases were usually small, and everyone in each category received the same increase.

President Hahn was able to increase the faculty salary average for 1964-1965 about 10 percent, making VPI more competitive nationally. Yet, more than simply raising all salaries, Hahn set out to reward faculty on the basis of their individual merit—with emphasis placed on their research productivity.

Especially in the beginning, the new administration put great emphasis on rewarding individual faculty who, during the previous year, demonstrated significant achievements in producing scholarly research

4.1 Merit increases and faculty research—When Marshall Hahn became president at VPI, the pay system was much like the salary scales for the civil service-type, nonacademic classified employees, except that faculty salaries were somewhat higher. (There also was a "critical scale" for certain fields in which competition for faculty was most intense, with salary steps somewhat higher than the normal scale.) The State Personnel Office and the State Budget Office in Richmond supervised the salary system rigidly; their approvals were required for special action salary decisions. Dr. Newman, and then Dr. Hahn after he became president, sometimes requested exceptional actions to resolve specific problems—often without much luck.

Hahn early on began a quiet campaign to convince John Garber, the state personnel director, that Virginia should use a new system for determining faculty salary averages at VPI—that the governor should authorize a faculty salary average based on the median salaries paid by comparable land-grant institutions across the country. It took almost a year, but Garber came around to supporting such a basis for salary averages.

Earlier, Hahn had set about to change the lock-step salary steps to a strictly merit system. "Merit increases represent recognition of outstanding performance in instruction, including extension activity, if appropriate, and productive research," he wrote in a memorandum to deans, directors, and department heads sent out right before fall quarter classes began in September 1962. Each department head was alerted that he or she would be expected to make a critical evaluation of each faculty member just prior to the date in the spring for considering salary increases, and to make appropriate salary recommendations to division directors and deans.

The memo did not say so, but the vice president and the president would review the deans' and directors' recommendations and approve or modify the final salary increase to be awarded each individual faculty member. It could range from zero to well above average, the average percentage increase depending upon funding available for salary increases that year. In

and in obtaining research grants. Hahn later explained, "We deliberately pushed harder on research at first, because it was necessary to change the thinking of the University."[1]

The change in the rewards system was one of President Hahn's most significant steps as he set out to build a comprehensive research university at VPI. It provided much of the leverage he needed to move people in the direction he wanted them to go. But he knew it was not the only place to focus.

cases where there were zero increases—and there were some—the lack of any salary increase at all tended to speak loud and clear of the low evaluation of an individual's performance. The reverse was true for above-average increases.

Hahn involved himself in the matter of pay raises from the beginning. In spring 1963 (for the 1963-1964 school year), he personally reviewed all of the recommendations for faculty salary increases, and he changed some of them significantly. When the process was repeated in spring 1964 (for the 1964-1965 school year), however, Stuart Cassell looked at the results and suggested in a handwritten note to a colleague that "it makes a laugh out of getting rid of the scales." Cassell said that two-thirds of the faculty received either a $600 increase (instructors and assistant professors), or an $800 increase (for associate and full professors). (Hahn papers, 1963; Cassell note, 15 May 1964)

As the system began to take effect, it nonetheless became apparent to the faculty that the rewards system was changing—not only in a move toward merit pay raises but in the heightened emphasis on research. The fact that many members of the faculty saw identical raises belied another fact, that people who stood out, those with exceptional activities to report in a given year, were rewarded with more.

Many faculty members didn't like it; others thought it was great. Looking back on it all many years later, Warren Brandt mused about those times that "they were good for some people, and not good for others. A lot of people get crushed in that type of thing. People have come in expecting it to stay a sleepy old institution, and then all of a sudden it changes, and they are not equipped to deal with the changes. They wind up getting poor raises and left out of things. It's no fault of theirs, the institution changed.... Yet when they were hired they were okay. Doing what we did, you hurt some people."

"Where the Leverage Was"

In many ways, the VPI faculty President Hahn inherited from President Newman was quite respectable, with fine teachers and researchers. Some departments sported considerable interest in research and a number of externally funded research projects.[2] Yet some faculty had never published a word—and never would. In its entirety, the faculty was by no means of the quality necessary for the development of the kind of university Marshall Hahn—or Walter Newman, for that matter—had in mind.

The new president was no stranger to most of VPI's department heads, but many, no matter how strong or how weak, were approaching retirement. In Marshall Hahn's perspective, the department heads would be the key to strengthening the faculty. "That's where the leverage was," Hahn would say many years later. They were the frontline lieutenants of the institutional leadership—they were appointed from the top, not chosen by the faculty in their departments—and their strong support was essential. Hahn could have tremendous influence in selecting the new department heads, and they in turn had tremendous say in recruiting new members of the faculty. Then Hahn's other means of leverage—the

4.2 Filling vacancies and finding new faculty—In the early 1960s, significant numbers of senior faculty and staff reached retirement age. In September 1963, somewhat more than fifty people were added to the faculty ranks—some to fill new positions, most to fill positions vacated by retiring faculty. Some, with varying degrees of teaching experience, had recently earned a master's or Ph.D. at VPI. Most of the instructors employed for 1963-1964 came with no graduate degrees; in particular, the math department's roster carried many part-time, temporary instructors. By contrast, some on the 1963 new faculty list held doctoral degrees from distinguished universities. It was quite a diverse faculty group in its training and credentials. For the school year that opened in September 1964, nearly seventy new faculty members were added to the various departments. (VPI *Catalog*, 1964-1965)

Warren Brandt persuaded a former colleague at Purdue, Dr. Alan F. Clifford, to join him at VPI as head of the chemistry department in 1966. Dr. Wilson C. Snipes came from Mercer University to head the English department, and Dr. Joachim Bruhn became head of the new Department of Foreign Languages, newly separated from the English department. Dean Malpass recruited Dr. Robert A. Paterson from the University of Maryland in

rewards system—could go to work to reinforce the tendencies the department head had discerned in hiring the new person in the first place.

Warren Brandt's arrival in summer 1963 hastened the changes the new administration sought—perhaps most noticeably through faculty recruiting. Vacancies resulted from retirements, resignations, and new positions created to accommodate increased enrollments. In some cases the retirement or resignation was not entirely voluntary, for Warren Brandt, working with the president, on occasion found it necessary to encourage a department head or other faculty member to depart, however reluctantly.

President Hahn and his new chief academic officer, Dr. Brandt, agreed that faculty recruiting was a high priority, and they worked closely with the department heads and their respective faculty members in the recruitment process. Department heads sometimes suggested people whom Hahn or Brandt thought would make good potential candidates. In some departments, Brandt personally interviewed each candidate for a faculty position, and not infrequently he and Dr. Hahn separately would talk with a candidate.[3] By carefully screening all candidates for faculty openings,

1967 to head the biology department, and Paterson induced one of his colleagues at Maryland, Dr. Ernest Stout, a molecular biologist, to move to VPI as well. Years later in an interview, Paterson recalled his new colleagues as "good, enthusiastic people who were caught up in [the University's] development, and were excited about it." He later served as dean of the College of Arts and Sciences.

In filling vacancies, there were, of course, some internal appointments—although, in some cases, replacing from within still left a vacancy somewhere. When the Agriculture dean, Deet Dietrick, retired, for example, Dr. Hahn appointed Dr. Wilson B. Bell ('34), associate director of the Agricultural Experiment Station, to succeed him. In the Extension Service, of which Dietrick also was director, William H. Daughtrey ('27), a longtime Extension official, was chosen to replace him. When Harry W. Saunders ('16) retired in August 1963 as head of vocational education, Dr. Rufus W. Beamer ('38), who had come from the University of Tennessee the year before, succeeded him. Dean Carter, a sculptor who had been on the architecture faculty since 1950, was appointed acting head of the new art department, which was organizing a baccalaureate program (see chapter 20).

Hahn, Brandt & Co. set about to generate a quantum leap in academic quality.

Faculty recruiting was not easy. The kind of outstanding people Hahn, Brandt & Co. sought were for the most part already established in desirable situations at other universities. For example, among the new department heads on the campus in September 1964 was Dr. J. B. (J. Beverley) Jones, who came from Purdue University to succeed his uncle, also J. B. Jones (J. Bernard), as head of mechanical engineering. J. B. Jones had been reluctant even to consider returning to Blacksburg. A 1944 VPI graduate, J. B. had gone to Purdue after World War II, earned both his master's and Ph.D. there, and, after some industrial experience, returned to Purdue to begin a career in teaching and research. By 1963, he was well situated and had no thought of leaving.

VPI's repeated overtures, however, persuaded him to visit the campus, and Marshall Hahn's obviously able leadership broke down his reservations. Jones talked at length with Warren Brandt (whom he had known at Purdue), but it was the conversations in a larger context with President

4.3 Hatchetman—One of the vice president's more onerous tasks was to bring the bad news to faculty members who, for whatever reason, were given notice that their services would no longer be required beyond the following academic year. No one knows how many faculty members Warren Brandt actually fired in the six years he was on the VPI campus, but the number must have been significant. Some of them readily acknowledged their dismissal. Undoubtedly others who left the VPI faculty in the 1960s did so because of pressure from Brandt, who was dissatisfied with their performance. A "Reconciliation" Committee was in place to review serious arguments between individual faculty and administrators, but, especially in Warren Brandt's time at VPI, the real power remained with the administration. Dr. Brandt developed a reputation among the members of the faculty as Dr. Hahn's "hatchetman," the person who did the dirty work for the president.

Word evidently got around—beyond the faculty. On one occasion, Brandt remembered years later, a coed stopped by his office, and in the course of a pleasant conversation they talked about campus life, her classes, her academic goals, and such. She seemed quite interested, and he was glad to explore her feelings about VPI and about how she perceived her experience on the campus. Unexpectedly, however, Brandt recalled, she abruptly

Hahn that finally prompted him to accept the VPI position, he recalled many years later. Aside from the fact that "President Hahn had a lot of good ideas and the energy and capacity to make exciting things happen," Jones said, "I was most impressed with the clarity with which he distinguished between what he had accomplished, what he was pretty sure he could accomplish in a reasonable time, and what he hoped to accomplish in the future. He just didn't mix those things up at all, and he laid them right out." Jones also had been impressed with Hahn's realistic view of the time and resources necessary to achieve his goals for VPI.[4] Mechanical engineering at VPI achieved significant national recognition under J. B. Jones's leadership.

Another new department head was Dr. Leon W. "Lee" Rutland, recruited from the University of Colorado to succeed Dr. T. W. "Inky" Hatcher, who had retired as head of the mathematics department. Lee Rutland remembered, years later, receiving a call in 1963 from Warren Brandt. Rutland was happy at Colorado, he said, and when Dr. Brandt asked him to visit VPI, "I said 'you would be wasting your money.' But

changed the subject with a direct question: "What is a hatchetman?" Several people had told her that Dr. Brandt was Dr. Hahn's hatchetman, she said, and she wanted to be sure of what they were talking about.

Remembering those VPI days many years later, Brandt was a bit sobered; "I had that reputation, and had earned it fairly well," he said. He acknowledged that he sometimes wondered if he had made so many people angry that he was becoming ineffective—that the role had a limited shelf life. After six years at VPI, Brandt moved on to become the first president of the new Virginia Commonwealth University.

But the role itself remained important, to Brandt and to other institution builders—it was the flipside of the effort to bring in new talent. Dr. James E. Martin, who was recruited to VPI in 1966 by Hahn and Brandt to be head of agricultural economics, was later promoted to dean of the College of Agriculture but subsequently left and became president of the University of Arkansas and, still later, president of Auburn University, his undergraduate alma mater ('54). From Auburn, Martin contacted Hahn to inquire how he might obtain someone like Brandt to assist him there—that is, both to build up the stock of talent and to trim where he saw unpromising material. Hahn suggested asking Brandt, who accepted and went to Auburn for several years.

Warren insisted, and I went…. It turned out to be a real opportunity."[5] Rutland put together a strong math department.

Across campus in the College of Agriculture, Dr. James E. Nichols, professor of dairy science at Penn State, succeeded Dr. G. C. Graf, who had retired as head of dairy science. Jim Nichols had had no thought of coming to VPI when he was first contacted at Penn State about the dairy science headship. Years afterward, he said he refused for a time even to visit. When he finally agreed to do so, he found Hahn and Brandt quite persuasive, along with Dr. Wilson Bell, the new dean of Agriculture. But "Marshall Hahn was the real reason I came," Nichols recalled. "We just got

4.4 Peggy Hahn—Margaret Louise "Peggy" Lee was born December 17, 1923, on the family dairy farm in Dinwiddie County, Virginia. She was one of seven children of Travis Taylor Lee, a dairy farmer as well as rural mail carrier, and Nolie Dillon Lee, who in 1965 was named Virginia's Mother of the Year. In 2004 the dairy farm, part of the original colonial grant to the Lee family, was still operated by one of Peggy's brothers and two of her nephews, with help from one of her great nephews.

Peggy grew up on the farm and attended public schools in Dinwiddie County. She graduated from Madison College, today's James Madison University, with a major in home economics education, and then she taught home economics in Hyattsville, Maryland, until she and Marshall were married in 1948.

Dr. Hahn is quick to emphasize that "Peggy was enormously helpful" during his years at Virginia Tech. She was "the ideal wife of a university president, being very attractive, with a warm and friendly manner and unusual skill in making lunch and dinner guests feel very much at home." The Hahns hosted literally hundreds of lunches and dinners in their home—for alumni, students, political leaders, potential donors, visiting scholars, and prospective as well as current faculty. Peggy "managed these with skillful efficiency and friendly charm." She worked hard at it; she excelled at it; and she enjoyed it.

The former Virginia Tech president recalls that his "hard-driving approach to achieve rapidly as much progress as possible for the University sometimes left some ruffled feathers, and these were quickly smoothed by her charm." So she played crucial roles in institutional transformation—in Hahn's words, she "made easier to get done the difficult things that had to be done." He also credits her as playing a crucial role in "forging lasting and close friendships with so many persons important to the University," Governor and Mrs. Mills Godwin being prime examples.

caught up in his enthusiasm.... I thought something could be accomplished here." Nichols later became dean of the College of Agriculture and served there until his retirement.[6]

If J. B. Jones, Lee Rutland, and Jim Nichols all sounded like they were singing from the same script, it only went to show how involved President Hahn was in their recruitment—how indispensable his vision of the place was for their coming to Virginia Tech, serving as department heads, and playing the critical roles Hahn had in mind for them in building up the place.

"We Wanted to Build Quality"

As the institution grew, the numbers of new faculty employed each year became quite large. For the first few years, either Warren Brandt or the president interviewed every potential new faculty member. Warren Brandt recalled some of the reasons why:

> I was interviewing everybody in those days to try to teach the deans what we thought we ought to be looking for. Sometimes they would bring somebody in that really didn't look like quality.... It was a learning process, but it was also very deliberate on our part. A guy from a good school wasn't going to come to Tech as his first choice just in the normal course of events; we didn't have that kind of reputation. We had things that we thought we could accomplish [in terms of building a university]...but we weren't there yet. It was very deliberately a selling device on our part; they got to sit and visit some with the vice president...to hear the dream or whatever, to the point where they bought into it.[7]

Hahn and Brandt "felt in those years that was dreadfully important."

As the process developed and the deans became more comfortable with it, the departments began to identify individuals they would like to employ even before such candidates came for interviews. "We would set it up so that while we were doing certain things [during the candidates' visits], the department would have met and talked it over...and we would talk salary and make the offer before they left.... We would make them an offer right there on the spot. We did things like that...because we were recruiting above ourselves. We were recruiting people that were better than the institution was at that time, in considerable numbers," Brandt remembered. "We worked at it because we knew we had to have some edge to get the people we wanted."

The new faculty and staff who arrived on campus in the early 1960s were the first wave of hundreds who came to Blacksburg during the ensuing decade. Many of them can recall experiences with the Hahn/Brandt recruitment efforts similar to those J. B. Jones and Jim Nichols have reported. Of course, not all new faculty were recruited in such fashion; sometimes it was essential to see and talk personally to a candidate for a faculty position and then compare him or her with others who were interviewed. But for the top people, those whom Hahn and Brandt particularly wanted and knew so from the outset, the technique worked well.

Dr. James E. Martin, who came to VPI from Oklahoma State University in 1966 to become head of agricultural economics, is an excellent example. Jim came for an interview in winter 1965-1966, went through the interview process, and was offered the job on the spot. What he perceived, he later said, was that this was an institution on the way up, an institution that could make decisions and get on with the job. It was becoming vital, active, and it had great potential. When asked how long it would be before he made up his mind, he said "about twenty-four hours; all I have to do is talk to my wife."[8] Martin was one of a large number of faculty recruited from Oklahoma State University in the mid-1960s. Brandt and Hahn later chose him to become dean of the College of Agriculture.

Remembering all this many years later, Brandt and Hahn were still stirred by the excitement of that era. With rapid enrollment increases generating so many new positions, it was comparatively easy to turn a department around in a couple of years simply by outvoting "the old locked in types," as Brandt put it. The recruiting efforts focused on bringing in people from good schools, institutions such as VPI hoped to become, the two men recalled. "We wanted to build quality," Hahn said. "We wanted to bring in good people [and of course] some good people already were there."[9] After that, he attempted, he said, to create an environment in which they could be productive. The new emphasis on research and the annual raises that reflected impressive research activity provided an important stimulus. The entire undertaking turned out to be quite successful.

New Deans of Architecture and Engineering

Among the people recommended for the deanship of the new College of Architecture by Professor Len J. Currie, the departing director of the architecture program (see chapter 3), was Charles Burchard. After Burchard came to VPI as a visiting speaker for the architecture students, Currie wrote to Lou Pardue, with a copy to president-elect Hahn, that it was hard to be sure of Burchard's interest, "but our school and its program seem to have some real appeal" to him. Hahn, in encouraging Dean Whittemore in August 1962 to conduct a thorough search for "a truly outstanding person" to develop architecture as a separate school, said he would help in any way possible.[10]

President Hahn could, and did, help Dean Whittemore in the search for the first dean of the VPI College of Architecture. Hahn began looking into Charles Burchard's background and found an interesting architect with innovative ideas about architectural education. Burchard, a native of New York City, received an architecture degree from MIT in 1938. He went on to take his master's in 1940 from the Harvard School of Design, at that time under the chairmanship of Walter Gropius, who came to Harvard after fleeing Nazi Germany. He spent the war years as an airframe designer for Fairchild in Burlington, North Carolina, and then returned to Harvard to teach as well as to conduct a private practice. In 1953 he left Harvard to become a senior partner in the Cincinnati architectural firm of A. M. Kinney Associates, where he was doing creative work when Marshall Hahn began talking to him about VPI.

Dr. Hahn recalled years later that Burchard was soon recognized "as one of the really excellent people we wanted to bring to VPI, and that he could put together one of the centers of excellence we wanted to build." Burchard visited the campus in February 1963, and Hahn assured the prospective dean of his full backing in pursuit of nothing short of "placing VPI in the very forefront among schools of architecture." Finally Burchard agreed to accept the deanship—if he could delay his arrival until January 1, 1964, and if, after moving to Blacksburg, he could continue for a time to consult with his former firm. Hahn quickly agreed to both conditions.[11]

Meanwhile, Dean John W. Whittemore planned to retire early in 1963, so President Hahn moved quickly to find a new engineering dean. In anticipation of the vacancy, Hahn began writing to colleagues around the country soliciting nominations of possible candidates to succeed him, and associate dean S. H. "Buddy" Byrne was named acting dean. In recruiting for the engineering deanship, Hahn had described the position as one of the most important in the institution. As he wrote to Howard Miller at DuPont, he wanted to appoint "an outstanding engineer who can provide the level of leadership necessary to bring our engineering programs to the very forefront of advances in our technology."[12] In April 1963, Hahn announced the appointment of Dr. Willis G. Worcester, head of electrical engineering at the University of Colorado, as the new dean, effective July 1, 1963.

The president had to stretch a bit to obtain Worcester. The maximum salary possible under the state salary scale was $16,284, and Worcester was reluctant to come for less than $20,000. Hahn worked out an agreement with Governor Harrison to pay Worcester $20,000, with the additional $3,716 to come equally from state and private funds. As it happened, a prominent alumnus in Falls Church, R. J. Wysor ('06)—a retired president of Republic Steel Company as well as an internationally active industrial consultant—had sent in a contribution of 125 shares of Republic Steel stock. Hahn wrote to ask if he would mind if part of the gift were used to provide the supplement from private funds for Dean Worcester's salary. "This utilization of your gift would magnify its effectiveness, since it would result in a matching amount of additional state funds," Hahn wrote. Wysor readily agreed, and the college had a new dean.

The C. P. Miles Professorship in Arts and Sciences

In February 1965, the Board of Visitors approved, on the recommendation of President Hahn, the establishment of two named professorships—the John W. Whittemore Professorship in Engineering and the C. P. Miles Professorship in Arts and Sciences. No endowment funding was available for either; Dr. Hahn proposed that two state-funded positions each be supplemented annually with $2,000 by the Educational Foundation and that the total salary for each professorship, including the supplement, be $18,000 per academic year. The special professorships were effective September 1, 1965, and thus were available for the 1965-1966 school year.

The Whittemore Professorship of course honored Dean John W. Whittemore, whose death followed soon after his retirement in 1963. The Miles Professorship was named in honor of C. P. "Sally" Miles ('01), a legendary figure on the campus and then still very much alive.

4.5 C. P. "Sally" Miles ('01)—In his student days, Miles was an athlete, a star football player. Later he became graduate manager and athletic director. In the mid-1930s, he left athletics for a position in the classroom, teaching French. During World War II, President Burruss, amid administrative stress, appointed Miles dean of the College (VPI's third unit at the time, comprising the areas other than Agriculture and Engineering), so he had been responsible for roughly the same academic areas for which Burke Johnston was recruited as dean when he returned to VPI from Alabama in 1950—except by that time they had been organized into the School of Applied Science and Business Administration. By that point in his seventies, Miles returned to teaching, although part-time, in the Department of English and Foreign Languages. He finally retired from teaching, but he continued to serve as faculty chairman for athletics until his death in 1966.

In March 1965, Dr. Hahn announced that Dean G. Burke Johnston had accepted appointment to the C. P. Miles Professorship in English Literature, effective September 1, 1965. The announcement was something of a surprise for many of the faculty, especially Johnston's older colleagues, who had not been aware that Burke Johnston was contemplating leaving the dean's office. Nor had he been for long.

Dr. Brandt knew that more assertive leadership in the new College of Arts and Sciences was crucial in broadening VPI's curriculum as well as in providing the general education courses for students in technical and specialized fields. But he had been reluctant to move Burke Johnston. Brandt and Hahn both felt Burke had to be replaced, but the vice president was concerned that moving the much beloved Johnston from the dean's office would generate real problems, especially among the older faculty. Recalling the situation years later, Dr. Brandt put it like this:

[G. Burke Johnston] was obviously somebody the whole campus revered; he had a special position in people's minds…. They really felt strongly about Burke. I'm sure that, looking back on it, Marshall must have champed at the bit waiting for Burke to get something done…. Right from the word go, probably when I was interviewed, they commented that Burke didn't have it as a dean [and] it didn't take long to figure that out…. [But it took me a] year and a half to figure out how [to get it done], to get up my nerve to do it. I did a lot of them, but that was one I was really worried about. One, he was such a nice guy…. We were a bunch of young turks and one of us obviously had the reputation of a hatchet man. If we didn't do that one right, then it had the potential of upsetting the community really badly and interfering with what we were trying to do.

After President Hahn established the new named professorship, the appointment to which would be perceived among the faculty as an honor of considerable magnitude, Brandt said he finally felt he could move. "I think, in retrospect (and again, I learned from that one), that if you treat a man nicely a lot of them realize that they are not doing the job…. I think [Burke] felt much relieved when we finally took him out of the job, because he (my impression) knew he wasn't a good dean, but he couldn't resign. He couldn't come up front and volunteer that." Brandt, at least, believed Dean Johnston was glad to get out of administrative responsibilities and return to the classroom. "He was," Brandt acknowledged, "the epitome of the liberal arts scholar."[13]

Burke Johnston had mixed emotions, but he was glad to get back to teaching and writing. He had never fully left teaching even as an administrator. In later years, he described his departure from the dean's office as "a welcome change." It was clear to him that, in the kind of institution Hahn, Brandt & Co. was attempting to develop, the change was best for everyone concerned. He also clearly appreciated the way Dr. Brandt had handled the situation.[14] The Burke Johnston Student Center—known on campus as GBJ—commemorates his service to the University.

Recruiting Dean Malpass

Among the outstanding people for whom Hahn and Brandt were searching diligently, one was a successor to Burke Johnston as dean of the College of Arts and Sciences. He turned out to be Dr. Leslie F. Malpass, a psychologist originally from Hartford, Connecticut. Indeed the search apparently started even before Dean Johnston agreed to accept the Miles professorship. Malpass, initially contacted some months before, came to VPI for interviews at about the same time Dr. Hahn announced Burke Johnston's appointment to the Miles professorship.

Malpass earned his Ph.D. in clinical-experimental psychology at Syracuse University, where he had also done his undergraduate work. He had a broad range of experiences—Salvation Army officer, social worker, psychologist in a child guidance center for disturbed children. After eight years of teaching and research at Southern Illinois University, in 1960 he moved to the University of South Florida, at Tampa, where he was professor and chairman of behavioral sciences. In search of new opportunities, however, in 1965 he was just completing a year's post-doctoral internship in academic administration at the University of North Carolina and Stanford University. Two of the possible candidates for the deanship at VPI whom Dr. Hahn had attempted to recruit had declined, but one of them recommended his brother (then at another institution in Tampa), who wrote to Hahn to suggest Leslie Malpass as an attractive candidate. In early 1965, Malpass was invited for a visit to Blacksburg, where he had lengthy talks with Hahn and Brandt as well as other administrators and faculty.

Hahn and Brandt could be persuasive, and Malpass got the full treatment. He also was interviewing at Bradley University and at the University of California at Fullerton, but VPI seemed the better opportunity. Soon afterward, he was offered appointments at both Bradley and Fullerton, but he had heard nothing from VPI. When he called Warren Brandt "as a courtesy" before accepting one of the other positions, Brandt quickly came up with a counteroffer, and Malpass accepted it.[15]

Leslie Malpass joined VPI as dean of arts and sciences on July 1, 1965. Years later, he recalled being oriented to the campus that summer in regular meetings with Dr. Brandt. In September, Brandt began regular staff meetings with all of the deans. Remembering how the Hahn/Brandt team functioned, Malpass said they never told him what his college budget

4.6 W. E. C. Moore and the Anaerobe Lab—Among the significant research developments at VPI in the early years of the Hahn administration was the organization of the Anaerobic Bacteriology Laboratory, which later evolved into the anaerobic microbiology department. The Anaerobe Lab's founding director was Dr. Walter Edward Cladek Moore (1927–1996). In 1947–1948, Ed Moore worked at a hydroponics farm in Chosu, Japan, providing vegetables for the American occupation forces. (Also stationed at that farm in Japan was Warren Strother, and the pair found time to climb Mount Fuji.) Back in the States, Moore earned a B.S. at the University of New Hampshire in 1951; did graduate work at the University of Wisconsin, where in 1954 he completed a dissertation on anaerobes; and then moved to Blacksburg. Born the year after Marshall Hahn, he came to VPI the same year as Hahn.

By the 1960s, Ed Moore had developed an absorbing interest in anaerobic bacteria, the microbes typically found in large numbers in human and animal intestines, in soil or sludge—they thrive only in the absence of oxygen or oxidation products, and consequently little was known about them. Moore, by then a member of the research faculty in veterinary science, perfected a way, utilizing inert gases, to culture anaerobes routinely in an oxygen-free environment. But his tasks were just beginning; he and his colleagues had to develop a viable way to identify and classify thousands of different strains and substrains of such bacteria. The persistent work of Moore and his co-workers largely solved that problem by analysis of the fermentation products of each bacteria culture—acids, alcohols, and other material. Each strain left a precise pattern of fermentation products. Supplemented by tests for enzymes and growth requirements, this procedure made possible the precise identification of each strain of anaerobes.

This work generated some excitement—national and international—in the field of bacteriology, and in the mid-1960s it attracted several other scientists to Moore's operation. Joining the Anaerobe Lab in 1966 was Dr. Lillian V. Holdeman (later Lillian Holdeman Moore—Ed and Peg married in 1985), a research microbiologist at the US Communicable Disease Control Center in Atlanta, Georgia, and a national authority on botulism (food poisoning), with a Ph.D. from Montana State University. Dr. Cecil S. Cummins, from London (England) Hospital Medical College, came the next year, as did Dr. Louis DeSpain Smith, dean of the College of Graduate Studies at Montana State. Another star researcher, Tracy D. Wilkins, followed in 1972.

Moore also took over the work of Dr. Andre R. Prevot, a pioneer in anaerobic bacteriology research, at the Pasteur Institute in Paris, France. Moore had visited Prevot's laboratory twice earlier in the decade, and in the summer of 1967 he returned to Paris and purchased Dr. Prevot's entire collection, about 2,000 strains, collected and classified over the years. Prevot retired, happy that someone would carry on his life-long work, and Moore set about to build a national reference collection of anaerobes (W. E. C. Moore interview).

After Moore's death in 1996, his colleague Dr. Cummins wrote of him:

> His knowledge and expertise concerning anaerobes was distilled into the *Anaerobe Laboratory Manual*, edited by L. V. Holdeman and W. E. C. Moore, which first came out in 1972 and progressed to a 4th edition in 1977. Apart from giving detailed descriptions of morphological appearances and cultural characteristics of hundreds of species of anaerobes, it was a very practical manual illustrated by Ed Moore's own drawings (Ed was a very talented artist), and by very complete descriptions of how to prepare properly reduced media and to keep them reduced during storage and inoculation. He made many of the original pieces of equipment himself—he described a treadle-operated inoculator as "a good home shop project for a couple of evenings." Many of them were subsequently available commercially. Along with the *Manual*, he ran a series of courses for clinicians and medical technologists, through which the VPI *Anaerobe Laboratory Manual* and its methods became widely known and used.

A good part of the operational funding for Moore's lab came from the National Institutes of Health and the National Science Foundation; in fiscal year 1968, for example, NIH supplied $186,000 of its $315,000 total funding. But the lack of space was a big problem; the old veterinary science lab off Price's Fork Road became terribly overcrowded as the research expanded and the staff increased. Strenuous efforts in the late 1960s to obtain substantially greater funding proved partly successful. Construction money for the lab—$886,400—finally got into the state budget in 1968 as part of a statewide bond issue, and the NIH contributed another $376,000.

The work of the Anaerobe Lab continued for many years, but the lab itself—at one time "a world famous and world-class operation"—eventually came to an inglorious end. Faculty retired and were not replaced. The collection of microorganisms was scattered, distributed among various investigators. As for the building that once housed the Anaerobe Lab, "it still stands but is occupied by faculty in the College of Veterinary Medicine." (Communication from John L. Hess, department head of biochemistry, 29 March 2002)

would be until he actually received it. "Marshall sent the budget down through Warren, but it was Marshall's budget. That was the way Marshall let everybody in the institution know he was running [it]—by the way he, one, distributed the budget, and, two, distributed positions. Very simple administrative procedures, but he let everybody know clearly that he knew what was going on," Malpass said. "He could read quick and he could remember well. Once a year you got told how well you did."

Similarly, each faculty member was evaluated each year, Malpass remembered; Brandt would come to his office and work with each department head. "I had all the department chairs make their evaluations [of each faculty member] based on the usual criteria, instruction, research, and service—service defined only as scholarly professional service.... We were anxious that VPI become noted among the southern land-grant universities as one of the best. I got caught up with that. The opportunity was provided under Marshall's leadership to really demonstrate the kinds of salary increases you were going to get, merit salary increase, new offices, graduate assistants, and all those kinds of things that make a difference to those faculty chairs. You had it; you didn't have to worry about it. The money was there, so it was easy being a dean of arts and sciences," said Malpass.

The new dean was entirely supportive of the Hahn, Brandt & Co. emphasis on research. He had been heavily involved in research in various aspects of psychology at both Southern Illinois and South Florida, generating more than $1 million in research funding. "The whole idea in the 1950s of the universities in our society being the bulwark for the society's research was well grounded by then," he said.

But teaching was by no means undervalued. "Teaching," Malpass said, "was always considered number one, *always* number one, and it was expected that nobody was to be hired unless they could teach well. Granted the mathematics department, for example, sometimes had a very tough time and had to hire some foreign Ph.D.'s, because we wanted Ph.D.'s. We were willing to fight and scrap and pay for them, but we wanted Ph.D.'s. We had to hire some Orientals and some Indians, and sometimes their English wasn't so good. But every department was told, every year, 'teaching is the major function of this college, and you tell us for your area how teaching should be evaluated.'" Student evaluation of the various professors soon began, and Malpass said he began to encourage peer visitation at lectures so colleagues could also provide feedback on one's teaching effectiveness. Each department head also visited his faculty's classes, with or without invitation, and Dean Malpass himself frequently stopped in to visit as his faculty members taught. He also taught at least one course each quarter himself. "Teaching was considered very important," Malpass said, remembering his early days at VPI. "If the department head didn't give us good criteria for his people, and didn't apply it, he was let go."

Marshall Hahn and Warren Brandt both came to think highly of Dean Malpass. In mid-1967, after Malpass turned in his second annual report, Hahn replied with enthusiasm about such "an impressive statement": "Your leadership has become one of the University's most important

4.7 Another new recruit to the Tech faculty—J. Ambler Johnston was simply delighted. In spring 1967, Johnston wrote a note to President Hahn—and sent along a copy of another note, one from a friend at McLean, saying that James I. "Bud" Robertson would be returning to Virginia to join the history faculty at VPI. "It thrills me so that I cannot refrain from telling you.... Bud Robertson is one of my favorites, a learned historian, a fine fellow, and I predict will be a real asset to VPI," Johnston wrote. President Hahn, equally pleased, responded with a warm note of his own to "Uncle Doctor Leading Citizen Ambler."

Dr. Robertson grew up in Danville and earned his doctorate at Emory University. Then he had been staff director for the national Civil War Centennial Commission, and Ambler Johnston's Civil War Round Table work brought them together. After the centennial years ended, Robertson joined the history faculty of the University of Montana before accepting a position at VPI.

Ambler subsequently sent Lon Savage $150 and asked him to use it to pay for a "welcome Bud" party for Dr. Robertson at Grant's Tavern, then a popular place on Roanoke Road in Christiansburg. It was, indeed, a warm welcome for Robertson, held Tuesday evening, September 12, 1967, and presided over by President Hahn. Selected members of the faculty and staff were on hand, along with Ambler Johnston. The eighty-two-year-old Johnston couldn't have been more pleased. "I thought things went off right smoothly," he said in another note to Savage after he returned to Richmond. Totaling up the expenses, Lon wrote that, with everything included, the bill totaled $149.55. Ambler instructed him to give the remaining forty-five cents to Stuart Cassell, to use as he saw fit.

assets. I am impressed constantly with the way you have developed a full understanding of the spirit and direction of movement of the University, and have taken the leadership" in making the College of Arts and Sciences "one of the University's major strengths." Many years later, Brandt said of Malpass that he "was obviously the type of person that liberal arts people identified with. He spoke their language beautifully. He was well read. He had done a lot of research himself," and he "had a real interest in teaching." In sum: "From my standpoint we had an ideal person."[16]

Yet, remembering Les Malpass and his recruitment for the College of Arts and Sciences, Dr. Brandt suggested that Dr. Hahn initially didn't feel quite comfortable with Malpass. "It was not an academic thing," Brandt said; "it was a liberal-conservative thing. [That] was right about the time of the free speech movement, the start of the student uprisings, where we were just beginning to feel the impact of the Warren Court decisions, the change in individual rights versus community rights, and the ascendancy of the individual. Les came out of a liberal arts background, and he was widely read. Obviously he shared a lot of strong individual rights types of things which ran counter to a lot of things Marshall and I thought were important. I think that bothered Marshall. I guess he wasn't comfortable where Les would come down if push came to shove." Push did come to shove near the end of the decade, and Dr. Malpass's performance in the stressful periods of campus unrest removed any doubts Marshall Hahn may have had.

Recruitment, Research, Rewards

It is difficult, decades later, to recreate the excitement and energy of the mid-1960s on the VPI campus, when the momentum of the university's growth and development was so apparent. Lee Rutland, for example, was especially busy recruiting; he soon developed an impressive roster of newly appointed mathematics faculty from prestigious universities throughout the country. In spring 1965, he sent Warren Brandt a list of his new faculty for the 1965-1966 school year, which Brandt shared with Dr. Hahn. The president immediately dictated a warm congratulatory note to Rutland. "The most important responsibility of an educational administrator is that of locating and attracting outstanding people," he wrote.[17]

In September 1965, when the new school year began, some 20 percent of the teaching faculty were newly added to the faculty roster. The higher salaries made possible by the new state college and university salary system, related to national averages for similar institutions, had made a difference. "The new faculty represents an unusually strong group," Warren Strother summarized in the President's Report in summer 1966. "Their backgrounds range the whole of the United States and some foreign countries. When combined with the strong faculty already in the university's service, the new voices, new ideas, and new approaches provide a valuable stimulation for the entire institution."[18]

4.8 The geology department's recruiting class of 1967

—In spring 1967, Dr. Byron Cooper was hardly able to contain himself; his geological sciences department had had a banner recruiting season. Among the new faculty who would begin work in September, Cooper wrote in a note (8 April 1967) to Dean Malpass, were John Costain and Edwin S. Robinson, both from the University of Utah; Gilbert A. Bollinger, from Southern Illinois University; Richard M. Pratt, from Woods Hole Institute; and Charles Gilbert, from UCLA, who would come in 1968. "This staff undoubtedly constitute the greatest group of earth scientists between Penn State and the University of Texas," Cooper exulted. Recruiting such a group would mean "a giant step" toward the top twenty departments in the country, he predicted. President Hahn was pleased, too, and, in a note (15 April 1967) to Warren Brandt, he wrote, "There is little question about this area being one of our rapidly emerging nodes of national excellence."

The numbers of new appointments each year kept climbing, as did the total faculty percentage with doctorates. Warren Brandt worked up a data sheet on the teaching faculty in late 1966. It indicated that more than half—51 percent—of the 794 men and women on the faculty at that time had been hired since July 1962—that is, in the four years since the beginning of Dr. Hahn's administration. Moreover, 57 percent of all those with doctoral degrees had been employed since 1962. Some 165 new faculty members were appointed for fall 1966, of whom 113 were employed at the rank of assistant professor or above, and 102 (62 percent) had completed a Ph.D.[19]

President Hahn knew that recruiting a larger, stronger faculty—people prepared and committed to do substantial research, whatever its particular nature—was a high priority if he was to reach his goal and realize his vision of a new VPI. A university required a faculty engaged in research. Some among his faculty, even from the start, were already engaged in research, and with appropriate inducements—lighter teaching loads to leave more time for research, for example, and merit pay increases that clearly reflected the new emphasis on demonstrable research activity—others already on the faculty might also turn more of their energies to research. As for recruitment of new faculty, higher salaries certainly helped. Recruitment and rewards, Hahn knew, could combine to produce a far more research-oriented faculty, a far more research-oriented institution.

[1] Hahn interview, 10 February 1990.

[2] George Gray interview, 16 May 1989.

[3] Hahn interview, 10 February 1990; Brandt interview.

[4] J. B. Jones interview.

[5] Lee Rutland interview.

[6] James E. Nichols interview. Another Penn State professor, Dr. Houston B. Couch, succeeded Dr. S. A. Wingard as head of plant pathology and physiology. In chemical engineering, Dr. Gerhard "Gerry" Beyer came from the University of Missouri to succeed department head Dr. Fred W. Bull, who had been named director of the Engineering Experiment Station.

[7] Brandt interview.

[8] Martin interview; Brandt interview.

[9] Hahn interview, 8 July 1989; Brandt interview.

[10] Hahn papers, 1962.

[11] Hahn interview; Burchard/Hahn letters.

[12] Hahn letter, 5 November 1963.

[13] Brandt interview.

[14] G. Burke Johnston interview, 12 December 1990.

[15] Leslie F. Malpass interview, 31 March 1989.

[16] Hahn to Malpass, 20 June 1967; Brandt interview.

[17] Hahn letter, 12 April 1965.

[18] VPI *Bulletin* 59/8 (August 1966).

[19] Brandt noted that, of the institutions from which the Ph.D. degrees of incoming faculty in 1966 had been obtained, thirty-nine were in the South, twenty were Big Ten universities, and twelve were Big Eight universities; only one of the new recruits had earned his Ph.D. at VPI ("Data on VPI Faculty," fall 1966, Hahn papers, 1966).

Mrs. Hahn with College of William and Mary president Davis Y. Paschall. Courtesy of T. Marshall Hahn Jr.

Dr. Leslie F. Malpass, recruited in 1965 to VPI as professor of psychology and dean of the College of Arts and Sciences, subsequently served as vice president for academic affairs.

5: Looking for Money—Alumni and Development

President Walter Newman's best efforts left undone a number of major tasks, among them a strategy and organization to promote VPI's development. Efforts in the 1950s and early 1960s provided a base on which to build, but President Hahn undertook to centralize and reorganize development efforts—and to raise far more money. Various ideas that surfaced under Walter Newman were put in place by Marshall Hahn.

Efforts under President Newman

In the early 1950s, Dr. Jack Hutcheson initiated a campaign to raise funds for an adult education center on the VPI campus. Rather than try to put up a new building, Hutcheson proposed—and the Board of Visitors agreed—to convert the faculty apartment building across College Avenue from Squires Student Center into a continuing education center for conferences, short courses, and other continuing education activities.

The fund-raising for it had not been terribly successful. In 1958, Earl Fisher of Gloucester was hired as director of development, to be paid jointly by VPI and the VPI Educational Foundation. For some fifteen years, Fisher had been affiliated with the American City Bureau, and thus he brought considerable experience in fund-raising, although not in higher education. He worked up a "pre-centennial" campaign to raise $14 million in the fourteen years leading up to VPI's centennial in 1972. The money would be used for general college support, for the continuing education center, and for a new field house for physical education and recreation. By no means, however, did the campaign meet its goals.

The unhappy experience with Fisher had prompted Dr. Newman to seek outside advice on the matter of raising money for badly needed operating and capital purposes. His heart attack delayed the effort, but in 1961 Newman retained as consultants two highly regarded professionals (Mark Oliver had suggested both men) in the newly emerging field of higher educational fund-raising. They were Irving Youngberg, executive secretary of the Kansas Endowment Association at the University of Kansas, and Alan MacCarthy, director of the Development Council at the University of Michigan. The two spent several days on the VPI campus in December 1961 interviewing a good many people, and in January 1962 they sent a private memorandum to Dr. Newman, which they also shared with the president-elect at Kansas State.

The Youngberg/MacCarthy Memo recommended that the several fund-raising efforts on the campus—conducted by the development office, the Alumni Association, and the Student Aid Association (for funding scholarships for student athletes)—should be coordinated. They also recommended that VPI appoint two additional vice presidents. It seemed obvious, the two suggested, that Mr. Stuart Cassell should be named vice president for finance, for he was in effect already filling that position.

They recommended a second vice president for development and public relations, a person responsible for all VPI public relations and fund-raising. Such a person, Youngberg and MacCarthy suggested, should be a Virginian, a VPI graduate, someone with "the vigor of a young man, yet the stature and respect that comes with maturity...capable of representing [the president] and the institution in an able way in public gatherings of all kinds." The consultants made it clear that, in their opinion, Earl Fisher would not be suitable. Moreover, they noted, neither he nor his position would be needed if such a vice presidential position were set up.

MacCarthy and Youngberg also submitted a public report, which was widely distributed. It stressed the mechanics and philosophy of raising funds for a public institution, funds to supplement taxpayer support. It discussed the case for public support, campus and volunteer leadership, record keeping, and targeting specific publics in public relations work and in fund-raising.

The consultants said they found the environment favorable for fund-raising for VPI. "Neither of us has ever visited a campus where greater enthusiasm and support, both on a personal and professional basis, was indicated for the presidency than was evidenced at VPI for Dr. Newman and Dr. Hahn," they noted. VPI could and should make an excellent case for private support, they said. VPI's principal obstacle to effective fund-raising, MacCarthy and Youngberg concluded, was lack of effective organization.

Dr. Newman was not inclined to follow their advice, particularly about the vice presidents. As for Marshall Hahn, there were too many other things to deal with before he could consider the substance of the report. Meanwhile, President Newman sent a confidential note to the president-elect suggesting that Hahn might wish to discontinue the $8,000 salary supplement that the Educational Foundation paid Fisher and keep him on his regular $10,000 salary until his replacement could be found. Once in office, Hahn moved quickly. The Foundation supplement was promptly discontinued, and Fisher—who was given notice—was among those who "retired" December 31, 1962.

Alumni and Development: From Newman to Hahn

Alumni secretary Henry B. "Puss" Redd ('19) died on the first day of 1960, and Marcus L. "Mark" Oliver ('47), who had been assistant secretary of the Alumni Association for more than a decade, succeeded him. The alumni offices were in Memorial Gymnasium, which itself had been an alumni gift to the school in the 1920s as a memorial to the VPI men who died in World War I. Oliver reported in early 1962 to the Board of Visitors that the Alumni Association was anxious to see a comprehensive study of fund-raising and public relations at VPI, which the BOV had authorized. The relationships of the Alumni Fund, the Educational Foundation, and the Student Aid Association were friendly but unstructured, Oliver observed, and they should be reviewed in terms of VPI's current require-ments. For the previous year, 1961, he reported total contributions of $141,903 from 6,042 alumni.

In short, when Marshall Hahn returned to VPI, the Alumni Association already was providing significant support through its annual Alumni Fund, but at nowhere near the levels the new president had in mind. Shortly before relinquishing the presidency, Dr. Newman had reported that, during the previous year, the Alumni Fund had made the continuing education center project its major objective—so much so, many contributors had made three-year pledges for it, restricting their annual gifts for this purpose. Consequently the Alumni Association was $11,000 short in its own budget if it continued its support of various campus activities as in the past. This also would be the case in the following year, President Newman noted, since many of the three-year pledges had been only partly paid.

President Hahn quickly turned to the VPI newspaper, the *Techgram*, for his initial message from the campus to the entire VPI family. The paper, in a tabloid newspaper format, 9 1/2 by 12 1/4 inches, had been published since 1930 in cooperation with the Alumni Association. Bob McNeil, President Newman's director of public relations, was its editor, assisted by Jenkins Mikell "Jenks" Robertson. They gave the new president's message a prominent box on page two, under the heading "President Hahn's Own Greetings."

In a concise, to-the-point statement, Hahn said he would pledge to "all of the alumni, friends, and supporters of VPI that I will use all of my energies toward the continued advancement and strengthening of the institution we love." He spoke of VPI's heritage and rich tradition of service, and its multiple responsibilities of instruction, research, and extension. Meeting such responsibilities successfully, he said, "will require maximum and devoted effort from all of us." He outlined the challenges facing the University in enriching and strengthening all of its programs in the face of rapidly increasing numbers of students, and concluded by urging higher levels of "active financial and vocal support" from VPI's alumni and friends.

In early July 1962, President Hahn and Mark Oliver got together to talk about fund-raising. Prior to the meeting, Oliver sent Hahn a brief note that he said might help introduce the subject. After listing several things that institutional development is not, Oliver wrote that "the success of an institution of higher education depends upon all persons connected with the institution believing in, and working together for, the common goal of the institution." Consequently, the alumni secretary urged the new president to identify what VPI currently is, and what it should become, and establish specific goals to move the institution in that direction.

Dr. Hahn found it all interesting. In view of Dr. Newman's observations and the report of Alan MacCarthy and Irving Youngberg, all was obviously not well with VPI's organized fund-raising efforts. They badly needed coordination and strengthening. It was time, too, Hahn decided, to look closely at the relationship of the institution and its organized alumni. The Alumni Association activities at Mountain Lake, already scheduled for early autumn, would provide an opportunity to see what could be done.

Alumni Summit

The first major alumni get-together after Marshall Hahn became president was held at Mountain Lake, a secluded resort on the lake atop Salt Pond Mountain in Giles County, not far west of Blacksburg. The weekend festivities took place Friday and Saturday, September 21–22, 1962. These included a program for alumni chapter officers, a regular meeting of the Board of the Alumni Association, and the unveiling of a portrait of President-emeritus Walter Newman, commissioned by the Association. Dr. Hahn accepted the painting on behalf of VPI; the portrait would, he said, serve continually as a reminder "of an outstanding man who had given the most productive years of his life to the institution we all love" and would symbolize "the tremendous progress" VPI had achieved under Dr. Newman's leadership.

In addition to Dr. Hahn's public remarks—the basic stump speech with which he routinely sought to build public and political support for strengthening Virginia higher education—he had been invited to meet with the Board of the Alumni Association. It was an opportune time, for the Association had been attempting to reexamine its relationships with VPI and its reason for being. As it happened, a Board committee chaired by Jim Cargill ('36), a Richmond advertising executive, had been appointed two years earlier to review and revise the constitution and by-laws of the Association. The committee, which also included J. Ambler Johnston ('04) and G. B. "Bill" Hawkins ('10), had made little progress. A draft report submitted for discussion at the Mountain Lake meeting asserted that the Association existed simply "to further the cause of VPI" under direction of the institution's president. Consequently it would be inappropriate to revise the constitution and by-laws until VPI's president could "define the role of the Alumni Association."[1]

Cargill's draft report concurred with the Youngberg/MacCarthy Report that a single fund-raising body should be established at VPI (although it said that "for obvious reasons" the Student Aid Association would continue to raise money for athletic scholarships). The committee stressed, however, that "the Alumni Association is not and should not be a fund raising organization. Its role is on a higher plane." The draft report recommended that VPI's president "define a specific role" for the Alumni Association in the school's development program. If the president could not personally head a development program, he should "select an individual of sufficient stature and capacity to insure the program's success." The report also said the Association should be responsible to the VPI president for effecting a development program. The Association's "major role" should be that of projecting the college's image to students and alumni, although it also should assist in soliciting funds from alumni. Committee members might collect data and express their views, but actual drafting of the constitution and by-laws should be done by someone with better skills.

The Cargill committee met immediately prior to the Alumni Board meeting with the executive committees of the Board of Visitors and the VPI Educational Foundation, along with Dr. Hahn, Tom Rice, Gene Rowe, and Mark Oliver. This was an exploratory session on VPI's overall development, and its alumni and public relations concerns, in the light of the Youngberg/MacCarthy report.

The president's discussion with the Alumni Board at Mountain Lake generated some interest, and references to it surfaced from time to time among the VPI staff for years afterward. With the passage of time, it was increasingly difficult to find agreement on what the president had actually said, but the record is well preserved in Mark Oliver's minutes. First, Dr. Hahn spoke of the dedicated support and demonstrated value of the Association to VPI over many years—and of the loyalty and interest of individual alumni. The Alumni organization, the Educational Foundation, and the Student Aid Association all were interested in strengthening VPI, he said. But there was a widespread absence of recognition and respect for the quality of the University, both in Virginia and elsewhere. The new president urged everyone interested in VPI to work hard to strengthen the reputation and public perception of the University.

Development, Dr. Hahn said, means much more than simply raising money, and alumni are the essential element in any successful development program. Alumni should seek to "generate support of a non-financial nature" among business and professional groups, industry, legislators, and influential people generally—"must generate enthusiasm for VPI." In addition, alumni serve as "agents for the infusion of ideas into the institution," and innovative ideas were needed to help make VPI the kind of top-ranking institution it could become. Finally, alumni could contribute personal financial resources in support of VPI and help in the work of raising money from other sources.

Speaking further of VPI's organized development program, the president said a new start had been made and a renewed momentum must be generated. Accordingly, he proposed a series of steps. First, he said, recruit as soon as possible a director of development and public relations, a person young enough to be energetic and vigorous, yet mature; his job would be to assist the president in putting together a coordinated development program. The initial salary should be $15,000, supported equally by VPI, the Foundation, and the Alumni Association. Second, organize a VPI development council, composed of the executive committees of the Board of Visitors, the Alumni Board, and the Board of the Foundation, plus the president of the Student Aid Association. The existing leadership structure of the Alumni Association, the Educational Foundation, and the Student Aid Associations would be retained, he said. And third—the Foundation should perform this function—the school must develop necessary systems to maintain appropriate records on an institution-wide basis for centralized control of fund-raising and for receiving, holding, and managing gifts and investments.

Under such a system, Dr. Hahn said, the annual budget of the Alumni Association first would go to its Board for approval and then to the Development Council, which could grant the money from unrestricted funds. The Student Aid Association scholarship program for student athletes should continue separately, in coordination with the Development Council. Student Aid should not, however, engage in capital fund drives, Hahn said. He also suggested that a major role of the Development Council and the development director would be to work with the VPI administration and the Board of Visitors in formulating the institution's long-term objectives. Also, the development council could appoint advisory committees to work with the respective deans in assisting the several schools.

In the discussion that followed, Dr. Hahn stressed the need for a system of acknowledging, tabulating, and analyzing the contributions made to VPI, including gifts of equipment as well as securities and money. The reaction of the Board members appeared quite positive, although at least one, L. A. Hall ('24), stressed "the importance of retaining the developed relationship between the individual alumnus and the Alumni Association." Charlie Harris ('29), a manufacturer in Charlotte, North Carolina, summed up his reaction in a word—"terrific." That sentiment, Oliver wrote, "seemed to be generally shared by all of the members of the Board of Directors."

Dr. John E. Scott Jr. ('48), a member of the engineering faculty at the University of Virginia, promptly made a motion "that the Board go on record as...enthusiastically and wholeheartedly" approving Dr. Hahn's proposals; pledge to "move effectively to cooperate with [him] in working out the details of the proposal"; and "commit our treasurer to the extent of $5,000 per year for one third of the salary of the director of development and public relations." The motion was adopted unanimously. It was agreed in open discussion that the Executive Committee of the Board would work with Dr. Hahn in the early stages of the proposal and would involve a committee on the constitution and by-laws when it became appropriate.[2]

The timing of the Mountain Lake meeting appears to have been excellent. The Alumni Board was attempting to rethink the Association's basic reason for being and the role the Alumni Association should play in the life of the institution. At the same time, a new president had come aboard who was more than willing to give the Alumni Association a specific role, focused on generating financial and other support for much more rapid development of VPI.

It was not, however, a philosophical approach the Alumni Association had traditionally embraced. The VPI Alumni Association was an independent organization headed by its own Board of Directors, in partnership with alma mater. The relationship Marshall Hahn seemed to envision for it was more subordinate to the College, or as Hahn was increasingly disposed to call it, the University. Many years later, Dr. Hahn remembered the Mountain Lake meeting as an effort to get everyone pulling as a team. He had sought to promote "a vision of the Alumni Association being a powerful arm of the university's development efforts."[3]

At the Mountain Lake assembly, Tom Rice concluded his two-year term as president of the Alumni Association; he already had been named rector of the Board of Visitors at its summer meeting. Gene Rowe succeeded him as Association president; Jim Cargill was first vice president. They, together with Mark Oliver, Vernon Eberwine, and Bill Moffett, constituted the Executive Committee.

Gene Rowe was enthusiastic about President Hahn's scheme for coordinating VPI and Alumni Association efforts, especially the proposed development structure. Writing a few days later from Danville to Dr. Hahn about the Mountain Lake meeting, he put it like this: "Your presence and remarks to the several groups assembled…engendered an enthusiasm for development among alumni such as I have not previously observed at VPI. We thank you for coming and giving our Association a practical and inspiring program to pursue." The Alumni Board, Rowe said, had instructed its Executive Committee to work with Hahn in the early stages of the rearrangement of development work, and later the Association's constitution and by-laws would be appropriately revised.[4]

Dr. Hahn wrote back to thank Rowe and to congratulate him upon his election as alumni president. Hahn said he looked forward to working with all of the alumni leaders to form a successful development program at VPI.

"This Is Wonderful News"

The Alumni Board's enthusiastic approval of President Hahn's proposals at the Mountain Lake meeting in September 1962 was all he needed to begin a high priority development effort. VPI, the Foundation, and the Alumni Board all soon approved the proposed development council and the joint employment of a new development officer. The Board of Visitors approved the plan at its November 2, 1962, meeting. By the time the Executive Committee of the VPI Educational Foundation Board got together in late November to reconfirm the Mountain Lake agreements, President Hahn was working hard at fund-raising. He needed money. He looked for it from alumni, from other private citizens, from corporations, and from the state.

5.1 C. Eugene Rowe—C. Eugene "Gene" Rowe ('33) was elected president of the VPI Alumni Association in early autumn 1962, a few months after Marshall Hahn became president. It was a most fortunate development for the new president, for the story of VPI in the 1960s might have been different had another person, less amenable to the direction in which Hahn sought to move VPI, taken on that position. Among the most supportive and committed alumni VPI has produced, Gene Rowe gave the new president tremendous encouragement and support. A soft-spoken, even-tempered man with a ready smile and a twinkle in his eyes, he quietly did the things he believed would be most helpful to his alma mater, its students, and his fellow alumni. The Rowes and Hahns became close friends.

Rowe was a native of Northumberland County, son of the county treasurer. He had had to borrow money to enroll at VPI in 1926 as a business major. Active in a variety of extracurricular activities, he was a founder and first president of the VPI chapter of ODK, the student leadership fraternity, and was editor of both the student newspaper and the yearbook. Also an officer in the Corps of Cadets, Rowe graduated in 1933, in the depths of the Great Depression, with academic honors.

Rowe's first job was with the Continental Oil Company in Richmond, in accounting. Two years later, he began a twenty-year association with Burlington Industries in North Carolina. During those years, he met and married Mary Lewis Johnson, a native of Salem, Virginia, and a graduate of Vanderbilt; had a son and daughter; and completed Harvard University's advanced management program. He then joined the Baldwin Piano Company in Cincinnati, Ohio, for several years before moving to Dan River Mills (later Dan River, Inc.) as secretary-treasurer, first at Danville, Virginia, and later at Greenville, South Carolina. At his retirement in 1976, he was Dan River's vice president and chief financial officer.

Gene Rowe early became a dedicated and active alumnus, so much so that Mary Lewis used to say, "I guess I married an institution as well as a man." A founding member of the original Central Carolinas alumni chapter, Rowe was also a founding director of the VPI Educational Foundation (now the Virginia Tech Foundation). He was one of the prime movers in the planning and fund-raising for the World War II memorial chapel at VPI, and before that he outfitted a small YMCA chapel in Squires Student Center (see chapter 9). Having been elected to the Association Board in the early 1950s, he served as vice president in 1958-1962 and president in 1962-1965. He later (1968-1976) served two successive four-year terms on the VPI Board of Visitors. Rowe served successively as president (1972-1982) and chairman (1982-1985) of the Virginia Tech Foundation, and he remained active in alumni and university affairs until his death in 1987.

As VPI sought to generate more widespread support, the school often solicited major gifts to be earmarked for specific projects, but unrestricted gifts were essential, too. For example, just before Christmas 1963, Stuart Saunders, president of the N&W, wrote Hahn that his Board had authorized a $10,000 unrestricted gift to VPI. "This is wonderful news," Hahn replied, "and I deeply appreciate both the gift and the confidence it represents."

Among major projects, the president first wanted to complete the funding for the continuing education center, for which VPI had been attempting to raise money for nearly fifteen years. By late 1962, Dr. Hahn had learned that the State's Capital Outlay Study Commission would recommend that the 1964 General Assembly appropriate $850,000 for the project, to be matched by an equal amount from VPI sources. Hahn reported that about $786,000 had been raised, and sufficient pledges had been received to make the total at least $850,000.

VPI would request the $850,000 state appropriation through the normal budget process, Hahn told the Foundation leaders, and the chances of obtaining the funds were good, especially in view of the Capital Outlay Commission's recommendation. Because the project already had been so long delayed, therefore, he proposed that the Foundation, using funds already contributed, go ahead and engage an architect to begin preparing plans under normal state capital outlay procedures. He assured the Executive Committee that he would first obtain state approval for doing so.[5]

Hahn did his own development work, personally soliciting a small list of possible donors for contributions. Later, in autumn 1963, it was announced that the Mount Ararat Foundation (established by F. Donaldson Brown of Port Deposit, Maryland, a VPI alumnus and former General Motors vice president) had made a $100,000 gift to VPI to assist in strengthening Newman Library.

Other significant projects urged along by President Hahn included a longer runway at the VPI airport (see chapter 11). The biggest project of all, however, was a proposed new football stadium, expected to cost approximately $3 million—and relying on private gifts for its financing.

A New Stadium

The old stadium, Miles Stadium, was located immediately south of Memorial Gymnasium. Although it had served long and well, its time had gone, Hahn concluded. It had serious structural problems, and the space it occupied was badly needed for student residence hall construction. The Board of Visitors had concurred in the desirability of building a new stadium, and at its November 1962 meeting it approved Dr. Hahn's idea of quietly approaching a small number of individuals to seek commitments for major gifts for the proposed stadium.

The proposed new stadium would be constructed on a site southeast of the new coliseum where there was adequate space for it. Hahn, writing to potential contributors, said that $1 million was being sought for the first phase, and a gift of $300,000—or 10 percent of the entire cost—would be enough for the stadium to be named for the donor. At that point, he said he had received $250,000 toward the initial $1 million. One of the early donors for the stadium was John W. Hancock Jr., of Roanoke Electric Steel, who pledged $50,000, payable over five years. Thanking Hancock in December 1962, Hahn said that three early pledges, including his, totaled more than $100,000 and would be invaluable in generating additional gifts.

Construction contracts were let for the new stadium and for demolition of Miles Stadium at the end of the 1964 football season. But the contracts had termination clauses, so that if fund-raising fell too far behind, construction could be stopped without further liability. The first-phase construction contract, for the press box tower and approximately 6,800 seats for spectators, was about $665,000, most of which had been raised or pledged. A loan—guaranteed by the VPI Educational Foundation—was negotiated with the First National Exchange Bank for about $700,000 for the completion of the west stands.[6]

Construction was sufficiently advanced to permit the home games of the 1965 season to be contested in the new stadium, although only a part of the stands had been completed. The west stands were completed that year, and additional bank loans were authorized to permit beginning of construction of the east stands. The first contract for construction on the east stands, about 7,000 seats, was let early in 1965, to be completed before the 1966 football season. Student fee funds were authorized by the Board of Visitors in 1965 to permit long-term financing; major contributions for the stadium construction also continued to come in.[7]

The stadium subsequently was named Lane Stadium, in honor of Edward H. Lane Sr. ('12), head of the Lane Company, who had made a series of gifts totaling about $300,000 toward its construction.

5.2 Visiting Scholars Program—Near the end of the 1962-1963 school year, President Hahn announced that an anonymous donor had contributed $300,000 to fund a ten-year visiting scholars program. The funds were to be used to bring nationally and internationally known scholars to the campus for lectures and other programs for the students and faculty. A good many years elapsed before the identity of the donor was made known following his death: John Lee Pratt of Stafford County, a former General Motors executive who gave generously to many institutions. He had already made significant and undisclosed gifts to VPI, would make many more, and it did not take President Hahn long to identify him and to encourage the funding of the visiting scholars program.

The visiting scholars gift suggested the scope of the new president's interests. The program would attract public attention with high-profile visiting scholars and was broad enough to encompass any field. Dr. Hahn invited Mark Van Doren, the renowned critic, poet, and biographer, to the campus for a convocation, offering to pay expenses and a $600 honorarium. The cultural programs of the campus were being upgraded "to bring in...some of the country's most distinguished scholars," Hahn wrote, and Van Doren would initiate the series. Van Doren readily agreed and on 24 October 1963, he came to VPI for a reading/lecture convocation. Another prominent visiting scholar, Allardyce Nicoll, came from England and spoke on "Shakespeare Today."

While Dr. and Mrs. Hahn were in Kansas, they developed an interest in the paintings of Streeter Blair (see box epilogue.2), a retired Kansas schoolteacher then living in Los Angeles who took up "primitive" style painting in his seventies. The Hahns began corresponding with him about acquiring some of his work. Blair came to Blacksburg in May 1965 for a weeklong series of seminars, lecture-demonstrations, TV interviews, and receptions, all handled as a part of the Visiting Scholars program. After spending part of his stay as houseguest of the Hahns, he wrote them from California, "The Prince of Wales could not have been better treated." (Hahn papers; Mrs. Hahn interview)

"Dear Friend"

President Hahn could readily see, from the beginning of his administration, that annual gifts from alumni had to pick up, especially unrestricted ones. The Alumni Association budget was in difficulty, so it could not provide much support for scholarships, the campus YMCA, or other activities. Gene Rowe wrote the president in January 1963 to review the situation. In March, Hahn met in Richmond with the Alumni Fund Council (the Alumni Association's fund-raising committee), which included Tom Rice, Ambler Johnston, Graham Claytor, Gene Rowe, and half a dozen other senior alumni leaders. And the next month, shortly after his April 4 inauguration, Hahn arranged with Mark Oliver to send another in a series of "Dear Friend" letters to alumni.

In that letter, the president described his inauguration as a "humbling experience." The opening months of his presidency had convinced him, he wrote, that "the future holds no limit to the greatness of [VPI], provided every alumnus, friend, and supporter…makes available the maximum support." Those who wanted to see VPI take its place among the nation's top universities, he exhorted, would have to help create a "climate of support" among the institution's natural publics, together with "a free exchange of ideas" among alumni and friends.

As the new president put it, "The most urgent need of VPI is continuing, annual investment in a greater VPI—at an ever increasing rate." So he called upon VPI's alumni and other friends to make "unstinting investment of personal resources"—"to invest in the future of VPI with as large a check as you reasonably can write." The future would not be easy, he concluded, but "it *is* an exciting and worthwhile one."

The search for a new director of development also began to intensify during the spring of 1963. During the search, Hahn and others interviewed R. Craig Fabian, a supervisor of educational programs for Westinghouse, in Pittsburgh. In July, Fabian was appointed director of development and public relations, with a salary of $15,000, subject to periodic review and raises for good performance. Plans for the immediate future included no crash fund-raising program or capital gifts campaign, Hahn wrote him. Rather, "emphasis is being placed on annual, informed, enthusiastic support for VPI on a continuing basis."

Fabian was a crew-cut, friendly person with a ready smile and easy laugh. He loved to talk, and his non-stop conversations were punctuated with laughter. He was a graduate of the College of Wooster, in Ohio, and had a master's degree from Syracuse University. A veteran of World War II, he was a lieutenant commander in the Navy when he left the service. He was an admissions officer at Rider College for five years, and then an industrial relations officer for the Naval Air Turbine Test Station in Trenton, New Jersey, before going to Westinghouse. [8] The VPI job brought him back to academe.

Fabian was at work in Burruss Hall by early September 1963, when Hahn wrote him a note to ask that he put together a pamphlet or leaflet to explain the 1964-1966 budget requests that VPI would be presenting to the General Assembly. "In considering the development of financial support for the university, we must always keep in mind that our greatest source of support is from taxpayer funds. This should be an ever-present component of our philosophy in all development and promotional efforts," the president stressed. Some privately funded edifices were constructed at VPI during the Hahn years—chief among them Lane Stadium—but Hahn remained a firm believer that, where a state institution is concerned, the state should be the primary source of construction funding.

[1] Preliminary Draft, Report of the Constitution and By-laws Committee, Alumni Board, forwarded to members of the Alumni Board, 11 September 1962, by Mark Oliver, copy included with the minutes of the Board meeting at Mountain Lake.

[2] Mark Oliver letter, 11 September 1962; minutes, Alumni Board, 21 September 1962.

[3] Hahn interview, 8 July 1989.

[4] Rowe letter, 26 September 1962.

[5] Minutes, executive committee, VPI Educational Foundation, 21 November 1962.

[6] Minutes, 11 December 1964.

[7] Minutes, 11 December 1965.

[8] VPI news release, 5 September 1963.

C. Eugene Rowe ('33) gave loyal support to VPI in a great many ways, from 1970 to 1975 serving as rector of the Board of Visitors. Photo by Fabian Bachrach.

6: President Hahn and State Policy, 1962-1965

It was one thing for President Hahn—as he pursued his vision of a new VPI and, indeed, a new approach to higher education in Virginia—to secure the support of his Board of Visitors, at least neutralize the State Council of Higher Education, and regularize and energize fund-raising activities. Much of his agenda could be achieved, however, only if he could bring the state government around to his view of things. Much of Hahn's energy during the first few years of his presidency was directed to that larger objective, played out in that larger arena.

The General Assembly that met in early 1964 was a central feature of those efforts. It enacted one major change that he desired—related to the VPI connection to Radford College—and it called for a statewide study that might lead to substantial further change.

Radford and Blacksburg

The VPI/Radford relationship had complicated the reality of both institutions ever since they had joined in 1944. An initiative of Governor Colgate Darden that year primarily involved the University of Virginia in Charlottesville and Mary Washington College in Fredericksburg, making MWC a female "coordinate" college such that undergraduate women would not be attending the Charlottesville campus. But the same law also linked VPI with the State Teachers College at Radford, which was renamed Radford College and designated the women's division of Virginia Polytechnic Institute. The law made both campuses the responsibility of the same governing board, the VPI Board of Visitors, which was enlarged to sixteen members (later reduced to fifteen), four of whom were to be women. Despite the linkage after 1944, the new arrangement preserved Radford College's identity as a separate institution. Radford retained its own president and administrative structure; the president of VPI was the chancellor of Radford College.

Marshall Hahn was not unfamiliar with this institutional family relationship when he returned as president, having observed it close-up during his earlier years at VPI. He had seen the practical difficulties generated by the partial merger of two different institutions. The negotiations necessary to find solutions to specific questions and problems involving both Radford and VPI were often protracted and frustrating.

One consideration driving President Hahn's determination to separate VPI and Radford College was his concern about faculty salaries. To compete nationally for top-flight faculty, he would have to be able to pay competitive salaries (see chapter 4), and he knew that Radford College's affiliation would make it all the more difficult. There always would be the question of equity between the two faculties; at Radford, faculty continued to gain promotion to associate professor when they earned a doctorate. Separation would end that problem as well as others—for example, the Radford relationship inhibited the broadening of VPI's curriculum into the humanities and social sciences.

There were, of course, some women students at VPI—there had been since 1921. A few were graduate students. According to the 1944 arrangement, undergraduate women, too, continued to matriculate at VPI, if they could slip through certain legal loopholes—they were residents of the Blacksburg community and lived at home, or they were at least twenty-one years old, or they were studying engineering, which was unavailable at Radford. The female percentage remained no higher than 5, however.

President Hahn decided early on that the best thing to do was to legally separate the two institutions, for Radford College would make virtually impossible the institution-building tasks, difficult enough under the best conditions, that he saw ahead. Not only was the matter of faculty salaries a pressing concern, but, if Hahn were to create at VPI the university he envisioned, it would have to be coeducational, and that would not be possible with the existing VPI/Radford relationship.

6.1 Kinnear on Hahn and the Radford connection

—Lyle Kinnear—who had taught courses in Radford as well as in Blacksburg—later recalled about VPI's connection with Radford College that one of the first things President Hahn did, in 1964, was "he broke that relationship. He didn't say so publicly, but privately he said, 'We'll never grow with the fence we got built around us.'"

Looking back another twenty years to 1944, Kinnear explained, about the legislative act that put the two institutions together in the first place, that John B. Spiers, who represented Montgomery County and the City of Radford in the House of Delegates, had written the bill. The man "who drew up the plan for the union of the two institutions" was "quite efficient as a legislator, but he was a native of Radford. He drew the plan in such a way that—he openly said publicly, published it, didn't pick any bones about it—that it would not hurt VPI but would help Radford. I still get a little bit wrangled at what happened on that, because they built a fence around VPI and its expansion." That is, "the provision for this consolidation included that VPI was not to offer any of the work in the humanities that could rightfully be done at Radford." Moreover, the Blacksburg campus was "not to offer any education courses other than the vocational. Women were excluded from most of the vocational courses [that] VPI would offer in the field of vocational education, unless they lived within Blacksburg. Girls could attend these courses of education if they lived in Blacksburg. But if they didn't, they'd have to go to Radford. So that was the plan on which they operated."

Kinnear had his own recollections of how the relationship worked. He went on about the extraordinary range of courses he taught (during one trying term, Mondays, Wednesdays, and Fridays on one campus; Tuesdays, Thursdays, and Saturdays on the other; all different courses—fall, winter, spring, and summer). Among those courses, "I would teach a course in curriculum instruction, school administration, school supervision, school finance, and school law. I did not try all of those at one time, but over a period of time I'd done all of them…. When Radford decided that they wanted to offer a master's degree in school administration, the man who was to teach it actually wrote to me and wanted to know if I would furnish him my syllabus and outline and how to teach it. He said, 'Since we're one institution, let's just trade it back and forth.' They got the benefit, I did the work. That actually happened." (Dunn interview with Kinnear, 12, 13, 19)

Hahn would need BOV support on the Radford initiative. Wyatt Williams, then a newly appointed BOV member, remembered visiting with Marshall Hahn in summer 1962, before their first Board meeting in

August, and the tenor of their conversations with respect to Radford College. Williams tended to agree with the new president. Strongly impressed by Hahn's vision and his readily apparent strength and determination, he was inclined to support the president's initiatives.[1]

Radford College president Charles K. Martin wrote almost immediately after Hahn assumed the VPI presidency to suggest they get together to discuss institutional relationships.[2] The young VPI president was pleasant, courteous, and not at all intimidated by his older colleague, as Martin quickly learned. Martin and VPI officials earlier had made tentative agreements that in 1962-1963, Radford women would have all the privileges of VPI students with respect to athletic events (after payment of athletic fees), including eligibility to be elected cheerleaders and the opportunity for the Radford College band to perform at athletic contests.

The new VPI president would not concur, however. He said the band and cheerleader questions were quite separate from attendance at athletic events. Martin insisted that, in this context, Radford students should have the same privileges on the VPI campus as VPI women. Reporting all of this to the Board of Visitors, Martin recommended that the Radford College "reluctantly withdraw from the [VPI] athletic program." Radford student leaders, sensing a new uneasiness in the relationships of the two institutions, wrote to rector Tom Rice in October 1962 to inquire why. Why, for example, were Radford women no longer invited to participate in VPI homecoming activities?[3]

Shedding a Sister

Early in 1963, no doubt with Marshall Hahn's encouragement, Rector Rice appointed a Board committee—composed of himself, Bill Erwin, Ed Lane, Paul Saunders, and Jane Wilhelm—to look into the question of separating VPI from Radford. After discussing the matter with faculty leaders from the respective campuses as well as the two presidents, the BOV committee decided that it would be best to legally separate the two institutions. They had, after all, never been consolidated; they still functioned largely as separate institutions; and the linkage was getting in the way.[4]

The full Board, at its May 1963 meeting, adopted a resolution recommending the separation. Citing Radford College's growth and maturity, it observed that Radford was the largest women's college in Virginia—larger than Longwood, Mary Washington, or Madison College. The growing programs of both institutions, the resolution noted, "require greater investments of time and energies than is possible by a single administration and governing board."

President Hahn again went over the matter with the Board in August 1963. Shortly thereafter, he wrote to John Boatwright, at the Statutory Research and Drafting office at the capitol, to ask that he initiate the drafting of proposed legislation to separate the two institutions. One of the two schools should be designated Virginia Polytechnic Institute, Hahn wrote, and the other Radford College, and the bill should retain for the VPI Board of Visitors as many of the members of the existing Board as possible. Hahn suggested that the statute take the general form of the one that, just a year earlier, had separated Old Dominion College in Norfolk from its prior status as a branch of William and Mary.[5]

Hahn assured Boatwright that Governor Harrison was well aware of the matter, as Tom Rice had discussed it at length with the governor. Boatwright drafted the bill, and, enacted with virtually no opposition in the 1964 General Assembly, it became effective in July 1964. Beginning with fall quarter 1964, all courses on the VPI campus were open to women students. Separated from Radford, the Blacksburg campus could—and would—become much more fully coeducational than ever before.

Just as VPI's programs and schools changed their identities, then, so did the students who enrolled in them, and the school's policies and practices soon reflected the changing student population. Back in 1952, during the Newman administration, VPI had begun recognizing a "Campus Man of the Year." In 1965, the school began naming a "Woman of the Year" as well, and Carol P. Schuck, from Arlington, was so recognized that inaugural year.

The 1964 Legislature

Despite the impressions that the VPI president had made upon Governor Albertis S. Harrison Jr. and the legislators during his budget presentations, Marshall Hahn found the governor's recommendations to the 1964 General Assembly for VPI funding distressingly low. "I must confess I am deeply disappointed, concerned, and even shocked," Hahn wrote to Joseph C. "Joe" Hamrick at the Division of Industrial

Development on January 13. The proposed Virginia Tech appropriations for 1964-1966 were "cut to a point where I don't see how we can operate."

Hahn promptly went to work to see how much he could persuade the General Assembly to improve upon Governor Harrison's recommendations. Much of what went on remains unrecorded, but Marshall Hahn and Stuart Cassell were much in evidence in the halls of the capital in January and February 1964. Walter Newman's work, entirely confidential, is also unknown, but Hahn undoubtedly found his advice and assistance useful.

Erwin Will, chairman and CEO of Virginia Electric and Power Co. and a member of the VPI Board, was no stranger to legislative and executive lobbying. Remembering those days much later, Will said Hahn had been busy in Richmond during winter 1963-1964. "He knew he couldn't get very far unless he had the backing of the legislature, and set out to get it," Will recalled. "Hahn was the first [VPI president] I know of who really set out to get acquainted with the legislators and to get to the point where he was persuasive enough to get the financial backing...that he needed. He was that much political. We were asked to help, and we did; we got a very receptive audience. VPI stood right high when Marshall was there."

Some of the effort is in the record; a personal note in Hahn's 1964 files indicates that a letter and a summary information sheet were sent to each VPI alumni chapter in Virginia; to 100 selected members of the Richmond chapter; to 125 key extension constituents through Extension Director Bill Daughtrey; and to each of the academic departments. The material contained Hahn's analysis of the governor's recommendations: "For an increase of more than 1,000 in enrollment (19.5 percent), the recommended increase in General Fund appropriations for maintenance and operations, exclusive of salary adjustments, was only 4.1 percent. This amount will not provide for continuation of instructional programs without serious decline in quality. Virginia cannot afford such loss in higher education." Hahn similarly went through the governor's recommendations for the experiment stations and the Extension Service, as well as the branch colleges, stressing what he perceived to be drastic underfunding.[6]

In his discussions with the House Appropriations Committee and the Senate Finance Committee, Hahn agreed to trade-offs to improve the situation to some degree. Despite his earlier insistence that student fees not be increased, he agreed to raise them to provide additional salary funding.

He also had to do some horse-trading to find a way to obtain more money for building construction. The General Assembly had traditionally appropriated one-half the cost of dormitory construction; Hahn agreed to underwrite all, instead of one-half, of the dormitory construction costs from revenue bonds to be paid from residence hall fees. He was especially anxious to proceed with the continuing education center project, to build new facilities for Home Economics, and to begin enlarging the administration building, Burruss Hall.[7]

Hahn later wrote to Ed Givens, president of the Agricultural Conference Board, and requested a special meeting of the Executive Committee. On February 10, Givens wrote to the members of the Committee and outlined assignments for their work with individual members of the House Appropriations Committee. Each was given the names of several members. For example, Earl J. Shiflett, then director of the Association of Virginia Cooperatives, was assigned Chairman Howard Adams of Eastville and Delegate Tom Frost of Warrenton, and he was also asked to work with the Richmond group on Richmond Delegate Fred Pollard.[8] The results suggest that the Conference Board's work was helpful.

There was concern, meanwhile, on the part of the Agricultural Conference Board about its lobbying activity for general VPI funding. It was interested, of course, in agriculturally related aspects of the VPI budget. After a meeting on that subject later in the year in which Warren Brandt and Stuart Cassell participated—Hahn had to be elsewhere—the president wrote to Howard H. Gordon, the Conference Board secretary, to suggest the most important result of the meeting was improved communications. "The particular interest of the Conference Board in the agricultural side of the budget request of VPI is of course easily understood and most appropriate," Hahn wrote. "At the same time I do feel our most effective approach is for all our interested publics to support the total budget request."[9]

Hahn's Assessment of the 1964 Legislature's Work

In early March, after the session had adjourned and the dust had settled, Hahn had his public relations office send out a news release on the General Assembly's appropriations for VPI. Most important, it stressed, were the faculty salary increases and the new merit system. Faculty salary increases in the two years would raise the faculty salary average to the national average for land-grant universities, with half the cost from the State General Fund and half from increased student fees and other special revenues. General Fund appropriations for maintenance and operations for the instructional programs were increased 8.1 percent over 1962-1964, as compared to Governor Harrison's recommendation of 5.6 percent. For the Engineering Experiment Station, the increase was 29.7 percent, "thanks to the House Appropriations Committee." General Fund maintenance and operations appropriations for the Agricultural Experiment Station and the Extension Service had been increased 6.9 percent and 5.8 percent, respectively, in addition to salary increase funds, the release reported.

Appropriations for building construction included $850,000 for the continuing education center (to be matched with the same amount from private funds for a total of $1.7 million); $750,000 for the first phase of the Home Economics building; and $45,000 for plans for the initial addition to Burruss Hall; aside from authorization for construction of three new dormitories to be funded with bonds. Other capital outlay items in the VPI 1964-1966 budget included $273,000 for books and equipment; $427,000 for utilities and site development; $295,000 to complete the renovation of Davidson Hall (the chemistry building); $316,000 for the completion of the coliseum; $350,000 for the renovation of McBryde Hall; $42,000 for plans for the new architecture building; $200,000 for an addition to the laundry; and $150,000 for greenhouse construction.

Hahn was fairly blunt, at least in the Virginia context, in the news release: "The level of appropriations for the coming biennium provides for significant progress in a number of areas, but significant increases in appropriations for both operations and capital outlays must be made available in future biennia if the increasing numbers of Virginia youth seeking high quality educational opportunities at VPI are to be accommodated."

President Hahn was nonetheless careful to thank Governor Harrison for his "assistance and support" during the 1964 legislative session. "Although there are some areas in the various budgets of VPI and its associated agencies where funds will be rather limited during the coming biennium, the majority of our most pressing needs were met, and I do deeply appreciate your helpful counsel and patient assistance," he wrote the governor on March 11, 1964. Hahn deemed Harrison's program for bringing faculty salaries up to national averages "the most important step taken in higher education in several biennia." He stressed, however, that if the full potential of the state's economy were to be realized, much more substantial state support for higher education would be required.

In a similar letter to Lieutenant Governor Mills Godwin thanking him for his help with the General Assembly session, President Hahn said he counted heavily on future legislative sessions to help make up for some of the funding that could not be achieved in 1964, especially considering the flood of would-be students seeking admission to Virginia's institutions of higher education. Godwin, responding in a "Personal" letter March 17, said he believed the outlook quite good for more adequate state support in future legislative sessions for Virginia's institutions of higher learning, although he alluded to "some problems among our leadership" that had been discussed previously. "I honestly believe," Godwin wrote, "the people of Virginia are willing to go along with a reasonable program of increased activity. You and others can do a lot to help solidify this program, and it can be done without being too critical of what we have done or what we are now doing. The facts of life are such that the demands are greater and the needs are imperative."

Godwin then turned to overtly political matters. He went on to thank President Hahn for his personal support with respect to Godwin's political aspirations. "As of now most signs appear encouraging," he wrote, but acknowledged that political winds can change quickly. Godwin suggested he had to be careful in coming months if his political plans were to become viable; he urged Hahn to be "frank and free" in his political advice. "I do not have the heart or desire…to undertake a campaign for Governor without the backing and support of the organization as we know it in Virginia," he said. As things developed, Mills Godwin was elected governor in November 1965—setting the stage for what President Hahn had reason to view as a particularly productive legislative session in 1966 (see chapter 10).

The Statewide Study

The focus of a good deal of Marshall Hahn's interest in the legislative goings-on in the capitol in the winter of 1964 was a Senate Joint Resolution, SJR30, the chief patron of which was Senator Lloyd C. Bird of

Chesterfield County. The proposed resolution would mandate a thorough study of Virginia higher education by a legislative commission. Generating large questions about statewide higher education were such considerations as the state's rapidly growing population, its urbanization, rapid changes in technology, and the governor's industrial development program. Marshall Hahn was especially interested in the development of a long-range plan for Virginia higher education, in which VPI would function as a comprehensive land-grant university. The study resolution was adopted without significant opposition in the Senate, and readily concurred in by the House (where Delegate French Slaughter of Culpeper took the lead in support of the proposed joint resolution). It was necessary, the lawmakers agreed, "to evaluate higher educational objectives, needs, and resources, and to develop a program of long-range planning for [Virginia] higher education."

Few things could have more delighted Marshall Hahn—he left no obvious footprints in his efforts to see that the Resolution was adopted, but he later acknowledged that he had worked very hard to help make it

6.2 Hahn and the Byrd Organization—Senator Harry F. Byrd Sr. early in 1964 announced that with his wife's concurrence he had changed his mind and decided not to retire after all (see box 2.2). Marshall Hahn, joining in the chorus of hallelujahs, wrote Byrd in March that the announcement of his continued service in the US Senate "is wonderful news, indeed! ...Your fine leadership is badly needed." Hahn wrote that Byrd had his "full support" and that he would help in any way possible in the election; "of course, your reelection is assured," he noted. It was, and once Mills Godwin had made certain that he had the Organization's full support, so was his election as governor in the 1965 campaign.

President Hahn was hospitalized briefly in autumn 1964 for minor surgery, and Mills Godwin wrote him a note, hoping the hospital stay would be brief. A WRVA radio commentator named Joe Weeks had made reference to Mills Godwin's political ambitions, and Hahn sent the lieutenant governor a note inquiring whether Godwin thought Hahn's close association with him was unhelpful. President Hahn suggested he would be glad to modify the tone of his public speeches to accommodate whatever emphasis the lieutenant governor thought would be politically helpful. In mid-October, Hahn urged Godwin to announce as a candidate for the governorship before Christmas. ("Personal" letter, 10 December 1964)

happen. Senator Lloyd Bird, an outspoken advocate for higher education, was one of the key people who won approval for the joint resolution. Senator Bird and President Hahn became good friends early on. The dynamic young president was impressing many people in the House and Senate and already had many friends in both houses, though his brashness also put some people off. Once the commission study was under way, Hahn made sure that its members had a good understanding of what VPI was undertaking and why.

The study group—designated the Virginia Higher Education Study Commission—was appointed by Governor Harrison and the presiding officers of the two houses of the legislature. Its membership included the State Council of Higher Education and eleven other people, several chosen from the state at large. Senator Lloyd Bird was named chairman, and Sol W. Rawls Jr., a Suffolk businessman and a member of the State Council, was elected vice chairman. It was an able panel, with men such as Joe Blackburn (also of the State Council), general counsel for the C&P Telephone Company; Delegate Sam Pope of Southampton County (who had so long urged that Virginia adopt a sales tax that he was often called "Sales Tax Sam"); and T. Edward Temple, city manager of Danville. Some were educators themselves, such as Dr. Robert P. Daniel, president of Virginia State College; Dr. Woodrow W. Wilkerson, state superintendent of public instruction; and John D. Richmond, a well-known district superintendent. Bill McFarlane, staff director of the State Council when the commission was appointed, also was a member. The staff of the State Council was to serve as the Commission's secretariat.

Dr. John Dale Russell, a nationally known educator, was selected as director of the study. Russell's degrees were from Indiana University (where his Ph.D. dissertation was "Efficiency in College Management"). He had taught at several universities, including the University of Kentucky, and had extensive experience in administration and state educational finance. In the 1930s and 1940s, he had been a professor of education and an associate dean of social sciences at the University of Chicago. In the late 1940s and early 1950s, he served for a time in the US Office of Education, first as director of the division of higher education and later as assistant commissioner of education. Having retired in 1961 as director of institutional research at New York University, he then

6.3 Graduation 1964—Back in Blacksburg, the second commencement of Marshall Hahn's presidency took place in June 1964. The commissioning ceremony for new military graduates was held Saturday, June 6, with Air Force Lieutenant General Thomas P. Gerrity, deputy chief of staff for systems and logistics, doing the honors. The commencement exercises were held in the VPI coliseum the next day, with Dr. George J. Harrar, president of the Rockefeller Foundation (and a former member of the VPI faculty), the principal speaker.

Dr. Harrar emphasized the responsibilities that young Americans had to face in a rapidly changing world. The new graduates, he said, "have a great opportunity to help make those changes positive." Harrar stressed that the many new and emerging nations would need help to gain a decent standard of living, and he urged VPI's newest alumni to help: "Involvement in the problems of the less fortunate people in the world should be part of a person's human experience."

President Hahn conferred degrees upon 1,228 undergraduates and advanced degree recipients before an assembly of some 9,000 parents, relatives, friends, faculty, and other onlookers. Class President Robert E. Russell of South Hill presented greetings from the senior class. Russell, the Corps regimental commander, earlier had presented a check for $3,500 during a Corps formation as the class gift, to underwrite the costs of installing two flagpoles at Lane Stadium, then under construction. Reverend Alfred C. Payne, newly installed as assistant dean of students (see chapter 9), gave the invocation and benediction for the commencement ceremony; in the years that followed, Payne's campus prayers became something of a legend.

George Harrar was the president's houseguest during his stay and planned a return visit to the VPI campus on December 3, 1964. Harrar returned the $1,000 honorarium VPI paid him for the commencement address; it was deposited to the president's discretionary fund in the alumni accounts (Hahn letter to Harrar, 8 June 1964). Dr. Hahn left for California soon afterward to attend to his ill father.

Among the graduates in 1964 was Homer H. Hickam Jr., an industrial engineering major from Coalwood, West Virginia. First inspired by the Soviet launch of *Sputnik* in October 1957, he experimented with rockets while in high school and then enrolled at VPI. After a tour in the US Army that took him to Vietnam, he worked for ten years as an engineer with the US Army Missile Command, and then seventeen years as an aerospace engineer with NASA, where his projects included the Hubble Space Telescope. Hickam wrote a memoir about his youth, *Rocket Boys*, that was made into the 1999 movie *October Sky*.

returned to his hometown of Bloomington, Indiana. He was seventy-nine years old at the time of his appointment as the project director.[10]

As study director, Dr. Russell turned out be honest, tough-minded, and able. Much the same could be said about Lloyd Bird, the Commission chairman, as a political leader. The staff collected bales of data on funding, enrollments, administrative structures, faculties, physical facilities, students, and other aspects of Virginia's public colleges and universities. Russell or one of his colleagues visited every state institution of higher education in Virginia, often more than once, during the yearlong study, and consultants looked at special problems. Detailed studies by the Commission staff and consultants were published as staff reports, so the information collected was readily available to anyone.[11]

Dr. Russell visited Virginia Tech and Roanoke Technical Institute in June 1965. In what Dr. Hahn called "one of the basics of building good relationships," he sent Pop Warner and a co-pilot in the *Hokie* (regarding the VPI plane, see chapter 11) to fly the visitor from Bloomington to Blacksburg. At the suggestion of Lon Savage (Hahn's new executive assistant), the president, Warren Brandt, Stuart Cassell, and Mike Lacy (dean of admissions and records) got together to prepare for Russell's visit, especially with respect to Roanoke Technical Institute and the rivalry in the Roanoke Valley between VPI and the University of Virginia. When the group went with Dr. Russell to Roanoke to visit the Institute, Dean Lacy brought along detailed enrollment data.[12]

Recalling the overall study—and the relationship between two big state schools—a quarter century later, Marshall Hahn looked back with some satisfaction. "It was a timely opportunity," he said; "there was enough fluid dimension to the whole picture of higher education in Virginia that it was clear [that the Commission study] was the place to input and deal with questions like the two-year [branch colleges] and the role of the two state universities. I took the position right then, with the Governor and with Senator [Lloyd] Bird…that we had two state universities—we didn't want to dissipate the limited resources we had by those two institutions fighting one another—and that we ought to lay down a master plan."[13]

Divergent Visions

Both the energetic young president of VPI and Dr. Edgar F. Shannon, the genteel scholar who presided at the University of Virginia, were able and likable men, but their differences were impressive. Theirs was no simple contrast in appearance or conflict of personalities. The kind of state system of higher education Marshall Hahn envisioned for Virginia differed significantly from that toward which President Shannon and the University of Virginia seemed to strive.

Hahn later said it this way: The University of Virginia envisioned a single state university with a network of two-year branches under its control—branches whose graduates would rarely gain admission to the Charlottesville campus. Hahn rejected the vision as bad for VPI and bad for the state, a plan that "would have severely limited, I think, educational opportunities in the state, and what VPI could develop in years to come." By contrast, Hahn explained, "I visualized two state universities" plus "a community college system that would reach the many people that the two state universities couldn't reach," and the "community college system would be feeding those two state universities. Which pretty much came to pass" (see chapter 10).[14]

Marshall Hahn envisioned a statewide community college system to insure every young person the opportunity for post-high school work, to the limit of his or her ability and interest. Those in the college transfer programs at the community colleges who could successfully complete their first year or first two years of academic work could go on to a four-year institution, and perhaps even to graduate work.

The University at Charlottesville, evidently intent upon developing an extensive system of branch colleges, was already operating branch colleges at Wise (Clinch Valley), in Lynchburg, in Fairfax in Northern Virginia, at Wallops Island on the Eastern Shore, and at Martinsville. With a statewide general extension operation and numerous "extension centers" much like the University of Virginia Center in Roanoke, the University was in a position to establish others when it seemed advantageous. Branch college students, however, rarely could qualify if they wished to transfer to the University at Charlottesville.

VPI too had branch colleges—two-year institutions at Danville and Roanoke, and newly developing two-year branches at Wytheville and Clifton Forge-Covington. Students who successfully completed their work at the VPI branches, unless they were in a two-year technical program, were expected to go on to VPI to complete their upper-division undergraduate work. As President Hahn saw it, a statewide community college system with this same relationship to the senior colleges and universities would open up higher educational opportunities for young people in virtually every community in Virginia. Moreover, when it came to selling his vision in Richmond, he observed, "We had a lot going for us because we had done a pretty good job—and this had been done before I got [to Tech]—with Roanoke and Covington-Clifton Forge and Wytheville. There was a good record of transfers into VPI from those institutions."[15]

The Bird Commission Report, 1965

A draft study report written by Dr. Russell and Jim Connor, his assistant director, was reviewed and approved unanimously by the members of the Commission. Released in December 1965, just before the 1966 General Assembly session, it was submitted, as Senator Bird wrote, "in the hope and expectation that the adoption of these recommendations will be influential in the continued improvement" of higher education in Virginia.[16]

6.4 Higher education in Virginia and the nation—As an index of how Virginia's higher education system compared nationally, the Commission report noted, the state had 2.2 percent of the national population and controlled slightly less than 2 percent of the nation's economic resources. Virginia reasonably should bear about 2 percent of the national load in higher education. Although Virginia had 1.9 percent of the total personal income in the United States, state and local tax collections were only 1.5 percent of the national total. Virginia fell well below 2 percent in most measures related to higher education, the Commission found. In financial support, its percentage was 1.7. Total enrollments in higher education in Virginia were 1.5 percent of the national total: In 1964, Virginia's colleges and universities awarded 1.7 percent of the nation's bachelor's degrees, 0.9 percent of the master's degrees, and only 0.8 percent of doctoral degrees. To raise the total to 2 percent in the fall of 1964, an additional 25,000 students would have had to be admitted, the equivalent of doubling the enrollments of the four largest institutions in the state.

The Commission declared that Virginia, as compared with national benchmarks, was failing to provide higher education within its borders to the extent it should. and unless public education in the state was substantially strengthened, the situation would quickly worsen. A rapidly increasing college-age population, together with a rapidly increasing proportion of young people seeking higher educational opportunities, compounded an already difficult problem. The Commonwealth would have to at least double its higher education system in the next ten to twelve years, the Commission concluded, pointing out that similar trends in population and educational patterns were apparent throughout the United States.

Such conclusions were hardly revelations, for Marshall Hahn had been saying the same thing, from every rostrum he could find, in the three and a half years he had been VPI's president. Now the message would reach a larger audience—and perhaps be more readily received. As for VPI, Hahn sent his faculty a long memorandum in mid-January 1966 summarizing the Commission's recommendations.

The Higher Education Study Commission's first priority was development of a statewide community college system in Virginia. Under the proposal, the new State Board of Technical Education (established in 1964) would be enlarged to twelve members and reconstituted as a state community college board. The proposed new community college board's first task would be to develop a statewide plan for community colleges. Such a plan, the Commission urged, would incorporate most of the two-year branch colleges of the existing four-year institutions; the "technical institutes" being planned (one was already being developed at Arlington) by the Board of Technical Education; and the post-high school vocational programs.[17]

One of the current two-year branches of four-year institutions was Roanoke Technical Institute. Complicating the Roanoke situation was the competition between VPI and the University of Virginia, so the Commission urged the merger of Roanoke Technical Institute with the University of Virginia Extension Center to form a comprehensive community college on a single campus. "The city of Roanoke would seem to be an ideal location for the operation of an excellent institution of the community college type," the report observed.

Only George Mason College (the University of Virginia branch college in Northern Virginia) and Christopher Newport College (the two-year branch of William and Mary in Newport News) were to be excepted, pending final decisions on current movements to make them four-year colleges. The Commission report suggested that George Mason College might serve as the foundation on which to develop a major state university to serve the Northern Virginia area. Similarly, Christopher Newport College should become a four-year school to serve the North Hampton Roads area as an urban college, with programs focused on that objective; it thus would not duplicate or compete with nearby William and Mary at Williamsburg. If such four-year institutions were developed, parallel community colleges would be required in both Northern Virginia and the Newport News area as part of the statewide community college system, the Commission report noted.

The Commission's intensive review of Virginia's system of public higher education resulted in numerous other recommendations. Among them was the development of a comprehensive university for the Richmond area by consolidating the Medical College of Virginia with Richmond Professional Institute, both for expansion of undergraduate day and evening programs and for development of a strong and comprehensive graduate school in addition to the medical school. When implemented, this recommendation led to the establishment of Virginia Commonwealth University.

Another recommendation was the restoration of Mary Washington College, the women's college of the University of Virginia, as a separate institution (echoing the division between VPI and Radford). The Commission recommended, too, that the Norfolk branch of Virginia State College be made a separate institution with its own governing board as soon as its programs were strong enough to warrant separate accreditation.

The Commission urged the adoption of admissions policies calculated to provide opportunity for every high school graduate to prove he or she could successfully undertake college work. To insure diverse enrollments, such policies should avoid arbitrary limits on admission of out-of-state students at Virginia institutions. Far more Virginia students were going to out-of-state institutions than out-of-state students were coming to Virginia.

Another recommendation was to avoid the establishment of single-sex restrictions in the future and, in fact, to repeal all current single-sex restrictions, especially for the former state teachers colleges (Radford,

Madison, Longwood, and Mary Washington). The Commission declined to go so far as to recommend that all single-sex institutions be made coeducational, although such change, it said, should be voluntary.

In addition, the Commission urged a series of initiatives intended to broaden and strengthen graduate-level education in Virginia public institutions. Existing graduate programs were concentrated in the sciences, mathematics, and several professional fields, the report noted. State funding was needed for broadening and strengthening graduate work, especially in the humanities and social sciences.

There were numerous other recommendations, including concerns about the need for larger numbers of people trained in specific fields (many related to medicine and health), library use and administration, the evolving utilization of television and computers, and sponsored research. Regarding the latter, the Commission report urged that a way be found to pay especially attractive salaries to a small number of research faculty and thus attract a few top-flight people. These in turn would attract graduate students, research grants, and colleagues and begin a steady expansion of sponsored research. The Commission also urged that the faculty salary program based on averages for peer institutions be continued and strengthened.

Among the Commission's more important recommendations were those concerned with statewide coordination of the higher educational system. It found the statutes creating the State Council "basically sound," but urged that they be strengthened to insure more effective coordination—especially with respect to development of extension programs and branch colleges and in reviewing institutional biennial budget requests. The State Council, the Commission stressed, should be the chief advisory body to both the governor and the General Assembly in developing statewide policies, promoting long-range planning, and coordinating current activities with future planning.

Marshall Hahn, VPI, and State Policy at Mid-decade

In early 1964, at the first legislative session following Marshall Hahn's assuming the presidency at VPI, he had a tremendous impact. Regarding funds, he did not get everything he wanted, but he got far more than the governor's proposed budget offered—and far more than any previous VPI president had managed. He obtained authorization for the break with

6.5 Virginia's public institutions of higher education—In the 1960s, Virginia confronted its history as it reconsidered the configuration of public higher education and the specific constituencies and missions that had characterized higher education in the past. When the University of Virginia opened its doors in 1825, only white men could attend the school, whether they pursued undergraduate studies or a course of legal study. Virginia Military Institute, when it began operations in 1839, had a different curriculum, but it, too, admitted only white men as students.

After the Civil War, the state modified the old policy, not by permitting new groups to attend the state university or VMI, but by opening or supporting schools for other groups. In 1872, the federal land-grant money under the Morrill Act was divided between a school for white males, Virginia Agricultural and Mechanical College, and a school for black men and black women, Hampton Normal and Agricultural Institute. In the 1880s, the legislature established a public institution for black Virginians, known at first as Virginia Normal and Collegiate Institute; created a public component, designed to train white men as public school teachers, at what was then a private school, William and Mary; and took over what became Longwood College to train young white women to be public school teachers.

The first half of the twentieth century did little to modify the traditional policy. Having established Longwood College in the Southside, the legislature founded a similar school for each of the state's other quadrants—the institutions that became Mary Washington College in Fredericksburg, James Madison University in Harrisonburg, and Radford University in Radford. In perhaps the most striking change, William and Mary became a public institution—one that continued to exclude African Americans but accepted white women as well as white men. Beginning in the 1930s and 1940s, several schools, white or black, established branch campuses—William and Mary had a branch at what became Old Dominion University, for example; Virginia State College, in Petersburg, had what became Norfolk State University; and the University of Virginia had what grew into George Mason University.

Female students sometimes attended the schools that started out all-male; the University of Virginia began admitting women to its law and medical schools in 1920, and VPI began enrolling small numbers of women the following year. Similarly, male students sometimes attended the women's schools—male students from the community, who could commute to school, were graduating in the early 1950s from Madison College, for example—but they were unusual; the school provided no housing for male students; and, in the aftermath of the Supreme Court's 1954 decision in the school desegregation case, *Brown* v. *Board of Education*, the institution banned male students for some years.

The Commission faced this history when it made recommendations regarding such matters as single-sex institutions.

Radford College, so he was free in that respect to go his own way with the Blacksburg campus.

And the General Assembly established a commission to take a long, careful look at the entire system of public higher education in Virginia, with the responsibility of recommending such changes as seemed advisable for the next legislature to consider. Moreover, the new president continued to strengthen his relationship with the lieutenant governor, Mills Godwin, who became the next governor. All in all, it was an extraordinary performance with the promise of even more to come.

1 Wyatt Williams interview.

2 Martin letter to Hahn, 2 July 1962.

3 Martin report to the BOV Executive Committee, 1962; letter to Tom Rice from the presidents of the sophomore, junior, and senior classes at Radford College, 15 October 1962.

4 Letter of 28 March 1963.

5 Hahn letter to Boatwright, 14 August 1963; Sweeney, *Old Dominion University*, 66-72. Hahn also asked that the bill provide that not more than three Board members be out-of-state residents.

6 Hahn memorandum, 29 January 1964.

7 Ibid.

8 Hahn letter, 14 January 1964; Givens letter, 10 February 1964.

9 Hahn letter, 19 October 1964.

10 *Who's Who in American Education*, 22d ed., 1965-1966 (Nashville: Who's Who in American Education, Inc.).

11 These were (1) *Prospective College-age Population in Virginia, by Subregions, 1960-1985*; (2) *Statewide Patterns of Higher Education in Virginia*; (3) *Geographical Origins of Students Attending College in Virginia* (which Russell himself wrote); (4) *The Two-Year College in Virginia*; (5) *Instructional Programs in Virginia's Institutions of Higher Education* (also by Russell); (6) *Instructional Programs in Virginia for Fields Related to Health*; (7) *Extension Services, Television Instruction, and Research in Virginia's Colleges and Universities*; (8) *The Faculties of Virginia's Colleges and Universities*; (9) *Library Services in Virginia Institutions of Higher Education*; (10) *Instructional Plants in Virginia's Institutions of Higher Education*; and (11) *Control and Coordination of Higher Education in Virginia* (also by Russell).

12 Savage memo, 22 May 1965; Hahn memo, 28 May 1965.

13 Hahn interview, 31 August 1989.

14 Ibid.

15 Ibid.

16 Commonwealth of Virginia, *Report of the Higher Education Study Commission*, December 1965.

17 Following the recommendations of the 1963 Commission on Vocational Education, the 1964 General Assembly created a State Board of Technical Education to develop and operate new area vocational and technical schools. The 1963 Commission also had recommended that—in conjunction with the State Council, VPI, the University of Virginia, and the College of William and Mary—the new technical education board make a thorough study of the feasibility of developing a system of comprehensive community colleges. All this was preempted by the creation of the Higher Education Study Commission and its subsequent recommendations (*Report of the Commission on Vocational Education*, House Doc. 9, Commonwealth of Virginia, 1963).

The Hahn children—Anne, Betty, and Bill—at the Duck Pond on campus. Courtesy of T. Marshall Hahn Jr.

.

7: Athletics to Advance Academics, 1962-1967

President Hahn perceived a prominence in intercollegiate athletics as a necessary complement to eminence in academics. Partly it was a matter of gaining national visibility for the institution. In large part, it was a matter of generating support for the school.

Participating in the first meeting of the first Hokie Club in the Washington Metropolitan area just as he assumed the VPI presidency in summer 1962, Dr. Hahn urged support for a strong intercollegiate athletics program. The meeting—a social event at the Arlington home of Robert Bruce ('31), a Student Aid Association regional vice president—attracted more than fifty VPI enthusiasts, spouses, and other guests, among them four corporation executives, a rear admiral, a general, and two colonels. A top-flight athletic program at VPI would generate greater interest in the school and facilitate its development as a major university, the new VPI president told the group.[1]

Two years later, Hahn repeated the chorus to that song. "Nothing can be more successful in solidifying support from all our publics than a successful intercollegiate program," he wrote to athletic director Frank O. Moseley in July 1964, after reviewing the Athletic Association's annual report that year. Hahn went on to congratulate Moseley on the progress being made.

Dr. Hahn was actively interested in athletics in the same way he was interested in other aspects of the institution's development. In fact, the president also wrote routinely to potential athletic recruits to invite them personally to VPI, usually in response to suggestions from VPI enthusiasts who became aware of promising talent. Moreover, he was extremely competitive in every activity, athletic or otherwise.

Backdrop to the Hahn Years

A basic long-range plan for improving VPI's athletic and recreational facilities was drawn up in the early 1950s and approved generally by the Board of Visitors in 1954. It involved relocation of barns, experimental plots, and other agricultural areas farther from the central campus to provide space for athletic facilities.

Stuart Cassell and his associates began to implement the plan as resources became available and soon built a good baseball field in what had been a cow pasture south of the central campus. Heavy earthmoving equipment readjusted terrain right and left, obliterating all traces of barns, barnyards, horse show rings, and other agricultural installations. The famous old water tower disappeared in 1957 after the VPI-Blacksburg-Christiansburg Water Authority's facilities began delivering New River water to campus. Washington Street was extended westward beyond the greenhouses and the meat-processing laboratory (now the food science department). On the other side of campus, a nine-hole golf course was completed in 1958 on part of what had been the college apple orchard and agronomy plots.[2]

The big problem had been the urgent need for new facilities for basketball. The varsity games were played in the crowded, inadequate, and outmoded Memorial Gymnasium, constructed in the 1920s by the Alumni Association as a memorial to VPI men lost in World War I. The varsity basketball court in the old gym was a veritable pit with a terrible reputation. Athletic Director Frank Moseley and the Athletic Association offices were crammed into building.

Miles Stadium—the football playing field located on the hill immediately behind Memorial Gymnasium—also was built in the 1920s. At least football players could compete there without undue hazard to life and limb, but it, too, was old and inadequate. The stadium could accommodate barely 20,000 fans even when students and other spectators "were hanging from the trees and crowding the hillsides."[3]

President Walter Newman had brought Moseley from Kentucky in 1951 as athletic director and head football coach at a time when VPI football was a lost cause. Coach Robert C. "Bob" McNeish had quit in mid-season in 1950, the third of three seasons in which VPI won only one game. In a few years, Moseley had VPI football back on a winning track. The 1954 team went undefeated—the only undefeated football team in Tech history—although it was tied by the College of William and Mary, so it ended the season at 8–0–1, ranked #16 in the AP national rankings. After the initial rebuilding in the early 1950s, Moseley's teams were consistent winners for most of the decade in which he coached. They faltered in 1957, when the Gobblers were 4–6, but a year later they were back in the winner's column with a record of 5–4–1. In 1959 and 1960, Moseley's final years as a coach, they won six games each year. But by that time some of the alumni were becoming restive, and Moseley took Walter Newman's advice and gave up coaching to concentrate on athletic administration. In January 1961 he hired Jerry Claiborne, Coach Bear Bryant's top assistant at Alabama, to take over VPI football.

7.1 Frank "Mose" Moseley

—Frank Moseley—the top assistant to Coach Paul "Bear" Bryant at Kentucky—was induced to come to VPI in 1951 only after having been offered the athletic directorship as well as the head football coach job. W. L. "Monk" Younger gave up the athletic directorship and stayed on for a several years as business manager. To help Moseley with coaching and to raise money for athletic scholarships, H. Macauley "Mac" McEver—an old VPI hand who had left in the 1940s to venture into the pro football business in Richmond and other endeavors in eastern Virginia—also returned in 1951 (McEver interview).

Best known to friends and associates as "Mose," Frank Moseley had a surprising number of important connections in intercollegiate athletics, many of whom were old friends. Some who did not know him well, however, no doubt concluded that he was a fractious, irritable individual with a poor opinion of the whole human race. Sometimes difficult to understand, he seemed moody and stern looking with a stubborn streak. Given adequate provocation, Mose could indeed be difficult. But actually he was much like Stuart Cassell; beneath a stern exterior, each was a generous, kind-hearted man. Both shared another trait, too. They kept close track of any money for which they were responsible. Frank Moseley, no doubt with Stuart Cassell's help, made sure that the Virginia Tech Athletic Association managed to live within its means. Moseley served as Virginia Tech athletic director from 1951 to 1978—through most of the Newman years and all of the Hahn years.

Coach Claiborne won four games but lost five in his first season. VPI defeated Virginia in Roanoke and Florida State in Blacksburg, but lost to VMI in the Thanksgiving Day game in Roanoke. The new coach was putting together a strong defensive squad and also began developing an outstanding quarterback in Bob Schweickert. Unfortunately for VPI, Schweickert was hurt early in the season and did not play in another game for more than a year.

A New Basketball Facility

Cassell and his colleagues began site preparation in 1958 for a new athletic facility, then identified in institutional and state planning and budget documents as the "student activities and physical education building." The plans for the building—which Carneal & Johnston, Ambler Johnston's old firm in Richmond, put together—envisioned a huge structure built into the hillside site, with a great arched roof anchored with a series of flying buttresses. The structure would contain some 187,000 square feet; the basketball playing floor, set some two stories below street level, would be surrounded by more than 9,000 seats, placed on concrete risers stretching upward toward the huge arched ceiling. A big circular foyer surrounded the arena. Aside from the steeply climbing arena—space to accommodate the basketball court, the sidelines, and nearly 10,000 spectators—the building would contain what seemed like acres of office space, dressing rooms, corridors, utility space, clubrooms, two complete practice gyms, and even several handball courts.

It was an unbelievable building in the context of the era in which it was planned. The entire student populations of VPI and Radford College combined could have been seated in the arena at one time and still have had space for all the members of both faculties. State officials in Richmond found it difficult to believe that—for any purpose whatever, at least outside a football stadium—anything approaching 10,000 seats would be needed in one place in Blacksburg.

Despite the skepticism of Richmond officialdom, Stuart Cassell and President Newman worked long and hard to win approval and develop funding for the building. Money was always short, initial bids came in high, and the plans were revised to reduce costs. The architects at Carneal & Johnston struggled mightily with the design of the huge roof to build it within financial constraints. They finally hit upon great laminated wooden arches to span the building and support the roof. The wooden arches were anchored to the flying buttresses, which arched out from the walls for greater support.

The original plans were not changed substantially in the cost-cutting efforts, and Stuart Cassell scrounged money for the structure wherever he could find it. His perseverance and tenacity ultimately prevailed, and the big building finally took shape. Funded largely by a combination of state appropriations and bond financing, it ultimately cost $2.8 million. Construction began in September 1960 and was nearly complete in summer 1962, when Marshall Hahn came back from Kansas.

The building (now Cassell Coliseum) officially was designated "the coliseum" by action of the Board of Visitors late in the Newman administration. The first basketball game was played on the new basketball court in January 1961 against Alabama—VPI won, 91–67—with the seats yet to be installed and some of the exterior walls not yet completed. The 7,000 spectators sat on the concrete risers. The question about who would use nearly 10,000 seats in Blacksburg was readily answered the following month, when at least 10,000 people, again seated on concrete, packed the coliseum to watch Virginia Tech defeat West Virginia, 85–82. The seats were not installed for a year or two; Mr. Cassell had to find the money, somewhere, to pay for them. A total of 9,360 seats initially were installed.[4] Additional concrete risers and seats later were added high up in the four corners, paid for from a $316,000 state appropriation in 1964 for finishing work on the building.

Basketball under President Hahn

In basketball, Coach Chuck Noe resigned as basketball coach, ending a successful run, shortly before Marshall Hahn began his presidency. VPI teams won 109 games and lost but 51 in Noe's seven seasons, and the 1961-1962 season ended at 19–6. In spring 1962, however, South Carolina offered him its coaching job. Before the Hahns moved to Kansas, Noe had been their next-door neighbor in Blacksburg, and Hahn later characterized him as "an outstanding coach and close personal friend." As incoming president of VPI, Hahn attempted on the telephone from Manhattan, Kansas, to persuade Noe to stay. South Carolina hadn't been able to lure Marshall Hahn as its president, but Hahn wasn't able to keep Coach Noe from going there.[5]

William B. "Bill" Matthews ('56), who was Chuck Noe's chief recruiter, scout, and freshman coach, succeeded Noe as basketball coach. Matthews, himself a standout player in his student days, as a senior had been the leading scorer on Noe's first Virginia Tech team. Inaugurating the Matthews era, the team "electrified the sports scene with an opening 80–77 victory over third-ranked University of Kentucky," as Professor Lyle Kinnear described it, but it ended the season at 12–12.[6] In summer 1963, Matthews picked up some help when Charles R. "Charlie" Moir signed on as his assistant for scouting, recruiting, and freshman coaching. Moir came from high school basketball; in his 11 years coaching at Stuart, Virginia, and Jefferson and Mt. Airy, North Carolina, his teams had won 224 games and lost but 43.

In Matthews's second year (1963–1964), his basketball team put together a 16–6 season. But VPI was eliminated in the first round of the Southern Conference tournament—falling to George Washington University, with which the VPI had split a pair of games in the regular season—and VMI went on to win the tournament, something else that made some people unhappy. Matthews was relieved of his basketball coaching

7.2 Roundball altercation—When Bill Matthews's 1962-1963 basketball squad played at VMI in Lexington on February 1, 1963, the traditional VPI-VMI rivalry got a bit out of hand. A VMI cheerleader, dressed as a VPI cadet, engaged in such provocative antics during the pre-game warm-up that he and a member of the VPI team came to blows. The Keydets came out of the stands, and a general melee ensued. Coach Matthews pulled his team off the floor, but order was finally restored, and VPI won the game, 77–66. A few days later, Frank Moseley wrote to VMI athletic director "Duke" Ellington that it appeared unwise for VPI to send its basketball team back to Lexington, although VPI would be glad to play again in Blacksburg. Some prominent alumni from each of the schools got involved: Elmond Gray wrote E. H. Lane Sr. about the problem, and Lane wrote to President Hahn, enclosing newspaper clippings. Dr. Hahn, responding, said he would try to get the matter smoothed over with VMI commandant General Shell, who had been present when the fight broke out. "I hope we can avoid further deterioration of the relationships between VPI and VMI," Hahn wrote. However much the president may have tried, the two schools did not meet on a basketball court again until they played—in Roanoke—early in the 1971-1972 season. (Moseley letter, 11 May 1963; Hahn papers, 1963)

responsibilities and moved over to become field secretary of the Student Aid Association under Mac McEver, and also to help out in the AD's office when Frank Moseley needed assistance. The head basketball coaching position remained vacant for some time, although Charlie Moir, with Matthews's help, continued recruiting student athletes.

For the new head basketball coach, President Hahn had suggested a friend from his Kansas State days as a likely candidate—Howard P. "Howie" Shannon, assistant to Kansas State Coach Tex Winter. Frank Moseley wasn't too keen about that possibility, and he put off a decision, hoping to find someone he liked better. Moseley did bring in Shannon for a visit, along with his wife, Pat, who charmed everyone. Shannon himself, though, was a quiet, rather introverted man. After several other possibilities fell through and Dr. Hahn grew impatient, Moseley gave up and hired Shannon.[7]

No doubt, in Dr. Hahn's view, Howie Shannon was a better fit than Bill Matthews, at least with respect to the president's aspirations for a first-rate university in Blacksburg and a first-rate intercollegiate athletic program to go with it. Shannon had been captain and won All American honors on Kansas State's first Big Seven championship team back in the late 1940s. A Texas native, he earlier had played at North Texas State Teachers College and also in inter-service competition for the Air Force. He was pro rookie of the year with the Providence Steamrollers (1948-1949) and then joined the Boston Celtics. He later coached high school basketball before going to K-State. In the 1960 Olympics in Rome, he coached the Puerto Rico team. In appearance and demeanor, Howie Shannon was a bit more polished than tall, laid-back, good-ole-boy Bill Matthews.

Football under President Hahn

Football coach Jerry Claiborne's second season at VPI was the new president's first. That year, 1962, VPI managed to upset the University of Virginia in the Harvest Bowl game and also won its Homecoming game with the University of Richmond. But VMI again won the Thanksgiving Day game in Roanoke—losing to VMI always made VPI alumni and students unhappy—and the season ended with a record of 5–5.

In autumn 1963, by contrast, everything jelled behind quarterback Bob Schweickert's passing and fullback Silas Alex "Sonny" Utz's running, at least after VPI lost the season opener to Kentucky, 32–14. VPI defeated the University of Virginia 10–0, and, as Professor Kinnear recalled, took "sweet revenge" on VMI in the Thanksgiving game in Roanoke, 35–20.[8] The season ended at 8–2 as VPI won the Southern Conference championship for the first time ever. Coach Claiborne was voted the conference Coach of the Year, and Schweickert won All-American honors.

In 1964, Schweickert and Utz repeated much of their football magic, and the team ended the year at 6–4. At Homecoming, the Gobblers beat 10th-ranked Florida State 20–11. Later in the season, the Gobblers beat NC State, 28–19, in the last game played in old Miles Stadium before the wrecking crews tore it down to make way for new residence halls.

Exit the Southern Conference?

Virginia Polytechnic Institute was a member of the Southern Conference from the time it was organized in 1921; previously it had been part of the long-since defunct South Atlantic Conference. With the organization of the Atlantic Coast Conference in 1953 and other defections, VPI was the last remaining charter member when East Carolina joined in 1964. That year, VPI was the host school for the Southern Conference meeting in Roanoke, April 30-May 1. On the opening day of the meeting, the assembled crowd moved en masse via chartered buses from the Hotel Roanoke to the campus at Blacksburg for a big reception and dinner. Conference Commissioner Lloyd Jordan later wrote President Hahn to thank him and to tell of the "great enjoyment" everyone had had during their VPI visit, and the "splendid work" of Mr. Moseley and his staff.[9]

Marshall Hahn, Stuart Cassell, Frank Moseley, and others were gracious hosts for the Conference meeting, but they were growing restive with the SC affiliation. Hahn, in particular—intent upon building the institution itself into a nationally prominent university—felt strongly that the intercollegiate athletic programs should compete with institutions that were VPI's academic peers. The theme that emerged in the president's statements about athletics was the need for a balanced program, to develop at VPI the level of intercollegiate athletic competition to balance the growing strength and scope of its academics.

The Southern Conference affiliation seemed increasingly inappropriate. As Dr. Hahn put it at the time, "Virginia Tech is now competing academically on a national basis with many large private and state universities. The strengthening of Virginia Tech's academic programs will continue in the years ahead. It is essential that this same level of competition be maintained for Tech's athletic programs."[10]

In spring 1965, President Hahn decided to take VPI out of the Southern Conference, after having talked it over with the Athletic Association Board and with Dean Wilson Bell, the faculty chairman for athletics. In a letter to the president of the conference, Winston C. Babb of Furman University, Dr. Hahn described Tech's continuing development and said scheduling with Southern Conference schools had dropped to a point where "it is neither feasible for VPI nor in the best interest of the Southern Conference that we retain affiliation." Hahn sent the same letter to Commissioner Lloyd P. Jordan and to the presidents of the other schools in the conference.

7.3 "The Presidents' Box"—President Hahn often used athletic events to attract influential people to the campus to relax and enjoy themselves—and to provide an opportunity to talk with them. In spring 1963, he invited Ed Ould, Gordon Willis, Harry Wyatt, Stuart Saunders, Bill Armistead III, J. Douglas Bassett, Jack Hancock, W. P. Hazelgrove, Charles K. Lunsford, and others—all Roanoke business executives and prominent community leaders—to such an outing, along with their spouses. "Come over and philosophize in the sun during the afternoon, and have dinner with us in the evening," he wrote. "Those not interested in baseball and philosophy might be interested in spring football practice." Hahn suggested April 29, when a doubleheader with West Virginia was scheduled, as a good date.

Some came, some couldn't, and Hahn repeated the invitation to the entire group for May 4, in connection with the VPI-UNC baseball game at 2:30 P.M., following the First National Exchange Bank Board meeting in the morning. Those who had the afternoon free readily accepted the invitation, and Hahn also invited Frank Moseley, the athletic director, along with his wife, Edye.

Once the big three-level press box tower atop the new Lane Stadium became operational, football games provided even better opportunities for relaxing with special guests—and whatever politicking and other purposeful conversation might be appropriate. The second level down, originally designed for the president and his guests, was christened "The Presidents' Box," in honor of the ten VPI presidents who preceded Marshall Hahn. (The glass-enclosed presidents' box now on the third level from the roof of the press box tower was constructed later.)

Then President Hahn and his colleagues at VPI began an all-out effort to gain admission to the Atlantic Coast Conference. Dr. Hahn, Wilson Bell (then a member of VPI's Athletic Council), and Frank Moseley personally visited most of the ACC schools. They also invited the presidents, faculty chairmen for athletics, and athletic directors of the eight Atlantic Coast Conference members to VPI to discuss possible conference affiliation and to see something of the University's physical development, especially its athletic facilities. The conference members at that time were Maryland, Virginia, NC State, UNC, Duke, Wake Forest, Clemson, and South Carolina. ACC Commissioner James H. Weaver, who had not been on the VPI campus since 1919, did visit on June 3, and said he was impressed.

But not many people showed up for the ACC visitation scheduled for June 29–30, 1965, even though VPI provided air transportation. (Pop Warner flew the *Hokie* to Charlottesville, and Ken Brugh at Greensboro made an airplane available for those in North and South Carolina who wished to fly to Blacksburg.) Those who did come included President Thomas F. Jones of South Carolina, along with his faculty chairman for athletics, Dr. James A. Morris, and Marvin Bass, the South Carolina athletic director and football coach. A small group of University of Virginia people came from Charlottesville, including athletic director Steve Sebo, but President Edgar Shannon had other commitments. Gene Hooks, the athletic director at Wake Forest University, also came, but no other North Carolina institution was represented. Clemson, though a strong supporter of VPI's efforts to join the conference, did not send a representative. Maryland apparently had no objections but also was unrepresented. Those who came found President Hahn and his colleagues most hospitable.

When representatives of the Atlantic Coast Conference schools met in early December 1965, Virginia Tech was considered for membership, sponsored by Clemson and two other members, as required. Admission to the conference required a two-thirds vote, however, or six members. When it became apparent that six votes were not to be had, the motion by R. R. Ritchie of Clemson to admit VPI to membership was withdrawn. Clemson President Robert C. Edwards said the proposal would be resubmitted in the spring.

There was lots of talk about VPI and the ACC again in 1966, but not much happened to change anyone's mind. Earlier, NC State Chancellor John T. Caldwell had written candidly to Dr. Hahn that he doubted that "anywhere near a majority of the conference would favor this move." Virginia Tech's problem, he said, was demonstrating "that the addition of a ninth member to the ACC would be an advantage to the conference itself." At the spring ACC meeting, the matter was assigned to a study committee, and nobody heard of it again for months. At the conference's

7.4 Bob Schweickert ('64) and Frank Loria ('67)—Arguably the two greatest football players at VPI during Marshall Hahn's first six years as president were Bob Schweickert ('64) and Frank Loria ('67). Schweickert played from 1962 through 1964, mostly at quarterback but also on special teams. In 1963, the year VPI won the Southern Conference championship, he set a conference record with 1,526 total yards offense and was named conference player of the year. Though he missed a number of games due to injury, he completed 133 passes in 266 career attempts, for 1,725 yards. He also racked up 1,723 career yards rushing on 337 carries—including 204 yards on 29 carries against the University of Richmond in 1963. His six longest career touchdown runs were for 59, 59, 63, 66, 74, and 96 yards. What's more, he once returned a punt for 82 yards. And in VPI's 1964 victory over Florida State, he kicked punts of 51, 58, and 65 yards. (Colston, *Hokies Handbook*, 27-29, 146-52; Doughty and Lazenby, *'Hoos 'n' Hokies*, 81-86)

Frank Loria played from 1965 through 1967, mostly on defense, where he hit with spectacular precision and force and also caught seven career interceptions. He also returned punts—four of them for touchdowns (three in 1966). During his three years playing varsity football, VPI went 22–7–1. An exemplary student, too, he twice earned academic All-American honors. A West Virginian, from Clarksburg, he had been spurned when his home state university was recruiting from high school because of his small size (he grew to 5'9" and 175 pounds). A consensus All-American player in 1966 and 1967, he was spurned again, this time by the National Football League, so he went into coaching. He was in his second year as an assistant coach at Marshall University in West Virginia when, coming back into Huntington on a Southern Airways DC-9 on November 14, 1970, he and the entire team died when the plane crashed short of the runway. In a eulogy to the fallen warrior, Coach Claiborne said of Loria, "No other athlete has brought as much recognition and honor to the university during his playing days as did Frank Loria." (Colston, *Hokies Handbook*, 31, 35, 152; Doughty and Lazenby, *'Hoos 'n' Hokies*, 86, 88-91)

December 1966 meeting at Hilton Head, South Carolina, the matter was brought up again—and again postponed.

By this time Marshall Hahn, Stuart Cassell, Wilson Bell, and Frank Moseley had had enough. The president sent telegrams to everyone involved that VPI had withdrawn its application for membership.

7.5 VMI and VPI: The annual Thanksgiving tradition
—Year after year, thousands of Virginians looked forward to the football game between VMI and VPI, held each year in Roanoke (midway between Lexington and Blacksburg) on Thanksgiving Day. But the two schools were diverging in many ways, and President Hahn concluded that the time had come to amend the tradition.

In 1965, there was much discussion in the Roanoke press about the discontinuance of the annual Thanksgiving Day football game in Victory Stadium. President Hahn's mail increased considerably. The Roanoke Touchdown Club adopted a formal resolution asking that the Thanksgiving Day games be continued. President Hahn responded with sensitivity and patience, but he held fast. The Thanksgiving Day game eliminated two possible Saturday games in November, those before and after Thanksgiving Day, he explained. That made scheduling difficult because it required starting the season too early. The VPI-VMI game would remain in Roanoke, but it would be contested on a Saturday. For some years—the then current commitment with VMI extended through 1970—the VPI-VMI games continued each November in Roanoke, but attendance dropped off.

A New Stadium

In the 1965 football season, quarterback Bobby Owens attracted a lot of attention. So did the new stadium, Lane Stadium (see chapter 5), which opened that fall—although, aside from the playing field, only the press box tower and the west stands were completed. The Gobblers started the fall campaign by defeating Wake Forest in Roanoke, 12–3, and ended it by beating VMI, also in Roanoke, 44–13, for a 7–3 record. In between, VPI inaugurated play in the new stadium in Blacksburg on October 16 by defeating William and Mary, 9–7. The new stadium was dedicated during the first Governor's Day program, on October 23, when the Gobblers defeated the University of Virginia Cavaliers, 22–14.

7.6 "Governor's Day" football—In spring 1965, President Hahn and his staff began planning a special program in conjunction with a selected football game each autumn to which lots of well-placed people throughout the state could be invited. "Governor's Day" seemed an appropriate title, provided Governor Albertis Harrison would agree and participate. Blacksburg was fairly remote from the state's more urban north and east, and most Virginians had little idea of VPI's rapid development in the 1950s and 1960s. Virginia Tech had, and has, a beautiful campus in an especially beautiful part of the world. The new coliseum and an extensive construction program, with big buildings going up left and right, all suggested a vitality and dynamism that one had to see to believe. A popular football game in autumn, when colorful leaves transform the tree-clad mountains, seemed an ideal time. The Virginia Tech-University of Virginia game, scheduled for October 23 that year, filled the bill.

The University of Virginia for some years had held its "Commonwealth Day" each autumn for similar purposes, and the College of William and Mary had an annual "Burgesses Day," named for colonial-era legislators. Governor Harrison readily agreed to the "governor's day" designation for the VPI program and said he would be pleased to participate. (Hahn letter to Harrison, 1 July 1965, and the governor's reply)

The first Governor's Day weekend attracted hundreds of special guests and was a big success. It began with a cocktail party and dinner at the Roanoke Country Club on Friday evening, October 22, for more than 300—paid for, of course, with private funds. The guest list included many members of the General Assembly, local and state governmental officials, several congressmen, a large contingent of journalists from across the state, members of the VPI-related boards and the University's administration and faculty leadership group, and special friends from near and far, including spouses and other guests. Stan Kingma's new Glee Club (see chapter 20) put on a lively after-dinner concert that seemed especially enjoyable and appropriate.

The festivities continued on Governor's Day itself with a luncheon in Owens Dining Hall on the campus. Governor Harrison was unable to get to the Friday night party, but he and Mrs. Harrison were honored guests at the luncheon. The Governor, President Hahn, and President Edgar Shannon, who headed a delegation from the University of Virginia, that day began what became a tradition of lighthearted and sometimes tart exchanges. Governor Harrison was gracious and appreciative, but he and Presidents Hahn and Shannon made the most of a keen institutional rivalry.

Once the special guests were in the stadium, the glass-enclosed Presidents' Box atop the west stands served its purpose well. There was lots of room in which to move around, find refreshments, and talk, as well as to sit and watch the game. Outdoors, the weather was cool and a bit blustery, after two wet days, but there was no rain. The outcome of the football game—at which Governor Harrison at half-time made a brief dedication speech—could not have been more appropriate, at least from Virginia Tech's perspective: VPI 22, Virginia 14. The half-time ceremonies also included a reunion of most of the twenty-five-man football squad from 1926 that had helped dedicate Miles Stadium with another VPI-Virginia game—VPI had won that game, too. After all the excitement of the day, Bill Bradley's big, modernistic home on the edge of the plateau overlooking the Ellett Valley was opened for a post-game party for the visiting press people and other selected guests.

Athletic Life as an Independent

Despite the ACC disappointment, the athletic enterprise prospered; Virginia Tech's independent status did create scheduling opportunities. The 1965 baseball season, contested while VPI was still in the Southern Conference, ended with a 13–10 record, and the team lost in the semifinals of the conference tournament. In basketball, Howie Shannon's squad—competing for the first year as an independent—pulled off a big surprise at the All College Tournament in Oklahoma City, where it defeated Texas A&M, 101–74, and top-seeded Wichita, 91–90, before losing to Oklahoma City, 99–90. It ended the 1965-1966 season with a 19–4 record, 7–1 against Southern Conference opponents and 5–2 over ACC member schools. The squad went to the National Invitation Tournament but lost to Temple, 88–73, in the first round.

In spring 1966, the VPI baseball team compiled a 10–6 record, and the golfers came out on top 9–2 with their third straight state championship. The track team, at 4–1, had its best season since 1956, although the tennis team went 4–5.

The 1966 football season turned out well, despite the opening loss to Tulane, 16–0. Regular season play concluded with a 70–12 defeat of VMI in Roanoke, a seven-game winning streak, and an 8–1–1 record. Coach Jerry Claiborne's squad included sixteen seniors, paced by tailback Tommy Francisco. The impressive season finale prompted an invitation to the Liberty Bowl in Memphis, Tennessee, on December 10, 1966, to play Miami of Florida.

7.7 White players at a white school—The two extraordinary seasons Coach Shannon and the basketball team put together in the mid-1960s attracted some attention. The players—including Ted Ware, Chris Ellis, Micky McDane, John Wetzel, and Ron Perry—were talented, enthusiastic athletes, most of whom Bill Matthews and Charlie Moir had recruited. They were also conspicuously white, although some of the schools with which VPI was competing (but not VMI, for example, or William and Mary) had increasing numbers of black students on their teams. There were in fact few black students on the VPI campus, and there were none at all at VMI until 1968.

In early summer 1966, the VPI Athletic Association Board adopted a statement reasserting a policy of recruiting student athletes "with high levels of academic and athletic ability, regardless of race." A short notice in the June 1966 *Techgram* said the policy statement was designed "to reassure Negro athletes that all recruiting decisions [at VPI] are made on the basis of ability and scholarship achievement, and that race is not a consideration." The statement itself was a far cry from the institution's earlier policies, when, into the 1950s, no black student could gain admittance to VPI, and then, for a number of years, none could play on a sports team for the school.

The campus soon was awash with excitement, and a large contingent of VPI's students, faculty, staff, alumni, and other friends converged upon Memphis, including the Highty-Tighties and much of the Corps of Cadets. Governor Godwin and President Hahn headed a big delegation of VIPs; Rector Harry Wyatt made available the Norfolk & Western airplane for the Memphis trip, supplemented by a charter flight.

When VPI lost to Miami 14–7 on national TV after a hard-fought contest, both Coach Claiborne and the football squad had every right to be proud. From the excitement of the alumni parties and after-game celebrations in Memphis, one might have thought that VPI had won. The national television exposure and favorable publicity were valuable for any athletic program. The Liberty Bowl resulted at least in a moral victory for the underdog Gobblers, as even Bill Brill acknowledged in the *Roanoke Times*. VPI ended the season at number 20 in the UPI national rankings.

Coach Shannon's 1966-1967 basketball campaign was equally successful. A 20–7 season earned the team an at-large invitation to the twenty-three-team NCCA tournament, where it won twice and reached the Final Eight before losing in the Mideast Regionals in overtime (see chapter 17).

7.8 Press facilities come down from the sky—The little press box—the architects had so carefully designed it up near the roof on the coliseum's west side—apparently made many of the sports writers who covered Virginia Tech basketball unhappy. As the tempo of the games increased in the 1966-1967 season, they began to complain seriously about their sky-high vantage point. Bill Brill, sports editor at the *Roanoke Times*, finally wrote to President Hahn asking that facilities for visiting writers and broadcasters be installed near the playing floor in the coliseum. Observers up in the press box, Brill explained, were unable to see the finer points of the game. In December 1966, Dr. Hahn went up to the press box during a game to see for himself, and he saw what Brill meant. Hahn wrote Brill that, now that he understood the problem, appropriate action would be taken. Tables and chairs soon were placed on the sidelines near the court to accommodate the sports press. The sideline press facilities are still in use today.

Within five years of taking over the helm at VPI, Hahn could see that great progress had indeed been made in athletics as well as academics. It all prompted much alumni mail, including a letter from C. G. Crowder Jr. ('48) of Madison, New Jersey, thanking Hahn for his "enthusiasm and strong support." Crowder also had written to congratulate Coach Shannon (with a copy to Dr. Hahn) on the successful basketball season. Basketball and football were both looking good. "Over the past few years you and Coach Claiborne have created at Tech something of which I believe we can all be very proud, a winning tradition," he wrote. Regarding VPI's athletic program in general and its basketball future in particular, President Hahn assured Mr. Crowder that VPI teams were of the caliber to play in the NCAA semi-finals and finals, and "we will be playing at that level in the future."

[1] *Northern Virginia Sun*, 3 July 1963.

[2] Robertson, *Historical Data Book*, 22, 101.

[3] Wendy Weisend interview.

[4] James R. Beck (retired architect for Carneal & Johnston) interview, 17 October 1990; *Techgram*, 15 January 1962; VPI news release, 29 March 1964.

[5] Hahn letter to George H. Burton, 8 August 1962.

[6] Kinnear, *The First 100 Years*, 420.

[7] Mac McEver interview; Bill Matthews interview.

[8] Kinnear, *The First 100 Years*, 427.

[9] Jordan letter to Hahn, 6 May 1964. According to one later view, had VPI been playing better

football in the early 1950s, it might have been invited to join the ACC as a charter member, but the undefeated season in 1954 came too late for that (Colston, *Hokies Handbook*, 24). According to another, the explanation dates back to a refusal by VPI to support the inclusion of fellow Southern Conference members Maryland and South Carolina in the new ACC (Doug Doughty, "ACC's Chance to Add USC May Be Lost," *Roanoke Times*, 24 July 2003: C1).

[10] *Virginia Tech*, a promotional booklet published by VPI, spring 1965.

Dr. and Mrs. Hahn on the lawn at the Grove. Virginia Tech Special Collections.

8: Crisis over the Corps of Cadets

The Corps of Cadets and the military system at VPI had existed since the nineteenth century, and almost every president of the institution had wrestled with one problem or another associated with it.[1] Membership in the Corps had long been mandatory for many, even most, VPI students. Exceptions were medical exemption or former national military service. Membership was mandatory for almost all male undergraduates until 1924, when one major reform made the Corps a matter of choice for upperclassmen but—exemptions aside—left participation compulsory for male freshmen and sophomores. That policy persisted into the 1960s. Women students—admitted to VPI in small numbers ever since 1921— had always been excluded from the Corps.

President Newman struggled for years with problems with the military side of campus life and found no answers. In the early 1950s especially, civilian students, mostly veterans, agitated to change the system and even adopted the slogan "The Corps Must Go."[2] Yet when Newman turned the presidency over to Hahn, the military tradition remained such an important aspect of life at VPI, especially in the minds of many upper-class cadets and former students, that any suggestion that the system be changed generated opposition—vocal and vehement—on campus and off.

8.1 Chris Kraft's recollections of VPI and the Corps of Cadets—Christopher C. Kraft entered VPI in 1941 and, in view of the fast-track scheduling of courses during World War II, graduated in December 1944, in aeronautical engineering. His recollections of the Corps and the education he received at VPI are revealing of the importance alumni ascribed to both VPI and the Corps in enabling them to become the people they did, and they suggest the general attitudes among alumni when the mandatory Corps became a policy issue in the 1960s.

> Those who survived [the rat year] developed a strong camaraderie, supported each other, and came together as a unit. And that, of course, was the purpose of it all.... One of the joys of being a sophomore is not being a rat.... When I was a twenty-year-old senior, I was elected president of the Corps of Cadets.... From my secure vantage point in the twenty-first century, I can see what the Corps of Cadets, and particularly that senior year, did for me. It gave me my first, and almost only, training in leadership.... I know beyond doubt that my own leadership skills were honed by the direction, example, and practices of the Corps of Cadets. Experience is a great teacher and the Corps gave me those experiences when I was still young and impressionable. To this day, I encourage young men to recognize and take advantage of this aspect of military training. Some won't be suited for it. But many others will, and the military experience will become an invaluable part of their core person through whatever career or profession they follow....
>
> By the fall of 1944, it was time to graduate. I would get one of the first degrees in aeronautical engineering granted by VPI, and my B+ average was good, if not spectacular. I was a kid, but I felt ready to be a man. Somehow I knew that the jewel of a college education wasn't in the knowledge I'd gained, but in the process I'd gone through. We were all lucky on that campus. The process was delivered by professors who understood the difference between teaching and learning. We learned the formulas and the theories. But we learned, too, that it all can become obsolete overnight and that we have to be ready to encounter new technologies and to discover new truths. We had teachers, particularly in aeronautics, who knew how to measure us, how to quiz us and stroke us and confront us and sometimes even to bully us into thinking through a problem. That kind of teaching is a real art. That kind of education—the Corps, the dance weekends, baseball, and learning not just facts, but learning how to learn—was a jewel that I hold forever precious. Virginia Tech, the school that I hadn't even wanted to consider, took this boy from Phoebus and made him into the man I would become. (Kraft, *Flight*, 17, 23-25)

8.2 The first commandant of the Corps of Cadets—Regarding the Corps of Cadets, the one significant change on Newman's watch came in 1952, when the Board of Visitors, seeking to strengthen the Corps, authorized employment of a full-time commandant of cadets. Previously, the US military officers assigned to VPI for the ROTC programs also had been responsible for supervising the Corps. The Board was responding to some of the problems of running a campus with two disparate student populations, one civilian, one military. The idea had been to provide strong, separate college leadership for both the military and non-military students in an effort to develop more coordinated and cooperative student life programs between the two groups. The first commandant was Major General John M. Devine, and Joseph Wiley Guthridge was promoted to director of civilian students and coordinator of student activities (Kinnear, *The First 100 Years*, 369, 371).

President Hahn and the Corps of Cadets

When Dr. Hahn began his presidency, he had, he has said, no preconceived notions about changing the Corps or the military system at VPI. To the contrary, that there might be a serious problem he would have to address simply "wasn't obvious to me at the outset." As a professor and department head a few years earlier, he had been favorably impressed with cadets' academic performance. "They were committed; they were disciplined," he recalled years later. "They made good students, and I liked what I saw."[3]

Hahn said as much to some members of the Board of Visitors early in his administration. But he had seen the cadets as young men who had survived their rat year—all freshmen who resigned from the Corps had to drop out of school. As president, after observing the overall situation and coping with the strenuous objections of a good many unhappy students and parents about the mandatory Corps, Hahn saw a different picture. The demands of the military system on newly enrolled students—the rat system—generated serious problems. The dropout rate was disturbing, especially during the first few weeks of fall quarter, and the underclassmen who dropped out of the Corps were lost to VPI as well. Freshman and sophomore grades for cadets suffered by comparison with civilian students. In view of the mandatory Corps for freshman and sophomore men, many potential students refused even to enroll at VPI. All in all, Hahn came increasingly to realize, the costs just seemed too great.

Hahn mentioned these mounting concerns to the Board of Visitors from time to time, but he focused at first on the Corps itself to find a solution. He tried hard to convince the Corps leadership that, to preserve the benefits of discipline and leadership training that the Corps offered, the freshman system would have to be modified. But the Corps leadership refused to change the system, Hahn recalled. "The trouble was, one, the freshmen who survived the system felt that they had to make it at least as tough for the next generation, and, two, the alumni would reminisce about it and that was instilling a spirit of independence in the sophomores and upperclassmen in the Corps, so they simply wouldn't accept the statement from the management of the institution that this can't go on," he later explained. "I talked to the Board about it on more than one occasion. Finally, we had a pretty extensive discussion at a Board meeting, with no recommendation from me. Those who were strong Corps supporters took the position, well, just keep working on it," Hahn recalled. The fact that such discussions were occurring and the Board had not acted naturally leaked out, he said, and if anything the Corps position became even more resistant to change.[4]

8.3 **President Hahn on his early lessons about the Corps**—In a conversation long after the facts, Hahn recollected how, in contrast to initiatives he came to his job intent on pursuing, he had to learn on the job that the Corps would have to be renovated as well: "As soon as I got here [in 1962] I started to be hammered on by parents of these freshmen who were being hazed to the point that their studies were suffering. There was a high drop out rate and [a clear] conflict between the level and intensity of the freshman disciplinary type activities and the academic side. You had students suffering academically. You had students leaving the institution. You had also top students who wanted to study in areas of academic concentration offered [in Virginia] only at [VPI] who were going out of state because of the Corps. You'll find plenty of that in the files. I don't know how much of my time the first year I spent dealing with that, learning how severe the problem was and then trying to work with the Corps to reduce the...excessive freshmen rat type activities" (Hahn interview, 8 July 1989).

President Hahn determined to recommend that the Corps be made voluntary rather than mandatory. Having talked it over with rector Tom Rice—who liked the system the way it was—Hahn discussed the issue with each of the other Board members to be sure that all were fully informed as to his reasons for the recommendation.[5] The matter would be the largest item considered at a meeting of the Board scheduled for May 18, 1964.

Whether to Convert to a Voluntary Corps

People who knew what was going on could see that Hahn's presidency might ride on whether he could pull off the big change he had in mind. Stuart Cassell, for one, was concerned—well aware that a rejection of Hahn's Corps recommendation would be in effect a vote of no confidence and that Hahn would have to leave. He urged the president to try to rally support for the change to a voluntary Corps, both on the Board and in the alumni ranks. Hahn refused, however. It would be inappropriate, he said, to make the Corps a public issue, because it was a policy matter for which the Board had ultimate responsibility.[6]

Marshall Hahn had talked it over with Peggy. He had considered how, if the change was not made, he could not build the university that VPI should become. He had to take the chance and hope for the best. "I thought I had a 50–50 chance.... I thought if it weren't done and I had to leave, it would probably set up the environment where it would then be certain to be done," Hahn said. "I knew by the time of the Board meeting that I had the votes, close, but I had the votes," Hahn later recalled. "At the time I talked to Tom [Rice] I didn't know at all."[7]

The Corps question was brought up in due course when the Board met around the conference table in Dr. Hahn's office on May 18, although it was not among the items included in "The President's Report to the Honorable Board of Visitors," which was prepared in advance for each meeting. The pre-prepared report to the Board—a practice Dr. Hahn had brought over from the Newman administration—usually included background information and discussion on matters the president wished to present to the Board. Rector Rice was presiding, and eleven other Board members were present: Blewett, Cochran, Erwin, Gibbs, Graham, Hancock, Showalter, Wilhelm, Williams, Wyatt, and ex officio member Wilkerson. Lane, Will, and ex officio member Wampler were absent.

Considerable business was dispatched—the new faculty salary program; residence hall names honoring President-emeritus Walter Newman and Dean C. P. Miles; renovation and construction projects for 1964–1966.

Then it was time to consider the climactic item, the Corps. Dr. Hahn again outlined the difficulties with mandatory enrollment of male underclassmen in the Corps. After extensive discussion, Wyatt Williams offered a motion that—effective September 1964—enrollment in the Corps be made an elective opportunity, rather than compulsory, except that it continue to be required for students in ROTC programs. Jack Hancock seconded the motion. George Cochran then made a substitute motion, seconded by Mrs. Graham, that the previous resolution be considered at a special meeting of the Board, to be held within thirty days. The vote on the substitute motion was evenly divided, 6–6; Rector Rice ruled that the substitute failed. The ensuing vote on the original motion was 8–3, with one abstention. The Board had approved the change to a voluntary Corps.[8]

Tom Rice could not conceal his bitter disappointment; both Hancock and Williams vividly remembered his distress. A few days later he asked Governor Harrison not to reappoint him to the VPI Board when his short term expired. The governor apparently talked him out of it, for Rice was reappointed to a full four-year term beginning July 1, 1964. In any event, the voluntary Corps issue proved terribly divisive among VPI alumni and even among students. Those who opposed the action were especially vocal; they fired off letters to newspaper editors, to Dr. Hahn, to the Board members, to Governor Harrison, to the State Council of Higher Education. A delegation called on Governor Harrison in Richmond asking that the Board reconsider the matter in a special hearing.

8.4 W. Thomas Rice ('34)—Tom Rice, the Board rector, had graduated from VPI in 1934. His experience in the Corps, with its discipline and camaraderie, had been valuable to him in shaping his personal and professional life. He did not want to see that experience lost for VPI students, he recalled much later, and he and Marshall Hahn "had a definite difference of opinion as to the type of school we wanted in Blacksburg," he said.

Tom Rice was, and is, a soft-spoken gentleman, quiet, gracious, a friendly smile on his face, his blue eyes glinting. Despite his charm and ability to put one at ease, he is a strong person; he spent a good part of his professional career building a railroad empire. A native of Westmoreland County, Rice graduated with the highest academic average in his civil engineering class and was one of only two seniors in the class who had a job offer upon graduation, in the midst of the Great Depression. In late summer 1934, he started out with the Pennsylvania Railroad as a civil engineer, and he stayed with the railroad until 1942, when World War II interrupted his career. He spent most of the war years running the Iranian State Railway System for the US Army. In 1946 he left the service as a much-decorated lieutenant colonel and joined the Richmond, Fredericksburg, and Potomac Railroad, "that lovely little railroad between Richmond and Washington," as he later described it. Rice moved up rapidly, and in 1955 he took over as president. When the Atlantic Coast Line Rail Road was looking for a new executive in 1957, it chose Tom Rice, then forty-five years old. Both the ACL and Tom Rice prospered. Ten years later, Rice was one of the key players in the merger of the ACL and Seaboard Coast Line Railroad, and he became president of the merged railroad, the Seaboard Coast Line.

He was elected chairman and CEO of the consolidated railroad and several affiliated corporations in 1970. When he retired seven years later he was much involved in another merger, that of the Seaboard Coast Line system and the Chessie system; the merged rail systems became the present CSX Corp. The one-time VPI cadet reached the rank of major general in the US Army reserve before he retired. Always busy, he served on a long list of bank and corporate boards and the boards of subsidiary companies of the railroads he headed. Even in retirement, Rice remained active, maintaining an office at Seaboard Coast Line Industries at One James Center in Richmond. Rice was active in many civic and educational organizations during his long career. For some years he was chairman of the educational committee of the Virginia Chamber of Commerce.

While continuing active in retirement, Tom Rice garnered much recognition at Virginia Tech. In 1981 the University awarded him the Ruffner Medal. In his honor CSX established a W. Thomas Rice Professorship at Virginia Tech. A unit in the Corps of Cadets, first established in 1996, was renamed the Major General W. Thomas Rice Corp of Cadets Center for Leader Development, and it was headed by communications professor Robert E. Denton, who held the W. Thomas Rice Chair. Moreover, having been president of the Alumni Association in 1960 when the War Memorial was first dedicated, Rice gave the keynote address in 2001 when the memorial and chapel, having been nicely refurbished, were rededicated. The class of 2005 named its ring collection after Major General W. Thomas Rice.

Would the Policy Change Stick?

Dr. Hahn, presiding at a regular meeting of the Academic Council on May 19, the day following the Board action, reported the Board's decision to make the Corps voluntary. The deans and others on the Council were strongly supportive, and Dean Wilson Bell moved that the Council "heartily endorse" the action as a major step in VPI's progress in achieving academic excellence. The motion was unanimously approved.

President Hahn turned to the *Techgram* in June to attempt to make sure the alumni understood what was involved in the Corps decision. In an open letter addressed to alumni, parents of students, "and other friends of VPI," Hahn outlined the reasons for the decision and "the details of implementation" of the voluntary Corps concept. The new policy was intended, he wrote, "to achieve the continuation of the strongest possible Corps program simultaneously with meeting the increased educational obligations of VPI to the taxpayers and youth of Virginia."

Hahn cited high failure rates among freshman cadets and the refusal of many good students even to consider entering VPI as "problems of increasing magnitude." The explosion of knowledge in recent decades had intensified the academic demands of college work, and consequently a major conflict had developed between the demands of the military program and academics, the president wrote. He stressed the high dropout rate for freshman cadets, their lower academic achievement level, and especially the severe criticism by parents of struggling cadets who were forced to remain in the Corps until they had to drop out of school because of poor academic work. "There was no alternative to making participation in the Corps of Cadets an elective opportunity if VPI was to meet its legal and moral responsibilities as a land-grant institution," Hahn wrote, in a striking reversal of a traditional understanding.

An account of the Corps decision in the news columns of the *Techgram* acknowledged that "from the standpoint of tradition and long-established image, the de-emphasis of the corps will not be easily accepted by many. All traditions, and particularly military traditions, die hard." But it quoted Dr. Hahn expressing his belief that a stronger corps would evolve because students participating in it would be doing so by choice.

The divisive Corps issue reverberated throughout alumni chapters. Craig Fabian's frequent and lengthy memos to the president were full of reports, rumors, and quotes from various alumni leaders about chapters adopting resolutions or otherwise taking sides. One such, from June 18, was a message that Jack Hancock had visited Bill Blewett at the Newport News Shipyard, where a group of alumni leaders in an informal vote had favored the voluntary Corps decision, 12–2.

Governor Harrison called in Dr. Hahn and Mr. Rice to discuss the matter; Rice was upset about the decision, Hahn recalled, but courteous and honest in the way he presented it. It was a mistake, Rice told the governor, and he hoped a public hearing would be held for further consideration. President Hahn, though he sensed at first that the issue could be politically damaging for Governor Harrison, soon concluded that such a hearing would prove more therapeutic than harmful.[9]

Public Hearing

At the governor's request, the Board scheduled a public hearing for 9:00 A.M., June 29, 1964, in Burruss Hall auditorium on the VPI campus. When the hour arrived, the 3,000-seat auditorium was pretty well filled, and scores of people, some of them faculty members, made statements. Among those who spoke were Gene Rowe, president of the Alumni Association, and Charles O. Gordon, a member of the Alumni Board. E. H. Lane and Erwin Will, who had been absent from the May meeting, were present; Mr. Wampler and Mr. Blewett were the only absent members. After the hearing, the Board reconvened around the conference table in the president's office.

Gene Rowe and the Executive Committee of the Alumni Board had met with Dr. Hahn at that same table just before the hearing. Rowe was a bit unhappy that Hahn had not informed him prior to the May Board meeting of the impending decision on the Corps. Hahn explained that he considered it improper to "put pressure on the Board."[10] The president said that, if he had erred in not informing Gene Rowe, he apologized, but he was attempting to be ethically careful. In any event, the Alumni Board meeting with Hahn that morning resulted in a resolution that Tom Rice read at the meeting of the Board of Visitors that immediately followed the public hearing.

By majority vote, the Alumni Board had resolved that "in our opinion the long identification of the Corps of Cadets with VPI has produced values for its members, the institution, the state, and the nation"—values that continued to be desirable—and "[we] enthusiastically recommend the continuation and active support of the Corps of Cadets on the VPI campus today and in the future." Recognizing, however, that "the increasing opportunities and responsibilities facing VPI require that its final decisions—as must be true of any honorable educational institution—must be made without threat, pressure, or other interference from any source by the authority established for this purpose," they urged that the Board of Visitors "make such decisions for VPI as they are moved to make." They expressed a willingness to "accept the volunteer Corps concept," at least if it included two provisions—that "in order for one to be admitted to ROTC he must be in the Corps of Cadets" and that "there be a committee of the Board of Visitors to work with the Alumni Board and representatives of the administration to seek ways and means of strengthening the Corps program on the VPI campus."

Tom Rice suggested that the Alumni Board didn't really mean it, but did want to avoid embarrassing the Board of Visitors. Earlier he had asked Dr. Hahn to clarify the recommendation that ROTC be made optional and available only to members of the Corps. It was clear from the discussion that mandatory membership in the Corps for male students for the first two years would be dropped, and that only members of the Corps would be permitted to enroll in ROTC, the national officer-training program.

Harry Wyatt then offered a motion that the Board reaffirm its May decision. Mr. Lane amended the Wyatt motion to limit the voluntary Corps to a one-year trial period. Lane's motion to make the change a temporary experiment was voted down 10–2 with one abstention; Mr. Wyatt's motion to reaffirm the May decision was carried, 10–3. The Board then adopted a motion by Mr. Hancock that enrollment in ROTC be limited to students in the Corps, and also a motion by Mr. Cochran that a committee with no more than nine members be appointed from the Board of Visitors, the Alumni Association, the administration, and the students "to study the operation of the new Corps policy and to report to the Board such recommendations as they feel may lead to strengthening of the Corps of Cadets."[11]

The deed was done; the unthinkable had happened; and Tom Rice was desolate. Elva Redding's minutes put it like this: "Mr. Rice dictated a news release, after which he stated that he would like for the members of the Board to elect a Rector at this meeting, and declared the chair vacant." After some discussion it was agreed that the election would be by secret ballot, and the election would be only for the time remaining until the regular summer meeting in August, when new Board officers normally would be elected for the following year. Mr. Rice was promptly reelected.

Before the meeting ended, it was agreed that Rector Tom Rice should confer with the president in appointing the special committee to recommend ways in which the Corps might be strengthened. Then the Board dealt with several remaining items (including approval of individual faculty salaries for the 1964–1965 school year), but the high drama of the day was over and done. VPI alumni were badly divided on the Corps issue, and it would require some years for the hurt to heal.

On July 1, 1964, President Hahn, responding to a request from Governor Harrison, wrote a four-page letter to the governor that supplied background information on the Corps question and the Board's initial decision in May. He included a mass of data showing the comparative performance of civilian and Corps students, faculty votes on the question, and a summary of the Board's final action following the rehearing. Hahn sent copies to Senator Harry F. Byrd Sr. and Lieutenant Governor Mills Godwin for their confidential information, along with others to Warren Brandt, Craig Fabian, and also Mark Oliver in the alumni office.

Beginning with fall quarter 1964, mandatory participation in the Corps of Cadets came to an end. The Corps continued to be an important part of campus life, but it did so for a markedly smaller fraction of the student population. Even among male freshmen and sophomores, most students every year after the 1964 decision were civilians. A central dimension of the institution's history suddenly faded. Although a military component of student life certainly persisted, VPI became an increasingly civilian community. Two years into his presidency, Marshall Hahn survived the biggest challenge to his tenure as president, and he pushed on to make other changes.

Transition to a Voluntary Corps of Cadets

Going into fall quarter 1964, it remained to be seen whether, or to what degree, the transition of the VPI Corps of Cadets to a voluntary military organization would take place smoothly. Would sufficient numbers of incoming freshmen opt to come into the Corps? And how many of them would stay?

8.5 Tom Rice—after the 1964 decision—The June 15 *Techgram* account of the 1964 commencement program made no mention of participation by Rector Tom Rice. President Hahn earlier had written the rector to invite him to stay with the Hahns during commencement weekend and to bring greetings to the graduates from the Board, but Rice did not attend. Sorely hurt when the Board majority overruled him on the issue of the mandatory Corps, Rice became largely inactive in VPI affairs in the years immediately following. Governor Harrison, however, had already reappointed him to a second four-year term. At the August meeting, which Rice did attend, Harry Wyatt was elected the new rector in a secret ballot vote.

Years later, Mr. Rice said he became so terribly busy with his railroad work that it simply wasn't possible to get to many meetings, either of the Board of Visitors or the board of the Alumni Association. "My main problem was trying to get a merger through the Interstate Commerce Commission, and through the courts, plus running the railroad," he said. "I was terribly busy with many things.... I went [to board meetings] whenever I could," he explained, but "because of my job commitments it was difficult to be very active."

But as busy as he was, it is difficult not to conclude that Mr. Rice's philosophical differences with Marshall Hahn and his personal hurt regarding the Corps had as much to do with his absences from the campus during those years as his preoccupation with the ACL-Seaboard merger efforts. He did manage to get to some of the VPI-VMI football games, and he maintained some contacts with his VPI friends (Sol Rawls Jr. interview). In the 1970s and early 1980s, Rice served two four-year terms on the Virginia Military Institute Board, appointed at VMI's request. "VMI's mission was completely separate and different from that of VPI," Rice said, "and there never was any conflict of interest." Tom Rice later was to renew his VPI interests and resume active participation in alumni leadership. He also remained a great friend and admirer of Marshall Hahn. "I admire him exceedingly and have a great respect for him.... We simply had a very positive difference of opinion as to the type of school we wanted VPI to be," he observed (Rice interview).

The Corps strength dropped from about 2,150 in early 1963–1964 to 1,611—614 of them first-year students—at the beginning of fall 1964. The drop-off in freshmen and sophomore cadets was ominous, but in mid-October, General M. W. Schewe, the commandant, reported that not many more students had dropped out of the Corps than in the previous autumn. Fred Loeffler, the state editor of the *Roanoke Times*, visited the campus and published an encouraging story from the Corps' point of view on October 12. The student leadership, under Cadet Colonel James H. Powell of Petersburg, seemed to be adapting well to the organization's volunteer status.[12]

Corps enthusiasts were talking about an ideal size of 2,200, enough to fill the Upper Quad (the north dormitory area). One of the principal changes was an emphasis on more time for the Corpsmen to study, Loeffler wrote. Meanwhile, the VPI Board had approved the addition of a deputy commandant to augment General Schewe's staff, and Colonel Thomas M. Larner ('31), a retired Army Colonel who earlier headed the Army ROTC unit at VPI, was appointed to the position. But it became increasingly clear that the transition in the Corps at VPI had come at a difficult time, as the national environment regarding military concerns grew increasingly cool. In the second half of the 1960s, opposition to the war in Vietnam grew ever greater. Willingness to enroll at VPI grew ever greater, too, but willingness to participate in the Corps diminished.

Enrollment in the Corps dropped sharply in autumn 1965, when 403 freshmen opted for the Corps, and overall beginning strength dropped from 1,611 at the beginning of 1964 to 1,330 a year later. Even the "Highty-Tighties," the Corps' famous regimental band, attracted fewer musicians. The regimental band had received considerable national recognition and publicity in 1964, when it was among the bands selected to participate in the opening day parade of the World's Fair in New York.

George Cochran's resolution in the BOV had called for a committee to study ways and means of strengthening the Corps once it began functioning on a voluntary basis. Wyatt Williams, the committee chairman, got together periodically with his Committee on the Corps to discuss possible ways to strengthen the Corps. Early on, there seemed general agreement that lots of promotional and public relations work was needed to attract attention to leadership training opportunities in the Corps. The group also seemed to agree that, once the transition to a voluntary Corps was completed, the Corps could be—if provided sufficient support from the University administration and the civilian student group—a better organization than ever.[13] Not much, however, appeared to come out of the committee's work.

The Corps leadership itself made determined efforts to reverse the declining enrollment. In order to institute modifications more attractive to incoming students, it undertook an intense review of Corps customs,

8.6 The Committee on the Corps—The membership of the Committee on the Corps was announced in October 1964. After discussing it with the new rector, Harry Wyatt, President Hahn appointed Warren Brandt and Jim Dean to represent the VPI administration, together with two students—Cadet Colonel James H. Powell, regimental commander of the Corps, and Frank W. Nolen, president of the civilian student body. Alumni members were W. S. "Bill" Moffett of Staunton and Charles O. Gordon of Johnson City, Tennessee. Representing the BOV were Wyatt Williams as chairman, together with Jack Hancock and Erwin Will. Subsequently, Cliff Cutchins of Norfolk, when he joined the Board of Visitors in 1966, joined the group, and the normal succession of student leadership meant that the cadet colonel of the Corps that year, Lewis R. "Ranny" Dixon and the SGA president, Garland Rigney, were the student members.

Wyatt Williams was not an ideal selection for its chairman, at least from the Corps' point of view. In later years, Williams was quite candid about his selection, looking back. "That was about the dumbest appointment they ever made," he said, and he made it clear that he knew President Hahn had done the appointing. Williams, not particularly interested in the Corps, did not provide vigorous leadership.

Charlie Gordon ('42), who headed a furniture manufacturing firm in Johnson City, was the most ardent Corps supporter on the committee. He felt strongly that the Corps' discipline and leadership training had been invaluable in his own education. He was disappointed with the committee's inaction, and in later years said he believed it was stacked against the Corps. Warren Brandt, especially, was outspoken in his opposition to the Corps of Cadets, Gordon recalled. Brandt "didn't like the Corps and thought it should be done away with," Gordon said. "I always felt that behind the scenes Warren was working against us." Over all, the Committee wasn't active. "Those were frustrating years in that we couldn't get anything done in a positive way, and the Corps was diminishing," Gordon recalled (Gordon interview, 16 October 1988).

traditions, and regulations. In an effort to attract top-ranking students, rules and regulations increasingly stressed academic achievement. During the annual month-long summer orientation program for new students in 1966, military recruiting activity was much in evidence. General Schewe and Colonel Larner selected upper-class cadets and a good representation of the Army and Air Force ROTC personnel to work, along with student personnel and academic staff, with orientation sessions.

The VPI publications office prepared a simple but effectively designed recruitment brochure for the Corps, and copies were printed in sufficient numbers to be distributed—accompanied by ROTC recruitment materials—to each of the 1,950 entering freshmen in 1966. General Schewe sent copies of them to Mike Lacy, director of admissions and records, along with a draft letter outlining the policies governing the voluntary Corps and "the strongest possible recommendation that this proposal be approved, and the material indicated be expeditiously furnished to all entering male freshmen." Dean Jim Dean, Dean Les Malpass, and the

8.7 Scholarships for cadets—To help attract students to the voluntary Corps program, Samuel E. Bonsack (vice president of the C&P Telephone Co.) and other alumni leaders loyal to the Corps began raising money for Corps scholarships. Hahn wrote to Bonsack in January 1965 to congratulate him on the Corps scholarship fund-raising; a *Techgram* story would identify the initial donors and, Hahn hoped, would attract additional contributions.

The VPI News Bureau in January 1965 sent out announcements of the scholarship program for top-ranking high school seniors interested in going into the Corps. The $500 scholarships would be awarded to incoming freshmen whose high school records demonstrated "superior academic and leadership qualities." It was anticipated that the scholarships would be renewed each year for four years if the recipients maintained satisfactory academic and military achievement. The release was vague, though, about how many scholarships would be awarded, since that depended on how much money was contributed toward them.

Initially, Bonsack collected $1,550, and three scholarships were awarded. Contributors included Tom Rice, Erwin Will, Charlie Gordon, Jim Cargill, Marshall N. Pearman (also a C&P executive), and Stuart Shumate, president of the RF&P Railroad. The Corps scholarships were awarded by the University's Scholarship Committee, just as other scholarships were. No great outpouring of funds for the Corps scholarships developed, however, and few scholarships were awarded.

Charlie Gordon later said he took it upon himself to do some quiet fund-raising on his own—quite aside from the alumni fund-raising for scholarships for Corpsmen—that no one ever knew about. The money raised, Gordon said, was channeled directly to the Commandant's office "for use at his discretion...working with the regimental staff to make recruiting trips to high schools, or to do whatever they needed to do with it."

respective ROTC officers for the Army and Air Force units all concurred.[14] The Corps and ROTC recruiting materials were distributed.

Despite it all, the strength of the Corps continued to decline. The number of cadets fell to 1,288 in 1966–1967, barely topped 1,000 in 1967–1968, and in 1969–1970 fell to 932.

8.8 Farewell to one commandant, greetings to another—In June 1967, after six years as commandant, Brigadier General M. W. Schewe retired a second time and moved to Leesville, Louisiana, "to do a little fishing," as he expressed it. A thanks-and-best-wishes letter from President Hahn arrived at Leesville even before the general did. The entire 1,200-man Corps of Cadets chipped in and bought the departing general a farewell gift, a camping trailer (*Techgram*, July 1967). General Schewe was succeeded by Major General Francis T. Pachler, who had just retired from the Army after a long and distinguished career. He was a West Point graduate who, immediately prior to his retirement, had completed a tour of duty as chief of staff of the US Army in Europe. President Hahn wrote a warm letter of welcome. "I look forward to the continued strengthening and development of the Corps under your fine leadership," Hahn wrote.

President Hahn himself grew concerned about the Corps situation, and, in spring 1966 he appointed a subcommittee of the University Council to consider the Corps' problems.[15] The subcommittee reported back to University Council in February 1967 with a series of recommendations. Tutorial assistance and increased study time for cadets, it said, might improve Corps members' academic performance. Easing up on minor requirements for first-year students as well, and creating military ranks for all four classes to reward outstanding cadet performance, might enhance morale. A weeklong orientation for incoming freshmen cadets prior to fall registration might ease their transition, and improvements in recruiting for the Corps, with primary emphasis on high school juniors, might yield more VPI students intent on joining in the first place.

President Hahn welcomed the report and generally approved it. He did, however, delay implementation of the extra-week program for new cadets in the fall. Without advance notice, imposition of such a program might severely impact freshman enrollment in the Corps, rather than enhance it, he said.

A Rocky Transition to a Voluntary Corps

"We had some disappointments...in the four or five years following the transition" to a voluntary Corps, Charlie Gordon recalled. There always seemed some roadblock in the way; the promotion and publicity the Corps needed somehow didn't come through. "I always felt that particular committee was stacked against us...that Wyatt Williams never functioned like he should," said Gordon, still morose and regretful at the lost opportunities. "I don't think he had very strong feelings in support of the Corps."[16]

Looking back many years later, Hahn acknowledged that Wyatt Williams's leadership did not help much in efforts to strengthen the Corps. Hahn said he had tried hard to persuade the regimental staff that it had to provide an environment in which students could be attracted into the Corps, "not to eliminate the freshman system, but let up to the point where [the freshmen] could handle it.... We worked at it." The shift to voluntary participation provided an opportunity for the Corps to grow, Hahn said. Every year, there was such a much larger student population from which to draw.[17]

Yet the struggle to maintain the Corps of Cadets as a viable component of VPI continued throughout the Hahn administration. The big change, something President Hahn had come early to see as absolutely essential to the growth of the university, had perhaps overshot the mark. In view of the enormous opposition to such a change, even the considerable uncertainty as to whether pushing it might destroy his presidency, the accomplishment was extraordinary. It carried considerable costs, however, even as it fostered the momentum toward a new VPI.

8.9 Consternation leads to a prodigious history by Colonel Harry D. Temple —The Corps of Cadets came on hard times at Virginia Tech in the years after the policy change in 1964. Harry Downing Temple (1911–2004), a 1934 graduate in industrial engineering, had spent thirty-two years in the US Army, including combat service in World War II and the Korean War, and had retired as a colonel, when, in 1973, the thought struck him as to what he should do in light of talk of—and so dismal a prospect as—disbanding the Corps. He set out to "preserve for posterity" the Corps' hundred-year history; and Henry J. Dekker (a member of the class of 1944 and a combat veteran of World War II himself) assured him that, if he researched and wrote the history, Dekker would see that it got published.

The task proved far greater than Temple had anticipated and took far longer than the five or six years he had figured on. In 1996, he published volume 1—taking the story down to 1900. Then each year, he published another fat volume. In December 2001, volume 6 came out—it covered his four years in the Corps and completed the story through his graduation in 1934. By that time, Colonel Temple had produced more than 5,000 published pages, including more than 3,000 photographs. Finally deciding to retire a second time, this time at the age of ninety, he handed on the rest of his twenty-eight years of research to another graduate of the Corps, Lieutenant Colonel John A. Coulter II (retired), class of '76. (Kevin Miller, "Corps Historian Passes the Torch," *Roanoke Times*, 20 December 2001, New River Current 1)

---

1 Temple, *The Bugle's Echo, a Chronology of Cadet Life*, vol. 1, *1872–1900*, esp. 28; Kinnear, *The First 100 Years*.

2 Kinnear, *The First 100 Years*, 370.

3 Hahn interview, 8 July 1989.

4 Ibid.

5 Hahn interview, 10 July 1989. Hahn and Rice differ somewhat in recalling their initial conversations on the matter. Hahn remembers telling Rice there was no alternative but for him to bring the Corps problem to the Board for full discussion, and that he would have to recommend it be changed, that enrollment in the Corps be made voluntary. Rice recalls Hahn speaking of bringing the matter to the Board for discussion, but does not remember the president saying that he would have to recommend that the system be changed. It may have been simply a hearing problem; Mr. Rice has had hearing difficulty for many years.

6 Hahn interview, 8 July 1989. If Dr. Hahn would not buttonhole Board members and try to persuade them of the merits of a voluntary Corps, some of his friends on the Board certainly would. Jack Hancock and Wyatt Williams spent a good part of the evening before the May 18 meeting with the four female members of the Board—Gibbs, Graham, Showalter, and Wilhelm—seeking to obtain commitments for their votes for the voluntary Corps. They had some success, and they believed, at least, that the vote the next day might have had a different outcome had it not been for their efforts (Hancock interview; Williams interview). Mr. Hancock died in 1994.

7 Hahn interview, 8 July 1989.

8 Board minutes, 18 May 1964.

9 Hahn interview, 8 July 1989.

10 Ibid.

11 Board minutes, 29 June 1964.

12 *Roanoke Times*, 16 October 1964.

13 *Techgram*, 1 April 1965.

14 General Schewe letter to Dr. Lacy, 16 February 1966.

15 Dean Wilson Bell was named chairman; other members were professors Ogden H. Hall (business administration) and George Litton (animal science), along with Willis Worcester, Mike Lacy, Les Malpass, General Schewe, and Jim Dean, as well as students William L. Coulbourne of Parkersburg, West Virginia, and Cadet Colonel Randolph Sinclair of Abingdon.

16 Gordon interview, 16 October 1988.

17 Hahn interview, 8 July 1989.

9: Transition in Student Policy, 1962–1966

President Hahn's first few years at the helm launched tremendous change in many areas, but—as far as the school's student population and student services were concerned—the continuity was, at first, as great as the change. Hahn had correctly anticipated the influx of student applications that would result from the baby boom, but, then again, even the first cohort, born in 1946, would not be knocking at the door until 1964, and the cohort born at the high point of the baby boom, 1957, would not turn eighteen until 1975. The Hahn administration had a brief period to focus on more immediate needs, though it had to be mindful of the surge that would soon appear.

Regarding female undergraduates and male civilian underclassmen, too, the changes in the student population took some time to kick in. By the time the 1964 decision on the Corps of Cadets took place, students had already made up their minds whether to apply to VPI for admission that fall and, if admitted, most had already decided whether to enroll, so the big change in that respect did not materialize before 1965. The split of VPI from Radford College in 1964 had immediate implications, but, as women students from the 1960s are quick to point out, the change in policy to full coeducation could not be fully implemented until ample housing came on stream, and there was little increase in housing for women students until at least 1966—initially by converting men's dormitories into residence halls for women.

In view of the end to the mandatory Corps of Cadets, the policy change to full coeducation, and the implications of the baby boom, the institution's student policies would have to undergo substantial change in the 1960s. Alterations in personnel and practice combined to bring other changes, too.

Preliminary Changes in Admissions and Enrollment

In preparation for the anticipated onslaught of would-be students, the new president moved to strengthen the admissions office. In 1963, Dr. Paul Farrier was moved up to a new position, director of admissions and records, and when Farrier retired a year later, Dr. M. P. "Mike" Lacy ('51) succeeded him. Yet far more was involved than the numbers of students or the personnel in the admissions office. As the admissions office staff was strengthened, the screening process for applicants seeking to enroll intensified, with a view to raising the caliber of incoming freshmen and transfer students. Soon after Hahn became president, he instituted new procedures for admission. In particular, beginning with the 1963–1964 school year, VPI required all applicants to take College Board examinations in both English and math.[1]

Whatever the admissions requirements, enrollment growth at VPI during the Hahn years was tremendous (see chapters 16 and 20 and appendix 1). In 1964–1965—after mandatory enrollment in the Corps of Cadets for male freshmen and sophomores was dropped, and all courses of study were opened to female students—enrollment increased by 750 over the preceding year, and the freshman class numbered about 1,400. In fall 1965, VPI enrolled about 1,800 freshmen. By 1966–1967, total enrollment was 9,064—already up 43 percent from the 6,358 four years earlier, in the first year of Hahn's presidency—and total female enrollment reached about 650, double the figure just two years earlier.

People and Policy in Student Services

Significant changes in student services personnel were already under way when Marshall Hahn left VPI in 1959 and even more so by the time he returned as president three years later. Early in 1959, President Walter Newman brought Dr. James W. Dean to Blacksburg as director of student affairs and dean of civilian students. Dean worked alongside the commandant of cadets, who by 1961 was Brigadier General M. W. Schewe,

9.1 Women citizens, female scholars—In rough outline, and certainly with regard to the enrollment of women, VPI's trajectory through the twentieth century in general, and the 1960s in particular, resembled that of other white Southern land-grant institutions. Maryland State College (later the University of Maryland) awarded its first degree to a woman in 1920, VPI in 1923, and North Carolina State College in 1927. A half-century after the South's land-grant era began, more and more schools were making space for women as well as men.

On the gender front, the last great battle over enrollment was fought at Texas A&M, a school that replicated Virginia Tech's history though with its own twists. The question of coeducation was tangled with the question of compulsory military education. Texas A&M confirmed its stand in the 1950s and stood alone not only in maintaining a mandatory participation in the military for virtually all undergraduates but also in remaining all-male. Change came in the 1960s. Women filed a lawsuit seeking coeducation that went to the U.S. Supreme Court, but the judiciary looked the other way. The board of directors, acting on its own, decided in 1963 that women could be admitted to the school provided they were the wives or daughters of students or faculty, pursued a program of study unavailable elsewhere in Texas, or did graduate work. By 1971 women were admitted with no such restrictions, and in 1972 a women's dormitory opened on campus. Meanwhile, in 1965, Texas A&M abolished compulsory participation in its Corps of Cadets.

As other land-grant schools took on new identities, they adopted new names, much as VPI would in 1970. Texas Agricultural and Mechanical College became Texas A&M University in 1963. In 1971 Texas A&M advertised itself as "a coeducational university admitting all qualified men and women to all academic studies on the same basis without regard to race, creed, color or national origin." During the 1960s, Texas A&M underwent the kind of transformation under President James Earl Rudder that Virginia Tech did under President T. Marshall Hahn (Dethloff, *Centennial History*, ch. 25). To a degree, other schools like VPI did much the same, among them Clemson Agricultural College, which was renamed Clemson University in 1964.

U.S.A. (Ret.). Paul N. Derring had long served as the YMCA secretary, but in 1958 President Newman moved him to a new post, director of campus religious activities, and Rev. Alfred C. Payne came to VPI to replace Derring at the YMCA. So the lead team in student services in 1962 included Dean, Schewe, Derring, and Payne. Increasingly in the 1960s, Dean was the dominant figure.

The student affairs director, the commandant, and their staffs were housed in Squires Student Center, then better known as the student activities building, or SAB. Squires Student Center was bursting at the seams. The VPI Bookstore occupied much of its ground floor, behind the great brick stairway leading up to the red brick arches that spanned the main entrance at the second floor level. The YMCA offices, the little YMCA chapel, and a good many student organization offices were also crowded into the building. Before the decade was out, Squires would be greatly expanded, as would student services—and the student population.

During the first few years of Marshall Hahn's presidency, the structure and content of student services underwent a collection of significant changes. Some changes in policy and personnel reflected the changing student population—its far larger size, its increasingly civilian nature, the growing number of women. Some changes represented a determined effort to bring more student services and student activities directly under the control of the VPI administration. Later, pressure from undergraduates mounted to create an environment in which the school had less say, rather than more, over what students did. During the 1960s, everything—the role of the YMCA, the question of fraternities, dining hall policies—was put up for reconsideration by someone (see also chapter 16). As with so much else, change continued throughout the Hahn years and beyond, but the big break with the past came in his first four or five years as president. After an interlude during Hahn's first year or two, a cluster of changes came between 1964 and 1966.

The YMCA at VPI

When Marshall Hahn became VPI president in 1962, much of the student services work at the institution took place under the direction of the campus YMCA. There it had long been. Virginia Agricultural and Mechanical College opened its doors in 1872, and the YMCA dates its beginnings on the VPI campus from a year later. Almost as old as the institution itself, the Y had long been a central feature of campus life, and so it remained into the 1960s.

The stone edifice that, at the dawn of the twenty-first century, served as the Performing Arts Building—located on the edge of the Upper Quad, between McBryde Hall and Major Williams Hall—had been built a century earlier, in 1899, a very early example of Hokie Stone construction when all the other Upper Quad buildings were made of brick. It was financed with contributions and built as the campus home of the YMCA, and it remained the home of the Y until the Student Activities Building (later Squires) was constructed during the Great Depression, when the Y moved into the new building.

During forty years as YMCA secretary at VPI—from 1918 to 1956—Paul N. Derring initiated many student service programs. In addition to its regular Y activities for students, the YMCA managed the programs of the Student Center, and it sponsored a Religious Emphasis Week that brought a series of well-known speakers to campus each year. The organization also ran orientation programs for new students—a freshman camp each fall as well as a program to help meet the needs of newly-arriving foreign graduate students. Although the school had begun to appoint individuals to student counseling and other official responsibilities, it is not too much to say that, into the 1960s, the Y—together with academics, athletics, and, for many students, the Corps of Cadets—remained at the center of students' activities on campus.

In October 1939, the YWCA was organized at VPI as a counterpart to the YMCA. Virtually all the women students were members that first year, and the separate groups persisted for twenty-five years. In the early 1960s, the YWCA was working with the YMCA to sponsor Religious Emphasis Week, and a Big Sister-Little Sister program paired a junior or senior woman with an incoming female freshman or transfer student to help with the transition to college life. In 1964, the two groups merged into the YMCA at Virginia Tech, and in 1968 the combined group elected Susie Shertzer as its president. The group styled itself as open to "students of any or no religion, male or female, and regardless of race or nationality."[2]

The YMCA was well integrated into the structure of VPI, although it was autonomous, with its own board. It received some institutional support, which Hahn, early in his presidency, valued at about $20,000 annually, largely in rent-free office space, secretarial support, and some funding from student fees.[3]

Paul N. Derring

Paul N. Derring (1894–1973) came to VPI in 1918, during World War I. A 1917 graduate of the College of William and Mary, he wished to contribute to the war effort but, totally blind, he could not volunteer for the military, so he worked for the YMCA. His service at Virginia Tech, at first with soldiers as well as civilians, continued with students, as secretary of the Tech YMCA, through the entire quarter-century presidency of Julian Burruss and on—past a celebration during the Second World War of his twenty-five years at Tech—well into the Newman years.

Countless students recalled Derring as "my daddy while I was at VPI" or "a Dad away from home." They knew him as the man who supplied wise and generous counsel when they were students—at first in his office in the YMCA building and later in the Student Activities Building—and who instantly recognized them by their voices when they stopped by campus even many years later. Derring started freshman orientation in 1927. He brought many speakers to campus, and the YMCA "Chariot" took students to meetings far from Tech. After one such meeting in Greensboro, North Carolina, in the late 1930s, a female student there asked him, "Mr. Derring, just what is your job at VPI?" When he replied—condensing his Christianity and his job description—"To save young men," she squealed, "Oh, please save me one!"[4]

Derring remained the YMCA secretary for forty years, and then President Newman appointed him director of campus religious activities. Derring continued in that capacity from 1958 into the Hahn years, until February 1964, when he turned seventy years old and faced mandatory retirement under state personnel rules. In September 1963, President Hahn wrote to Gene Rowe, the Alumni Association president, about Paul Derring's difficult retirement. The religious affairs position that Derring occupied had created problems, Hahn explained. State personnel officials had never permitted salary increases for Derring because they questioned the propriety of using state resources for religious purposes, and Derring occupied the only such position in state service. Derring's anomalous standing prevented him from getting pay raises—thus hurting his retirement benefits—yet he was subject to the state's mandatory retirement policy. Moreover, it seems that Derring and Dean had clashed on multiple fronts, and Derring may well have had misgivings regarding the direction VPI would go after he had left.

Derring Hall memorializes the longtime YMCA secretary's service to VPI. In view of Derring's close connection to student affairs and not to geology or, indeed, any academic discipline, it might well have been more appropriate to name the Student Activities Building after him; the timing was off, however, as the name Squires had become attached to the building in 1949.

Rev. Alfred C. Payne

Al Payne (1916–2003), a native of Georgia, earned a bachelor's degree from Clemson in 1938 and—after World War II, where he participated in the Normandy landing in France—a divinity degree in 1946 from Yale. He then came to VPI in 1946, during Dr. Jack Hutcheson's presidency. Appointed associate secretary of the YMCA, which was directed by secretary Paul Derring, he ministered in particular to the hundreds of veterans who had enrolled under the GI Bill. He loved to discuss things, and to mediate conflict, and he proved adept at every task he undertook. He did not stay long, though, for he left in 1949 to head up the YMCA at the University of Pittsburgh. And then he left there, too, to participate from 1954 to 1958 in the Southern Area YMCA Council, which was seeking to help the faculty and students at historically-white institutions of higher education across the South accept racial desegregation.

Payne returned to VPI in 1958, recruited to take Paul Derring's place as YMCA secretary when Derring left the Y to fill the new post of coordinator of campus religious activities. Hahn determined, after Paul Derring's retirement in 1964, to abolish the religious affairs position Derring had held and transfer its functions to the dean of students' office. Therefore, Hahn put Payne into a new position as an assistant to the dean of students, so Payne resigned his position with the Y in 1964—Buford E. "Butch" Trent succeeded him—to join the VPI student services staff. There he carried out a campus role very much like the one with the Y—mostly working with the campus religious programs—and he served until his retirement in 1981. In his long career at Virginia Tech, Payne had an impact on the campus and the community that compared with Derring's. Payne Hall, a residence hall, was named for him in 1993.

In a conversation between Warren Strother and Warren Brandt some years after Al Payne had retired, Brandt said that Payne "had the most magnificent invocations." Payne had sent a copy of his book of prayers to Brandt because, Brandt explained, "I was one who said 'hey, why don't you write these down? They are just superb.' After a pretty good one I would congratulate him each time. I just thought he had a way of expressing things so succinctly…just marvelous invocations." Payne had the "ability to just slice right through it and come up with the essence of everything, very brief, with tremendous impact." As for Strother, he had helped select the invocations and had recruited "an excellent book designer, who designed that book for us and it came through beautifully," he told Brandt. "I was proud of that book. Still am."

Religious Concerns

In the autumn of 1962, primarily at Paul Derring's initiative, a number of senior faculty and staff had a weekend conference at Mountain Lake to consider campus religious concerns. Among those in attendance were YMCA secretary Al Payne; deans Jim Dean, Bill Mitchell, Burke Johnston, and Laura Harper; agronomy professor Roy Blazer, religion professor Guy Hammond, and engineering mechanics professor Frank Maher; and, for part of the weekend, President Hahn. Mark Oliver chaired the conference, a kind of brain-storming exploration of ideas as to how the religious needs of the students might best be met, including the role of the Campus Y. The meeting itself highlighted the importance of religious concerns in the everyday life of the institution in the early 1960s. In its aftermath, Dr. Hahn appointed or reappointed a number of members of the Religious Activities Advisory Committee, with Paul Derring as chairman.[5]

In January 1963, the Y-sponsored Religious Emphasis Week presented a long list of speakers headed by former Congressman Brooks Hayes, then special assistant to President Kennedy. According to Al Payne, in an assessment that he sent to President Hahn, the visiting leaders had appreciated the program, and some were "amazed at the response...both in quality and large numbers of participants." Payne also stressed the values of dorm discussions, faculty coffees, faculty lectures, and meetings with off-campus groups. President Hahn had given a reception honoring the visiting speakers.

A year elapsed following the Mountain Lake conference before Hahn appointed the Committee on Religious Programs and made Dr. Brandt its chairman. When the committee first met October 21, 1963, Hahn outlined its charge—"the development of the strongest programs possible within the confines of the church/state relationship." He reviewed the work of Paul Derring and the autonomous YMCA Board; all the services the Y had provided; and their gradual incorporation into the dean of students' programs. The president also outlined his plans for Al Payne to join the staff of the dean of students. He urged the group to take a hard look at all of the religiously oriented aspects of campus life and to make recommendations to improve them.

In his new role, Al Payne joined the Committee in early 1964, and in March he attempted, he said, to clarify the basic goals agreed upon in committee. "Stated briefly, the committee feels that the university should be vitally concerned with the religious development of all students, not merely those who show interest in a particular religious 'activity'; and, that this concern includes an effort to cultivate the 'moral dimension' throughout campus life." Payne's free-wheeling prose revealed considerable discussion and varying points of view. He stressed that the university "must scrupulously avoid an 'official' religious view point"; "avoid any semblance of compulsion in religious programs"; and "avoid discriminatory treatment or favoritism toward any sectarian group." On the relationship between church and state, the draft suggested there was no problem "as long as the spirit of voluntarism is preserved and the university does not show partiality to any particular church or sect." These various statements more or less summed up the thinking among the people most concerned with the role of religion in campus culture in the early years of the Hahn administration.

Campus Ministers—"Chaplains"—and the Hahn Administration

In the 1950s, a number of Blacksburg's churches ran programs for VPI students, and four had hired "chaplains"—denominational ministers assigned to work with VPI students—to look after these programs, and President Walter Newman put Paul Derring in charge of coordinating the various activities. The Methodists broke ground for their new student center, the Wesley Foundation building, in the spring of 1962. During Hahn's first few years as VPI president, the chaplains—John Coffee at the Wesley Foundation, Hugh "Woody" Leach of the Presbyterian Church, Baldwin Lloyd of the Episcopal Church, and others—sought, under the sponsorship of their respective churches, to help meet the religious needs of VPI students.

Marshall Hahn, before he left for Kansas, had been chairman of the Wesley Foundation Board at Blacksburg Methodist Church, and he became active in the church again after he returned. Nonetheless, policy and practice regarding the chaplains were modified under the Hahn

9.2 The YMCA chapel in Squires—Gene Rowe (see box 5.1) inquired of Marshall Hahn in September 1963 about the little YMCA chapel in the Squires Student Center that Rowe had earlier helped make possible with a substantial donation. Hahn suggested, as tactfully as possible, that the completion of the War Memorial in 1960—with its fine chapel opening onto the Drill Field—almost eliminated the need for the little chapel in Squires, In any event, Hahn wrote, a committee would be appointed under Warren Brandt's leadership to study the total on-campus religious program and make recommendations as to "those steps which can best be taken to strengthen the religious experience on campus for VPI students." Saying he already had talked to the Y Board about the study, Hahn suggested that the campus YMCA might want to undertake a similar study of its mission and purpose, for some aspects of the Y program might need to be revised in light of changing conditions.

The Y Board already had agreed to give up two rooms in the Student Activities Building, space that would be used for a new Counseling Center. It would be well to avoid any other reassignment of space in the terribly crowded SAB until both the VPI study and the YMCA Board study could be completed, President Hahn had written to Rowe, and he suggested that Rowe defer any new contribution for the Y chapel until the studies were completed. Rowe was understanding and gracious. The YMCA chapel that he and his wife, Mary Lewis, had largely contributed was used for some years before (as well as after) Memorial Chapel became available in 1960, and that, Rowe wrote, "gave us all the satisfaction one could ask from a project."

administration. In spring 1965, Warren Brandt sent a memo to President Hahn, Stuart Cassell, Jim Dean, General Schewe, Al Payne, and Lon Savage referring to a May 14 meeting regarding VPI's relationships with the campus ministers. First, Brandt said, the dormitory programs were the University's responsibility. If campus ministers to students wished to participate in VPI programs, they were welcome. But, although of course they could visit individuals in the dormitories, he said, they must not initiate their own programs. Second, the ministers to students were visitors to the campus. Accordingly, although they were free to drive on the campus, they were not to be issued staff parking permits. Third, the relationship between the school and the ministers was to be "not quite laissez faire"; Al Payne would be the chairman for development and maintenance of rapport. Finally, as for tickets to athletic events, the chaplains would receive them again that year, Brandt said, but not after, in view of the financial factor, considerations of morale (some people felt that the privilege was being abused or was not in line with other policies), and a lack of space as enrollments increased.

Warren Brandt had ended a long career in academe when he was asked in the late 1980s about the religious programs committee assignment Dr. Hahn had given him back in 1963. He could remember very little of it, but "it related probably to the Paul Derring era," he said. "A lot of people still thought that we ought to have that type of presence on campus. Campuses were changing in those days, and we moved past that type of thing. Even at the time…that type of model was no longer acceptable on most of the campuses around the country. That must have been what we were trying to do."

Recalling the chaplains, Dr. Brandt suggested that Jim Dean and he were "trying to just gradually run that out." As for Dr. Dean, who reported to Dr. Brandt in those early years, there was little doubt of his hostility to the chaplains. Al Payne, who remained on Dean's staff until his retirement, caught a good deal of that hostility, for Payne more than anyone else at VPI personified religious concerns at the institution.

A New Look to Student Services

Early in his presidency, Marshall Hahn began shifting responsibility for student services from the YMCA to Jim Dean. In the summer of 1963, he assigned Dr. W. H. "Bill" Cato and the Placement Office to the Office of Student Affairs, with no change in either the title of the office or the director. "This administrative realignment represents additional progress in the consolidation of the various student services under one administrative office," Hahn said. Cato had earlier written to Hahn to say that he had no objection to the realignment. "For many years," Cato wrote, "I have advocated the consolidation of student services under one administration."[6]

The student counseling part of Cato's Guidance and Placement Office (which had been housed in some small offices behind the Burruss Hall auditorium) was split off into a separate unit, however. The new Counseling Center was moved to the SAB, in the space previously used for the YMCA chapel, and in 1963 Dr. Harry J. Canon was brought in from the University of Nebraska (where he had completed his Ph.D. that year) to run it. The remedial reading program, in which Charles H. "Hank" Powers worked so effectively, was incorporated into the Counseling

9.3 Dr. James W. Dean—Dr. James W. Dean, director of student affairs and dean of civilian students, joined the VPI administrative staff in 1959. Jim Dean had taken his Ph.D. in education and student personnel at Penn State University in 1956. He was assistant dean of men at Penn State for a couple of years, then worked for a year as dean of men at Coe College before joining Westinghouse, in Pittsburgh, where he was assistant manager of the company's education center and supervisor of its personnel program. As one of the Westinghouse people who helped recruit young engineers, Dean had occasion to visit selected engineering schools. Through his visits to VPI, he came to know President Walter Newman, who invited Dean to join his staff at VPI (*Techgram*, January 1959; Dean interview).

Dr. Dean was a complex man, often difficult to understand. He smoked a curved-stem pipe, the cleaning, filling, and lighting of which seem to occupy a good deal of his time. He loved to talk, and he put a lot of energy and expression into his words. He often spoke in long, involved, complex sentences that seemed to have no endings—all of which sometimes left the impression that his verbal circumlocutions were purposeful, intent upon generating anything but clear understanding.

Jim Dean's strengths were many. Though he ran off a number of recruits to student services, one of his major strengths over the years turned out to be his ability to recruit good people with which to staff the student personnel organization, men and women with whom the students could work effectively. Though he had weaknesses, President Hahn perceived that, all in all, Dean was doing a good job; the likelihood of finding someone who could do better was a stretch; and besides, given the rivalry between Warren Brandt and Stuart Cassell (see chapter 13), shedding Dean, who reported to Brandt and worked well with him, would give Cassell a victory that Hahn could not permit. Hahn needed Brandt and Cassell to continue to work together, regardless of their frictions, and he needed someone to continue to do the kind of work that Dean was accomplishing in student services. Dean stayed on, well beyond the Hahn years.

Center. A year later, Dr. Thomas E. Cook (who had just earned his Ed.D. at the University of Missouri) was recruited as associate director. One of the first projects the two psychologists undertook was the development of a psychological profile of VPI's freshman class, to get a better feel for students' needs and concerns. But Harry Canon and Jim Dean simply could not long coexist; Canon soon resigned and returned to Nebraska; and Tom Cook then served as director of the Counseling Center.[7] He held that post until shortly before his death in 1993, and the unit was subsequently renamed the Thomas E. Cook Counseling Center.

New deans of men and women were appointed in the mid-1960s. In the summer of 1964, J. Gordon Brown, dean of men at Emory and Henry College, was appointed to a similar position at VPI. A graduate of East Tennessee State University, Brown had earned his M.S. in educational administration and supervision from the University of Tennessee. Brown was assigned responsibility for student housing and the resident men's counseling program. In 1966, David C. Hill, an ex-marine who had just earned a master's degree from the University of Alabama, was recruited as assistant to Gordon Brown for selective service and orientation programs.

A resident advisor system was installed in the civilian dormitories, along with a related cadet system in the Corps dorms, and it was reported that the improved dorm supervision resulted in "gratifying improvement in student performance." Gordon Brown set about designing a dormitory governance system for the students in the civilian dorms, but found it very difficult to come up with something that Jim Dean would approve. Dean was uncertain of what he wanted himself, as the administration felt its way in new directions, Brown concluded.[8]

After VPI's separation from Radford College, female enrollment steadily rose, and in the summer of 1965, Audrey Rentz, a New York native who had earned an M.S. in counselor education at Penn State University that year, joined the staff as dean of women. Rentz resigned, however, before the end of the school year. In part, she was young and inexperienced, but her major problem, as Gordon Brown recalled years later, was Dr. Dean, whom she could not please no matter how she tried. In 1966, Martha Harder, who had been dean of students at Lander College in Greenwood, South Carolina, succeeded Rentz as dean of women. Eggleston Hall's East and Main wings, newly converted for women students, were reopened in September 1966, and West Eggleston opened the following January. Myra Howze, appointed head resident for Eggleston Hall, reported to Dean Harder and, with the help of the housemother, floor leaders, and organized house councils, was responsible for programming for the Eggleston residents.

In sum, the rapid expansion of the student personnel staff corresponded with VPI's rapid growth. Larger numbers of students required corresponding growth of the student personnel staff as well as the faculty.

Moreover, ever more facets of student services were brought under the control of Jim Dean. Dean, who also dealt with disciplinary problems among the civilian students, generally sought to maintain order among an ever larger population of civilian students. Together with assistant dean Al Crawford, Jim Dean worked with the student leaders and the scores of student organizations. Crawford, who continued his counseling responsibilities in the non-cadet dormitories, also monitored the accounts of the student organizations to make sure that the funds allocated for student activities were properly accounted for. In one among many harbingers of the future, Dr. Dean's office also started a program to assist students who sought housing in the Blacksburg community.

Student Activities Committee

While the new staff people settled in and began their work, Vice President Warren Brandt began his own work. President Hahn altered Brandt's responsibilities so that Dean reported directly to him. The Student Activities Committee also was reorganized. Warren Brandt chaired it, and both Dr. Dean and General Schewe were members, as were two faculty members and five student leaders.

The Student Activities Committee, with strong student representation, was the principal forum for student concerns and interests at that time. Its agenda usually was filled student issues and various student-related matters that Dr. Dean and his staff brought up for discussion. Jim Dean was secretary of the committee and worked very closely with chairman Warren Brandt, although Dean's verbal circumlocutions were no doubt often something of a puzzle to the students.

One of the Student Activities Committee's major tasks was the annual revision of the University's basic policies for student life. These were the rules and regulations for students in residence halls, dining halls, and practically everywhere else, for *in loco parentis* was still much in vogue on many American college campuses in the mid-1960s; the University was a kind of substitute parent. The Committee's recommendations for revisions in student life policies were sent on to University Council, which sometimes made significant changes in them.

In early 1966, University Council approved plans for a more extensive summer orientation program for new students admitted for the 1966–1967 school year, along with their parents. For several years, one or

9.4 Warren Strother's impressions of VPI students in the mid-1960s—The student leaders and indeed most students in those years were bright, attractive, and thoughtful young people. Generally they didn't quarrel too much with the rules of the game, at least until they felt badly mistreated. They seemed naturally friendly, exchanging greetings with passersby and the like. Virginia Tech in those years was in many ways a quite conservative institution. Although the radicalization of the American campus was well under way, its manifestations were fairly limited in Blacksburg.

It was still a college campus, however, and collegians can get into trouble. Many did. Gordon Brown, the dean of men, and his staff had their share of troublesome students who were not much concerned about transgressions of student life policies. Every violation was carefully investigated and documented, and Brown imposed the appropriate penalty. Rarely was he overruled. Scores of students each year were called on the carpet for possession and consumption of alcoholic beverages, creating undue disturbances in the dormitories, drunk driving convictions, or even bringing discredit on the University by their behavior on visits to other campuses. Most intoxication violations resulted in disciplinary probation, and a second violation meant automatic suspension.

After Eggleston and Campbell became women's residence halls, along with Hillcrest, Martha Harder similarly had her hands full as dean of women. The coeds sometimes failed to sign out, or they signed out to fictitious destinations. Young women found to have entertained male friends in their rooms were severely punished.

more of the colleges had organized orientation programs for new students at some time during the summer. The previous summer, four colleges (Agriculture, Architecture, Business, and Engineering) had each offered an orientation program for new students and parents at various times during the summer, in addition to the usual orientation and registration as school opened in the fall and the traditional YMCA Freshman Camp. But 1966 would be the first year that all six colleges would do so. The program that first year, for about 2,000 first-year (freshmen and transfer) students and many parents, took place in July and addressed almost every aspect of student life and academic concerns.

A Unified Student Government?

Big policy changes back in the 1920s led to big changes in student government. In the late 1920s—soon after the first women were admitted as

VPI students in 1921—female students organized a Women's Student Organization. After civilian male students—their numbers greatly increased after the 1924 decision to exempt upperclassmen from the Corps—organized the Civilian Student Union as a student government but excluded women from it, women organized a counterpart Women's Student Union. As the three factions jockeyed—cadets, male civilians, and females—they might align themselves according to male and female or according to cadet and civilian, but they could not do both at once. In 1939, to counter the cadets' power in student government, the male civilians invited the women to join them in a combined Civilian Student Union.

So it was that VPI entered the Hahn years with two student government organizations. One was superimposed over the military structure of the Corps of Cadets, and the other was the civilian student government. During the 1964–1965 school year—immediately following the decision to end the mandatory Corps—there were efforts to bring the two student government organizations together, and a referendum was held on the question on March 16, 1965. Civilian students easily approved the proposal, 1,007 to 239, but, by a similar margin, it failed to win majority approval in the Corps, which voted against it, 954–173. Disappointed, senior class president Frank Nolen suggested that it was the work of the regimental staff and did not reflect the feelings of the rank and file. President Hahn shared Nolen's sentiments and said Nolen's work undoubtedly had "brought us closer to realizing a unified student government."

Indeed, the next year a new combined Student Government Association went into effect. With an assist from some hard work by Kendall Clay of Hillsville, the civilian student government president in 1965–1966, the Corps reversed itself in early 1966 and voted to participate in a single governance system for all students. M. Garland Rigney ('67), a history major from Madison Heights who was elected the first president of the unified student body in May 1966, was delighted. He looked forward, he said in a letter to Dr. Hahn, to taking "an even bigger step toward making our university one of the best in the nation."9

From Paul N. Derring to James W. Dean

It was a long way from the world of Paul Derring to that of Jim Dean, from the YMCA to the school's new system of student activities and student services, from the former dominance of the Corps of Cadets to the new combined Student Government Association, just as it had earlier been a big change from the old YMCA Building to the new Squires Student Center. Already by 1965 or 1966, much of the change of the Hahn years had taken place, but much more was soon to come. Into the 1970s, student life grew more and more different from what it been in 1962.

[1] At about the same time, it also was decided the diplomas awarded to VPI graduates were much too large. Thereafter the size of the document was greatly reduced—from 17 by 14 inches to 11 by 8 1/2 inches—and the diplomas were enclosed in an attractive leatherette cover.

[2] *Bugle,* 1940, 1964, 1968; Benjamin T. Breland IV, "The YMCA at Virginia Tech: Serving a Changing University during the Payne and Trent Years," in Wallenstein, *Essays, Spring 1978.*

[3] Hahn letter, 20 September 1963.

[4] Webster, *I Remember Paul,* 23, 29, 54.

[5] Hahn letter, 13 December 1963.

[6] Hahn note to Dean and Cato, 16 August 1963; Cato letter, 9 August 1963.

[7] Dr. Cato and Dr. Dean had little interaction. Bill Cato largely ignored the man to whom he was supposed to report, and Jim Dean bothered Cato hardly at all. Cato retired from the Placement Office in 1972, after long and effective service (Tom Cook, Bill Cato, and Jim Dean interviews).

[8] *Annual Report,* 1964–1965, 7; Gordon Brown interview.

[9] General Schewe letter to Charles O. Gordon, 17 May 1967; Rigney letter to Dr. Hahn, 10 May 1966.

10: The 1966 Virginia General Assembly

During the two-months between Mills Godwin's election as governor in November 1965 and his inauguration in January 1966, he and Marshall Hahn discussed at length many of the major issues facing the Commonwealth. Godwin was an occasional houseguest in the president's home on the VPI campus, and, in lengthy conversations in Blacksburg, the two explored one another's thinking in depth on numerous matters of public concern, as both men years later acknowledged.[1] The VPI president was very much encouraged by the coming inauguration of the new governor. Hahn was, to be sure, only one of many influential people with whom the governor-elect discussed such matters. But no one could have been happier than Hahn was with Godwin's vigorous leadership as governor, especially his focus on education. The 1966 session of the Virginia General Assembly was an extraordinary time, for Virginia and for VPI.

Governor Mills Godwin and Public Education

Governor Godwin proposed a series of significant initiatives, along with new revenues to pay for them. In his inaugural address, the new governor declared, "We can take no rest until all our public schools—not just some—will compare with any in the nation; until all our colleges and universities—not just some—can hold up their heads in any company"; and until "all our sons and daughters—not just some—have the same chance to train their minds and their skills to the utmost."[2]

Addressing the newly convened 1966 General Assembly, Governor Godwin outlined a "positive plan of action" to meet the needs of the rapidly changing state. He urged much stronger support for Virginia's public school system—in a state that, only a few years earlier, had gone on record as committed to closing any public elementary or high school rather than permit it to be desegregated. A mere seven years after the Massive Resistance program had been overturned in the courts and abandoned in 1959, an Organization man was proposing to put far greater resources than ever before into the school system.

The governor also proposed an extensive highway construction program, along with sharply increased funding for mental hospitals, higher education, and other programs. To begin with, he asked the General Assembly to approve an emergency $34 million appropriation to speed up construction of projects, already planned, at state colleges and mental hospitals.

Governor Godwin strongly endorsed the recommendations of the Higher Education Study Commission and the proposed legislation to implement them. Among these were a new statewide community college system, together with expansion of existing institutions of higher education, and the merger of the Medical College of Virginia and Richmond Professional Institute to form a new state university for metropolitan Richmond, a school that became known as Virginia Commonwealth University.

The governor stressed, however, that, in building new institutions, he was not suggesting that existing ones be diminished. "I would steadfastly oppose any reductions in the standards of our long-established colleges and universities, or any limitations on their capacity to meet their obvious needs. I will support their growth in size, in stature and in quality," he said. To promote the growth of graduate education and associated research programs in the state's universities, the governor proposed a $1 million graduate incentive fund. To facilitate more effective statewide planning in higher education, he urged the strengthening of the State Council of Higher Education.

A Sales Tax?

To provide the necessary funding, Governor Godwin proposed two separate sales taxes. A statewide tax on retail sales could supply the funds to support increased spending on education—the item in which President Hahn had the greatest interest. In addition, an excise tax on the sale of automobiles might fund new highway construction.

Governor Albertis S. Harrison Jr.'s budget recommendations to the General Assembly as he left office also had included a proposed sales tax, and Governor J. Lindsay Almond Jr. had tried but failed to secure passage of a statewide sales tax back in 1960. By the beginning of 1966, some fifteen Virginia cities already had adopted local sales taxes, and both the outgoing and incoming governors were apprehensive that, unless the Commonwealth acted soon, the cities would perhaps have preempted the tax and certainly would have made it difficult to enact on a statewide basis. Passage in 1966 seemed urgent, then, not only because enhanced funding seemed necessary but because the opportunity to gain passage at all might soon be lost. Godwin later explained that otherwise "the state never would be able to impose its own sales tax and we would be in a real straitjacket financially."[3]

Meanwhile, Hahn had not been silent on the sales tax issue. He was well aware that, if Virginia was to face up to changing demographic and economic realities, it would have to significantly broaden its tax base. By early summer 1965, Hahn's correspondence made clear his view that enactment of a statewide sales tax was essential. During the statewide political campaign in summer and autumn 1965, Hahn was in close touch with Lieutenant Governor Godwin, then the Democratic candidate for governor. Godwin, careful in the campaign not to express opposition to a sales tax, said he would not hesitate to seek new revenues if necessary.[4]

President Hahn, in his frequent speeches throughout the autumn, maintained a strong advocacy of a statewide sales tax, undoubtedly with Godwin's approval. Hahn's speaking schedule was as hectic as ever, and he lost no opportunity to cite the urgent need to strengthen the state's educational system.

The sales tax issue dominated the opening of the 1966 General Assembly session; funding questions had to be answered before other issues. Early in the session, Governor Godwin was somewhat relieved to see a delegation of Tidewater legislators, led by Senator Edward L. Breeden of Norfolk, come calling. The delegation proposed to support the governor's state sales tax proposal if he in turn would support a 1 percent sales tax for the localities. "That was the beginning of being able to pull the thing together and get it passed," Godwin later recalled.[5]

There were switched votes and close calls, but in the end, the sales tax legislation passed easily, along with the excise tax on sales of autos and trucks. The sales tax measure imposed a 1 percent state sales tax (with half of the proceeds distributed to localities on the basis of school age population), a 1 percent sales tax for the localities, plus another 1 percent state sales tax to become effective in 1968, when additional state revenues obviously would be needed.[6]

Marshall Hahn Goes to Richmond

Just as had been the case two years earlier, President Hahn found Governor Harrison's 1966–1968 budget recommendations to the General

Assembly disappointing, especially for capital outlays. VPI had requested about $13.3 million in state general fund appropriations for building construction, but Governor Harrison recommended only $7.4 million. The budget recommendations for maintenance and operations were somewhat more generous, although there were problems, especially with the Agricultural Experiment Station. Marshall Hahn, turning his attention to VPI's budget concerns, lost little time in getting the attention of key legislators. Together with Stuart Cassell, who knew his way around the capitol as well as anyone in Virginia, Hahn made the most of his opportunities. His close alliance with the newly inaugurated governor proved helpful.

In early February 1966, the Richmond Chapter of the VPI Alumni Association held its traditional biennial party for the General Assembly. Back in September 1965, the president had alerted members of his Board of Visitors of the upcoming date, February 9, and the place, the Hotel John Marshall. Governor and Mrs. Godwin were among the guests, along with many legislators, prominent VPI alumni, Board members, and other university and state officials, plus members of the capitol press corps and spouses or friends. Everybody with any influence was working hard to leverage it. The following week, Dr. Hahn wrote to alumnus Bernard E. Cooper of Richmond to thank him for everyone's help. It was an extraordinarily successful affair, he said, and he wrote glowingly of comments made by the governor and many legislators—some of whom were suggesting that the 1968 party would need to find a larger room.[7]

After the legislative session was completed, Dr. Hahn could report General Fund appropriations for resident instruction for 1966–1968 of $13.8 million, up 52 percent over 1964–1966, primarily to accommodate substantial enrollment increases. Similar appropriations were approved

---

10.2 Ambler Johnston misses a party—One disappointed would-be party-goer in Richmond in 1966 was Ambler Johnston. Johnston had attended such legislative receptions for years, always putting in a good word for VPI with his numerous friends. He would be out of town when the 1966 reception was held, however, so he wrote to a selected list of legislators and urged them to be sure to attend. In a note to Dr. Hahn, Johnston added: "Maybe the legislature will go right on whether I am there or not, but I hate to miss this one." In his reply, Hahn assured him that the situation in Richmond looked reasonably good.

from student fees and other non-tax revenues. The General Fund appropriations for the Agricultural Experiment Station for 1966–1968 totaled $4.8 million, up 6.5 percent; for the Cooperative Extension Service, $7.5 million, up 20 percent. For the Engineering Experiment Station, the general fund appropriation was $483,000, more than double the 1964–1966 funding.[8]

Fast-track Action on Capital Funding

The 1966 General Assembly appropriated about $10 million for new buildings and related capital outlays at VPI. Dr. Hahn wrote in mid-March to the board of the Alumni Association that the Assembly actions would provide for "significantly more rapid progress toward achieving the quality and scope of educational opportunities so essential to the advancement of the entire Commonwealth." He also noted that "additional appropriations were requested in several areas where there were problems, and in every case the General Assembly made additional appropriations available."

In May, the *Techgram* reported that $11.6 million in new construction and renovation projects would get under way on the campus by late autumn, increasing the VPI construction program to more than $25 million. New projects included a $3.7 million classroom-laboratory building, a $2.9 million addition and renovation for Squires Student Center (about half of which was funded by revenue bonds to be paid off from student fees), another $1.1 million addition to Burruss Hall (the administration building), a $1 million architecture building, a $1.1 million home economics building, and a $720,000 addition to the food processing laboratory.

One reason the construction program advanced so rapidly was Governor Godwin's fast-track funding for the $34 million appropriation under an emergency clause for higher educational institutions ($28.3 million for college buildings) and the mental hospital system ($5.8 million). The General Assembly readily agreed with the governor's recommendation, and nearly $8 million of the emergency appropriation was earmarked for VPI's facilities in Blacksburg. In addition, $2.7 million was appropriated under the emergency legislation for classroom buildings at Roanoke Technical Institute and at the Danville and Wytheville branch colleges, all three of which were still part of VPI.

10.3 A five-day workweek?—The University's 1966–1968 appropriations helped resolve the workweek problem for its support staff, an irritant that had caused much unhappiness for some years among non-faculty employees. By the early 1960s, a five-day, forty-hour workweek had become standard for most employers and employees, but Virginia Tech was an exception, with generally a five-and-a-half day, forty-four-hour week. The faculty had a similar schedule, which included classes on Saturday mornings as well as weekdays. But faculty members had much more flexible schedules, and they earned considerably higher salaries than most non-faculty employees, who had grumbled for some years about the long week. After 1960, when the state mental hospital system adopted a five-day workweek for its employees, the issue began to heat up on the campus.

In May 1964, Edward B. Evans, then the VPI personnel officer, wrote Dr. Hahn to advise that the problem had to be addressed. Aside from overt employee complaints, he said, it was becoming difficult to fill vacancies in some job categories, as the longer workweek made it difficult to compete with other employers. Stuart Cassell was not sympathetic. He and J. Russell "Russ" Abbitt, the buildings and grounds director, sometimes exchanged heated opinions on the subject. Abbitt, whose staff was almost entirely classified (non-faculty), cited growing morale problems and the loss of key people.

The pressure intensified. In May 1965, Abbitt forwarded to Evans a petition signed by more than 90 percent of his work force urging a five-day, forty-hour workweek. The unhappy employees also generated political heat. Delegate Kenneth I. Devore, who represented the Blacksburg area in the House of Delegates, wrote to President Hahn in summer 1965 to express his concern. VPI employees were holding the state responsible, Devore said, but as far as he knew the institution had never requested funding for a five-day workweek. He offered to go with Dr. Hahn to the governor to try to resolve the problem. "I need Help!" he wrote in longhand across the formal letter.

President Hahn, who knew a problem when he saw one, promptly requested Board approval to institute a five-day, forty-hour week for classified employees. The Board of Visitors readily agreed, contingent upon necessary appropriations by the General Assembly (BOV Minutes, 24 June 1965). Stuart Cassell announced in the *Techgram* in June 1966 that, for non-faculty employees, the five-day week would be instituted July 1, the first day of the new budget year. The academic calendar, with five-and-a-half-day class schedules, persisted for several more years.

The emergency appropriations had their roots in the 1965 gubernatorial campaign and some earlier spadework by the presidents of Virginia's public colleges and universities. The Council of Presidents of the public institutions in May 1965 released a special report, "Virginia's Crisis in Higher Education," citing the urgent need to strengthen the state's system of higher education. "The Commonwealth is facing a crisis in public higher education, precipitated by an extremely rapid population growth and the demands of a changing economy," the report began, and it went on to cite a series of facts and figures on the inadequacies of current funding.

For example, the report said, Virginia was fifth from the top among fifteen southern states in per capita personal income, but third from the bottom of those fifteen states in college enrollments as a percentage of college-age population. It cited, too, Governor Harrison's statement that Virginia's total state and local tax rate, in relation to personal income, was the lowest in the nation. The Council urged substantial increases in state appropriations for public institutions of higher education, both for capital outlays and for operating budgets.

The Council of Presidents, of which Marshall Hahn was an active member, had issued an initial special report in 1963 on "Higher Education and Economic Development in Virginia." Beyond citing then-current statistics on Virginia's relative position in higher education, the report highlighted the urgent need to strengthen Virginia's higher education system if Governor Harrison's economic development program was to achieve significant results. The 1963 report had attracted widespread editorial comment in the state's newspapers, almost all of it strongly supportive. The 1965 special report stirred up another round of editorials on the subject of Virginia's higher educational concerns—precisely what the presidents and the staff people at the public institutions who put the reports together had in mind. Paul Saunier Jr., assistant to President Shannon at the University of Virginia, and Warren Strother at VPI, working with their colleagues at several other state schools and their respective presidents, had put the special report together.

Governor Harrison anticipated a substantial surplus at the end of the budget year on June 30, 1966. (His proposed 1966–1968 budget, submitted just as he left office, estimated the surplus at about $96 million.) In summer 1965, the governor called a special session of the General Assembly to redistrict Virginia's congressional districts, to comply with a federal court order. Meanwhile, in light of all the concern about "the crisis in public higher education," a number of people began to urge the governor to open the way for the General Assembly's special session to make emergency appropriations for college construction projects and thereby speed up construction on the campuses. Prominent among them were a number of legislators from Northern Virginia: Harrison Mann, Leroy Bendheim, Robert Fitzgerald, Omer Hirst, Guy Farley, Dorothy McDiarmid, and Katherine Stone.

Governor Harrison, however, was not at all interested in opening the special session to other issues, particularly with the regular 1966 session coming up in a few months. For one thing, he said, there was no shortage of capital outlay funding. As of late August 1965, the unexpended balance in the General Fund for campus construction projects—plus funds available from bond issues for dormitories and other bond-financed projects and some $25.4 million in planning funds already released to accelerate construction on the state college campuses—all added up to more than $75 million. Aside from that, Governor Harrison told the legislators assembled in special session, the Higher Education Study Commission's recommendations likely would result in the development of a long-range plan for Virginia higher education. It would be the better part of wisdom, he said, to await the Commission's guidance before making further capital appropriations for individual colleges. Governor Harrison declined to open the session to any emergency funding.

President Hahn, surely as anxious as anyone to obtain speeded up state funding for building construction, had nonetheless agreed with Governor Harrison. In a talk to the Agricultural Conference Board in July 1965, just before he went on vacation, Hahn reported that planning was under way for more than $10 million in construction projects at VPI for 1966–1968. If appropriations for the projects could be made available early in the 1966 legislative session, he said, those projects could be expedited. But since plans for the buildings would not be completed much before the end of 1965, there would be little advantage from action at the General Assembly's special session in August.

Reporter George Kelly of the *Norfolk Virginian-Pilot* filed a special story for the *Washington Post* in late July 1965, recounting Hahn's position on the possible special session appropriations, and noting that it was the first break in the ranks of the Virginia college presidents on the issue. Dortch Warriner, the Republican candidate for attorney general, promptly charged that Marshall Hahn "had been forced to parrot the

Harrison-Godwin line." Delegate Harrison "Hank" Mann of Arlington sent Dr. Hahn a note, along with a clipping of the *Post* story, with the cryptic statement: "Thanks for cutting the ground out from under us! It's your privilege, but a little stupid." President Hahn's response carefully spelled out the reasons for his position. In reply, Mann insisted that emergency appropriations in August could in many cases make up to a year's difference in when the buildings could be available. Most of all, however, Mann said, "It would provide a psychological impetus to the entire capital outlay program" and generate a widespread feeling that "concrete steps were being taken...to meet the needs of the people." "I suggest," Mann wrote, "that having paid your justified respect to the Republicans, you chalk this one up as an error and get ready for a new ballgame." He urged Hahn to avoid the "creeping frame of mind [that] so often afflicts executives and public officials...to look for 16 reasons why we shouldn't do something."

Linwood Holton, the Republican candidate for governor, wrote to President Hahn in early September to inquire if anyone had made assurances to him that emergency legislation, requiring a four-fifths vote, could be arranged in early January 1966. Such a scenario was unrealistic, Holton asserted. With both Republicans and Democrats supporting emergency appropriations, Hahn responded, it ought to be easily possible. Linwood Holton lost the 1965 gubernatorial contest with Mills Godwin (although Holton was successful in another bid four years later). VPI and other state institutions did get their high-priority buildings funded on an emergency basis early in the 1966 legislative session; President Hahn's confidence had not been misplaced.

A System of Community Colleges?

The 1966 General Assembly had a crowded agenda; Governor Godwin's initiatives gave it a heavy workload in addition to other concerns facing the legislators. It was late in the session before the bills on the proposed community college system were taken up, although Godwin had them introduced early. Even the proposed sites of the individual community colleges had been publicized to generate local support for the community college plan. The community college bills, though easily approved in the House of Delegates, ran into a roadblock in the Senate. There, though some branch colleges had been excepted from the proposed new system—William and Mary's Christopher Newport College in the east as well as the University of Virginia's George Mason College in Northern Virginia and the college at Wise in the southwest part of the state—a few senators wanted to keep out additional branches.

The proposed legislation brought into direct conflict two different approaches to the structure of higher education in Virginia. Marshall Hahn had been long convinced of the value of the comprehensive community college to provide educational opportunity for all students who might seek it. More than two decades later, Mills Godwin was still impressed with Hahn's extraordinary efforts on behalf of the community college bills. "All during the [1966] session," Godwin said, "Marshall was going from here to there to other places promoting" the legislation.

It was apparent, however, that powerful elements of the University of Virginia opposed a statewide community college system. Early in the session, the University of Virginia BOV issued a statement describing the statewide community college system proposal as "commendable" in terms of broader educational opportunities, but asserting that the University's branches "are not community colleges…but instead are branches of the University and are serving as regional colleges." The branch colleges were operating with "the enthusiastic support" of the communities in which they were located, the Board's statement noted, and "the University is prepared to continue" these relationships so long as doing so "appears to be in the best interest of education in the Commonwealth."

In the final week of the session, the community college bills were hung up in the Senate Education Committee, going nowhere. Senators William F. Stone and E. Almer Ames, both of whose districts included branch colleges of the University of Virginia, were blocking them. Governor Godwin recalled summoning State Superintendent Woodrow W. Wilkerson as well as Presidents Hahn (VPI), Shannon (University of Virginia), Paschall (William and Mary), and Robert Smith (Medical College of Virginia) to an early morning meeting to see if the roadblock could somehow be removed. Hahn, Godwin recalled, was downright eloquent as he spoke to the urgency of the legislation. Paschall and Smith also indicated support, but "Shannon was reluctant; he just wouldn't say much," according to Godwin.[9]

The governor threatened to go public: "If this community college bill is not voted upon because it is bottled up…I am going to have to call in the press this evening and tell them why this bill is not moving," he later remembered telling the group. In short order, Senators Stone and Ames agreed to a compromise. If the University of Virginia branches at Martinsville and Wallops Island were excluded from the community college system until they could gain independent accreditation (apart from their University affiliation), they would withdraw their objections. The two state senators had been arguing that, if the branch colleges were immediately transferred to a community college system, they would have serious accreditation problems. This was nothing more than a smoke screen, Governor Godwin asserted, the situation still vivid in his mind after nearly a quarter century. In any event, the compromise was agreed to. The bills were voted out of the Senate Education Committee and passed the Senate, 39–0. The House concurred in the Senate amendments, and the bills went to the governor's desk, where they were promptly signed into law. The governor named Dr. Dana B. Hamel to direct the new community college system, which grew very rapidly in the next few years.

Looking back at the community college fight more than two decades later, Marshall Hahn took pride in what he had been able to do to. "I had built a lot of [friendships] in the General Assembly by then and I just went down and pulled out all the stops," Hahn recalled. "Mills [Godwin] didn't ask me to; we didn't ask each other to do things. We could almost anticipate what needed to be done. I went down and…cashed in all the chips I had. Mills called me in after the bill passed and said there was 'no way I could tell you how helpful you have been.'"[10]

Continuing Momentum from the 1966 Session

When the 1966 legislative session was over, the General Assembly had approved a $2.3 billion budget for 1966–1968, about $980 million of it in State General Fund appropriations, along with a new general sales tax and other revenue measures to pay for it. The sales tax was consistent enough with Virginia's traditional "pay-as-you-go" approach during the many years of the Byrd Organization—but it revealed a far greater willingness to pay. Far greater investment in higher education than ever before included massive increases in the money President Hahn could work with at VPI. The new system of community colleges meant that Hahn had largely seen his policy wishes legislated into existence, and it meant, too, that VPI would thereafter be focusing on the Blacksburg campus. The scattered branches would be administered on their own.

In June 1966, Governor Godwin arranged with the Virginia Association of Broadcasters to put together a statewide network of radio and TV stations for an announcement from the governor's office. He used

10.4 VPI and a new system of community colleges—Three of VPI's two-year branch colleges—Roanoke Technical Institute (which became Virginia Western Community College), Wytheville, and Clifton Forge-Covington—were transferred to the new community college system in 1966, and the Danville branch was to follow two years later. The communities in which the schools were located, however, were quite reluctant to sever their affiliations with the senior institutions. Local community leaders perceived a university branch college to be a more prestigious institution than a community college.

Hahn had moved quickly to try to calm their apprehensions after release of the Bird Commission report. On January 5, 1966, he wrote to each member of the local advisory board for each of the branch colleges and invited them all to a joint meeting in his office on Saturday, January 8. This was just before the 1966 General Assembly session would convene. The Commission recommendation for a statewide community college system that would include existing branch colleges was of great concern, Hahn wrote, and he asked that they get together to look at "all of the ramifications" of such a change. Dr. Hahn also invited all twenty-seven of the local board members to dinner on the campus and afterward to watch a basketball game with the University of Pittsburgh, all as guests of the university.

A few weeks after that discussion, Dr. Hahn wrote to all members of the local advisory committees again, this time to convey VPI's formal position on the community college issue as adopted by the Executive Committee of the Board of Visitors on January 15, 1966. The Committee statement supported the Bird Commission report generally, and it "strongly endorse[d]" the Commission's recommendations for a statewide community college system. Although existing VPI branches had filled a real need, the statement continued, and although the relationships of the branches, the university, and the local communities were excellent, "if the recommendations of the Commission are implemented...VPI will cooperate, and will stand ready to serve both the communities and the Commonwealth in any ways appropriate" (Hahn letter and statement, 9 January 1966).

Thinking about it almost a quarter century later, the former VPI president recalled it like this: "I did maintain contact with [people associated with the community colleges] during the period of the battle, and kept saying it could mean more, not less. They weren't fully convinced, but they didn't feel that anyone was working behind their backs" (Hahn interview, 31 August 1989).

the broadcast to outline plans for a statewide conference on education in fall 1966 to look at Virginia's educational system and better prepare for its future. "Virginia has in the past jumped from crisis to crisis—plugging the dikes for next year or the year after against the flood of new knowledge and against the waves of new young people more anxious than ever to acquire that knowledge," he said.[11]

With the resources made possible by the new sales tax, the Commonwealth should be better able to plan for the future, the governor said. "Virginians must not be swayed by any thought that Virginia cannot afford public education in modern times," he asserted. "The truth is nearer the axiom that Virginia cannot afford ignorance in modern times." For one thing, Governor Godwin wanted to make sure that the people understood why a sales tax had been needed and how the money would be spent.

A statewide conference on education to generate greater support for educational in the Commonwealth would be desirable, the governor believed. He had promised during his 1965 gubernatorial campaign to do all he could to improve education—because of its importance to Virginia's future as he saw it, and no doubt with Marshall Hahn's strong encouragement.

The Council of Presidents of the State-aided Institutions of Higher Education—which was at least partly responsible for the governor's June announcement—assisted in preparation for the event. The idea was new for Virginia; no governor had ever attempted to rally support for education at all levels in such fashion, and to enlist the help of leaders in business, industry, and the professions in putting it together. More than a score of business, professional, and educational associations joined in sponsoring the governor's conference, along with six former governors all the way back to Colgate W. Darden Jr., Virginia's governor during World War II, a former president of the University of Virginia who at that time was a member of the State Board of Education.

The official call for the conference came on September 15, 1966, when Governor Godwin announced that it would be held at the Mosque Auditorium in Richmond on October 5. Nearly 2,000 special invitations were sent to legislators, local governmental officials, business and community leaders, and other citizens. Moreover, a general invitation went out to all interested citizens.

The governor named Virginius "Vee" Dabney—editor of the *Times-Dispatch*, the morning newspaper in Richmond—chairman of the conference. Dabney headed a sixteen-member Steering Committee of political, business, and educational leaders, including Fred G. Pollard, the lieutenant governor. There had been strong media support for the idea when Governor Godwin first announced it, and interest and enthusiasm intensified during the autumn. Opening the conference before a packed hall, Vee Dabney called it "the greatest upsurge of interest in better education that has been seen in the State in generations." It would, he said, "seek to lay the foundations for the future educational progress of Virginia"— exactly what the governor and a good many others had in mind.[12]

10.5 The Governor's Conference on Education, October 1966—Governor Godwin's brief keynote address set the tone for the day. He had called the conference, he said, "out of a firm belief that the time had come to inscribe new and higher bench marks by which to measure education in Virginia." It was time, he went on, "to examine education as we never have before, to find its weakness and its strength, to assess its needs in the light of the Virginia which is taking shape around us, and of her place in a nation speeding to new heights." He urged his listeners to go forth "as advocates, apostles, and prophets" in the cause of education.

Then Tom Boushall—Thomas C. Boushall, the effervescent, curmudgeon-like board chairman of the Bank of Virginia—began what amounted to a sermon on Virginia public education. Comparing Virginia's support for education with other states, Boushall was blunt. The Commonwealth, he said, ranked fourteenth in population and thirty-fourth in total income, but thirty-eighth or lower in per pupil expenditures, current expenditures for elementary and secondary schools, percent of people fourteen or older classed as illiterate, and median school years completed by people twenty-five or older. Virginia ranked forty-fifth, he pointed out, in per capita tax collections. Deriding the paltry funding the state had long put into educating its citizenry, he declared, "Virginia has no way to go but up!" (Andrews, *No Higher Honor*, 100)

Boushall spoke of school divisions in the state that were outstanding in their performance—and much larger numbers that were poor. He noted the steady migration of people to urban areas looking for work, totally unequipped to find employment in a rapidly changing economy. Noting that he came as a businessman, not as an educator, he asserted that "the education of its people is the most productive investment any state or nation can make." If Virginia wished to become economically strong, with per capita income in the nation's upper quartile, he insisted, the only possible way was to continue investing in education.

Boushall considered it strange that school divisions statewide found it effective to borrow funds with which to build schools and pay off the debt over twenty years, while, at the state level, capital funding for educational institutions had to come out of current income. Consequently, he proposed that the state constitution be amended to permit bond issues limited to public education. The bank board chairman's long and effective sermon was much like the message President Hahn had preached ever since he came back to Virginia. The conference could hardly have had a more eloquent spokesman for the cause of education.

For higher education, the conference planners had invited back Dr. John Dale Russell, the Indiana educator who had directed the Virginia Higher Education Study in 1964–1965. Dr. Russell congratulated everyone concerned with the giant steps taken in Virginia's higher educational system in 1966—instituting a community college system, taking initial steps in developing a major university in Richmond, and positioning Northern Virginia's George Mason College and Southwest Virginia's Clinch Valley College to develop as separate institutions. Less visible, but equally important, he said, was the legislation strengthening the State Council of Higher Education.

Dr. Russell took as a good sign the increased levels of support for the public colleges and universities in the 1966–1968 budget (up 56 percent from the previous biennium). He saw the $1 million special appropriation for strengthening graduate programs in the state as especially significant. Warning, however, that Virginia's efforts to significantly strengthen public higher education were only beginning, he said nonetheless that the presence of so many people at a conference focusing on education indeed was encouraging. Underscoring many of the recommendations included in the 1964–1965 report, Dr. Russell urged continued attention to strengthening faculty salaries, expanding the number and quality of graduate programs (especially by strengthening the faculties of Virginia's institutions of higher education), and maintaining diverse admissions polices so as to accommodate a wide range of students.

Media reaction to the conference was enthusiastic. In February and March 1967, regional conferences were held throughout the state—at Richmond, Farmville, Bristol, Roanoke, Fredericksburg, Alexandria, Harrisonburg, and Norfolk. Governor Godwin attended each of them, stressing his view that the sales tax was essential in building a stronger and more effective system of education in Virginia. Later, in the autumn, he urged that the task of building a stronger educational system be given top priority in the 1968 General Assembly. (Andrews, *No Higher Honor*; proceedings, Governor's Conference on Education, 5 October 1966)

In the afternoon, President Shannon of the University of Virginia, President Paschall of William and Mary, and President Hahn of Virginia Polytechnic Institute offered three different perspectives on higher education. Dr. Paschall spoke with characteristic eloquence of the values and joys of the liberal arts. Dr. Shannon described the urgent need for Virginia to build strong programs in graduate education, as Dr. Russell had documented in his yearlong study of Virginia higher education. Dr. Hahn finished up with "Education for Industry," a recognition of the rapidly changing technology undergirding the society, and Virginia's rapid population growth. "It makes sound economic sense," he said, "to educate all of our citizens to their fullest capability of contributing to our economy and society, regardless of economic or social, or ethnic background." The progress made in the 1966 General Assembly session was welcome and necessary, but, he cautioned, it was "the first step in a long road."

Vee Dabney picked up that theme in his closing remarks. Senator Hunter B. Andrews of Hampton made a motion requesting that Governor Godwin appoint a citizens committee to promote regional conferences to spread the word, and the governor promptly agreed to do so. "I extend to you the gratitude of all the people of Virginia, and particularly that of your Governor. You have indeed warmed my heart," Andrews told the audience.

An Interim Report—VPI, 1966

The 1966 General Assembly session was one of the more stimulating times for Marshall Hahn in his VPI career. He delighted in the give and take of the political process, and that process could hardly have been more active in a General Assembly session in which Governor Godwin initiated a legislative program designed to bring the Commonwealth into the modern era. In the 1950s, Marshall Hahn had perceived Virginia as a sleeping giant. In the 1960s, he had reason to believe that he was seeing it awaken.

In the first four years of his presidency, Marshall Hahn found solutions to a variety of difficult problems—the Radford College question, faculty salaries, coeducation, the Corps of Cadets situation, and the emerging community (branch) colleges. The 1966 General Assembly, with Governor Godwin's leadership, had developed the funding, based on the new sales tax, with which to build a strong statewide educational system involving the public schools, the new community college system, and the state's public four-year colleges and universities. The opposition of the State Council of Higher Education and its staff to VPI's development as a comprehensive institution had largely disappeared.

The basic plan for the development of Virginia public higher education in the years ahead—a plan President Hahn had heavily influenced—was put together by the Bird Commission in 1965 and generally approved by the General Assembly in the opening months of 1966. VPI's development as a major land-grant university was, unmistakably, a part of that plan—operating and capital appropriations for 1966–1968 provided good confirmation. The Assembly had also approved new statutory bases for VPI's extension and research programs, the Extension and Research divisions, establishing a statewide context for the University.

No lack of problems remained, however. The stresses from the Corps issue, which so badly divided the alumni, still reverberated, and the Corps struggled to maintain its strength. The 1965–1966 self-study provided a ready forum for the faculty and staff to articulate their concerns, and many did. It was an extraordinary beginning, but much work remained.

10.6 The SACS report: President Hahn's first four years—The SACS Visiting Committee that came to VPI in October 1966 (at the close of the self-study) pronounced its amazement at the changes taking place so swiftly and, at the same time, cautioned that the many tasks were still in progress: "It is evident both from the self-study report and [from] interviews with staff and students that implementation of this fundamental change in institutional purpose, [hardly] four years in process, is being accomplished efficiently and rapidly. The Visiting Committee commends President Hahn's administration for the signal progress which has been made toward achieving the new objectives. New programs, new faculty, and new buildings are evident.... But generalizing the scope and significantly adding to the fundamental quality of a century-old technical and applied institute is not accomplished in four years.... The Committee feels that notable as the progress has been, much remains to be achieved." (Southern Association of Colleges and Schools, Visiting Committee, *Report on Virginia Polytechnic Institute, October 23–26, 1966,* 6)

[1] Hahn interview, 31 August 1989; Godwin interview, 14 March 1989.

[2] Text of Governor Godwin's inaugural address, reprinted in the *Richmond Times-Dispatch*, 16 January 1966, and subsequently in Godwin, *Selected Speeches* (this paragraph is on p. 4).

[3] Andrews, *No Higher Honor*, 55.

[4] Hahn letter to Ronald E. Shibley, 25 June 1965; Andrews, *No Higher Honor*, 55.

[5] Godwin interview, 14 March 1989.

[6] Wilkinson, *Harry Byrd*, ch. 11.

[7] Hahn letter, 14 February 1966.

[8] *Techgram*, April 1966.

[9] Godwin interview, 14 March 1989. Delegate Roy Smith of Petersburg, chairman of the House Appropriations Committee, made sure that William and Mary's Richard Bland College at Petersburg also was excluded from the community college system; Smith and others had aspirations for another four-year college there in addition to Virginia State College (Roy Smith interview).

[10] Hahn interview, 31 August 1989. For more on the beginnings of the Virginia system of community colleges, see Dana Hamel interviews; Vaughan, *Pursuing the American Dream*; and Cristo, "Community College System in Virginia."

[11] Andrews, *No Higher Honor*, 98–99.

[12] Proceedings, Governor's Conference on Education, 5 October 1966.

11: Getting Around and Getting Away

Marshall Hahn worked hard as president of VPI—his daily schedule would have quickly exhausted most people. He traveled often, and when he was home he often worked into the night. He could be found almost every evening after dinner in his personal office, going through materials for immediate attention that Lon Savage or others had brought over from the president's office in Burruss Hall. He dictated letters, worked the phone, and otherwise fought the fires and dealt with the demands of the moment.

Moreover, his travel was unrelenting, for he was always scheduled somewhere—to make a speech, see the governor, attend a meeting or conference. To get expeditiously around to his many scattered appointments, in Virginia and elsewhere, he had to be able to travel quickly. A VPI airplane, available for official business, made it possible to move at something approaching the speed he wanted and needed.

To stay fresh at the job, he had to get away from it on occasion, go on vacation, with buddies or with his family. Getting around was vitally important. So was getting away.

A Longer Runway for the VPI Airport

One of the high-priority projects to which Marshall Hahn, early in his presidency, called the attention of the Educational Foundation and the Board of Visitors was the improvement of the VPI airport, including construction of a new 4,600-foot runway. This item no doubt surprised some of Hahn's colleagues, but he had in mind a new airplane, a multi-engine executive aircraft that would comfortably seat five or six passengers. VPI's southwest Virginia location, fairly remote from Washington and Richmond—and indeed from the growing urbanized areas of the whole state—made extensive travel burdensome and time-consuming. A dependable all-weather airplane would be invaluable. There was no doubt that there would be extensive travel; the necessary trips to Richmond seemed to multiply with each passing month, to say nothing of other travel.

Hahn first brought the airport expansion project to the Executive Committee of the Educational Foundation in fall 1963. Hahn asked the Foundation to earmark $50,000 for airport improvements, to be used only when total airport funding, approximately $500,000, had been developed. When a Federal Aeronautics Administration grant of $275,000—half of the eventual cost—was approved in 1963, and state

11.1 The early years of the Virginia Tech airport—The VPI airport originated in 1929—when the school supplied the site and half the cost of construction and the state picked up the other half—and began operations in 1931. In 1935, Carmen Venegas ('38), a female engineering undergraduate from Costa Rica, proposed formation of an Aeronautics Club, and it was in place before she graduated. More than that, the facility fostered the VPI curriculum's development as well as VPI's role in world affairs.

The eruption of World War II affected developments at VPI. For about six years beginning in 1939, VPI cadets—among them Julian Ashby Burruss Jr., son of President Burruss—trained as airmen for the Navy and the Army. Among the flight instructors was Kenneth V. Brugh Jr. ('40). A grant from the Works Progress Administration in 1940 supplemented school funds to pave the runway and build a hanger, as a Great Depression public works agency helped fund a facility that the War Department deemed an emergency national defense project with the war threatening to draw the United States in.

In 1942, after the nation entered World War II, VPI inaugurated a major in aeronautical engineering—newly separated from mechanical engineering, a field in which aeronautics had been an option since 1936—and Jane Hardcastle changed her major from ME and graduated in aeronautical engineering that December. (W. H. Byrne [airport manager], "Brief History Virginia Tech Airport, 1929 to 1983"; Geoffrey Buescher, "Virginia Tech Aviation, 1929–1945," and Meredith Cook, "Progress...or Not? Virginia Tech's Women Engineers, 1921–1997," both in Wallenstein, *Essays, Fall 1997*)

funding followed, the project was assured. Construction on the new runway was begun in 1965 and completed the next year.

Meanwhile, Hahn's persistent efforts to obtain an appropriate airplane for executive travel paid off. In autumn 1964, he received a check for $35,000 from John B. Rich, president of the Broseco Corporation, in Baltimore, as a "contribution." Rich instructed Hahn in turn to send a check for $35,000 from the VPI Educational Foundation to Penrose Production Company, in Fort Worth, Texas, and the airplane would be his.

That is how—through the generosity of F. Donaldson Brown of Port Deposit, Maryland, a wealthy 1902 VPI graduate and retired DuPont and General Motors executive—VPI acquired the gift of a Queen Air Beechcraft, a twin-engine executive aircraft seating five passengers and two pilots. The plane arrived at the VPI Airport early in 1965. After being thoroughly checked out and serviced, it became available for official use in May. In a July letter to Brown, Hahn mentioned the airplane "you so generously made available to us," and from then on he had a faster and easier way to get where he needed to go.

The chief pilot, recruited from North Carolina where he was between jobs, turned out to be Spurgeon "Pop" Warner, a one-time Navy aviator with years of experience in multi-engine aircraft. Pop Warner was prematurely bald, had a ruddy complexion, and possessed a wild sense of humor. His laughing eyes and mischievous nature made life anything but dull, and he loved flying. His co-pilot most often was William H. "Billy" Byrne, one of the pilots already employed at VPI.

Marshall Hahn thought he might do a little flying, too, but Harry Wyatt, the BOV rector, put a stop to that—the VPI president would be a passenger, not a pilot.[1] He and his colleagues used the aircraft, soon dubbed the *Hokie*, for rapid transportation whenever it was cost effective. The president used it the most. He seemed always on the move, and the light-hearted banter between him and his pilots soon became something of a tradition.

Getting Away

Ambler Johnston and Jack Hancock introduced the Hahns to the joys of the Chesapeake Bay during summer 1963, and Hancock loaned Marshall Hahn his big boat based at Deltaville while the Hahns rented a

11.2 The *Hokie* and its pilot, Pop Warner—Spurgeon "Pop" Warner had flown full-time most recently for Octave Blake, president of Cornell-Dubilier Electronics (and also president of the Grand Circuit Harness Racing Association). Blake retired in January 1965, though, and Warner found himself out of a job. Though he picked up a little work with Burlington Industries, he was looking for permanent employment. That's where Ken Brugh—a VPI graduate who operated Greensboro Air Service, a substantial aviation dealership and air service company—came in. Brugh's mechanics and technicians had checked out and serviced the Beechcraft plane immediately after its delivery to VPI. Brugh made sure Pop Warner knew about the VPI situation and vice versa. Warner was happy to move to Blacksburg and fly for Marshall Hahn and his colleagues. (Personal Warner family records; Billy Byrne interview, 3 August 1994; Mrs. Warner interview; Hahn Papers, 1965)

The aircraft was to be used only "when efficiencies and economies" could be realized. The cost, billed to the using department, was $45 per hour, plus out-of-pocket crew expenses. Lon Savage was assigned the task of scheduling the plane; it didn't quite recover cost, and the hourly rate was soon raised to $50 (Hahn memos, 15 May 1965, 13 December 1965). Dean Laura Jane Harper, anxious to recruit an especially well-qualified candidate for her faculty, early on sent the plane to State College, Pennsylvania, to pick up the visitor. There was a small delay, Dean Harper recalled, while a bird's nest was removed from under one of the engine cowlings.

cottage on Tabbs Creek, near Kilmmarnock. Marshall Hahn and Jack Hancock also spent several weekends fishing on the Chesapeake during the months that followed. So by summer 1964, sailing the blue waters of the Chesapeake was not a new experience for Hahn, and he had bought the *Spindrift*, a 34-foot cruiser. As Mrs. Hahn later observed about summers and the Chesapeake, "We used to go down and stay about two weeks, live on the boat, and we would just go out during the day and come back to the marina to spend the night," still on the boat.

But some trips took them much farther away from Blacksburg. Busy couples often try to convert travel to multiple purposes and combine business with pleasure. President and Mrs. Hahn went to Florida in April 1966 when Dr. Hahn was the speaker for a meeting of the VPI Gold Coast Alumni Chapter. After the scheduled event, he and she took a Sunday afternoon fishing trip. He landed a 105-pound creature. "It took nearly an hour to bring in," he wrote in a letter, and the catch was reported to be "one of the largest white Marlins caught so far this year." Mrs. Hahn hooked a sailfish, but it got away before it could be landed.[2]

That summer, the entire family spent time in California visiting Marshall Hahn's parents. Marshall Hahn Sr. was in poor health, and the

---

11.3 Lifesavers and the Chesapeake—In late August 1964, Marshall Hahn and his family went to Deltaville, on the Chesapeake Bay, for their vacation—two weeks aboard their cruiser, the *Spindrift*. Having checked out the engine and equipment, they would head into the Bay each day for a family outing. On one occasion, though, they seemed to vanish. After cruising several hours, the engines sputtered and died, and the craft stopped dead in the water. Marshall was unable to get it started again and contacted the Coast Guard on the radio to request a tow, identifying his location with the number on a nearby buoy. As luck would have it, the channel buoys had been renumbered that summer, so the Coast Guard went searching in the wrong place and came up empty. Subsequent attempts to make radio contact were unsuccessful; as Mrs. Hahn recalls, "the radio went out." So there was nothing to do but wait and try to hail a passing ship for a tow. It was a long wait—until late afternoon—before a fishing boat answered their distress signal and towed the *Spindrift* back into Deltaville.

Meanwhile, news of the Hahns' disappearance spread, as the Coast Guard's failure to find them, after having been notified of their troubles, made it seem clear that something was wrong. Peggy's parents in Dinwiddie County were terribly worried; so was Governor Harrison; and so were a good many others in Richmond and Blacksburg who had come to know and admire the young VPI president. The family's safe return did not come to anyone's attention right away, though. The fishermen had assured the Hahns they would notify the Coast Guard of their towing the *Spindrift* in, and the Hahn family settled down for the night safely anchored. But the message somehow never got through, and it was the next day before anyone else learned that the missing Hahn family was safe and sound, not drowned. Lieutenant Governor Mills Godwin sent Hahn a note to say how relieved he had been to learn that the family was safe. Hahn wrote back to thank Godwin for his concern and to express regret at having alarmed his friends.

The story of Marshall Hahn's misadventure at sea—what Peggy Hahn calls "the boat story"—generated all kinds of light-hearted merriment among his friends and colleagues. State budget director L. M. Kuhn presented Dr. Hahn a little red toy boat filled with candy "Lifesavers" and suggested he take them with him the next time he went sailing. (Hahn papers, 1964; Hahn interviews, 22 March 1989, 14 November 1989; Mrs. Hahn interview)

---

children had not seen their grandparents for some years. Peggy thought it wise to go, and they found Hahn Sr. somewhat improved.[3]

About once a year, Dr. Hahn accompanied a group of Roanoke friends to a hunting preserve at Swan Island, North Carolina, to unwind, relax, and shoot ducks. A stag affair, it always included Jack Hancock, the Roanoke industrialist and civil leader, as well as other good friends in the Roanoke business and professional community. Years later, Hancock looked back on those excursions to Swan Lake with fond memories. "We'd go down and spend four or five days," he said. "It was a private hunting preserve owned by a bunch of New Englanders, south of Back Bay. Marshall went many times with us, and really enjoyed it."

Dr. Hahn himself wrote about one such trip in late 1966. It began when the group assembled for a hunt breakfast in the Virginia Room of the Hotel Roanoke, after which they departed for Swan Island. That particular invitation came from two Roanoke physicians, Dr. Edgar N. Weaver (the neurosurgeon upon whom Hahn had called for emergency attention the night of Lou Pardue's accident on Christiansburg Mountain) and Dr. R. Earle Glendy. Afterward, Hahn wrote to the hosts and the participants to express his appreciation for the opportunity to share in the experience. To Hancock, he wrote that "without a doubt, last week at Swan Island was one of the most pleasant periods I have ever enjoyed…. I cannot thank you enough…. The shooting, the food, and above all, the fellowship, were superb. When I left Blacksburg…I really felt the accumulation of several months of working at maximum pace every day." But he returned, he said, "with renewed vigor and energy."[4]

The Bahamas

In 1967, the Hahn family went all the way to the Bahamas for their summer vacation. For two weeks in early August, they rented a house at Hope Town, Abaco, accessible by boat taxi from Marsh Harbor, which had daily airline service. Dr. Hahn described the Hook House, which they had rented for $100 a week, as "well located on the beach, cool and comfortable." They had hired a fishing boat, along with a professional fisherman, for the best part of one tide, four or five hours, for $20, including boat and tackle. The family thrived on good seafood. Eight lobsters could be purchased for $2, "and we ate lobsters nearly every day," Hahn reported. "You can't beat it."[5]

So delighted were the Hahns with their vacation in the Bahamas that they rented the same house during the last week of June and the first week of July the following summer. Afterward, Hahn reported to Ambler Johnston that the trip was "delightful, although we didn't catch any large fish. We did catch many smaller ones, ranging from 9 feet on down."

The Bahamas surely captivated some members of the Hahn family, perhaps all. Later in 1967, Hancock and Hahn each purchased a half-interest in the Bowen White House in Hope Town. Described as a good rental property, it was a modern house on the beach with a separate guest· cottage. An agent in Hope Town maintained the property and also managed the rental business when the Hahns did not have the houses reserved for their personal use or for the use of invited guests. Hahn occasionally expressed disappointment that Governor Godwin and his wife were never able to take a vacation at the Hope Town house. As for Jack Hancock, he had readily agreed to invest in the property with Marshall Hahn, but he and his family almost never went to the Bahamas, and when they did go they stayed at a hotel. Hancock joined in the venture primarily as a favor to Hahn, for the two by then had become close friends, and Hancock was pleased that the property enabled Hahn and his family to get away on occasion from the great pressures of the VPI presidency.

The family returned each summer, just about the only time, as Mrs. Hahn later explained it, Dr. Hahn could get away. After their first sojourn, three weeks in the new place, Hahn reported that "the fishing was excellent, and I spent a total of fifteen days" at it. "We caught sixteen different kinds…with the largest weighing more than 60 pounds. We caught quite a few bonefish, and I had a great time catching one in the surf which weighed about eight pounds." Writing another friend, Hahn said about the Bahamas vacation that it had been wonderful. As a result, he felt "much better prepared for the coming year."[6]

The next year, 1969, they were back in the Bahamas. Upon their return, President Hahn wrote Governor Godwin that they had had "a delightful three weeks." His hands were "literally calloused" from so much fishing, he reported. "The nicest fish I caught was a 66-pound Wahoo, which I landed from an 18-foot open boat." Another of his catches was a bonefish, weighing more than 10 pounds, right in front of the house. As for Anne, his youngest daughter, he reported proudly, she had caught "a

27-pound barracuda on tackle so light that it may go into the Bahamas record books."[7]

Still Farther Afield

The Hahns enjoyed their place in the Bahamas for a number of years, but by the 1970s they rarely managed to get there, and in 1973 Hahn and Hancock sold it. During summer 1972, Dr. and Mrs. Hahn, together with youngest daughter Anne and Hahn's mother, flew to England, and Marshall brought back some antiques. Another time, Marshall and Peggy went alone, and he brought back more. As for Hahn's travels on business—sometimes related to university research or outreach—those, too, could take him even farther away than the Caribbean. One trip took him to the Philippines in 1967, another to Antarctica in 1973 (see chapter 19).

Regarding his vacation activities, Hahn sought to maintain privacy. Expressing delight with the visits to the Bahamas when writing good friends was one thing. To others, he referred to his times on vacation as having "been out of the country" or some such. The rest of the world need not know about his downtime—his private time with family or his respite from Blacksburg that permitted him to return, as he said, "with renewed vigor and energy" and "much better prepared for the coming year."

[1] Billy Byrne interview, 20 June 1991.
[2] Hahn to William D. Saunders, 22 April 1966.
[3] Hahn to Reverend John I. Prather, 18 July 1966.
[4] Hahn letters to Hancock, Dr. Glendy, and Dr. Weaver, 7 December 1966.
[5] Hahn to J. C. Wheat Jr., 27 March 1967.
[6] Hahn letters, 16 July 1968 and 21 August 1968.
[7] Hahn to Godwin, 14 July 1969.

The Hokie Bird image flew high on Marshall Hahn's aircraft in the 1960s. Unable to get assigned the number presenting *pi* (it had already been claimed), physicist Hahn obtained the value of *e* (rendered more precisely as 2.71828), the number used as the base of the system of natural logarithms. Virginia Tech Special Collections.

12: Construction Everywhere

A tremendous amount of new construction went up on the VPI campus during the 1930s and again during the 1950s. Even more impressive was the pace of new construction on President Hahn's watch. A series of new buildings went up through the 1960s and into the 1970s. The new buildings addressed the urgent need for far greater dormitory space as well as far greater space for classrooms, laboratories, and faculty offices. They reflected Hahn's astute and energetic politicking in Richmond, and they fostered realization of his vision of a large research university in Blacksburg. Other construction brought VPI new athletic facilities—Lane Stadium, the Rector Field House—and renovation changed the face of what became a continuing education center and a new and enlarged Squires Student Center.

In May 1964, at the same meeting in which the Corps decision made history, Dr. Hahn recommended to the Board of Visitors that the university be authorized to proceed with the construction and renovation projects funded by the 1964 General Assembly and also the planned dormitory construction and renovation. The Board readily did so.[1] These projects included the construction of new dormitories—completing the Presidential Quad—as well as the renovation of Eggleston Hall (the dormitory adjacent to the drill field east of Memorial Gymnasium) and its conversion into a women's dorm. All these activities would be funded from revenue bonds and/or borrowing from the Virginia College Building Authority.

Marshall Hahn had also obtained a $316,000 appropriation to complete the coliseum at last. In 1962, Dr. Newman had been successful in obtaining a $500,000 appropriation for additional work on the Student Activities and Physical Education Building (as it was then officially known) and for equipment.[2] Two years later, most of the building was completed, but the 1964 appropriation provided such items as additional equipment and construction of concrete risers high up in each of the arena's four corners, together with installation of more than 600 additional seats—bringing the coliseum's total seating capacity to more than 10,000 (see chapter 7). The coliseum was the venue for President Hahn's inauguration in April 1963 and his first commencement in June 1963. The building was finished in December 1964.

12.1 Construction with federal financial support during the New Deal— During the 1930s, the New Deal brought all kinds of federal programs designed to put people back to work, often on public works projects, including many at universities across the nation. President Julian Burruss strove mightily—and with great success—to obtain federal funding for new construction at VPI.

To list the buildings at Tech that went up with federal aid during the 1930s is to take a tour around the drill field. On one side of the drill field, a giant new building went up—called at the time the Teaching and Administration Building but later named Burruss Hall after the college president who made it happen. Work began in 1934, and the building opened in 1936 in time for that year's commencement exercises to fit comfortably in the new 3,000-seat auditorium.

Diagonally across the drill field from Burruss is Hutcheson Hall, completed in 1940 as Agricultural Hall. Behind it is Smyth Hall, the Natural Science Building or "Aggie Annex," completed in 1939. On one side of Smyth are Seitz Hall, completed in 1937 and originally called the Agricultural Engineering Hall; the Home Economics Building, completed in 1939 and now known as Agnew Hall; and the Dairy Building, completed in 1931, even before the New Deal, and later named Saunders Hall.

At another corner of the drill field is the Eggleston complex. East Stone Dormitory Number 1, as it was called at first, was completed in 1935, and the east and west wings were added by 1939. In back of Eggleston is Owens Dining Hall, also (in its original form) a product of the 1930s.

Housing

In fall 1962, the Corps of Cadets was housed on the Upper Quadrangle, and the cadets took their meals in Schultz Dining Hall, which had opened for business that fall. The civilian students were housed in the Lower Quad—in newly constructed Vawter and Barringer Halls as well as Eggleston and Campbell (the older dormitories bracketing Memorial gymnasium)—and took their meals in Owens Dining Hall. Freshmen civilian students were housed for the first time in all-freshman dorms. As a result, "disciplinary problems decreased drastically and academic records improved," the institution reported.[3]

In the early 1960s, decisions regarding new student housing took place in the context of a small school, as can be seen in the architecture of

Nor does this exhaust the list of monuments to the New Deal on the Tech campus. Holden Hall, originally the Mineral Industries Building, dates from 1940. So does Hillcrest, a women's dormitory (immediately dubbed the "Skirt Barn") that, unlike other buildings, never acquired anyone's name and that today, though still a dorm, also houses the University Honors program and other academic activities.

The list goes on, as did the construction. The Student Activities Building, now known as Squires Student Center, opened in 1937, and Paul Derring and the YMCA office moved there then. Faculty obtained new housing on campus—and thus benefited from more than new buildings to teach in—when the Faculty Apartments, or Faculty Center, opened in 1935. Since enlarged and renovated, as Squires has been, the Faculty Center subsequently became known as the Donaldson Brown Continuing Education Center and then the Donaldson Brown Hotel and Conference Center.

Seitz Hall offers a glimpse at the way in which construction of these new buildings drew on the energy of the community as well as the expertise of the college—and how both could benefit. The faculty in agricultural engineering designed their own building. Then they trained workers, as necessary, in such skills as carpentry, electricity, masonry, plumbing, and stonecutting, and they supervised the construction.

A tour of the Tech campus would not be complete if it did not include the Duck Pond. In addition to all the major construction itemized here, the 1930s brought significant landscaping and tree planting and the construction of new walks, roads, and what, because of the feathered life forms that also flock there, came to be known as the Duck Pond.

the new student housing constructed during the first half of the 1960s. Sometimes known collectively as the Presidents' Quad, five new buildings went up on the hillside between Newman Library and the coliseum, quite some distance from either the original Upper Quad or the Agricultural Quad. All five opened between 1962 and 1966.

The initial building in the quadrangle, Barringer Hall, was largely constructed during the Newman administration, as was nearby Vawter Hall. Both opened for fall quarter 1962 at the outset of Hahn's administration. Barringer was named for Paul B. Barringer, VPI's fifth president; Vawter honored Charles E. Vawter, a long-term rector of the Board back in the 1890s. The two dormitories housed about 550 men students.

Two other dormitories—authorized by the 1962 General Assembly, which also appropriated funds to pay half their total cost—were under construction by the time Barringer and Vawter opened. Completed in the late spring 1964, they were later named Newman Hall and Miles Hall in honor of Walter Newman and "Sally" Miles ('01), and together they, too, housed a little more than 500 men students. The last of the five buildings in the complex was approved by the 1964 General Assembly. Later named Johnson Hall, after J. S. A. Johnson (see box 12.3), it housed another 185 men. Completing the quadrangle of three-story stone dorms at the corner of Washington and Kent streets, it was opened to students for winter quarter in January 1966.[4]

In the continuing construction after 1966, a new architecture of student residence halls matched—stood as a metaphor for—the multiple transformations in student population and student policy. Johnson Hall, which opened in 1966, was among the last of the three-story, Tudor-style residence halls built at VPI (nearby, a few additional such buildings went up later, including Payne Hall and Peddrew-Yates Hall), for with rapidly growing enrollments the University had switched to big, high-rise dormitories. Three such structures—rising to as many as eight stories and built even farther away from the original Upper Quad—were under construction in the background when the dedication ceremony was held that spring. One of them would be named for Ambler Johnston, the main speaker at that ceremony. Lee Hall, Pritchard, Ambler Johnston—these represented the future of residence halls on the campus of the university that Marshall Hahn built.

12.2 Construction in the decade before Marshall Hahn's presidency—In the aftermath of World War II, VPI put up three new cadet dorms, each named for a former VPI student who had died in the war and had been awarded the Congressional Medal of Honor—Robert E. Femoyer ('44), James W. Monteith ('41), and Herbert J. Thomas ('41). In the 1950s, additional construction in the Upper Quad increased the size of what was named Major Williams Hall—named after Lloyd W. Williams ('07), who had died in World War I—as well as Shanks, Brodie, and Rasche halls. In order to make space for these new sections of various barracks buildings, the old First Academic Building and Second Academic Building were torn down in 1957. Those buildings were replaced when new academic buildings were constructed away from the Upper Quad.

Considerable construction took place on the VPI campus in the decade before Marshall Hahn returned as president. Memorial Chapel was completed in 1960, and, above it, Memorial Court memorialized former VPI students who had died in each of the nation's wars. A new classroom building, Williams Hall—named for John E. Williams, a mathematics professor from 1903 to 1943 and also a dean from 1924 until 1943—was opened in 1953. The Carol M. Newman Library, named for a professor of English, 1903-1941 (he was also considered the patron saint of extracurricular activities at VPI), opened in 1955; it remained in its original configuration through the 1960s, and then doubled in size in the 1970s. What was at first called Commerce Hall opened in 1957; in 1969 it was renamed Pamplin Hall, in honor of Robert B. Pamplin Sr. ('33, business administration)—CEO of the Georgia-Pacific Corporation and a major benefactor of the university—and in the 1980s it was expanded, with an atrium connecting the original building with a new section.

Also completed in the 1950s were several large buildings that housed classrooms and laboratories for science or engineering. One of these was Randolph Hall, named for Lingan S. Randolph, professor of mechanical engineering from 1893 to 1918 and, for the last six of those years, dean of engineering. A new Physics Building—a project launched while Marshall Hahn was department head—was completed in 1960; in 1968 it was named Robeson Hall for Frank L. Robeson, who headed the physics department from 1923 to 1954, when Hahn succeeded him. A new Biochemistry and Nutrition Building was completed during fall 1961 and later named for Ruben W. "Charlie" Engel (see chapter 19), who was recruited to build up the department of biochemistry and nutrition and served on the faculty from 1952 to 1977. The Engineering Building—later named Norris Hall to honor Earle B. Norris, dean of engineering, 1928-1952, and director of the Engineering Experiment Station, 1932-1952—went up in stages, with one wing completed in spring 1960 and a second, connecting with Holden, in summer 1962, in time to welcome the new president to campus.

12.3 Dedication of the last five small dorms—In May 1966, when spring was at its loveliest in the highlands, the university community took time to dedicate a cluster of five three-story stone dormitories that filled the southwest corner of Washington and Kent streets, extending down Kent almost to Owens Dining Hall. They were Barringer, Johnson, Miles, Newman, and Vawter halls, all opened during President Hahn's administration, although Barringer and Vawter were nearly completed when Dr. Hahn arrived in summer 1962. Johnson Hall, the newest dorm, finished just a few of months before the dedication, completed the quadrangle.

These attractive dormitories were named for Paul Brandon Barringer, VPI's president 1907-1913; Colonel J. S. A. Johnson ('98), a long-time member of the faculty who had also served as commandant of cadets, head of mechanical engineering, and alumni secretary; Dean C. P. "Sally" Miles (who had died only a few weeks earlier), known to generations of VPI students as a student, athlete, coach, athletic director, and dean; Walter S. Newman, president-emeritus, the man who as president laid much of the foundation on which Marshall Hahn would build a university; and Charles E. Vawter, a member and rector of the Board of Visitors for many years in the late-nineteenth century—when the school recruited President John McLaren McBryde, took on the name Virginia Polytechnic Institute and Agricultural and Mechanical College, and launched a graduate program, an intercollegiate football team, and an annual student yearbook.

It was to be a grand occasion, and J. Ambler Johnston ('04), who personally had known all five of the men for whom the buildings were named, agreed to make the dedication remarks. The leadership of the whole university family was invited to the ceremony on May 16 and to the dinner following in the Yellow Room of Owens Dining Hall—all the official boards; faculty, staff, and student leaders; and all known living descendants of those for whom the buildings were named.

Walter Newman was still very much alive in Blacksburg, and J. S. A. Johnson's son, Adger S. Johnson ('28), was a vice president of Union Carbide Corporation as well as a member of the VPI Board of Visitors (he maintained homes in both Blacksburg and Englewood, New Jersey). The Walter Newmans and the Adger Johnsons were of course present. Governor Godwin and the members of the General Assembly all were invited. A scattered representation of the Assembly was on hand for the occasion, but the governor, though he had initially agreed to participate, later had to back out under the press of urgent business.

The gentle, sloping courtyard encompassed by four of the dormitories, crisscrossed by sidewalks and stairsteps, makes a kind of natural amphitheater, though the ceremony may have been its only theatrical production.

Ambler Johnston—his white hair and round face graced with a cherubic smile—was much in evidence, along with his trusty cane, and he made the most of the occasion, reminiscing about the five men. He permitted himself a small complaint that President Hahn had given him only twenty minutes to cover sixty-five years of VPI history, but then he proceeded. "One's immortality is gauged by the effect of that person on succeeding generations," he said; "our naming these buildings for these people is simple, tangible evidence of their intangible, quiet immortality. We are honored by doing so.... They were all just good, plain American hard-working citizens, doing what they saw fit and proper and their duty at the time; and I am sure not a one of them would care to be in any way eulogized."

One by one Ambler Johnston dedicated the five dormitories to the five men, with remembrances from the past—Captain Vawter's talks to the Corps of Cadets; President Barringer's lectures in chapel; Sally Miles knocked senseless in a football game; a dear friend, Bill Wine, designating Walter Newman the tenth president of VPI; the towering Colonel Johnson of Ambler Johnston's Corps days, who also was to become a dear friend.

President Hahn, who presided, took special pains to recognize his predecessor, Dr. Newman, and to ask a moment of silence in memory of Sally Miles, who everyone had hoped would be present. His recent death lent an air of sadness to the otherwise happy occasion. Ambler Johnston ended the proceedings with a story about a famous country doctor, after whose death forty years earlier his surviving friends and one-time patients could still feel his immortality. It was, he suggested, easy to "feel the immortality" of the men being honored that day. No one enjoyed the afternoon more than Ambler Johnston, not even Marshall Hahn. Later, a small publication was prepared on the afternoon's proceedings and was distributed far and wide. (VPI *Bulletin* 59/7, July 1966)

Plans

Planning for the university's academic growth in the latter half of the 1960s and early 1970s required plans for physical facilities, and the state Budget Office asked each state institution to project its building needs for the next three biennia, 1966-1972. President Hahn released the capital outlay plan in December 1964 after it had been submitted to the governor's office, and he invited news reporters and editors to the campus to discuss it. The plan was based on rapidly increasing enrollments—from an estimated 1964 fall enrollment of about 6,500 students to a projected figure of approximately 13,700 in 1974. The enrollment projections, Dr. Hahn stressed, as extraordinary as they seemed in 1964—the projected ten-year growth of VPI alone at that time was far larger than the total enrollment at any existing college or university in Virginia—were actually conservative. In fact, VPI's enrollment in 1974 totaled 17,470, including 2,266 graduate students.[5]

Even with the anticipated enrollment increases, Dr. Hahn told the visiting news people, it was already clear that substantial numbers of qualified Virginia applicants would have to be turned away because of the Commonwealth's rapid population growth and the growing proportion of college-age young people seeking higher educational opportunities. If the state's young people were to be provided essential higher educational opportunities, said Hahn, all of Virginia institutions of higher education would have to develop additional facilities and expand their enrollments.[6]

The plan committed VPI to the construction of additional residential facilities to accommodate 2,830 beds during the next six years, plus several renovation projects—and with no public funds required. The bond-funded construction—to be paid for, as the new buildings were being used, by student rental fees—was intended to make it possible to house and feed about 70 percent of VPI's students. The private sector would be expected to accommodate the remainder in private homes and apartments.[7]

As for instructional and research facilities, the 1966-1972 plan by biennium envisioned an equally extensive construction program. For 1966-1968, it included completion of the home economics building (Wallace Hall); the architecture building (Cowgill Hall); a big classroom/laboratory/office building (Derring Hall) for the departments of biology, geology, and education; and various renovation projects (including McBryde Hall). For 1968-1970, the plan proposed construction of three major classroom/laboratory/office buildings, a heating plant addition, a bond-financed dining hall, and numerous renovation projects, and funding also would be requested for essential land purchases. Then, for 1970-1972, the plan included three more big classroom/laboratory/office buildings.[8]

The 1966-1972 capital plan also included the proposed funding of the Burruss Hall addition, for which planning funds were appropriated in 1964. It indicated that additional student service facilities (such as the renovation and expansion of Squires Student Center) would be funded during 1966-1968 from revenue bonds and student fees.[9]

The 1965 Site Plan

Once the expansion of the physical plant began, it seemed to take on a momentum of its own. With the accelerated physical growth of the campus, Hahn, Cassell & Co. felt it advisable to revise the basic directional site plan, which previously had been updated in 1960. Again, the Board of Visitors agreed. In early summer 1965, the task was assigned to Carneal & Johnston, in conjunction with Architects Collaborative, Inc., a Massachusetts firm that had extensive experience in campus planning and the design of university buildings. The revised site plan, completed in December 1965, was keyed to the six-year institutional development plan prepared a year earlier.

The funding, design, and approval processes for the buildings themselves might mean some delay, but Stuart Cassell made sure building sites were ready when construction could start. The area behind Burruss Hall, for example, where the new architecture building would be located, was a jumbled mix of utility structures used by the buildings and grounds department, although further east both sections of Randolph Hall were already in place, constructed in the 1950s. To the west, several big "temporary" World War II structures were still in use.[10] The utility buildings gradually were removed, the site graded, and utility lines installed. Once a construction contract was let, there were no further impediments.

Facilities

In the aftermath of the 1964 session of the legislature, the biggest state-funded project was the continuing education center, for which the General Assembly had appropriated $850,000, to be matched by an equal amount from the VPI Educational Foundation (which was holding funds for the project contributed over nearly fifteen years). The faculty apartment building known as the Faculty Center, across College Avenue from Squires Student Center, would be renovated as continuing education center space, along with construction of a major addition to the building.[11] Carneal & Johnston Inc. were already at work on plans for the structure.

The $270,000 appropriated in 1964 for utilities and building site development was put to good use, as bulldozers and other earth-moving

12.4 The 1965 plan's later years—The 1965 plan has been revised many times. It initially projected a large academic area for classroom/laboratory/office buildings to the northwest, well into where the big commuter student parking areas are located today. (At that time that area, out to Price's Fork Road, was privately owned and already developed with houses and apartments, but Stuart Cassell was gradually buying individual parcels as they became available.) The plaza between the new architecture building and Burruss Hall was first visualized in the plan. The first outline of the big u-shaped building that Architects Collaborative would design for the biology/geology/education building, with an auditorium at the base of the "u" near Greenhouse Road (now West Campus Drive), also appeared on the plan, although only one side of the "u"—Derring Hall—was constructed. Another academic area east of what then was Greenhouse Road, south of Biochemistry (now Engel Hall), also was envisioned, as was another big dormitory, a mirror image of Pritchard Hall. That proposed dorm finally became Ambler Johnston Hall.

Among the many concerns of the 1965 site plan was the continuing proliferation of automobiles on the campus. There were about 5,000 automobiles on the campus in 1964, about half of which had faculty/staff registration. The planners projected about 15,000 vehicles on the campus by the early 1970s, 10,000 of them with student permits. They recommended construction of additional parking lots and the use of athletic parking lots near the stadium and the coliseum for student parking when they were not needed for athletic purposes.

equipment seemed always to be changing the contours of the campus. During fall 1964, the bulldozers began systematically destroying the beautiful reflecting pool and landscaped garden separating the Faculty Center and the University Club, preliminary to construction and renovation work for the new continuing education center. In the spring, the Faculty Center and its famous old dining room were closed, the dining room wing was razed, and construction began. In the end, the construction costs totaled $1,806,703 for the new hotel-like building and its integration with the older Faculty Center structure.

The quickening tempo of campus construction was apparent in winter 1964-1965, when contractors began tearing out Miles Stadium, and farther to the southeast, beyond the old baseball field, construction began on what would become Lane Stadium. After Miles Stadium was torn down, the area between Memorial Gymnasium and Washington Street was regraded. Construction on two high-rise residence halls began in that area in 1965 and was completed in autumn 1966.

The 1964 General Assembly also spurred along other projects. Capital outlay projects included nearly $300,000 to complete the refurbishing of Davidson Hall, the chemistry building. The first phase of a home economics building, for which $425,000 initially had been appropriated, included planning funds for the structure, and Dean Laura Harper was much heartened. Home Economics then was crowded into Agnew Hall, squeezed between Saunders and Seitz.[12] Another appropriation supplied $45,000 for planning an addition to Burruss Hall, the central administration building.

The 1964 General Assembly appropriated $42,000 for planning a new architecture building. It didn't take long for the architects to get busy, as Stuart Cassell, who was skilled in finding shortcuts in the state's complex capital outlay procedures, worked effectively with state budget director L. M. Kuhn to get through the paperwork.[13] Carneal & Johnston did not win the planning contract for the home economics building, which went instead to Smithy & Boynton, a Roanoke firm (Henry B. Boynton was also an alumnus, class of '21). But Ambler Johnston's old firm did plan the addition for the west side of Burruss Hall.

A Norfolk architectural firm, Schriver & Holland, won the contract for designing a building for the new College of Architecture. Dean Charles Burchard, himself a distinguished architect, undoubtedly had a good deal to do with the selection of that particular firm and the ultimate design of the building. As it turned out, the new architecture building was the first structure in the central campus to abandon Ambler Johnston's neo-Gothic designs, which had used native limestone. Cowgill Hall—as it was eventually named, in honor of Clinton H. Cowgill, founder and head of the department of architectural engineering (1928-1956)—turned out to be a contemporary structure, a crisp, rectangular, flat-roofed building with exposed aggregate concrete panels and a glass-enclosed lower floor. The building was partly surrounded by a moat-like area to accommodate its first-floor windows. Some students later termed it "Burchard's national bank" for its modernistic design facing the broad plaza separating it from Burruss Hall. (The plaza later became something different when an underground addition to Cowgill was constructed underneath.)

Appropriations for other capital outlay projects included $350,000 for major repairs and renovations of McBryde Hall. Old McBryde Hall, built in 1914-1917, was the original building of native stone with which Ambler Johnston began the neo-Gothic architectural style that characterizes the central VPI campus. McBryde's graceful arches and Gothic flourishes helped conceal the foundry and other shops it originally housed. By the 1960s, it was something of a shrine on the VPI campus, but not only was it outmoded, it was found to be in bad structural shape. Harold F. Meade, VPI's building inspector and a member of the team that evaluated the technical aspects of the question of renovation versus demolition for McBryde, concluded that the building wasn't physically sound enough to warrant renovation and modernization.[14]

McBryde Hall was eventually torn down, and the $350,000 reappropriated to help fund the building that became the new—and very different—McBryde Hall. The new McBryde, begun in 1970 and largely completed the next year, functioned as a metaphor for the great changes at Tech since its A&M days. The original McBryde Building of Mechanic Arts was a shop building, complete with lathes, saws, forges, and planes. The McBryde of the 1970s and 1980s housed the departments of history, political science, and sociology as well as math and computer science.

By the early 1970s, two other academic buildings began to go up, with the first phase of each completed in 1971. An additional building for engineering, Whittemore Hall, was named for a longtime professor (1928-1963) and dean (1952-1963) of engineering and architecture, John W. Whittemore. Cheatham Hall, a new building for forestry and wildlife sciences, was named for Julian N. Cheatham ('33), a director of the Georgia-Pacific Corporation. A classmate and roommate of Robert B. Pamplin Sr., he and his brother Owen Cheatham as well as Robert Pamplin built up the Georgia Hardwood Company, which developed into Georgia-Pacific. The building served as home to the curriculum that appropriately reflected Cheatham's long career related to wood products.

Additional new construction, together with enhancements and other renovations, could be found around campus. One example was Derring Hall, which opened in 1969 as the new home of a number of academic departments in the College of Arts and Sciences; it was named for Paul Derring, who worked with students as YMCA secretary and in other capacities from 1918 to 1964. Also opening in 1969 was the new home economics building, Wallace Hall, named for Maude E. Wallace, who served as state home demonstration agent and then assistant director of Extension between 1929 and 1959.

Among other construction, Burruss gained additional space at the back, as did Hillcrest to the east. Lane Stadium gained thousands of new seats, and the Rector Field House opened. In 1973, the old YMCA building was converted into a Performing Arts Building. By 1973, a huge addition was being planned for Newman Library. Moreover, planning was under way for a new College of Veterinary Medicine.

Dormitories: Put 'Em up Fast, Put 'Em up Cheap

In the late 1960s, at VPI as at other colleges and universities across the country, new residence halls were constructed at what often seemed breakneck speed. At VPI in August 1964, Dr. Hahn obtained authorization from the Board of Visitors to borrow $225,000 from the State treasury to be used to finance the quarrying of building stone, the preparation of plans, and other preliminary work to expedite various dormitory projects.[15] In this fashion, the time-consuming sale of bonds to finance the dormitory construction and the renovation of Eggleston Hall could be postponed until construction actually began.

Marshall Hahn and Stuart Cassell came up with an effective idea for the funding of bond-financed residential and dining halls. In 1965, they established a consolidated dormitory and dining hall revenue bond system in which appropriate revenues from all of the dormitories and dining halls were pledged to pay off bonded indebtedness for the entire system, regardless of whether any indebtedness remained on a particular structure. In this fashion, new bonds could be sold at lower interest rates, and dining hall and room rental fees would be lower, than if bonds were sold to finance individual buildings. In May 1965, VPI sold $9.6 million in bonds, and all the prior dormitory and dining hall issues outstanding were incorporated into the system. It was an open-ended scheme so that additional bonds could be issued as needed.[16]

The two larger dormitories, later named Lee and O'Shaughnessy halls, together would house about 1,200 students. They were big, seven- or eight-story structures (depending on the section), named respectively for Claudius Lee ('96) and Louis O'Shaughnessy, both well-known faculty members from an earlier era. Claudius Lee had stayed on after graduation to teach electrical engineering for fifty years.[17] O'Shaughnessy, who taught applied mathematics from 1918 to 1954, also served as head of civil engineering and director of graduate studies.

By that time, an even larger dormitory was well underway, west of O'Shaughnessy and Lee. To be named Pritchard Hall, it was a huge structure containing more than 201,000 square feet, with a capacity of more than 1,000 students; the cost was $3,262,240. Its name honors Samuel R. Pritchard, a faculty member whose tenure extended from 1893 to 1935 and who served as department head of physics and electrical engineering and dean of Engineering. Pritchard Hall was opened for fall quarter 1967.

In the meantime, the renovation and conversion of Eggleston Hall for women students were completed, and 524 coeds occupied the building in 1966. Eggleston, the first women's dormitory since Hillcrest (which opened in 1940 to accommodate 108 women), was followed by others, starting with the renovation of Campbell Hall (on the other side of the Memorial Gymnasium) in 1967-1968.

Another dining hall, Dietrick, went up near the high-rise dormitories. Begun in 1968 and completed in 1970, it was named for Leander B. Dietrick, who served for many years on the faculty (1923-1962) and as director of Extension and dean of Agriculture. A huge facility, it could feed 3,000 people at one meal. Three decades after it opened, it remained a central place for students to meet and eat on campus.

Yet another high-rise residence hall went up in the early 1970s. Construction began in 1971 on Slusher Hall, planned for women students and named for registrar-emerita Clarice Slusher ('27).[18] Upon the completion of Slusher as well as Lee, Ambler Johnston (East and West), and Pritchard, the center of gravity of student residence on campus had dramatically shifted from the Upper Quad and the drill field (bracketing Memorial Gymnasium) to the area up the hill from Memorial Gymnasium and the old Agricultural Quad—in the general area where Miles Stadium had long been situated. And just as Schultz Dining Hall accommodated the Upper Quad and Owens Dining Hall suited the needs of the corner of campus where the Eggleston complex and the Presidential Quad were located, Dietrick Dining Hall made the new housing area more or less self-contained.

Implications and Complications

Marshall Hahn, Stuart Cassell, and everyone else involved were trying in those years—in every way they could—to build dormitories as quickly as possible. Large numbers of qualified applicants for admission were knocking on VPI's doors who could not be accommodated, partly because housing was not available. As the student population began to grow rapidly, the pressure for rapid residence hall construction also intensified, and so did internal stresses among the administrative staff (see also chapter 13).

Dean Dean's student personnel people, responsible for the daily operation of the residence halls, found them deficient in many ways, especially as the traditional three-story walk-up dormitories gave way to the seven floors—and even more—of the larger residence halls. The larger dorms continued in the same basic pattern of the older dormitories on the Upper Quad, the barracks-like design of the Corps residence halls. That meant long double-loaded hallways, with two-person rooms opening into the corridor from either side. The rooms did not have adjacent bathrooms, which meant big gang toilets and showers. The older dormitories such as Eggleston and Campbell, constructed as Works Progress Administration (WPA) projects back during the Great Depression, had generous lounge and foyer space, but the newer dorms had much less. Student life problems, according to the student personnel staff, were therefore predictable; the physical configuration of the dormitories, they argued, ought to be more carefully designed to produce better student lifestyles.

The pressure to build dorms quickly and at low cost, however, was not easily diverted. Warren Brandt and Jim Dean and his staff were on one side; Stuart Cassell, who controlled the funding and construction programs, was on the other. President Hahn wanted the dormitories built quickly and inexpensively, so the basic design remained largely unchanged for a good while. Cost was the most important consideration, Dr. Hahn later recalled, especially with the pooled funding that financed the construction, and more elaborate design would have required significantly higher residence hall fees.[19]

Bond-funded dormitories could be put up much more rapidly than state-funded buildings. For example, construction of the home economics building, later named Wallace Hall, did not begin until 1966 (the 1966 General Assembly appropriated another $675,000 for it), and it was not occupied until January 1969. Cowgill Hall, the architecture building, was also begun in 1966 (the 1966 General Assembly appropriated $1,050,000 for its construction), and most of it opened for use in 1969.

In the early to mid-1970s, people pushed ahead on plans for designing, funding, and building still other improvements and new structures. Massive new work was done, for example, on Memorial Gymnasium. Newman Library gained twice the space of the 1950s original, and the expanded library had a new entrance, facing a new bookstore. The old entrance, facing the drill field, lost its purpose and became a fossil appendage. Drivers lost the old connection between Kent Street and the drill field, for it vanished under a plaza between the new library entrance and the bookstore.[20] By 1974, moreover, plans were getting under way for a new complex, at a considerable distance from the central campus, to house a new College of Veterinary Medicine.

Access to the New VPI

The spread of the central campus stretched the distances from residence halls to classrooms. At the same time, it brought VPI within reach of thousands of students—young men and young women—for whom otherwise there would have been no space. Moreover, it remade Virginia Tech into the professional home of many hundreds of new faculty, who designed and taught their classes, and conceived and implemented their research projects, at VPI rather than somewhere else.

The construction of I-81, the interstate highway that runs past Christiansburg on its way from Pennsylvania to Tennessee, brought Blacksburg and Virginia Tech far closer in time than ever before to northern and eastern Virginia. Earth-movers were working on Christiansburg Mountain in 1969 at the same time that renovation continued at Squires. Once people made their way to the campus, new large outdoor maps—one each at the Lane Stadium entrance to campus and at the mall entrance leading from North Main Street to the Memorial Chapel and the drill field—guided them to their specific destinations.[21]

[1] BOV Minutes, 18 May 1964.

[2] President's report to the BOV, 15 May 1962.

[3] *Annual Report*, 1962-1963.

[4] *Historical Data Book*, 105, 107.

[5] *Annual Report*, 1974-1975. Graduate enrollments, included in the totals, were projected to increase from 768 in 1964 to approximately 2,000 a decade later.

[6] VPI News Release, 11 December 1964. Dr. Hahn proposed funding for the purchase of $500,000 worth of books in 1966-1968, $600,000 in 1968-1970, and $700,000 for 1970-1972. At that time, the Newman Library collection totaled only about 350,000 volumes; not until the mid-1970s did the collection exceed a million volumes. Continued strengthening of the library remained one of Hahn's top priorities as long as he was president.

[7] For one thing, the university made no plans for construction of housing for married students—President Hahn had no intention of entering the market for married student housing. With its ability to finance such construction with tax-free bonds, the University quickly could drive private builders out of the market, which was the last thing he wanted to do.

[8] Some of those classroom/laboratory/office buildings were originally conceived as being located near the dormitories for instructional use. Building instructional facilities near student housing areas would become essential as the total size of the university increased significantly, the president said. In the end, it hardly worked out like that, although there was some dispersal of classroom/laboratory/office space. In later years, because of cost-cutting requirements and intense space shortages, "campus in-fill" became a planning theme.

[9] 1966-1972 Capital Outlay Requests, 30 November 1964. Also noting the great need for buildings and grounds maintenance and service facilities, the plan proposed their construction in the area east of Lane Stadium, which itself was still under construction. A central garage (to service and control the numerous state-owned automobiles and other vehicles on the campus) was included, along with additional power plant facilities to heat the new buildings. With the campus expansion, extensive site development would be required, along with storm sewer construction, walks, roads, landscaping, and other facilities. A "substantial sum" would be needed in each of the three biennia for these purposes. Similarly, the planning document stressed, funding for the purchase of land would be required in each of the three biennia—especially for the purchase of farmland being leased, so that agricultural research could be planned on a long-range basis. Additional land-purchases also were required for the central campus in accord with the directional site plan. At Blacksburg, the Agricultural Experiment Station proposals included another addition to the food-processing laboratory, additional greenhouse construction, a plant pathology and entomology building, and several farm buildings. Capital proposals for the Engineering Experiment Station were for additional equipment. Although most of these projects were focused on the Blacksburg campus, the six-year plan also encompassed the dozen field stations of the Agricultural Experiment Station scattered across Virginia, for which proposals for extensive improvements were included. Also included in the capital outlay projections were funding proposals for the two-year branch colleges at Danville, Wytheville, Clifton Forge-Covington, and Roanoke, although the creation of the statewide community college system made those institutions the responsibility of others.

[10] In an earlier era, a big stone quarry was located near the area in which the architecture building was subsequently constructed. The quarry, long since abandoned, had been filled in the early 1950s (associate director of buildings and grounds Howard Price interview).

[11] The Faculty Center, containing about 39,000 square feet, was constructed in 1935 for $178,721. It was used as an apartment building for faculty and staff with a public dining room until it was closed in spring 1965 for renovation and construction for the continuing education facility (Robertson, *Historical Data Book*, 103).

[12] Dean Harper later recalled that, when Dr. Hahn called her from Richmond to say that the appropriation had been approved, she had difficulty sleeping that night because of apprehension that she and her faculty might not have the foresight to plan adequately for the future (Harper and Howery, "History of Home Economics at V.P.I.").

[13] Jimmy Beck (Carneal & Johnston architect) interview, 19 December 1990.

[14] Harold F. Meade interview. The walls of the concrete/stone building were noticeably bulging outward, Meade said. Other projects for which the 1964 General Assembly appropriated construction funds—a $200,000 addition to the laundry building and $150,000 for greenhouse construction—were begun as soon as Mr. Cassell could get the plans drawn and the bids advertised and awarded.

15 BOV minutes, 3 August 1964. See also Scott Carlson, "Colleges Struggle with a 60's Legacy: Ugly, Wasteful, and Outdated Buildings," *Chronicle of Higher Education*, 17 August 2001: A23, and Dober, *Campus Architecture*.

16 VPI Self-Study, 1965-1966, 1: IV9.

17 Claudius Lee, who taught at VPI from 1896 to 1946, occasioned considerable excitement on campus in fall 1997, when undergraduates in a class on the history of Virginia Tech, looking at old yearbooks, came across the 1896 *Bugle*, which Lee had edited and in which he presented himself as an officer, "the right hand of terror," in a campus organization, the "K.K.K."

18 *Techgram*, April 1974, June 1974. Upon her retirement, Ms. Slusher married Herman L. "Lem" Pritchard, a retired banker who stepped in and served the Alumni Association (see box 14.5)—not the Professor Pritchard for whom a nearby dormitory was named—so she was known subsequently as Mrs. Pritchard.

19 Hahn letter, 27 June 1994.

20 *Techgram*, October 1972.

21 *Techgram*, August 1972.

Slusher Hall, named for Clarice Slusher (B.S. '27, M.S. '36), VPI registrar 1937-1963. Construction began in 1971.

To accommodate the tremendous enrollment growth during the Hahn years, new construction on campus included far larger residence halls than ever before. This photo is of Ambler Johnston Hall under construction, 1968. Virginia Tech Special Collections.

The original McBryde Hall, named for VPI president John M. McBryde (1891-1907) and constructed of Hokie Stone in the 1910s as a shop building, was demolished in 1966 to make room for a new structure.

Constructed in 1970 on the site of the original McBryde Hall, the new McBryde Hall became home to history, political science, and other departments in the new College of Arts and Sciences.

13: Administration—Personalities and Personnel

In retrospect, 1966 was a watershed year in VPI's development as a comprehensive university. When the school year ended in June 1966, Marshall Hahn had completed his fourth year as president, and he could look back with some satisfaction on what had been accomplished. At the commencement ceremony, he characterized the years he had shared with the class of 1966—he and most of them had come through those four years together—as "among the most exciting and challenging of my life," and he admonished the graduating students to accommodate change as an essential part of life.

Much had been accomplished in President Hahn's first four years toward the great objectives he had in mind when he embarked upon his presidency. Yet during those four years, staff problems had appeared, had been addressed, and had recurred. An administrative structure for the burgeoning university was still emerging. These various administrative matters took up much of President Hahn's attention in his first four years, and they took up more in the next few years. By 1968, many of the problems had been worked out.

Staff Reorganization—and Vice Presidents for Administration and Academic Affairs

In spring and early summer 1966, President Hahn was negotiating a staff reorganization with John Garber, Governor Godwin's personnel director. The institution's rapid growth had enormously increased the workload of the administrative staff, and some relief was essential. Garber agreed, and in early August Hahn announced a reorganization of VPI's administrative leadership to foster "better services to the faculty and staff," "more effective long range planning," and stronger research and extension programs. Hahn promoted Stuart Cassell to a new faculty position, vice president for administration, and redesignated Warren Brandt vice president for academic affairs. Deanships were created for the new Extension and Research divisions, and also for admissions and records, reporting to Brandt. A new institutional research office, also reporting to the academic vice president, would be responsible for "expanded academic planning and analysis," Hahn said. Dr. Brandt thus would be responsible to the president for all academic administration. Reporting to him would be the deans of the colleges and the Graduate School, the deans of the Research and Extension divisions, the director of libraries, the dean of admissions and records, the dean of students, and the director of institutional research. Each collegiate dean also was authorized to appoint, on a full- or part-time basis, an associate dean for research.

13.1 Public information: from Bob McNeil to Warren Strother—Robert H. "Bob" McNeil retired as director of publications and editor of the *Techgram* in 1964 after some thirty-six years service. McNeil also had taught journalism, and just prior to his retirement the VPI Chapter of Pi Delta Epsilon presented him with a plaque for long and outstanding services to student journalism. Jenkins M. Robertson, assistant editor under McNeil, took over the editorship of the alumni newspaper. Their office also had been responsible for VPI public relations functions generally, except for the Agricultural Extension Service's information dissemination activities. Succeeding director McNeil was Warren H. Strother, a reporter for the *Richmond Times-Dispatch* who had come to know Dr. Hahn and Stuart Cassell in Richmond, especially during the General Assembly session the previous winter, when he was a part of the *Times-Dispatch* team covering the legislative session, and Hahn had attracted him to Blacksburg. Strother arrived in early September 1964, in the wake of the Corps controversy, and was initially assigned to Craig Fabian's office to organize a public relations program. In 1966, as director of the new information services group, Strother was assigned responsibility for public relations and information dissemination for all three major divisions of the University—Instruction, Research, and Extension—and reported to Mr. Cassell. (*Techgram*, 1 June 1964, 1 September 1964)

Stuart Cassell's old institutional business manager position (a state classified position) was retained at a lower level, and several new staff positions were announced, all part of the state classified service. They included a director of auxiliary enterprises and university services (food service, the dormitory system, the laundry, and so on). A new budget office, along with an office of physical plant planning, would be established. An information services division, to accommodate the University's public relations and communications needs, also was established. Stuart Cassell's appointment as vice president made him directly responsible to the president for all non-academic administration, including the computing center.

Dr. Hahn had proposed a vice presidential salary of $24,000 for Mr. Cassell, to make it equal to that of Dr. Brandt. But Governor Godwin approved an initial salary of only $23,000. Hahn wanted to get the two men on an equal footing, for he knew only too well the actual and potential areas of conflict between Cassell and Brandt. In large part, the 1966 staff reorganization followed the recommendations coming through the self-study—which emphasized the need to have subordinate administrators in place who could, without delay, make decisions for their areas of responsibility.[1]

The announcements of the reorganization did not mention the development office or Craig Fabian. Dr. Hahn's discussions with John Garber, however, made it clear that Stuart Cassell would assume primary fund-raising responsibilities, and Fabian would report directly to Cassell. In describing the impending reorganization in a letter to Gene Rowe, Hahn said he had been disappointed with the director of development. Fabian, he said, would serve as an assistant to Mr. Cassell, with his fund-raising efforts confined to corporate and non-alumni donors, and "we have advised him he will continue his work in that field for the next year, at which time we will review the progress to determine whether continuing opportunity exists for him."[2] The development director, not at all pleased with the president's decision, concluded that it was time to make other plans, and he resigned in January 1968 to return to his old department at Westinghouse in Pittsburgh.

In Dr. Hahn's letter to Gene Rowe, he also wrote that he regretted that the alumni director position had been open so long. He hoped that the Alumni Association's recent appointment of Bruce Ross as alumni director, coupled with an overall reorganization, would lead to "a well-organized approach with our alumni and an improved total development program." Ross would work under Dr. Dean, Hahn wrote, "who is capable of providing the leadership and training required for an effective alumni program."[3]

In October 1966, Dr. Brandt announced that an institutional research office was being set up to collect and analyze management data as an aid in decision making. There had been a mounting need to do institutional research, to conduct periodic self-study, to provide an empirical basis for institutional planning. At first, VPI tried to recruit someone from within the institution. Dr. Rhodes B. Holliman, professor of biology, opened the office, initially on a part-time basis, but he soon returned to full-time teaching and research. Two other faculty members briefly accepted responsibility for institutional research, Dr. Leo Padis (mechanical engineering) and then Dr. Carl Renfroe (chemical engineering). Then, in search of someone with experience at the task and a strong interest in pursuing it, the school looked outside. Dr. James R. Montgomery, recruited from the University of Tennessee (where his projects included a big book on that school's history), began a systematic institutional research and planning effort in 1968.

When the new administrative group finally was in place, it constituted a respectable leadership cadre for both its academic and administrative components, although adjustments were made from time to time. The administrative staff set in place by 1966 remained largely intact for the remainder of Dr. Hahn's administration, though Albin T. "Beanie" Butt came from the Norfolk Housing Authority as personnel director in 1967. The major changes were to come at the vice presidential level.

Research and Extension

It took a while before the new positions outlined in the administrative reorganization were filled. As for Research and Extension, a good deal of thought and discussion went into fleshing out the new divisions. In early summer, President Hahn convened much of the University's leadership group to look carefully at their objectives and how they could best be structured.[4]

The Extension Division was set up to put all Extension activities—including off-campus credit courses (graduate and undergraduate), the

13.2 Putting an administrative staff in place at VPI—In Mr. Cassell's non-academic group, Edward B. Evans, who had been VPI's personnel officer, was appointed business manager after a widespread search failed to produce other acceptable candidates. (The big problem, Evans said years later in an interview, was that at the time VPI was not paying high enough salaries to attract strong candidates. Evans had not even applied for the position when Mr. Cassell and Dr. Hahn offered it to him.) Evans, who had come to VPI from Richmond in 1955, took over some of the administrative tasks for which Stuart Cassell had been responsible—among them supervision of the University's accounting, purchasing, and treasurer's offices. Ed for some years also was the man with the unenviable responsibility of preparing the University's biennial budget requests prior to each General Assembly session.

Among the other key people on the staff at VPI, James F. Boon, the University's treasurer on Dr. Walter Newman's staff, had remained in that position when Dr. Hahn became president. Whitney L. Johnston, director of the computing center, reported to Mr. Cassell. William B. Sterrett ('47)—director of public utilities for Henrico County and a former Blacksburg town manager who came from Richmond in 1965 to succeed Russ Abbitt as director of buildings and grounds—similarly reported directly to Mr. Cassell. So did the new office of physical plant planning, to which H. P. C. Vandenberg, VPI's planning engineer, was appointed. Harold F. Meade, VPI's construction superintendent or inspector, was assigned to Sterrett's staff. When Fred O'Connell, VPI's chief accountant, left to join Dana Hamel's staff in Richmond, Ed Evans looked to the auditing office at Cornell University, the same place he had found O'Connell, and hired Carl Burke (Evans interview). Harry W. Swink, the VPI purchasing agent, was appointed director of university services and auxiliary enterprises. Jim Shotts, who had come from North Carolina a year earlier as Swink's assistant, was named purchasing agent. M. P. "Mike" Lacy, director of admissions records, who was made dean of admissions and records, put together an excellent staff.

traditional agricultural extension programs, and continuing education (including the continuing education center)—into one administrative structure. This was useful in a variety of ways. Perhaps most importantly, Hahn believed it would lay the foundation for greater political support, as well as provide a framework for broadening the mission of Extension. He saw it also as a way to expand general extension activity without having to set up a new structure for it, recognizing that later it might have to be changed.[5]

13.3 The Extension and Research divisions—President Hahn himself steered two measures through the legislative process in 1966, creating the University's Extension Division and Research Division. The former included the Cooperative Extension Service, the newly developing Technical Services program, and General Extension. The Extension Division bill was drafted by an institutional self-study committee, of which Dr. William E. Skelton was chairman. (The University's 1965–1966 Self-Study, an internal review and analysis required every ten years by VPI's accrediting body, the Southern Association of Colleges and Schools, was then in progress.) Early in 1966, Skelton was named director of Agricultural Extension, succeeding William H. Daughtrey, who retired at the end of 1965. In February 1966, upon Dr. Hahn's recommendation, the Board of Visitors redesignated the Agricultural Extension Service as the Cooperative Extension Service to indicate its more diverse activities and joint funding. The legislation creating the Extension Division empowered the division to "conduct educational programs and disseminate useful and practical information to the people of the Commonwealth of Virginia." The statute did not prescribe how the division was to be structured within the university. (VPI Self-Study, 1965–1966, 1: IX-2, IX-3)

The Research Division, also created by the 1966 General Assembly at President Hahn's request and with the approval of the BOV and the governor, consolidated the Virginia Agricultural Experiment Station and the Virginia Engineering Experiment Station into a major university division (along with the instructional and extension divisions). The Agricultural Experiment Station dated back to 1886, when it was established by the General Assembly in conjunction with federal legislation providing funds for agricultural research. Agricultural and agriculturally related research was and is conducted primarily through the departments, both at Blacksburg and a dozen research stations and research laboratories scattered throughout Virginia.

The Virginia Engineering Experiment Station initially was established by the VPI Board of Visitors in 1921; in 1950 the General Assembly enacted legislation establishing the station as a division of VPI. Under the new Research Division, the research programs of both the Agricultural Experiment Station and the Engineering Experiment Station were to be maintained and strengthened. Discussing the 1966 legislation more than two decades later, Hahn said he was primarily interested in laying the foundation for much greater funding of research outside of agriculture. A self-study committee on research, chaired by Dr. Fred W. Bull, dean of the Graduate School, saw the newly created division as "an organizational entity to provide an efficient administrative channel for handling all aspects of acquiring the facilities, auxiliary services, and funds for support and encouraging the growth of research at VPI." (VPI Self-Study, 1965-1966, 2: XI-6)

The group generally agreed on the structure of the two divisions, but Dr. Hahn initially deferred appointing a dean to head the new Research Division. Pending such appointment, he asked Dr. William B. Harrison and Dr. Coyt T. Wilson jointly to take over the leadership, with each being responsible for the same areas they had directed prior to the creation of the division. Dr. Harrison had moved to Virginia Tech a year earlier from Georgia Tech, where he was director of the School of Nuclear Engineering and head of the Experiment Station's nuclear division. Wilson Bell had recruited Dr. Wilson in 1964 from Auburn University, where he was assistant dean of agriculture and associate director of Auburn's Agricultural Experiment Station. Dr. Wilson came to VPI with the understanding that he would succeed Dr. Harold Young as director of the Agricultural Experiment Station, as he did when Dr. Young retired. The Research Division's administrative offices initially were set up in Hutcheson Hall, where the Agricultural Experiment Station had been. Dr. Harrison soon was named dean of the division, and Dr. Wilson became associate dean and director for agriculture, life sciences, and home economics research.[6]

Hahn himself saw the Research Division as a means of building statewide political support for research, facilitating the University's research programs, and significantly increasing sponsored research funding, especially non-agricultural research. Dr. Harrison advised the University faculty that the division would "provide assistance to those seeking outside sponsorship for research, and…administer those contracts and grants which are awarded by outside sponsors." An important objective, he said, would be "to encourage the interest in and recognition of faculty members performing high quality research, and aid in the creation of a campus environment conducive to research." One of the division's first concrete steps in that direction was to set up a new machine shop in Randolph Hall, under the direction of Donald N. Bodell, that would be capable of handling complex and sophisticated jobs beyond the capabilities of departmental shops. Similarly, an electronics and instrumentation service was organized, also in the basement of Randolph Hall, early in 1967 and directed by electronics engineer Carl Epley.[7]

Meanwhile Dr. W. E. "Bill" Skelton, whom Hahn had earlier appointed director of Cooperative Extension to succeed W. H. "Bill" Daughtrey, was appointed dean of the Extension Division. Skelton had worked closely with President Hahn on the legislation that created it, and in large part he drafted the bill the General Assembly enacted.[8]

In late autumn, Dr. Skelton appointed four directors for the division, each responsible for a specific administrative area. P. H. "Pat" DeHart, who had been associate director of Cooperative Extension, took responsibility for agriculture, 4-H, and youth programs. Dr. William E. Lavery—who a year or so earlier left the Federal Extension Service in Washington to join Dr. Skelton's Cooperative Extension staff as state leader for administration—took charge of administrative services and training. Dr. Roger L. Smith—who, then completing his work with the self-study, had headed the State Technical Services program in Virginia since its inception—was the new head of state technical services, general extension, branch colleges, and the continuing education center. Finally, Dr. George E. "Buddy" Russell, who had been state leader for resource development in Cooperative Extension, headed up resource development, home economics, and Title I programs.

Advice from Another Land-grant President

After the Visiting Committee of the Southern Association came to the campus in October 1966 for a firsthand look at VPI as the University concluded its 1965–1966 self-study, several of its recommendations concerned the University's top-level administrative structure. Dr. Herman Spivey of the University of Tennessee and others on the committee offered advice on Virginia Tech's administrative organization, but they acknowledged that the structure was changing even while the self-study was in progress. Before the group's visit, the 1966 administrative reorganization had taken place, with Stuart Cassell's appointment as vice president for administration. On some aspects of administration, the committee suggested, perhaps the most useful thing President Hahn could do was to find a president of a land-grant university much like VPI, one with long and successful experience, and ask his advice.

Despite President Hahn's heavy schedule and his preoccupation with here-and-now problems, internal and external, and increasingly heavy commitment of his time to the work of the Metropolitan Areas Study Commission (see chapter 19), he followed up on the suggestion the following spring. In March 1967, he invited Dr. C. Clement French, president of Washington State University, to spend a week on the VPI campus to

13.4 Centralized computing operations—Beginning in the 1930s, VPI had computing facilities—maintained in Hutcheson Hall by the Agricultural Experiment Station and the Department of Agricultural Economics for research purposes, and in Burruss Hall by the VPI business offices for administrative purposes. These separate systems—with their card punches, sorters, and tabulators—were updated over the years.

Centralized computing operations began to take shape in 1958 when a huge vacuum tube IBM 650 system was leased and installed in a big World War II "temporary" building (no. 365) on a site near where Derring Hall was later built. A computing coordinator reported to the associate director of the Ag Experiment Station, at that time Dr. Wilson Bell, but engineering faculty also made increasing use of the facility. In mid-1962, the Building 365 operation was enhanced with a larger-capacity IBM system; and the Burruss operation—still a separate operation whose unit manager reported to Stuart Cassell—was enhanced with the installation of an IBM system 1401 to expand administrative computing and record-keeping capabilities for various inventory, personnel, accounting, and student records.

In later 1962, after Marshall Hahn became president, an additional IBM computer was leased for the Computing Center in Building 365. The next year, Hahn appointed a Computer Committee—chaired by Warren Brandt—to help formulate policies and see how needed computer capabilities could be achieved. As a result, by the end of 1964 the two operations had been reorganized under the Computing Center, new equipment had been leased, and a fee structure was put in place so that units paid specified rates for various computer services. Although facilities were growing in size and sophistication, research-oriented members of the faculty—for example, in mining engineering—were often frustrated by technical and financial problems of getting their work done, though Robert C. Heterick, a young assistant professor of civil engineering, was able to help on at least one important initiative. (Wilson Bell interview; J. Richard Lucas interview)

In spring 1966, the center ordered more IBM equipment to upgrade its capabilities. In late 1966, at President Hahn's request, Governor Mills Godwin authorized VPI and the state computer coordinator to make a joint study of VPI's long-range computer needs. To facilitate the study, Dr. Hahn asked each administrative department head to make a six-year projection of the growth and expansion of computer applications and anticipated volume. Meanwhile, plans were under way for a major addition to Burruss Hall, where the computer facilities would be housed; and the 1965–1966 self-study—which had noted that the shift to Burruss might well occasion major changes in hardware—envisioned an online system of record-keeping and accounting as well as computerized procedures for admissions, registration, scheduling, and stu-

look at several matters and to make such recommendations concerning the University's central administration as seemed appropriate. Clement French had a good knowledge of VPI and where it had come from, for he himself had served briefly, in 1949–1950, as Walter Newman's vice president.[9]

Dr. Hahn invited President French to the campus for the week of April 2–8, 1967, and suggested that he could stay in one of the big guest rooms in the president's home, on a hill overlooking the campus. Dr. French was agreeable and spent most of the week talking to VPI administrators and faculty, especially Dr. Brandt, Mr. Cassell, and the deans. The houseguest arrangement also provided easy access to President Hahn, who facilitated Dr. French's visit by having dinners in the big dining room of the president's home on three successive evenings, where members of the administrative group and their spouses and Dr. French could get to know one another in a relaxed and pleasant setting.[10]

In mid-April, after returning to Pullman, Washington, Dr. French sent back a report on his observations at VPI. He could, he said, "only express amazement at the tremendous progress both in physical plant and in general attitude" that he had observed during his visit. "My over-all feeling is one of high approval of what has been accomplished, as well as pleasure at the degree of acceptance," he wrote. Recalling that President Hahn had focused with some intensity on the student service operations, Dr. French said Dean Dean had made it clear that he strongly believed his office "should have control of all aspects of the operation related to students." While this might be feasible for a small college, Dr. French wrote, it hardly seemed wise for a larger institution. The business operations involved in housing and feeding large numbers of students were far too extensive, he said. French agreed, however, that student personnel officers should be heavily involved in housing students and in planning facilities for the housing and serving of students.[11]

Dr. French also looked at the structure of the new Extension and Research divisions and at the question of faculty involvement in the governance of the institution. As for Extension, he simply congratulated Dr. Hahn for accomplishing a task that French had attempted unsuccessfully at Washington State. The research structure, evolving much more slowly, would take nurturing, Dr. French suggested; its success would depend upon how well the division dean and the academic deans worked together. As for faculty involvement and the development of a faculty senate, Dr. French was strongly supportive of the concept of a faculty senate and greater faculty participation in decision making, but he worried about the large numbers the faculty at VPI were talking about, "in effect a university faculty." The former VPI vice president was enormously impressed, he said, in the progress made at VPI in moving from the rigidly centralized administrative structure he had observed in 1949–1950. French was impressed, too, by the extent of the support for President Hahn that he found among many of the administrators and faculty with whom he talked.

Aside from the memorandum French sent Hahn, which might be shared with his staff, the consultant also wrote a confidential letter. In it he said, first, he would strongly advise against making the chief student personnel officer a vice president for student affairs. The student personnel deans on many campuses (including the one at Washington State) sought such status and authority, he observed, but "your present procedure is still the best way." Similarly, French said, he thought that the vice presidential level was not necessary for the chief research officer; separate deans for graduate research and graduate instruction might overlap a little, but that looked like the best plan.

Then, turning to another topic on which President Hahn had asked him to comment, Dr. French repeated what he earlier said to Dr. Hahn privately: "I found general concern for the possibility of a move by you away from VPI." Some people had expressed a fear that the institution would retrogress rapidly if Hahn departed; some worried about the difficulties VPI would have in finding an equally capable successor. Some faculty and staff also were critical of Hahn's frequent absences from the campus, with the vice presidents so often in charge. At the same time, French noted, they acknowledged that Hahn's work in Richmond and across the state had enormously benefited VPI. Indeed, he said, he found genuine concern that President Hahn might not be able, physically, to continue for long at such a pace.[12]

Dr. French's confidential letter concluded with a brief discussion of a topic about which he and Dr. Hahn obviously had talked a great deal during the consultant's visit—the Stuart Cassell-Warren Brandt problem. In sum, French suggested, the men were both exceedingly valuable in VPI's administration; but they were mirror images of each other in that their personalities tended to conceal their real abilities. Serious conflict between the two vice presidents was evident, he noted. Thanking the high heavens that it was not he who had to do it, Dr. French suggested what had to be done: "You must define unmistakably the areas of responsibility and…make clear the importance of a cooperative approach—and that you 'don't mean maybe.'" Neither should be senior vice president, he said, because for one to "win" over the other would not be good. Both must be made to realize that effective cooperation and coordination was mandatory, he stressed. All this added up to Marshall Hahn's "major operational problem," Dr. French observed.

Warren Brandt and Stuart Cassell

Dr. French's discussion of the Cassell-Brandt conflict underscored perhaps the most difficult and continuing problem with which Marshall Hahn had to concern himself through the first half of his presidency. French was correct in his assessment: Both Mr. Cassell and Dr. Brandt were enormously important in the ongoing growth and development of the institution; both contributed great strengths to the Hahn administration. No one was more loyal and committed to VPI than Stuart Cassell; virtually from the time he enrolled as a student in 1928, the institution had been a central part of his life. He had worked for many years in the Extension Service, had taught agricultural economics at VPI, and had served the institution as finance and business manager since 1945. Years later, Marshall Hahn was to say that the key to managing Stuart Cassell was Cassell's great love of the institution; one had but to convince Cassell of the value of a given course or action to VPI, and he would embrace it tenaciously. Dr. Brandt, the outsider, philosophically was Marshall Hahn's alter ego; their thinking on almost any question was virtually the same (with the exception of Stuart Cassell), and their approaches to the business of building a comprehensive university could hardly have been closer. Thus they could communicate easily, and there was little chance for misunderstanding.

Both men had personality traits that generated difficulties, however. Stuart Cassell was honest, and he tried to be fair in his dealings with anyone, superior or subordinate. But he was firm; once he made a decision, he stood by it, unyielding, barring overwhelming evidence that it was wrong. Dr. Hahn was right that Cassell's decisions always were based on what he thought was best for the institution. Those who worked closely with him and came to know the real Stuart Cassell, and to share his relaxed, reflective, feet-on-the-desk and hands-behind-the-head moments, came to love the man. But his reputation for toughness and rigidity pervaded the campus. Many people were intimidated without even meeting Cassell, and often they were not reassured after talking to him about whatever issue or concern had led them to his office.

Warren Brandt was probably as honest as Stuart Cassell, but his frame of reference was different. Brandt's student years at Michigan State University (B.S., 1944) and the University of Illinois (Ph.D., 1949), followed by his teaching, research, and administrative experiences at two other midwestern land-grant schools, Purdue and Kansas State, made his perception of higher education realities dissimilar to Stuart Cassell's.

Marshall Hahn, intent upon changing the essential nature of VPI, had brought in Warren Brandt as his principal agent in generating that change. One of the most important ways of changing the depth and scope of VPI's academic programs was to change people, to build a new faculty and new academic leadership. So one of Brandt's principal tasks was to encourage people who did not fit into the new academic realities of the

13.5 Stuart Cassell and getting things done—One of Stuart Cassell's favorite stories about his VPI experiences concerned the construction of the mall, the divided, four-lane street that now enters the campus from Main Street and runs to the War Memorial, with its tall pylons atop a beautiful little chapel at the head of the drill field. A grove of trees once stood in the area, with a winding road meandering through the trees to the campus, altogether a beautiful scene. But when construction of the mall began in 1951—to provide a new campus entrance with access to the new memorial (all of which would be completed by 1960)—it was seen as necessary to destroy many of the trees and regrade the area. It seems that many of the citizens of Blacksburg vigorously opposed cutting the trees.

Mr. Cassell told the story more than once, with a twinkle in his eyes and a sly grin—how he got the contractor to have his men at the site at 6 A.M., felling the trees before anyone was aware of what was happening. There was great hue and cry about the deed, he recalled, but by then there wasn't anything anybody could do about it. "Sometimes that's about the only way you can get something done," he chuckled later.

changing institution to move on. Warren Brandt's reputation as Dr. Hahn's "hatchetman" indeed had some basis in fact.

At the same time, Brandt had the task of positive leadership, helping generate on the campus the academic environment necessary for the rapidly growing faculty to become increasingly productive. Dr. Hahn and Dr. Brandt were intent upon not only insuring VPI's physical growth but in using a rapid-growth mode to dramatically strengthen the quality of the academic enterprise. It was a difficult task at best, but Dr. Brandt's personality characteristics made it even more so, for both Brandt and those with whom he worked. He had not learned well from Dr. Hahn, who seemed to control his reactions and emotions without effort. However difficult a situation might become, changes in the president's pleasant, relaxed demeanor were not easily discernible (at least by those who did not know him well).

Brandt's feelings and emotions were almost immediately evident, playing across his face like a thunderstorm. He was prone to disputation and argument, as if seeking to overwhelm an opponent with his bellicosity as well as with logic. Dr. Brandt on occasion was known to call a colleague in the evening after dinner to apologize and express regret for such behavior earlier in the day. A little of this also sometimes spilled over into Dr. Brandt's interaction with important external groups. Joe Blackburn, the C&P attorney who sat on the State Council of Higher Education in those years, remembered that, "if there was any way to antagonize any three people all at the same time, [Brandt] would do it. He was awfully hard to listen to…, his attitude was always 'I'm telling you,' rather than '[I want to] explain something.'"[13]

Quite aside from personality traits, the inevitability of serious and sustained friction between Warren Brandt and Stuart Cassell seems apparent. Particularly in the early years of their relationship, Mr. Cassell controlled all the things Dr. Brandt had to have in order to support his faculty and the academic programs—the physical facilities such as laboratories and classrooms, the support personnel, and, outside of faculty salaries and basic departmental budgets, the overall institutional budget. Early on, Mr. Cassell and his associates were even responsible for the internal coordination and preparation of the detailed biennial budget requests submitted through the State Budget Office (a division of the Governor's Office) to the General Assembly. Cassell knew his way around the corridors of power in the state capital as well as anyone in Virginia. First as business manager and later as vice president for administration, he was also in charge of the development of the physical plant—construction and maintenance of buildings, custodial services, landscaping and grounds keeping, campus planning, and so on. President Hahn provided overall direction and supervision, but the detailed decisions most often were Stuart Cassell's.[14]

Years later, in retirement, Warren Brandt remembered some of his frustrations with Stuart Cassell: "We were trying to move. We had visions of institutional quality that [were] at a different level from what we had before. There were a lot of things, just constant things, where the most frugal approach just didn't fit the scene for what we were trying to do. It didn't help us recruit the quality people we needed…. Over the years Stuart and I clashed…. We differed." Mr. Cassell and Dr. Brandt are not known to have ever raised their voices in dispute (Brandt cannot remember such an incident, and Stuart Cassell died years ago), but the two strong-willed men simply did not agree on many things.[15]

"Stuart just had such a lock control," Brandt remembered. "When you give one man control of positions for secretaries…control of the physical plant which can fix up your labs, fix up your offices, or whatever it is you need, and the whole personnel system…and then he's got the budget along with it, he's got your people locked up. [If] he decides he doesn't want to help somebody, they are just out there floating. There isn't anything that can be done for them." The friction between Mr. Cassell and Dr. Brandt grew intense in the mid-1960s. "It was probably the one thing that Marshall and I really saw different [for] three or four years," Brandt recalled.

And yet there was understanding as well as conflict between the two men. For one thing, Brandt recalled, "there were lots of times when Stuart would come across with the support when we needed it." Moreover, though Brandt didn't like the tension or the obstacles, he understood that Cassell had spent most of his career at Tech facing far greater financial constraints than the Hahn years had to confront. "Through years and years of just abominable funding, [Cassell] undoubtedly had managed because of his frugal practices to provide a lot of things they wouldn't have otherwise had." But, as Brandt himself put it, during the 1960s a new dispensation had come to town, and "we were trying to move." The old ways may have once been necessary, but necessity took on a new guise, and the utmost frugality came to carry a lower premium in getting things done.

President Hahn's ability to mobilize subordinates was particularly important with respect to Stuart Cassell and Warren Brandt. Looking back years later, he described the pair as "two very different individuals, who were unwilling teammates in the sense that when you put them in double harness they struggled, but I was strong-willed enough to harness them. And those two individuals contributed far more to the strengthening of this institution than most people want to give them credit for. Although they got a lot of credit, they deserved more."[16]

Clifford Cutchins—who served on the BOV from 1965 through the end of Hahn's presidency—said of Hahn and the University, "You know the great thing that Marshall had was Warren Brandt was running the academic side and Stuart [Cassell] was running the business side, and he really had an outstanding team that operated it." When Hahn took on the presidency, Cutchins added, VPI "was not really a university. It was a college, a military college which was on the verge of emerging." Making it all happen required "Marshall's leadership and Stuart's ability in that he understood how the state funded the University and he was able to stretch the dollars to probably produce more than most other people were able to do or would have been able to do."[17]

Differences over Dormitory Design

One of Mr. Cassell's major responsibilities was the University's construction program, along with campus site planning. Cassell's single-minded concentration upon getting buildings, and especially dormitories, constructed as easily as possible and as quickly as possible prompted much of the conflict with Dr. Brandt. Dean Dean and Dr. Brandt were not happy with the design of the residence halls—the interiors resembled the barracks that had housed the cadets in an earlier era. Mr. Cassell had expanded and modernized the older dormitories nearest the downtown area, the so-called Upper Quad, in the late 1950s during the Newman administration. Although they were multi-story buildings, they were barracks-like, with double loaded hallways and not much in the way of amenities. Two of them, Thomas Hall and Monteith Hall, were renovated and somewhat modernized in 1969–1970.

Meanwhile, all of the newer dormitories along Kent and Washington streets are of much the same utilitarian design. Even the interiors of the high-rise structures—O'Shaughnessy, Lee, and Pritchard, which are seven- or eight-story buildings—retained a good deal of the barracks look. The stone exteriors seemed attractive, but the huge dorms such as Lee and Pritchard—the latter houses more than 1,000 students—with their gang showers and toilets, generated real problems of management and maintenance. Too many young people with too much energy to burn were housed in too close proximity.

That, however, was not Cassell's primary concern when he worked with Carneal & Johnston, Uncle Ambler Johnston's old firm in Richmond. Rather, his primary concern was to build residence halls inexpensively and rapidly. President Hahn, anxious to enlarge the residence hall capacity as quickly as possible in order to accommodate larger numbers of high school graduates who sought college admission, urged him on. Dr. Brandt, Dr. Dean and his staff, and others had good reasons for wanting a greater voice in the design of the residence halls, so the structures could be better adapted to the psychological and social needs of the students and thus make management of the facilities less difficult. Early on, they had

13.6 Personnel, politics, and housing design—In an interview many years later, Dr. Dean described a wild scene early on, one in which Dr. Hahn, Mr. Cassell, Dr. Brandt, Dean Dean, the architects' representatives (even J. Ambler Johnston himself was said to have been present), along with G. L. Furr and some Board members, went over plans for four new dormitories. Dr. Brandt took strong exception to the plans, and Mr. Cassell suggested that this was "all we could afford." Dr. Dean said he began to express his opinion on the suitability of the plans when Dr. Hahn in effect told him to keep quiet. It was Dean's job to manage the dormitories after they were built, not to plan or build them, Dean quoted Hahn as saying. The meeting was said to have lasted seven hours. Dr. Dean's story, though by no means entirely credible (in fact, no such seven-hour meeting ever occurred), does suggest something of the realities behind the stresses evident in the Cassell/Brandt relationship.

Warren Brandt and Jim Dean were in close alliance—Brandt later recalled that he grew quite fond of Dean. But that alliance did little to help with Stuart Cassell, who remained unimpressed by the loquacious dean of students, although Gordon Brown (Jim Dean's chief lieutenant) and others were able to influence the situation to some degree. The larger dormitories were equipped with lounges, study rooms, and other amenities that somewhat softened the harshness of the interior. Later, when J. Ambler Johnston Hall, dormitory number 9 in the series—a huge residence hall housing more than 1,000 students—was constructed west of Pritchard Hall, the design was somewhat improved. Men were initially housed in the west wings, and women in the smaller east section, with lounges separating the sections. No one was able to eliminate the stark interior courtyard of Pritchard Hall, however. That was little more than a huge window well that students soon dubbed "the pit." Discarded items thrown from the windows of the student rooms that opened onto the courtyard soon made the interior a trash heap. Steel screens were later installed on the outside of the windows overlooking the enclosed yard below to stop the bombardment of trash.

The older stone-faced residence halls, Eggleston and Campbell, just off the drill field bracketing Memorial Gymnasium (originally constructed in the 1930s as part of the public works programs of the Great Depression), were converted to women's housing. Those facilities fared better; the interiors were redesigned attractively and comfortably. The renovated Eggleston Hall was opened with 524 women students in 1966. Before the conversion, it had housed 648 male students, but more generous lounge space, an apartment for a housemother, and other facilities reduced its capacity. Campbell Hall, west of Memorial Gymnasium from Eggleston, reopened as a women's residence hall in 1968, similarly equipped.

little voice. Mr. Cassell did exactly what Dr. Hahn wanted him to do—provide usable dormitory rooms as quickly as possible.

After 1968

Beginning in November 1968, four vice presidents reported to the executive vice president—Stuart Cassell as VP for Administration; Jim Dean for Student Affairs; Leslie F. Malpass for Academic Affairs; and William E. Lavery for Finance. Lavery earned a bachelor's degree from Michigan State and a Ph.D. at Wisconsin; worked for a decade in the Federal Extension Service; and first came to VPI in 1966 to work in Extension. Malpass moved up to vice president from his position as dean of the College of Arts and Sciences, where he had served from 1965 to 1968. Later, Malpass left the University, and John D. Wilson took his place as vice president for Academic Affairs.

Jim Dean and Stuart Cassell both continued in their new vice-presidential positions beyond the end of Marshall Hahn's presidency. Warren Brandt left Virginia Tech in 1969, however, to become the first president of Virginia Commonwealth University. Years later, remembering the administrative tussles of the 1960s, Brandt observed, "Stuart [Cassell] had such a lock because he had so many areas under his control. Ultimately breaking it up into the four vice presidents and an executive VP, I thought, was a tremendous step forward."[18] During and after their time together in Blacksburg, the University that Hahn, Brandt, and Cassell built continued to grow.

[1] The recommendations urged that vice presidents head the new Research and Extension divisions, but President Hahn did not follow the faculty/staff advice on that particular point.

[2] Memorandum to the faculty and staff, 8 August 1966; University news release distributed 9 August; Hahn letter to Garber, 20 June 1966; Hahn letter to Rowe, 20 June 1966.

[3] Hahn letter to Rowe, 20 June 1966. Bruce Ross had an unhappy eleven months on the job, and several years passed before the alumni situation was back on an even keel and the development program significantly improved. The unfortunate selection by the Alumni Association was compounded with Jim Dean's involvement.

[4] The participants, in addition to the president, included Mr. Cassell and Dr. Brandt, plus the deans of the colleges; William B. Harrison and Coyt T. Wilson, the directors of the Engineering Experiment Station and the Agricultural Experiment Station; Stuart Row, director of community (branch) colleges and General Extension; William E. Skelton, director of Cooperative Extension; and Roger Smith, who, though still director of the self-study, also was responsible for the State Technical Services program (Hahn letter, 2 June 1966).

[5] Hahn interview, 31 August 1989.

6 Dean Harrison did not immediately appoint a director for engineering and physical sciences, although he indicated that such a position ultimately would be filled. Dr. P. Howard Massey Jr., an assistant professor of horticulture who came from Cornell in 1952, served for a time as associate director of the new division for agriculture and life sciences. Hugh Duncan, who had been assistant to the director of the Agricultural Experiment Station, was appointed assistant to the dean of the Research Division.

7 For overall policy development, Dr. Harrison organized an advisory group called the Research Council. Its members included the dean of the Graduate School and the associate deans for research from the various colleges, plus two faculty members each from Engineering, Arts and Sciences, and Agriculture, and one each from Home Economics, Business, and Architecture, all nominated by their respective deans (Memorandum to the Faculty from Dean Harrison, undated but distributed late autumn 1966).

8 Dr. Harrison, who then was director of the Engineering Experiment Station, also had helped draft the bill which, when it became law, created the Research Division—knowing that it well might eliminate the job in which he was then working (VPI Self-Study, 1965–1966, 1: IX-2; Skelton interview; Harrison interview).

9 Dr. C. Clement French's undergraduate and graduate degrees were from the University of Pennsylvania, and he had been head of the chemistry department at Randolph-Macon Woman's College. He remained at VPI less than two years before leaving in 1950 to become a dean at Texas A&M.

10 Hahn letter to vice presidents, deans, and selected staff, 28 March 1967.

11 French memo to Hahn, 14 April 1967.

12 Confidential letter, 14 April 1967.

13 Blackburn interview.

14 The Cooperative Extension Service, which in 1966 became the Extension Division, had some measure of autonomy. So did the Agricultural Experiment Station and the Engineering Experiment Station, both of which were absorbed into the Research Division under the 1966 legislation. Technically, VPI operated as three separate state entities—Instruction, Research, and Extension—each with its separate state appropriation and accounting procedures.

15 Brandt interview.

16 Hahn interview, 24 March 1990.

17 Clifford Cutchins interview.

18 Taking Brandt's place for a time as executive vice president was William J. McKeefery, who had been serving as dean of academic affairs at Southern Illinois University when he was tapped to come to Virginia Tech.

Stuart K. Cassell (B.S. '32, M.S. '33), business manager (1945-1966) and then vice president for administration. Cassell Coliseum is named for him. The photo dates from 1968.

.

14: Alumni Reconciliation and University Development

In the early years of the Hahn administration, alumni relations had proven difficult—partly as the school developed a working relationship to the Alumni Association; partly as the Alumni Association itself attempted to secure reliable continuing leadership, mark a course, and follow through; and particularly in the aftermath of the policy change regarding the Corps of Cadets in 1964. In a meeting of the Alumni Board in March 1967, President Hahn declared that "the course of the University is set," but he made it clear that, as he saw it all, the rate of travel along that course would depend on alumni support.

In fact, the president was developing that idea in considerable detail and with growing emphasis. A long letter to Jim Dean in February 1967, followed by a talk to the Alumni Board in April, looked to VPI's emergence as a top-ranking institution of higher education—and it identified the alumni as a major source of the funding that would make such development possible. Early in Hahn's administration, he looked to the alumni for growing support, but he termed the state the major source of the kind of funding needed to grow the faculty and the physical infrastructure. Having obtained tremendously increased appropriations from the state in 1964 and especially in 1966, he looked again to the alumni.

The "substantial progress" of recent years, Hahn wrote Dean, had moved the University into a group of perhaps twenty-five to forty institutions each with the "strength and potential" that "could enable emergence to membership in the group of the nation's most outstanding universities." Further progress would be difficult, but it could be achieved. Support from VPI alumni would play a large role in determining whether the school could make the transition from a good state university to one of the best in the nation.

Among the great needs requiring enhanced alumni giving were academic scholarships (especially for attracting more students with high academic ability); scholarships for student athletes (who "must meet the same academic standards as all other students"); and money (not available from state funds) to purchase expensive scientific equipment for research programs. Essential funding categories also included library support (to build the collection to a million volumes); enhanced support for faculty development, particularly faculty fellowships; money to pay for high-quality programs in the soon-to-be-open continuing education center; and unrestricted giving that could be used to support the programs of the Alumni Association itself.[1]

Fund-raising from a Fractured Alumni

The decision to go to a voluntary Corps of Cadets generated a great deal of dissension among VPI alumni. It therefore altered the climate in which Marshall Hahn and his colleagues at VPI worked in the mid-1960s, especially in their fund-raising efforts. No one was more affected by disaffected alumni—people angry about what was happening to the Corps of Cadets—than Craig Fabian, the director of development and public relations. University fund-raising in the 1960s was difficult enough when alumni were reasonably happy. The split in VPI's alumni ranks was surprisingly balanced on each side of the Corps issue, although the older and more prominent alumni usually came down on the side of mandatory enrollment in the Corps. Many of them felt deeply about the issue and were in a position to make their unhappiness known by withholding financial support. Fabian reported a sharp drop in alumni support following the Corps decision.[2]

The leadership of the Alumni Association, however, remained generally level-headed and cooperative. In winter 1963–1964, before the Corps issue surfaced, Dr. Hahn had written to Gene Rowe suggesting it would be helpful if he could serve another two-year term as Association president. Under normal conditions, Richmond advertising executive Jim Cargill, the Association's vice president, would have succeeded Rowe as

14.1 The *VPI Historical Data Book*—Among the projects undertaken to help strengthen alumni support, one was a *VPI Historical Data Book* (VPI *Bulletin* 58/3, January 1964). The *Data Book* was a collection of historical data, sketches, lore, and other institutional information going all the way back to VPI's founding in 1872. The material had been collected and edited by Jenks Robertson. It was printed in spring 1964, prior to the controversial decision regarding the Corps. Dr. Hahn approved Craig Fabian's idea that it be widely distributed, and it was. A copy of the booklet, personally signed by the president, was sent to everyone who contributed to the Alumni Fund in 1963. In 1972, the University brought out a centennial edition.

Association president in 1964. There was a strong sense, however, that it would be a hardship on both the Association and Cargill if he took over as president amid VPI's larger transition from Walter Newman to Marshall Hahn, inasmuch as the vice president traditionally had not been heavily involved in the leadership of the Association until he actually became president. Most likely, Rowe wrote Hahn, after only one more year he would resign as president in favor of Jim Cargill. That way, if Cargill were reelected after he had served a year of Rowe's second term, each could serve three years.[3]

It was not to be. Cargill, who had previously attempted to resign from the Association Board, became less and less enthusiastic about Marshall Hahn's administration at VPI, and after a visit to Blacksburg in September 1964, he again urged that his resignation be accepted.[4] Gene Rowe remained president of the Association until 1965, when he was succeeded by Robert F. Willey ('27) of Washington, DC, regional manager for Bethlehem Steel.

Fabian sought to generate support for the university from whatever source he could, and of course he worked closely with Mark Oliver and the Alumni Association's annual fund efforts. The results, for a few years at least, were not especially encouraging, given the dissension about the Corps. But the VPI Development Council, incorporating as it did the senior leadership of the Board of Visitors, the Alumni Association, and the VPI Educational Foundation, had been envisioned as a unifying force. When the Council met with Dr. Hahn in September 1964, the president suggested that it coordinate fund-raising and take a leadership role in VPI's development efforts in general. The Council agreed that the imme-

14.2 Robert F. Willey ('27)—Robert F. Willey grew up in Front Royal, in the Shenandoah Valley, and majored in mining engineering at VPI, where he was a varsity baseball player and a drummer in the regimental band. At Bethlehem Steel, he began work as a design engineer and then, in 1934, moved to sales. He moved to Washington, DC, in 1942, soon became district sales manager, and in 1957 was named manager of the Washington office, where his responsibilities included a great deal of work with the federal government.

A tall, white-haired, distinguished-looking man, Willey looked the part, whether in his corporate home in the nation's capital or in a key leadership position for the VPI Alumni Association. In April 1965, he took over from Gene Rowe as president of the Association. Although he did so with some reluctance—his responsibilities at Bethlehem Steel were particularly heavy at that point—he served in that capacity, during a difficult period, for two years (Willey interview).

diate fund-raising efforts would be divided between the Alumni Association, which was responsible for annual alumni support, and the Educational Foundation, which would seek corporate and major gift support. Fuzzy Furr, still active, was elected chairman of the Council, and Stuart Cassell was elected secretary.

Finding a New Development Director

As Craig Fabian packed up to leave VPI and return to Pittsburgh early in 1967, President Hahn identified Gene Rowe as the perfect alumnus to succeed him as director of development—a successful businessman, widely known and much admired in the Alumni Association, who loved VPI with a passion and had contributed much to his alma mater. But one problem was money; the state salary level for the development position was $15,000, considerably less than Rowe was earning at Dan River Mills. Anyway, Rowe would not consider leaving Dan River immediately, although Dr. Hahn said he would be willing to hold the position open for some time if Gene would make the commitment.[5]

The president visited the Rowes in Danville in August 1967 to talk further about the possibilities, and he followed up with a letter. Rowe asked for a bit more time before further discussion. He and his wife, Mary Lewis, had planned a trip to Scotland in the fall, Rowe explained, but he would try to talk with Hahn again before leaving.[6]

Rowe finally decided to decline. In a "Confidential" letter to Hahn in October 1967, he asked to be withdrawn from consideration. He hoped, he said, that the time he had taken to consider the offer "will impress you with the seriousness of my approach, my love for VPI, and my great admiration for you and the leadership you have given and continue to give to our university." In response, Dr. Hahn acknowledged his disappointment,

14.3 "Operation Remembrance"—Craig Fabian came up with another idea he thought might appeal to the alumni, in what he called a "climate conditioner." When Miles Stadium was torn down in late 1964, Fabian suggested salvaging some of the wooden seats there and using them to make small flat desk pencil holders. These would be given to alumni contributors as a memento of the stadium and of VPI traditions. His idea was approved.

Salvaging the wood, assembling the equipment and workmen, and producing the pencil holders by the thousands proved a significant undertaking. The finished products were attractive conversation pieces—rich, cypress wood finished on top, bottom, and ends, with the weathered gray of the old stadium seats still apparent on their edges. Imprinted on each were the words "Miles Stadium—1926–1964" on the far side of the top and "Virginia Polytechnic Institute" on the top of the front edge.

The *Techgram* announced the project in a big way, with several photographs and an over-the-masthead story. "Every one of Tech's more than 25,000 alumni" for whom addresses were available, the newspaper announced, would "soon be receiving a small piece of wood from the seats in old Miles Stadium." The photographs included one of Dr. Hahn presenting the first of the commemorative pencil holders to C. P. "Sally" Miles ('01), the one-time star athlete who went on to serve as football coach, athletic manager, professor, and dean and, though retired by this time, still served as faculty chairman for athletics.

Fabian called the project "operation remembrance." A note from Marshall Hahn accompanied each pencil tray: "Here is a little piece of VPI for you—a pencil tray made from the seats of Miles Stadium. This familiar structure has given way to desperately needed dormitories. Just as the wood seems richer for its years of weathering service, so with VPI as it changes to meet the needs of Virginia's youth. Keep this remembrance with our very best wishes."

but he understood, he said, and deeply appreciated Rowe's thoughtful consideration of the position.[7]

A year and a half passed before the appointment of a new development director. In the interim, Lon Savage, Dr. Hahn's executive assistant, took on many of a director's tasks. Interested in fund-raising, especially as it concerned deferred giving, Savage corresponded with many alumni; encouraged some of the more affluent among them to include VPI in their estate planning; visited a number of possible benefactors; and produced a publication, "Effective Giving of Stocks and Bonds," to send to selected people.[8] As of July 1, 1968, Dean Wilson Bell accepted appointment as director of university development.

The Alumni Office

Into mid-1967, the Alumni office remained in some disarray. Bruce Ross resigned, as he reported in an open letter to members of the Old Guard (alumni who had been out of school fifty years or more). He said, however, that he was enthusiastic about the Old Guard—of whom thirty-three had returned to the campus for a reunion June 9–10, sixteen with their wives—and he urged that the reunion be made an annual event. At a meeting of the Development Council in Roanoke on June 13, 1967, Bob Willey announced that Herman "Lem" Pritchard would fill in until a new alumni director could be found. At this meeting, the "objectives and goals" that President Hahn had articulated since February were formally adopted as long-range goals for the University's development program. Those goals depended heavily upon increased alumni giving, but Willey had to acknowledge that alumni support had fallen off during the year and that unrestricted contributions were insufficient to meet the Alumni Association's budget.[9]

That summer, the Alumni Board elected Harry N. Gustin ('43), a Norfolk attorney, to succeed Bob Willey as president of the Association. Willey wrote to Dr. Hahn in early July 1967 to officially inform him of the election results. His letter was warm and appreciative, especially so in view of the difficulties he had faced in his two and a half years as Alumni president. Willey suggested that Hahn might want to get to know Pritchard and establish a working relationship with him "beneficial to the university as well as to the Alumni Association." President Hahn's response likewise was warm and cordial; he already had visited with Pritchard, he said, and planned to take him to lunch that week. Hahn was especially grateful, he wrote, for Willey's outstanding leadership "during a particularly difficult period."[10] Writing at the same time to congratulate Harry Gustin on his election as Alumni Association president, Hahn said he

14.4 President Hahn, fund-raiser—President Hahn, of course, always remained alert for possible sources of support, from whatever source. H. A. "Hobie" Weaver ('50), then assistant manager of the Western Electric Company plant at Winston-Salem, North Carolina, contacted Hahn occasionally offering used scientific equipment from Western Electric or Bell Labs. S. E. Davidson, owner of Davidson's in Roanoke and Blacksburg, stopped in to talk to the president about scholarships. The greatest need, Dr. Hahn later wrote him, was for scholarships that awarded at least $500 per year—with that much assistance, the typical student could get enough additional money from loans and work-study funds to get by. Davidson funded a $500 annual scholarship honoring his father, Joseph Davidson. In March 1967, US Steel renewed for two years, beginning in September, two graduate fellowships in engineering mechanics for $3,900 each (Hahn papers, 1967).

Sometime after the death of Harry F. Byrd Sr. in 1966, President Hahn was informed that Byrd had left $25,000 to VPI for scholarships. Hahn wrote Harry F. Byrd Jr. to inquire if the money should be put directly into scholarships or into an endowment fund, and the younger Byrd opted for the latter (Byrd letter, 22 February 1967). Meanwhile, a steady stream of corporate, foundation, and individual gifts came in, some earmarked for specific departments. Ed Lane and many others who had made pledges for the construction of Lane Stadium periodically sent in checks or contributed stock to redeem their pledges. A personal note of thanks from the president, over Hahn's signature, was sent for each gift of $200 or more.

President Hahn continued a playful correspondence with W. P. Tams Jr. (see box 4.6), in Tams, West Virginia. In summer 1967, Tams wrote to Frank Moseley (copy to Hahn), noting that estimates of the cost of the stadium kept going up. "It looks like Dr. Hahn will have to stop his other activities and go to beating the brush for the remaining stadium money," Tams said. Hahn wrote back that not nearly as much money remained to be raised as had already been raised. Tams responded, "there are just two kinds of people in the world—those who are worried about indebtedness, and those who let the other fellow worry." The former coal baron sent a check in December for $3,000, of which $1,000 was designated for the stadium and the remainder "to whatever fund applies to the care of retired faculty members" (Tams letters, 21 June, 15 December 1967; Hahn letter, 24 July 1967).

looked forward to working with Gustin in strengthening the Association and the continued development of the institution. The University and the Association needed to work closely together to accomplish their shared goals, Hahn said.[11]

Lem Pritchard's exuberant enthusiasm, the obvious dedication of the alumni officers, and their desire to get along began to ease the rough edges of alumni-administration relationships. Pritchard's enthusiasm came through clearly in his monthly column in *Techgram*. In one, he wrote appreciatively of Dr. Hahn's hosting the Association officers at a luncheon conference at the Shenandoah Club in Roanoke in August. In October the annual Chapter Officers Forum and the Association's annual meeting on the campus attracted good attendance. At the Alumni Association's autumn meeting, held November 3, 1967, in Roanoke, Pritchard reported he had been encouraged by his developing relationship with President Hahn. He had the feeling, he said, that "the door is discretely open" whenever necessary.

The Board, appreciative of Pritchard's work, gave him a renewed vote of confidence. Harry Gustin wrote to President Hahn in March 1968 to say that the Alumni Board sensed "increased harmony and progress." Hahn's hosting of executive committee summit meetings, and his innumerable constructive alumni contacts, had a lot to do with the changed atmosphere in which the alumni worked, the Alumni Association president said. President Hahn responded in the same vein. "An increasing spirit of harmony and progress" was evident, he wrote, and much of it was due to Gustin's "outstanding leadership."[12]

The Hall Report

In 1967, the Alumni Association Board undertook a reevaluation of its structure, policies, and operations, and as part of that process it retained a consultant to help in the evaluation. He was Thomas H. Hall III, director of resource development at Georgia Tech. Hall submitted his report in April 1968 following a visit to the campus and extensive interviews with Lem Pritchard, other alumni staff in Memorial Gymnasium, and President Hahn, Jim Dean, and Bill Skelton. Hall also had the opportunity to speak briefly with several other members of the administration and faculty and with a number of students. While on the campus, he attended the banquet at the annual meeting of the Women's Chapter of

14.5 Herman L. "Lem" Pritchard ('24)—Good fortune for the Alumni Association turned up in 1967 in the person of Lem Pritchard, a retired New Jersey savings and loan executive. Pritchard, a native of Norfolk and a 1924 VPI graduate, had retired as executive vice president of the First Federal Savings and Loan Association at Paterson, New Jersey. After his wife died—and hearing about the Alumni vacancy and anxious to move back south—he decided to explore the possibilities. He moved back to Blacksburg and agreed to fill in as staff director for the Alumni Association until a permanent director could be employed. Bob Willey announced that Pritchard was appointed associate director, effective June 15, 1967. (*Techgram*, July 1967)

The appearance of the tall, lanky, white-haired Pritchard was fortunate; he was soon busy getting the alumni activities back on track and getting to know Marshall Hahn. He also remarried in November 1967; his bride was Miss Clarice Slusher, the sprightly lady who had retired from the Registrar's Office early in the Hahn administration. The two had known one another when Pritchard was a student, back in the 1920s. He had been a striking young man, his wife remembered, and was editor of the student newspaper and captain of the band company. (Mrs. Clarice Slusher Pritchard interview)

the Alumni Association. He had not had, he said, an opportunity to talk with the members of the board's executive committee. The written report, submitted to the board on April 10, 1968, focused on several "areas of concern," as Hall expressed it.

The first was the relationship of the Alumni Association and the University administration. Hall rather bluntly called it "awkward, at best," characterized by a general feeling "that any close ties with the president will lead to a 'dependence' of the Association on the administration." Hall urged that the board's executive committee get together prior to the next board meeting and discuss the issue frankly. "It has not been my experience in alumni work, nor that of other successful alumni programs, that much can be accomplished without a mutual agreement on ways and means between the administration and the Alumni Association," he said. President Hahn had acknowledged that he badly needed the Alumni Association's help in accomplishing two main objectives, Hall wrote—providing a "supportive environment" and "the providing of material support." A major goal of any alumni association would be to maintain program objectives "which offer service to both the alumni and the [institution]," Hall observed. What the Alumni Association Board needed to do, he suggested, was get together with the administration and agree on "how the Association can best be of service."

In a lengthy discussion about the selection of a new alumni affairs director, Hall said it probably was the most important step to be taken in coming months, and he urged that the Board make the selection in close consultation with President Hahn. Hall submitted a list of qualifications for the position and suggested the board perhaps should avoid a retired military officer. As for the alumni staff, he said it was deserving of praise for carrying on in a difficult situation and maintaining the more traditional programs, such as class reunions, club meetings, and the Chapter Officers Forum. But after a new director had been appointed, a systems analysis should be made, and modern equipment installed to better facilitate record-keeping and other routine work.

Hall urged that immediate steps be taken to restore an active "annual giving" program as a major part of the Alumni program. He recommended the Association establish an aggressive and active fund committee to consult with the staff and assure that solicitations were timely and proper. Undesignated funds from alumni gifts were essential both for the operations of the Alumni Office and for the institution, he said. The con-

---

14.6 A home for the Alumni Association?—The increasing harmony in the relationship between the Alumni Association and the administration was welcomed by all. Many alumni felt strongly, however, that the Association ought to have a home of its own near the campus, an alumni house where former students could get together and visit, and which could house the Alumni Association staff. A good many members of the Alumni Board felt this way, and occasionally others tried to encourage the development of an alumni house at VPI. Bernie McGinnis ('50) of Nelson County earlier brought up the subject in a letter to President Hahn in summer 1967.

Dr. Hahn thought it unwise for the Association to seriously consider building or purchasing an alumni house, in view of the considerable expense of operating and maintaining such a facility. The new continuing education center, which would be opened for use in January 1968, would be available for alumni use, he noted—it could provide hotel accommodations, food service, and other facilities. VPI's development also would attract several higher quality motels, Hahn said; the University already was already negotiating with several motel chains (Hahn letter, 7 August 1967). Many years later, in 2003, the University broke ground for an alumni center.

sultant, as a professional development officer, also made specific recommendations for four mail solicitations to be made prior to the end of the fiscal year. He even included a draft of a suggested appeal letter and proposed a format for the reply card. On a related point, Hall reassured the Alumni Board that solicitations requesting that contributions be made payable to the VPI Educational Foundation were both proper and effective.

As for the general alumni program, Hall said he did not feel it was effectively meeting the needs of the institution and urged "new and interpretive programs, developed with the assistance and participation of the faculty." Such programs should provide "a sense of the vitality that exists on the campus" and "present a "comprehensive picture of VPI," he said. Alluding to the separate Alumni Women's Chapter, he urged "a concentrated effort...to unify the entire alumni body around one alumni program." An alumni magazine ultimately might be helpful, Hall said, but he recommended against attempting one until adequate resources were available to produce a good one. The consultant suggested that ways be found to add younger alumni to the board and that the board take pains to have some of its members visit in the Alumni Office during each year to keep in contact with the staff.

Noting some interest on the board in obtaining an alumni house near the campus, Hall urged that such a step be delayed, especially in view of the opening of the continuing education center, which could provide accommodations for visiting alumni. President Hahn's efforts to develop "a motel-like" facility near the campus might be helpful in this context, he said; in any event the board should make sure that the president was aware of the Association's long-range goal of having a suitable facility of its own.

Hall urged that the board immediately investigate the possibility of moving its offices from Memorial Gymnasium into Burruss Hall. He noted that President Hahn had invited the Association to move into the administration building, where available space had been laid out and renovated in line with the wishes of the Alumni Association. Mr. Pritchard should immediately request the necessary studies to determine if the move were physically possible, Hall advised. Concerns about fitting equipment and personnel into the space available could easily be resolved, he said. "Most alumni associations fight for space, any space, near the President's Office," he observed.

Finally, Hall observed that the Association had been fortunate to have the services of Herman L. Pritchard at a critical time. As associate director, Pritchard had earned everyone's admiration and respect, Hall said, and the man could continue to be of great service. But, as a retiree, he did not need the high-pressure, constantly demanding job as alumni director. Rather, the consultant concluded, he "needs the help of a director who is responsible for the total alumni program."

Hall came to the Alumni Board's spring meeting in Blacksburg in late May 1968 to discuss the report and respond to questions from board members.[13] Hall emphasized the concept that his report recommended for establishing a new and closer relationship between the Alumni Association and the University. He said it was obvious to him that the members of the board were concerned about the current situation. It was his feeling that the board should be a part of any planning that affected the future of VPI, that the Alumni Board should forge a new bridge to the University Administration so that the concerns of the Association could be part of VPI's future goals. There must, he said, be a spirit of mutual trust between the Association and the Administration. Mr. Hall observed that VPI had some 31,000 alumni who were concerned with the future of the University, and the Alumni Board represented them. He stated that Mr. Gustin should advise Dr. Hahn of the sincere desire of the board to function in this new concept. At the same time, though, the Administration should lend both financial and moral support to the operations and activities of the Alumni Association—salary help was essential. In addition, the Association, together with the director of development and the administration, should develop new and stimulating programs. Finally, he said, the Alumni Association should have a magazine and an Alumni Directory—projects for which the University should furnish financial assistance.

"Mine Eyes Have Seen the Glory"

At that same May 1968 meeting, following "a discussion by way of questions and answers," Pritchard's minutes reported, Tom Hall departed for Atlanta, and President Gustin introduced Wilson Bell, the incoming development director. Dr. Bell, who could count a number of his old VPI classmates among the board members, was pleased to be present, and he wanted, he said, to work closely with the Alumni Office and the board in his new position.

The board touched upon many other matters that afternoon and evening. Regarding plans for an alumni house, the property committee—though acknowledging that these would have to be deferred—urged that they be developed on a long-range basis. The committee also recommended that the Alumni offices be moved to Burruss Hall, once it was jointly determined that "proper and adequate space" would be available. Perhaps most importantly, the board deferred selecting an alumni director pending identification and evaluation of additional prospects.

Many of the Alumni Board members had assembled at the continuing education center the previous evening for what Ambler Johnston later called a "bull session" on Mr. Hall's report and related topics. They included Harry Wyatt, who was unable to participate in the board sessions on Friday and Saturday. The frank talk Thursday evening "laid the groundwork" for what followed, Johnston later wrote Dr. Hahn. Harry Gustin adjourned the Friday meeting at 10 P.M., to resume in the private dining room of the continuing education center at 8 A.M. for breakfast Saturday morning. Present as invited guests were Warren Brandt and Jim Dean, newly appointed as vice president for student affairs, along with Wilson Bell. According to Pritchard's minutes:

> Dr. Brandt and Dr. Dean spoke at length on the void which had existed between the Administration and the Alumni Association. The sentiments expressed by both were those of a desire for cooperation, regret for those differences of the past, and a sincere desire to work together for a greater VPI. Mr. Rice, as one who had unwillingly, but because of conviction and principle, represented the opposition of alumni to the Administration, replied in the same spirit of cooperation. With Tom Rice appearing reconciled at last, Mr. J. Ambler Johnston spoke for all present when he said, "This morning, mine eyes have seen the glory."

Later, in a *Techgram* column, Pritchard said Rice challenged the University administration and all alumni/alumnae to work in harmony.

They spoke of the need for closer cooperation, better communications, and unity of purpose through intelligent, long-range planning.[14]

Ambler Johnston returned to Richmond that afternoon. The next day, he wrote a brief note to Marshall Hahn:

> Things went so well at the Alumni Board meeting I can't wait for Monday—stenographer, etc.—but came to the office (instead of church) to get this off so you would have it Monday.
>
> 1. Thursday night so many more there that we had a "bull" session which laid the groundwork....
>
> 2. Friday, in full session the wind blew in the direction outlined in the two documents. I wish you could have been behind a curtain and, unseen, heard it all.
>
> 3. Saturday—Brandt and Dean made excellent presentations, after which Tom Rice caused me to say "mine eyes have seen the glory."[15]

Hahn, who was off on a speaking tour, later wrote Johnston that he also had written to Tom Rice to follow up on Rice's "statesmanlike and courageous move." All of the reports he had heard, Hahn said, "confirm both your favorable impression of the results of the Alumni Board meeting and your very significant contribution to the favorable outcome." Ambler Johnston had written, too, to Warren Brandt that Sunday, for in the following week Brandt responded with a thank-you note. Brandt wrote that he hoped the discussions "prove to be fruitful" in improving alumni-administration relationships, and he added, "I felt that Tom Rice stood tall in making the courageous and excellent statement which he did."[16]

The June 1968 *Techgram* carried a brief report from Alumni President Harry Gustin on Tom Hall's study and recommendations, as a result of which, Gustin said, the Association could expect "the early implementation of the recommendations, many of which are aimed at developing more effective cooperation between the Association and the University." Gustin also announced at that board meeting, however, that because of the growing demands of his professional work, he would not be able to serve a second year as president. In 1968, therefore, Charles O. Gordon became Association president.

14.7 Charles O. Gordon ('42)—Charles O. Gordon Sr. stands with Gene Rowe in the foremost ranks of enthusiastic and devoted alumni. He enrolled at VPI in 1938, from the family farm near Marion, and left an outstanding student record in industrial engineering. He became an officer in the Corps and was active in the German Club, then a formal dance club. After graduation in 1942, he went into the Army and was a glider pilot in the invasion of German-occupied France. He left the service a major and a much-decorated veteran, awarded the Silver Star, the Distinguished Flying Cross, and the Air Medal.

After the war, his father, who had long been associated with the Empress Furniture Co. in Johnson City, Tennessee, sold his interest in Empress, and father and son established Gordon's Inc., a new furniture manufacturing company. The new firm prospered, and young Gordon soon put all of the engineering and leaderships skills he had acquired at VPI to good use—laying out the plant site, grading, developing specifications, overseeing construction, installing equipment, employing a work force, and so on. Before long, Gordon's Inc. acquired a reputation for quality products at reasonable prices. In later years, the Gordons added other ventures, including an independent soft drink bottling company and another firm merchandising such products for the outdoorsman as boats and camping equipment. The eldest of his six children, Charles Jr., also an alumnus of Virginia Tech, took over the management of Gordon's Inc. when Gordon Sr. retired in 1983.

The contributions of Charlie Gordon—"Mr. VPI"—to Virginia Tech are legion. He was one of the alumni who helped plan, fund, and construct the war memorial at the head of the Drill Field, with its beautiful chapel and tall pylons. One of the organizers of the Student Aid Association, which funds athletic scholarships, he served as its president; and some years ago he and his wife, Evelyn, endowed an annual athletic scholarship. He served as president, and was named an honorary life member, of the Alumni Association Board. In 1973 he purchased the land on which the German Club Manor was subsequently constructed (see box 18.5). Beginning in 1976 he served two four-year terms on the University's Board of Visitors, and in 1981-1983 he was rector. In recognition of his service, in 1985 the University awarded him the Ruffner Medal. In 1999 he was a member of the first cohort of College of Engineering alumni to be inducted into the Academy of Engineering Excellence, and a professorship in the College bears his name.

Alumni Giving at a Land-grant University

Tom Rice's evident reconciliation with Marshall Hahn & Co. on that spring weekend in 1968, almost four years after the Corps decision, largely marked the end of the divisiveness and rancor among VPI alumni that had developed in its wake. It certainly helped heal the breach within the Alumni Association Board.

In the years that followed, the Association proved an increasingly important source of financial and other support as Marshall Hahn's VPI emerged as Virginia Polytechnic Institute and State University. The year 1972 saw contributions from private sources hit all-time high figures. More than 7,000 alumni that year contributed a total of $285,000 for the Alumni Annual Fund. In addition, the Virginia Tech Student Aid Association received $302,000 that year—another record high—for athletic scholarships.[17]

In spring 1973, at about the time the 1972 figures were announced, President Hahn spoke of the "improved quality of life" that he envisioned both on campus and off—enhanced programs for students at the Blacksburg campus and, moreover, new roles the University could take on to benefit citizens in the state at large. For all such efforts, he foresaw what he termed "the need for substantially increased private funds."[18]

The year 1973, too, saw new all-time high figures. Nearly 10,000 people that year contributed a total (when combined with employers' matching gifts) of $342,000 for the Alumni Annual Fund, and the Student Aid Association received $351,000.[19] These figures were far higher than those a decade earlier, when Marshall Hahn took on the presidency. By the late 1960s and early 1970s, the University had rapidly rising numbers of alumni, though the new recruits of the Hahn years had been out of school for only a short time and did not yet have the resources that many of their elders had.

In the early 1970s, participation in alumni giving to Virginia Tech was on a sharp rise, as were dollar contributions. The numbers were beginning to approximate Hahn's sense of the importance of private giving, especially from alumni, to make the University ever stronger—more able to function effectively regardless of the state's contributions and more able to undertake new initiatives that made it a better institution for a land-grant school's various constituencies, on campus and off.

[1] *Techgram*, May 1967.

[2] Contributions in 1963, from 5,200 donors, had totaled $146,300. As of November 17, contributions in 1964 totaled only about $70,800, from only 2,291 alumni.

[3] Dr. Hahn's letter to Gene Rowe had been drafted by Craig Fabian, who also had talked it over with Mark Oliver before Hahn sent it to Rowe. Rowe responded some weeks later; he had been working with Jack Bates (John W. Bates Jr., a real estate executive and alumni leader) in Richmond, he said, and he and Jim Cargill had agreed that, subject to Board approval, Rowe would stand for another term (Hahn letter, 5 February 1964; Rowe letter, 10 March 1964).

[4] Cargill letter to Rowe, 10 September 1964.

[5] Hahn letter, 23 January 1967.

[6] Rowe letter, 25 August 1967.

[7] Rowe letter, 2 October 1967; Hahn letter, 4 October 1967.

[8] Hahn papers, 1968.

[9] Ross letter, Hahn papers, 1967; council minutes, 13 June 1967.

[10] Charlie Gordon, the furniture manufacturer from Johnson City, Tennessee, and W. E. "Ernie" Norcross, a Bristol attorney, were elected first and second vice presidents. Lem Pritchard was named secretary-treasurer (Willey letter, 10 July 1967; Hahn letter, 17 July 1967).

[11] Gustin was a native of Woodstock, Ontario, Canada. An economics major at VPI, he had been a member of the German Club and of the regimental staff of the Corps, and then he went to the University of Virginia for his law degree. He had served in the Air Force during World War II, attaining the rank of captain. He and his wife Esther and their three children lived in Norfolk, where he was a senior member of the law firm Taylor, Gustin, Harris, Fears and Davis.

[12] Minutes, 3 November 1967; Gustin letter, 6 March 1968; Hahn letter, 12 March 1968.

[13] Harry Gustin convened the meeting Friday afternoon, May 24. Those present, according to Pritchard's minutes, were Jack Bates, Ping Betts, Jim Cargill, Graham Claytor, Bill Darnell, Vic duPont, Guy Furr, Bob Goodykoontz, Charlie Gordon, Charlie Harris, J. G. Hawkins, Ambler Johnston, Doug Petty, and Tom Rice. Lem Pritchard and Norene Essary were there for the Alumni Office staff. Dean Wilson Bell, whose appointment as the university's development director already had been announced, was an invited guest.

[14] Minutes, 24–25 May 1968; *Techgram*, July 1968.

[15] Johnston letter, 28 May 1968.

[16] Hahn letter, 3 June 1968; Brandt letter, 29 May 1968.

[17] *Techgram*, April 1973.

[18] *Techgram*, May 1973.

[19] *Techgram*, April 1974.

15: University Governance—Toward a Faculty Senate

When Marshall Hahn returned to VPI as president in 1962, the school's principal institutional planning and governance body was the Academic Council. It was an advisory group—the VPI president was by no means compelled to accept its decisions or follow its recommendations—but it was called upon to handle a wide array of academic matters.

In Walter Newman's presidency, the centralized authority in the president's office tended to be fairly obvious, but Marshall Hahn's methods were subtler. His skill and finesse in his relationships with those with whom he worked were legendary. When he presided over Council meetings, he seemed to have little difficulty in shaping Council consensus along the lines of his own objectives.

The emergence of the issue of a faculty senate came in the larger context of relations between the new president and the growing faculty. The report of the SACS' visiting committee in autumn 1966 near the end of the VPI self-study had found it remarkable that President Hahn was able to generate as much support as he had for the changes taking place at VPI.

The president no doubt commanded strong support among a major component of the faculty, but he—or his administrative style—also had detractors. Some viewed the president as making too many decisions without adequate consultation with the faculty. Dr. Coyt Wilson, years later, recalled that a significant number of the faculty felt Dr. Hahn's leadership was a bit too "high handed," though even they acknowledged that he was unusually effective in Richmond. He secured money for new positions, money for larger raises, money for better facilities.

Partly it was a question of style, partly one of process, and partly one of substance. People who were delighted at the direction the president was taking the institution could nonetheless take the position that he moved too fast—or not fast enough. Even if in agreement on all else, they could feel that their voices were not being heard—or that there was no mechanism in place to guarantee them access to the decision-making process. To be sure, in any case, a person with great power is not to be taken lightly, and Marshall Hahn had a way of keeping track of what was going on and urging that various things be changed. Moreover, as the school grew in size and complexity, and rapid change continued to unfold, it became increasingly clear that—at some points or on some issues, at least—old ways no longer sufficed to get things done expeditiously and well.

Academic Council

In autumn 1966, when university governance became a topic of considerable interest, the Academic Council was composed of Dr. Hahn and his major leadership group—including vice-president Warren Brandt, chief finance man Stuart Cassell, the dean of students and the commandant of cadets, plus the academic deans and at least one faculty representative from each college.[1]

In plain fact, the Council was overburdened. Curriculum changes, course proposals, or anything else concerned with VPI's academic programs had to clear the Council before they could be implemented. So did proposed changes in student life programs. With all the changes taking place on campus, the Council agenda lengthened markedly. Under less skillful leadership, the Academic Council workload well might have been overwhelming, and indeed it became ever more so.

Hahn and his colleagues usually managed to move through it all with dispatch—and usually without making too many people too unhappy. Thus, when Dean Burchard began making wholesale changes in the curriculum of the College of Architecture, he depended heavily on Dr. Hahn's assistance to win approval. "The way I got it all through," he recalled later, "was to convince Marshall Hahn that it all added up to a coherent program. Marshall took it from there, and we didn't have any trouble."

In early 1966, Professor Bill McCubbin and the Arts and Sciences curriculum committee submitted the proposed curriculum for a health and physical education major. Dean Malpass and the Arts and Sciences curriculum committee proposed a new core curriculum for all undergraduates. The other colleges, too, sought to expand and strengthen their curricula. It was all necessary. And it was all too much. The workload grew heavier, month by month, and as 1966 progressed, it became clear that a better mechanism was needed for faculty input on academic matters before they reached Academic Council. On September 20, the Council decided to change its name. On a motion by Dean Malpass, it redesignated itself the University Council.[2] Then it moved to create a faculty senate.

15.1 President Hahn and the VPI faculty—Marshall Hahn knew his faculty members well, individually, by name. (With his phenomenal memory, he also had little trouble remembering the names of spouses and children, something that often astonished people.) Not long after he became president, he began a practice of visiting one of the academic departments each month to talk with the department head and get to know the faculty there better. Later, he began writing formal memoranda following such visits, suggesting improvements, and sent them to the appropriate vice president or other responsible officer. Despite Hahn's efforts to become acquainted with the individual faculty and the multiplicity of units, there was in the central administration—among some members of the president's staff, at least—a touch of an adversarial relationship, Marshall Hahn & Co. versus the faculty.

Looking back years later, Dr. Hahn acknowledged as much. Really, he said, there were three groups—the older faculty who had been at VPI for some years; the newer faculty, "the very bright, very aggressive new people" whom Hahn, Brandt, and the deans and department heads were recruiting as rapidly as possible; and the people in the central administration.

Each had a differing perspective of institutional realities and potential; Hahn suggested that the administration's perception was somewhere in between. Some people wanted to see VPI become a Harvard, an MIT, or a University of Texas overnight, and it just wasn't in the cards; others found the rapid changes in which they were immersed threatening. But it wasn't clear-cut; some in each group were supportive of Hahn's leadership and the course he set for VPI's development as a comprehensive university. In any event, the president wasn't ready to turn over the reins completely; "a benevolent autocracy is a more efficient organization," Hahn observed with some levity (Hahn interview, 10 February 1990).

Calls for a Faculty Senate

At a meeting in November 1966 in Dr. Hahn's office, University Council unanimously approved a motion by Warren Brandt that a faculty senate be organized at VPI—"to make recommendations to University Council on University matters relating to academic affairs"—to become operational after a constitution and by-laws and been drafted, approved by the faculty, accepted by the Council, and subsequently approved by the Board of Visitors. Also approved were motions by Dr. Brandt to create a twelve-member steering committee from the faculties of the six colleges and to write such a constitution.[3]

Faculty sentiment for greater input into the formulation of academic programs and policies had developed steadily as the magnitude of the institutional changes generated by President Hahn and Dr. Brandt became increasingly clear. VPI faculty leaders had made sure that a strong recommendation for a faculty senate as an integral part of the governance system came through the 1965–1966 University Self-Study. Such a body would be concerned with "all matters of academic interest." The visiting committee of the Southern Association of Colleges and Schools similarly stressed the desirability of a school-wide faculty group primarily concerned with academic policies. The VPI Chapter of the American Association of University Professors strongly supported the development of a faculty senate, something it stated in a resolution adopted in November 1966.

In a national context, a number of college and university faculty members had affiliated with labor organizations and were engaged in collective bargaining. Although there appeared to be little sentiment for such an approach at VPI, Dr. Hahn and Dr. Brandt knew well that, as more and more faculty members were recruited from some of the stronger universities around the country, it would not be long before they insisted upon greater involvement in institutional governance. In part, then, Dr. Brandt's participation reflected his perception that, with the effort to develop a faculty senate gaining momentum, he and the president should join the parade so they could influence the outcome.

Some of Warren Brandt's thinking comes through the records. He sent Hahn a note early on suggesting that the best thing to do was work with the faculty and guide the development of a mechanism for greater faculty input so that it would be manageable. At a meeting of the Council of Deans in December 1966, Brandt emphasized the need for a faculty committee to which to refer such matters as tenure appeal and faculty dismissals. The group decided to define guidelines under which such a committee should act and get them properly incorporated into a faculty senate organization when it was formed. The Committee on Reconciliation, built into the Faculty Senate structure, was the eventual result.

Steering Committee and Interface Committee

Members of the Steering Committee were elected in December 1966 by the faculties of the respective colleges, pursuant to the University Council resolution.[4] Wybe Kroontje was elected to chair the Steering Committee. A bundle of energy, Kroontje became a driving force behind the Committee's deliberations. Even so, it was nearly three years before the Steering Committee and a University Council-Faculty Senate Interface Committee (chaired by Warren Brandt) came up with a proposed constitution for a Faculty Senate. While they were about it, they also had to put together a constitution for University Council, so that it would intermesh effectively with the new Faculty Senate. Early on, they decided it would be a "pure" faculty senate, composed entirely of faculty members.

Among the more difficult points at issue was Faculty Senate representation on University Council. Kroontje and his faculty colleagues proposed that fourteen representatives of the Faculty Senate (then envisioned to have a membership of about forty) sit on University Council. Warren Brandt, speaking for the administration, proposed that only one person directly represent the Faculty Senate on the Council, and other faculty representatives would come directly from the collegiate faculty associations. The two sides were hung up on the issue for some time. In the University Council Constitution, as it was ultimately approved, the numbers were six Faculty Senate representatives plus one faculty member elected by the faculty of each college, to be elected for three-year terms, staggered so that one-third were elected each year, as well as two administrators without a vote.[5]

Civil engineering professor George Gray was secretary of the Interface Committee, and he later became the second president of the Faculty Senate, following Wybe Kroontje. Years later, in retirement, Gray remembered long, wearisome days working across the summer as secretary of the committee. They met "twice a week"—Dr. Brandt, Dr. Kroontje, and the others—"to thrash out...our sense of how it should be, raising questions...of specific working [arrangements], I copiously taking notes, go back to the office and type it all out again, run it off, and have fresh copies to start with the next day."[6]

The Interface Committee worked with certain clear ground rules as it spliced together recognition of the president's ultimate authority and the faculty's need to have an institutionalized means of input. "There was never any doubt that the president of the University was the responsible leader of the University," Gray recalled many years later. The president "had to accept the responsibility, regardless," and there was a "sense of carefulness on his part not to give the faculty complete autonomy, no question about it." On the other side, Gray continued, "There was a lot of activity on the part of the AAUP to demand autonomy, authority, and to unionize the faculty," efforts that "both helped and hindered, because Marshall and Warren approached the formation of [the faculty senate] with caution." Hahn and Brandt "didn't want to encourage the faculty to take off and run the University, [but] on the other hand they recognized that unless they gave the faculty some responsibility in the university family, some voice, some recognition, some input into decision making…the faculty [might] turn to unionism."

A New System of Governance

In spring 1969, the VPI faculty overwhelmingly approved the proposed constitution and by-laws for a Faculty Senate and for University Council. In a unanimous vote, University Council promptly approved the documents and recommended that they be submitted to the Board of Visitors for final approval. The Board in turn gave its prompt approval as well as its congratulations.[7] The new governance system—the University Council, four subsidiary commissions, and the Faculty Senate—became effective September 1, 1969.

The formal development of the Faculty Senate required a top-to-bottom overhaul of the University committees that had existed prior to its organization. One of the innovative aspects of the new system was the commissions, reporting to University Council. Council, of course, could refer questions or concerns to the appropriate commission for extensive analysis or debate. If there was a significant matter of faculty concern, it similarly was referred to the Faculty Senate for consideration.

The four commissions were Undergraduate Studies, Research and Graduate Studies, Faculty Affairs, and Student Affairs. They were composed of upper-level administrators, representatives of the respective colleges, Faculty Senate representatives, and students. The vice president for academic affairs chaired the Commission on Undergraduate Studies, and the dean of the Graduate School chaired the Commission on Research and Graduate Studies. The vice president of the Faculty Senate was chairman of the Commission on Faculty Affairs, and the vice president for student affairs chaired the Commission on Student Affairs. The various university committees reported to one or another of the commissions. A number of student organizations, such as the Publications Board or the Interdormitory Councils, were directly represented on the Commission on Student Affairs.

The new governance system thus required the participation of all components of the University's leadership, be they faculty, administrators, or students. It was time-consuming; perhaps it was designed to be. Marshall Hahn, looking back twenty-plus years later, suggested that, for a university—a community of scholars—to progress, "you have got to get the input of a lot of people, and you can't get input without consuming their time."[8]

Recalling the situation that prevailed at VPI in the late 1960s, Hahn explained that "what I was trying to do—and I think, while it resulted in a somewhat cumbersome structure, it was one that did work—was strike a balance where you achieved a high level of faculty input," but the management of the institution "still had the ability" to manage it. "We didn't lose control, as many institutions have, and yet," he observed, "there was a well-balanced input from the faculty, and a generally…favorable reception from the faculty to the structure."[9]

In the decades since 1969, the governance structure has been considerably modified. But the foundations laid at that time have proved strong and durable. Wybe Kroontje, the first Faculty Senate president, was an activist, intent upon pushing faculty causes forward as rapidly as possible. (So much so, George Gray recalls, that Hahn and Brandt for a time had real reservations about the system.) Gray was much more low-key; "I was not so aggressive; we let the faculty play the game and grow with the organization," he explained. If members of the Faculty Senate were "responsible, they would get more attention, more authority," thought Gray. "The Faculty Senate initially was intended to be advisory," Gray said; "they had to earn their way." It "has grown very well," he concluded, and proved a "responsible group."[10]

Former president Hahn looks back with a good deal of respect for both Wybe Kroontje and George Gray. "Both made very significant contributions," he has said. They "were there at particularly important times."[11]

---

[1] Members of the Academic Council included the chief admissions officer; dean of students Jim Dean; General M. W. Schewe, commandant of cadets; and the academic deans—Wilson Bell, Agriculture; Charles Burchard, Architecture; Les Malpass, Arts and Sciences; Bill Mitchell, Business; and Willis Worcester, Engineering. The faculty representatives were George Litton, Agriculture; H. A. Elarth, Architecture; Luther Brice and T. F. Tilghman, Arts and Sciences; Otis Hall, Business; George Gray and Roger Smith, Engineering; and Oris Glisson, Home Economics.

[2] Academic Council minutes, 20 September 1966.

[3] University Council minutes, 7 November 1966.

[4] The members of the Steering Committee were W. L. "Hoot" Gibson, Maynard C. Heckel, and Wybe Kroontje from Agriculture; Harland W. Westermann from Architecture; Weldon A. Brown, Wallace D. Lowry, and Leonard McFadden from Arts and Sciences; Carl W. Allen from Business; Dan Frederick, C. H. "Huey" Long, and Robert H. Miller from Engineering; and Esther A. Martin from

Home Economics. Carl Allen, an economist, and Dan Frederick, from engineering mechanics, already served on University Council. A number of other faculty representatives on University Council also worked with the Steering Committee.

[5] Kroontje interview; University Council/Faculty Senate Constitution and By-Laws, April 1969.

[6] Gray interview, 15 May 1989. The Interface Committee included—in addition to Brandt and Gray—Wilson Bell, Dean Fred Bull, Hoot Gibson, Tom Gilmer, Huey Long, Wally Lowry, Esther Martin, Dean Jim Martin, Dean Bill Mitchell, and Harland Westermann.

[7] Minutes, 14 April 1969.

[8] Hahn interview, 10 February 1990.

[9] Ibid.

[10] Gray interview, 15 May 1989.

[11] Hahn interview, 10 February 1990.

16: Changes in Student Population and Student Policy, 1966–1974

Immediately upon assuming the presidency of VPI, Marshall Hahn set out to upgrade the quality of faculty as he increased their number. He did the same with regard to students. Within five years into his presidency, moreover, the key policy changes regarding Radford College and the Corps of Cadets were seeing dramatic results, and the changes in the student population continued to build through the late 1960s and into the 1970s. Year after year, the administration found that it had new policy decisions, large and small, to make. These included the inauguration of a new marching band, the recognition of fraternities and sororities, and the appropriate response to student unrest.

In the new regime, the proportion of civilian students would climb. There would be far more students than before—and far more women among them. Many of the new students would come seeking to take advantage of such traditional curricular strengths as engineering and business. Many, however, would come to follow the new programs of study that were opening up in the humanities and social sciences. Moreover, just as the female percentage could be expected to rise, so could the numbers of African American students. While there would continue to be a large proportion of white men taking classes, and their actual numbers would sharply rise, their numerical dominance would decline— a little on race, a lot on gender. In the new university environment, moreover, with its enhanced emphasis on research, the graduate population would grow as well. Although undergraduates would continue to predominate, it would be by a diminishing amount. In every respect, the student population of the 1970s could be expected to diverge from the norms of the past. The trends were evident from early on, and they were well in place by Marshall Hahn's fifth year as president.

President Hahn and Student Life

It continued to be true at VPI that most students were undergraduates, and most undergraduates lived on campus. In various ways, President Hahn tried to keep his hand on the pulse of the student population. Years later, David Hill (who was in the office of the dean of students for much of the Hahn presidency after 1966) remembered Hahn's easy relationships with individual students. "He could charm them to death, especially because of his memory," Hill recalled. "He could pick up on [points of discussion] and remember all of the details."[1]

Hahn early on began periodic meetings with student leaders to maintain personal contact with them and hear student concerns. At first, he met periodically, usually quarterly, with student leaders in his office. In spring 1966, however, he moved the meeting to the auditorium of Commerce Hall (now the old section of Pamplin Hall) and attempted to enlarge the group discussion. Initially, he did not have much success.

That fall, Hahn wrote to Garland Rigney, the first president of the Student Government Association, and a group of other student leaders suggesting that he meet with them—as well as representatives of the *Virginia Tech*, the student newspaper—in an open meeting that anyone could attend. Dr. Brandt, Mr. Cassell, and other selected members of the staff also were asked to attend. The meeting attracted a scattered group of interested spectators in addition to the student leaders and members of the student press. Dr. Hahn responded directly to questions. Often he asked an appropriate member of his staff to elaborate. The next year, in autumn 1967, the president's open meeting with student leaders was expanded even more, and WUVT, the student radio station, broadcasted it live. By this time, each of the deans also was invited to participate and respond to questions.

One question that interested the students was the rationale for a 10 percent charge on each ticket sold for concerts in the coliseum. Dr. Hahn explained that it was to cover direct cost of using the building in the evening (heat, light, janitorial services), plus debt service. When more difficult issues began to surface, the crowds at the president's quarterly student meetings grew considerably larger.

Many involved some aspect of residence hall life, with food perhaps the most frequent issue—dining hall policies, the quality of food, and the service. In 1967, a hot issue emerged after a student complained of finding a cockroach in his food. A photograph was sent to the Roanoke newspapers for publication, followed up by a letter to the editor about VPI's terrible food service and the inability of on-campus students to obtain meals elsewhere—or else pay twice, since meal plan fees were required for all dorm students. Improvements in both quality and service undoubtedly were made in the dining halls, within funding limitations. Income from student meal plan fees had to pay debt service on the

16.1 Tuition-free enrollment—Most Tech students in the 1960s did not pay tuition. In fact, from the late 1940s into the early 1980s, Virginia Tech charged in-state undergraduates no tuition. In 1967–1968, all students paid what was called a "university fee" of $140, and out-of-state students paid an additional $140 quarterly "tuition fee." In 1968, the school initiated a student activities fee of $15 per quarter and doubled the health fee to $10 per quarter. The health fee was designed to cover the rising costs of running the student infirmary, and the new activities fee was approved not only to pay for various student activities but also to contribute toward the enormous costs of renovating Squires Student Center. (*Techgram*, April 1968; William Charbonneau, "Tuition at Tech, 1872–1998," in Wallenstein, *Essays, Fall 1998*)

Many state schools, including Virginia, historically had some program of "state students," a finite number of grants to in-state students. A few years after World War II, VPI universalized this practice. Yet, across the nation, in the late 1960s and early 1970s, this legacy of free tuition was coming under attack, as states cut back on the extent to which they were able and willing to cover as much of the costs of instruction as had been the practice in the past. For example, the University of Connecticut, a northern land-grant school, began charging tuition in 1971–1972. Virginia Tech raised its fees but continued beyond the Hahn years to levy no separate tuition charge for in-state students. (Wallenstein, *From Slave South to New South*, 69–70, 164–66; George M. Kelley, "Higher Tuition Fees Detrimental to Education, Council Claims," *Roanoke Times*, 6 January 1972: 27; Terry Ryan, "College Tuition Skyrockets," *Roanoke Times*, 6 March 1972: 1)

buildings as well as food cost and dining hall operations. The controversy simmered for some time, and at one point an organized student boycott of all dining hall food for an evening meal had the support of the Student Government Association.[2]

Dr. Hahn had a habit of periodically visiting the dining halls, unannounced, to eat with students and to see (and taste) for himself what the food and the dining hall environment were like. Often, Stuart Cassell or Warren Brandt accompanied him. The president also liked to make unscheduled visits in the residence halls and talk informally with students he happened upon. As David Hill recalled years later, "he would call up and send shudders through [the staff]; 'I've got two hours this afternoon and I want to walk through a residence hall,' he would say, and off we would go." Hahn went to keep in touch with the students, and he wanted to see for himself what things were like. "If he saw something he didn't like, he would get you to correct it."[3]

Black Students—into Double Digits

On matters of race, Marshall Hahn was not Walter Newman, and the mid-1960s were not the 1940s or 1950s. Black students came to Blacksburg in 1966 and 1967, no longer just one or two or three at a time—as had been the case ever since Irving L. Peddrew III was admitted in 1953 to study electrical engineering—but suddenly in double digits. During the remainder of the 1950s, VPI had admitted seven more black students, all in engineering. The formula of "separate but equal" had become less exclusionary than before, but it was still in operation, and black students could not enroll at VPI for any program that was available at Virginia State College, the state's black land-grant school. Nor, through the 1950s, could they live on campus and in the barracks, even though, like other male undergraduates, they had to be in the Corps of Cadets their freshman and sophomore years. By the mid-1960s, all such restrictions vanished.

James D. Watkins, who came to VPI as a freshman in 1967, reveals both change and continuity on the racial front at Tech in the 1960s. When he arrived, the sound of "Dixie" seemed omnipresent; the Confederate flag hung from Cassell Coliseum; and black students in general—and black women in particular—were in short supply. During his freshman year, he and six other black students lived in O'Shaughnessy Hall, and all seven soon decided to transfer to another school, something Watkins has explained in terms of an overwhelmingly white campus in the South with "the Confederate flag and playing 'Dixie' and the fact that there weren't many black women here at the time." Moreover, "when we came to campus, there were no black athletes, that is no basketball players, and no football players. Jerry Gaines came in with me. He was the first black athlete, and he was in track." Watkins reported, "We had been told that the coaches here did not want black athletes." Well, he went on, if they "didn't want black athletes" at Tech, "when there were a lot of superstar black athletes, they certainly didn't want us here either."[4]

In the end, though, Watkins stuck it out, and he could see real change by the time he graduated in 1971. The most important change, one he had a major hand in organizing toward the end of his freshman year, was a black fraternity, Groove Phi Groove. The group got an off-campus house for parties, made contact with black women students at Radford and elsewhere, and began to create an alternate community for themselves. Groove Phi Groove therefore demonstrated how much was changing at VPI, yet it also reflected how little had changed and the considerable effort black students at the time put into bringing about more change. As for

16.2 Desegregation of white land-grant schools—The South's seventeen states, from Delaware to Oklahoma as well as from Florida to Texas, each had a dual system of education, including one land-grant school for whites and another for blacks. By 1965, the historically white schools—the land-grant schools and state universities alike—all admitted their first African American students. Some schools—among them Arkansas, Kentucky, Delaware, and West Virginia—did so easily by the mid-1950s, though it was in small numbers, without enthusiasm, and at first only at the graduate level. At some universities in the Deep South—for example, the University of Georgia—the first incidence of racial desegregation came with public pain, anger, and at least the threat of violence or of closing the school. By the late 1960s, nonetheless, this great transition was well under way. Among the historically white land-grant schools in the eleven states of the former Confederacy, VPI was the first to enroll a black undergraduate (Irving L. Peddrew III, in 1953) and the first to award a degree to a black undergraduate (Charlie L. Yates, in 1958). In March 2003, during a fiftieth-anniversary Black Alumni Reunion, Peddrew-Yates Residence Hall was dedicated in their honor.

academics, most of the time, he later recalled, he was the only black student in each class. Although, like all the eight black students who entered Tech in the 1950s, Watkins started out as an engineer, he had an option they did not. He switched to general science and then, having decided to go to dental school, majored in biology.

The puny numbers of black students at VPI—and the utter absence of black women among them—began to change in 1966. Six of the black students who enrolled at VPI that year were young women: Linda Adams, Jackie Butler, Linda Edmonds, Freddi Hairston, Marguerite Harper, and Chiquita Hudson. (From the school's origins in 1872, forty-nine years elapsed before the first white women enrolled; thirteen years went by between the first black male student at VPI and the first black women.) And, unlike their black male predecessors of the 1950s, all six lived on campus in the dormitories, whether Hillcrest or elsewhere.

Four of the six black women students of 1966 graduated from VPI. Chiquita Hudson, ill when she arrived as a freshman, died after that year ended. LaVerne "Freddi" Hairston, who, mid-way through her junior year, married a white student and moved to Minnesota, subsequently earned her bachelor's degree there. By the 1990s, as Dr. LaVerne Higgins, she served as business professor and academic administrator at LeMoyne College in upstate New York. Linda Adams, who came to Blacksburg as a junior after two years of study at VPI's Covington campus, earned a degree in statistics, class of 1968, and began a career with the US Census Bureau.

The other three graduated from Virginia Tech after four years. Graduating from VPI in 1970 were Jackie Butler, with a major in sociology, and Marguerite Harper, in history. Jackie Butler married a fellow black graduate of VPI, Eli Whitney Blackwell (mechanical engineering, '69). Marguerite Harper Scott went on to become an award-winning high school teacher. Linda Edmonds, who had planned to attend Hampton Institute, rather than a white school, graduated in clothing and textiles. She subsequently earned a Ph.D. in business ('79) from VPI; in the 1990s Dr. Linda Edmonds Turner was a professor and academic administrator at Dean College in Massachusetts; and in 2003 she was named president of the Urban College of Boston.[5]

Everything about Jackie Butler and Marguerite Harper embodied the new Virginia Tech. Not only were they female students, but they were

African American, and they majored in history and sociology, not engineering or, for that matter, such other curricula of long standing at VPI as home economics. Absolutely nothing of the sort could have happened before the 1960s.

Jackie Butler and Marguerite Harper did not just happen to come to VPI in 1966. They reflected the transformation of public policy across the state and the nation, as well as the new VPI. The partial desegregation that got under way in the 1950s could not suffice after 1964, when the Civil Rights Act was passed. Moreover, the school went out and secured a grant

16.3 The Rockefeller Foundation spurs desegregation—During fall 1965, President Hahn announced that VPI had been awarded a $100,000 grant by the Rockefeller Foundation for a new scholarship program designed to assist a number of "culturally disadvantaged" young people to go on to college. The initial four-year, $500 scholarships would be awarded to twenty-five selected students entering VPI in September 1966 and an additional twenty-five students entering in September 1967. The announcement indicated that additional funding would be sought for later phases of the program, which was designed to reach underprivileged youngsters in the Appalachian region, most of them white, as well as in eastern Virginia, most of them black. Students brought to VPI under the program also were to be assisted through existing loan funds, employment opportunities, and special counseling programs. The initial phase of the program was designed "to provide financial support for students of high academic ability who come from disadvantaged homes and are unable to afford college" (VPI release, dated 17 November 1965).

President Hahn said he was particularly pleased that Virginia Tech would be able to expand its scholarship programs with the Foundation grant. Such a program would "pay dividends in many ways," the president said. President Hahn and Dr. Brandt each wrote a warm, congratulatory letter to Dr. Randolph S. Thrush (head of the newly organized psychology/sociology department), who had prepared the grant proposal. A second grant from the Foundation, this one announced in May 1968, was for $250,000. Designed to continue the program through an additional five years, or through 1976, the second phase would assist students entering Tech in the years 1968 through 1972. President Hahn said the school would "at least match" the Rockefeller money. (*Techgram*, December 1965, May 1968; Christopher Johnston and William Charbonneau, "Virginia Tech's Rockefeller Foundation Grant," in Wallenstein, *Essays, Fall 1998*) from the Rockefeller Foundation that was designed, in large part, to attract black students to Blacksburg. Such scholarship assistance deflected black students like Linda Edmonds from black schools like Hampton Institute; without it, James Watkins would certainly not have come to VPI either. And it promoted President Hahn's vision of a university where no students were categorically excluded because of their gender or their racial identity. It was a people's university. Nor was it merely a matter of enrolling more black students, for, more and more, they became a part of campus culture, participating in it and changing it. By the late 1960s, black students were joining many of the clubs and teams on campus; Marguerite Harper, for example, was in student government.

Black students also began earning graduate degrees at Tech. In 1970, when eight students earned an M.S. in statistics, two of them were black students, Franklin McVie (who first enrolled in 1966) and Camilla Anita Brooks (who enrolled in 1968). Beginning in 1971–1972, a grant from the Ford Foundation and the American Society of Planning Officials funded twelve black graduate students in the College of Architecture's urban planning program.[6] Quite a number of people earning doctoral degrees in the 1970s—particularly in the College of Education, which was organized in 1971 (see chapter 19)—were African American. Among them was an educator from the area, Edwin L. Barnes ('76, Ed.D., vocational education).

Students versus Students, Students versus Administration

Southern schools with white traditions faced challenges from students—among them, Marguerite Harper and her black classmates at VPI—who objected when the band played "Dixie" at football games or the Confederate flag snapped in the wind. Black students at white schools encountered traditions they found objectionable, and whites were often bewildered when objections were registered.[7]

Over other issues as well, student unrest was not entirely a stranger to VPI in the late 1960s, though it tended to take more gentle forms there than on many campuses. Tensions developed, for example, over whether the campus infirmary should dispense contraceptives. In characteristic fashion, President Hahn proved a strong leader on such matters, whatever various individuals may have preferred for a policy outcome. Hahn took the position, as he remembered it, that the infirmary should "deal

16.4 Contest over a flag—Early one April morning in 1968, the flag detail, as usual, raised the flags of Virginia and the United States at Burruss Hall. Soon after 6 A.M., hours after the murder in Memphis of Martin Luther King Jr., a small interracial group of Tech students went to Burruss and lowered the flags to half-mast.

The *Virginia Tech* ran a story, "Students Stage Vigil at Burruss to Honor King," that told how the group stayed at their post at the flagpole to talk among themselves and to discuss issues with other students. One group member noted with approval afterward that they had occasioned considerable "thinking and talking." Around noon, however, a larger group of students forcibly raised the flags again. A short while later, President Lyndon Johnson directed that all US flags be lowered to half-mast. Math professor Ezra "Bud" Brown recalls a similar incident at LSU at the same time.

with medical emergencies and minor illnesses, and I didn't consider contraceptives falling into either category." Regarding the political considerations that did so much to shape his responses, he noted years later that he wasn't certain what position he might have taken "in a vacuum, but you had a Legislature, too." The "same faculty" who were writing letters calling for a change in policy, he went on, wanted more resources from the legislature for the university, including "higher salaries" for themselves, yet failed to consider what it "would have done to our appropriations...if we had started prescribing birth control pills in the infirmary with State funds."[8]

The nation's increasing division over the War in Vietnam heightened whatever unrest had emerged over other issues. The Vietnam War was long and costly, and thirty-six VPI students and alumni who died in that war have their names inscribed on the War Memorial. Through much of the decade of the 1960s, while student unrest rocked some campuses—notably Berkeley and Columbia—VPI remained largely serene. But in May 1970, student demonstrations at both VPI and the University of Virginia were front-page news. At Tech as elsewhere, there were other sources of unrest at the time—local issues of student policy and governance—and there were precursors. But the main events took place during the second week of May over events in Southeast Asia.

President Richard M. Nixon's widening of the Vietnam War—the incursion into Cambodia in May 1970—led to confrontations across the country, most notably at Kent State University, as opponents of the war demonstrated their fury, and military and law enforcement forces responded with violence. At Kent State University in Ohio, and at Jackson State College in Mississippi, young people were gunned down in hails of bullets fired by members of the National Guard or police. On Tuesday, May 5, President Hahn met, as he said at the time, with hundreds of students on the lawn at the Grove "and shared with them my own concerns and sadness." The "assembled students" asked that classes be dismissed that Thursday in memory of the dead at Kent State and for discussion of the widening war. Hahn promised to take the matter to the University Council. He did, and he also met again that Sunday evening, when "several hundred students again assembled on the lawn of the President's home."9

The events in May developed on top of earlier actions, and they came in a context in which the administration was fearful in light of warnings from the State Police and threats of arson that spring. After a hundred or so students disrupted a drill by the Corps of Cadets in April, the school had obtained an injunction—it named two professors and seven students—against interference with any authorized activities on campus. The next day, when news of the injunction reached the people at a "teach-in," a number of students marched on Burruss Hall demanding that it be rescinded. Later the Faculty Senate and the Student Senate both asked the administration to end the proceedings. And the administration did just that. President Hahn, together with attorney Allen Sowder, met with circuit court judge W. S. Jordan in his chambers in Christiansburg on May 11, and the judge agreed with their revised position and dismissed the injunction. Judge Jordan did so, though, with the express understanding that the administration could, if necessary, seek such an injunction again.10

That same day, things heated up on campus, as a continuing tussle between a substantial number of students and the major policy units reached an impasse. A group of students had insisted that the university send a telegram to President Nixon protesting the war policy in Southeast Asia, and the Hahn administration was having none of it—seeing taking any such a position as entirely out of order. Regardless, the Student Governing Association and the Graduate Assembly had proposed that students be given a number of options regarding their spring quarter courses. If they wished to go on strike—to protest the war in Asia and the deaths at Kent State—they might take a pass-fail grade in a class; take an incomplete grade; take their current grade in a class with a pledge to complete their work in the fall; or resign from the school without penalty. On Monday, the Commission on Undergraduate Studies adopted a narrower approach, recommending that students be allowed to defer exams until fall or resign from the school by the following Monday.

Students rejected what they termed the "watered down" version. That night, at about 4 A.M. Tuesday, twenty-three students occupied the architecture building, Cowgill Hall, where they issued a statement that expressed disappointment in the school's responses to their wishes regarding a strike. Shortly before 10 A.M., three school officials, including Architecture dean Charles Burchard, were let into the building. Dean Burchard assured the students that they could appear at the University Council meeting scheduled for that afternoon, and shortly after 11 A.M. the students left Cowgill, which then returned to normal. That afternoon, the campus was described as calm, although the word "strike" had been painted in red on various buildings, and state troopers were known to be just off campus in Blacksburg. At the meeting of the University Council, some of the twenty-three students from Cowgill did in fact attend, though President Hahn had told them that they would have to identify themselves and they would be subject to disciplinary action.

The meeting lasted more than six hours. Council largely adopted the Commission's recommendations. Students could resign "for reasons of conscience"—and thus escape failing grades—by the following Monday, but there would be no refund of university fees (the equivalent of tuition). All classes and other university activities would "continue as scheduled." (And professors would be barred from raising or lowering grades on the basis of class attendance.) In a provision that had not been part of the Commission's proposal, students were told that, if they chose to defer all exams, they would be considered as having resigned. Council's actions by no means settled the dispute.

The Takeover of Williams Hall, May 12-13, 1970

Sandy Hawthorne, president of the SGA, read the May 12 Council decision aloud to approximately 1,000 students gathered in front of Burruss Hall, and President Hahn informed the campus community over the local radio station. The Cowgill demonstrators had made it clear that, if Council rejected the students' strike plans, they planned to occupy another building. And indeed, shortly after the news went out, about 10 P.M., more than 100 protesters took over Williams Hall (home to the departments of English and mathematics), located adjacent to Burruss Hall. They took food and supplies with them, and they locked themselves in. Campus police closed the road around the Drill Field running past Burruss and Williams, but they took no other action through the next few hours.

A couple of hours after midnight, a student emerged from Williams, identifying himself as a reporter with the VPI student newspaper *Collegiate Times* (the new name of the old *Virginia Tech*), and carried a statement that, he said, came from demonstrators inside the building and set out "conditions for the return of the building" to the school administration: "We have occupied this building because of the unresponsive attitude of the VPI administration towards the Student Government Association strike proposals." The demands included that the University Council adopt the terms the SGA had framed for dealing with incomplete course work, as well as an amnesty for all students involved in demonstrations, including those at Cowgill and Williams.

During the night, as he recounted many years later, President Hahn spoke on the phone with Walter Ryland in the state attorney general's office in Richmond. Hahn has since recounted how he explained the need to act in a way that would avoid "violence or injury," maintain normal operations of the University, and bring to an end what he saw as a rapid series of "escalating disturbances." There had been blaring horns on campus late at night, phone calls threatening the use of bombs, and the breakout of occasional fires, as well as an incident when "a small number of students broke into the student personnel building in an effort to pour red paint (symbolizing blood) over the student records." Then came Cowgill Hall and, the very next night, Williams Hall. Cowgill was bad enough; Williams was worse; and who knew what might be next.

Jointly, as he recalled, Hahn and Ryland developed an approach that might work. They needed, as Hahn saw it, to find a way to "deal with the challenge of ending student disturbances without violating the rights of students to due process." Other universities had found that "if disciplinary procedures with due process were utilized, the students remained on campus leading to more disturbances. If the students were removed from the university campus immediately, the courts ordered their return because of lack of due process." Either way the cycle continued.[11]

The test of the new policy would soon be made. Students continued their occupation until dawn approached, but then the administration acted. The administration later explained: "The overriding concern…was to prevent violence and to make it possible for the university to continue operations. Williams Hall is the busiest classroom building on the campus. The possibility of violence occurring when students began arriving

16.5 "Taxpayers fed up with disorders at colleges"—In a press conference on Monday, 11 May 1970, Governor Linwood Holton recalled that students from a number of state-supported schools had converged on the General Assembly earlier that year asking for a substantial increase in funding for public colleges and universities—and they got it. Given the recent events at the University of Virginia, in particular, though, "the taxpayers," he said, are "mad," "ready to cut off appropriations," and students might want to keep taxpayer sentiment in mind when they expressed their dissent. The governor had been receiving "many calls…many letters," he said, and "people are saying bad things about students." One significant straw in the wind, he noted, was the recent call by the Virginia Farm Bureau Federation for a cut-off of state funds to colleges that had been disrupted by demonstrations. As for civil liberties, he insisted that, just as all students had a right to peaceful dissent, all students also had a "right of dissent from the dissenters." (Shelley Rolfe, "Holton Warns Protesters Taxpayers May Revolt," *Richmond Times-Dispatch*, 13 May 1970: A1; Wayne Farrar, "Taxpayers Fed up with Disorders at Colleges, Gov. Holton Warns," *Roanoke Times*, 13 May 1970: 13)

Later that week W. Roy Smith, the chairman of the Appropriations Committee in the Virginia House of Delegates, said he expected that his committee in particular, and the legislature in general, would be taking a hard look at state appropriations for campuses that were in turmoil. Smith insisted that taxpayers had the right to be assured that their funds "are not being squandered by students who do not study and teachers who do not teach." Moreover, if—perhaps as a result of student demonstrations or school closures—any school had smaller numbers of students or faculty the next year than had been the basis for the funding projections, then the governor, Smith pointed out, was authorized to withhold the appropriated funds. ("Prospects Grow for Squeeze on State Money for Colleges," *Roanoke Times*, 15 May 1970: 16; Melville Carico, "State Legislators Favor Firm Stand by Colleges," *Roanoke Times*, 16 May 1970: 1)

for 8:00 a.m. classes was very real, particularly since the building was sur-rounded by those sympathetic to its occupiers."

When police came onto the campus, there were at least sixty state troopers and local police, equipped with riot batons and accompanied by police dogs—Hahn insisted that there be a large enough force "to forestall any student resistance" and thus reduce the likelihood of injury to stu-dents. At about 6:25 A.M.., the occupants were ordered by loudspeaker out of Williams Hall, given ten minutes to vacate. No one left the building. Then a truck moved up, harpooned a locked door, and yanked it off. By the dozens, students walked (or, in some cases, were carried) out of the building and into two rented moving vans and a police paddy wagon. The students, as they left the building, were each handed a letter advising that they were "summarily suspended" from the university. The letter that morning of May 13 said:

> Because of your involvement in the occupation of Williams Hall, you are summarily suspended from the university.
> This is to advise you that you may make one trip to the campus to remove your personal belongings. Thereafter you will be regarded as a trespasser.

Briefly, some of the 100-plus people being arrested broke free of one moving van, as a student outside the truck opened its door and a number of people inside—estimates ran as few as four, as many as thirty—escaped. But then the door was closed again, and the three vehicles took their remaining cargo—107 people in all—off to the county jail, where they were booked and incarcerated.

Later that Wednesday, the arrested students were released on bail. At first, bail for trespassing was set at $500 cash or $1,000 in property, but county judge Kenneth I. Devore reduced those amounts. Out-of-state stu-dents had to put up $50 cash; in-state students were released on their own recognizance. By late afternoon, all had been released.

Meanwhile that day, President Hahn issued a statement (subsequent-ly published in the June issue of *Techgram*), described soon afterwards in the *Richmond Times-Dispatch* as "placing him in the forefront of major college administrators in Virginia publicly advocating stern resistance to disruptive student tactics." Hahn claimed that the occupying students had caused "significant damage" and had left behind "components for the manufacture of firebombs." He said that security personnel, including state police, would be remaining on campus "as long as necessary." And he said of the students who had been arrested at Williams Hall that they had "been notified that they may pick up their personal belongings on this campus and thereafter will be deemed trespassers."

Williams Hall, liberated by the occupying students, had been liberated in turn by the administration, restored to its more customary use as a classroom building. A second letter to the students who had occupied Williams Hall, three days after the first, detailed the rationale for the response to the takeover, and it also outlined students' right to appeal their suspensions (see box 16.6). As Hahn has noted, "the letter did its job and was upheld in federal district court in Roanoke." Beyond that, "The creative approach employed at Virginia Tech solved the problem [there] and became a template for other universities."

Feelings ran high. There was more than enough rage, and sadness, to go around. Hahn's statement was widely acclaimed, as were his actions, and he became a hero to many on campus and across the state. A representative letter to Dr. Hahn—dated May 14, from an alumnus of 1960—applauded the VPI president's response to the recent events on campus:

> I am proud of the action taken by you in arresting those persons occupying campus buildings illegally. Exercise of the right to dissent should not take away the right of the majority of students desiring to obtain a college education, nor should it allow destruction of the property of others.
>
> You have my support and I am sure the overwhelming majority of alumni share my attitude. You have shown yourself to be a leader among University Presidents since returning to V.P.I., and this latest action is a much needed step back to respect for the rights of all, not just a vocal minority.

Others, to be sure, decried what they saw as Hahn's heavy-handed response to the occupation of Williams Hall.

The students involved in the incident issued a response to President Hahn's account. In it they denied that there had been much damage, and they rejected the charge that they had contemplated the use of any kind of incendiary device—beyond candles in the event that the power was turned off. But a comparison of the two statements reveals common ground—some damage took place, certainly in the erection of barricades inside against the doors, but not a great deal, and some cleanup was required (students pointed out that, having had had to leave abruptly, they

16.6 President Hahn's letter to students who had occupied Williams Hall — Dr. Hahn's May 16 letter to suspended students, following up the short letter of May 13, was designed to contain campus unrest and address the question of due process—protect individual students as well as the wider university community:

As you were advised in my letter of May 13, 1970, a copy of which is enclosed, you have been summarily suspended from the university because of your involvement in the occupation of Williams Hall. This strong step was necessary to maintain public safety and to continue operations of the university. Because of continued campus unrest this suspension must stand as long as there is potential disruption of the normal operations of the university.

In addition, it appears you may be in violation of the following prohibitions of University Policies for Student Life, specifically violation of the following prohibitions appearing on page 8 of the publication, *University Policies for Student Life 1969–70:*

Direct disobedience of orders by authorized university officials;

Actions which interfere with the rights of other members of the university community, including the disruption of essential functions of the university;

Entering or being present in locked university buildings without proper authority.

Disciplinary proceedings will be administered as set forth on page 13 of the above publication with due process and protection of individual rights and freedoms. These proceedings will be administered by the Vice President of Student Affairs and his designated

had had no opportunity to complete any cleanup); also, the continuing demand for amnesty specified a third, earlier occurrence, not played up in the University's version, at the student records office. Where there was no common ground was whether the occupation of a campus building—let alone shutting the school down—was an acceptable tactic in the expression of dissent, no matter how much a matter of conscience.

As for the degree of division on campus, Hahn later pointed to one measure of support for his actions. "Faculty morale and attitude were best

staff. In accordance with University Policies for Student Life you may request that your case be considered by a panel of faculty, administrators and students.

Disciplinary proceedings will be initiated as soon as possible consistent with maintenance of normal operations of the university and assurance of fair treatment of your case. You should contact the Vice President for Student Affairs to arrange a mutually convenient time for your disciplinary proceedings.

If you wish to waive in writing to the Vice President for Student Affairs your right to disciplinary proceedings as set forth in University Policies for Student Life, he will advise you immediately of the disciplinary action taken.

If you do not submit prior to June 6, 1970, a written request for disciplinary proceedings, the Vice President for Student Affairs will advise you of the disciplinary action taken.

After all the proceedings are completed, the university will provide appropriate arrangements and redress should any academic inequity remain as a result of being summarily suspended from the university.

The disciplinary appeals procedure is set forth on page 14 of the publication, *University Policies for Student Life 1969–70,* as follows [and here the relevant sections are quoted]:

The university regrets that your actions necessitate these proceedings.

Copies of the letter to each suspended student went as well to parents and/or guardians, the executive vice president, the vice president for academic affairs, the vice president for student affairs, and the registrar.

evidenced that next day at the meeting in Burruss Hall auditorium I called of the entire university faculty to ensure there was full understanding of the events of the previous evening. When I entered the auditorium I was given a strong and lasting standing ovation." Another incident, at a campus event not longer after, pointed up some reconciliation with the Corps of Cadets as a consequence of the events in May: Hahn found himself, to his great surprise, given an enthusiastic ovation by members of the Corps. He'd never expected to see that happen, he said. They'd never expected it either, was one response from the group.[12]

Feelings continued strong, even a third of a century later, whether it was (among Hahn's opponents) a former graduate student who still expressed disgust at Hahn or (among Hahn's supporters) Warren Strother's rueful statement that "it was a long spring" that year. What remained imprinted in Strother's mind was Hahn's sustained effort to see that no permanent damage come to either the institution or the dissenters who challenged his control of it. Countless faculty did what they could to see that students have an opportunity to make up final exams and complete their coursework that spring. Students were charged with misdemeanors, not felonies. And they were suspended from school, not expelled, and hearings established a timetable for their possible return to campus as students.

The next January, Jim Dean sent Marshall Hahn a memo to catch him up on the status of the students who had been suspended as a result of the Williams Hall incident. "Out of the 107 who were found guilty of trespass," Dean recounted, 100 were undergraduates. Three would not be permitted to return until spring quarter that year, but the other ninety-seven were eligible to return to campus that winter—and his figures showed that, so far, forty had done so. At least half of the returning "Williams Hall students" would be living on campus, Dean noted, and residence hall personnel would be "discretely" monitoring "their readjustment to University life."[13]

Years later, Hahn characterized his administration's actions when, regarding the larger context of student unrest at universities during that time, he noted: "those institutions that caved, rather than deal with it forthrightly, had much longer running problems. The institutions that dealt forthrightly and even-handedly, but firmly, put the problem behind them much sooner, I think, than the institutions that caved."[14]

In the biggest challenge to Marshall Hahn's presidency since the Corps of Cadets controversy in 1964, he had acted with characteristic decisiveness. Any and all among a number of considerations can explain the approach he took to the occupation of Williams Hall over the night of May 12–13, 1970. One could say that President Hahn had invested so much in building up the University that he was not about to see it threatened by its beneficiaries. One could say that, with one eye always on the state's political climate, more particularly on attitudes in the legislature, he was intent on protecting a public institution against attack from the outside—and therefore had to protect it from assault from within. One could say that his conservative tendencies controlled his responses. One could conclude, as he has said, that his primary concern was that bloodshed might erupt between one group of students and another—in particular, civilians and Corps members might not be safe from one another—and he could not chance such a development. Violence must be avoided, and the school would stay in full operation. It was, and it did.

Fraternities and Sororities?

Major student issues that emerged in the 1960s also involved the question of fraternities and sororities; access to alcohol; visiting privileges in the residence halls; and representation in university governance. Fraternities and sororities were not recognized or authorized by the University, although groups of students tended to get together and rent one of the older homes in or near Blacksburg and call themselves fraternities, complete even with Greek-letter signs. VPI officially had banned social fraternities back in the 1880s, and recurrent attempts to reestablish a Greek system had been unsuccessful.

President Hahn resisted the development of a fraternity/sorority system at VPI. In spring 1966, his point of view on the fraternity/sorority question was summarized in response to a letter from four students who identified themselves as Richard Emanuel, Vernon Elhart, Mark Londner, and Martin Levin. First, the president wrote, he was well aware of the "social problem" on the campus. The lack of adequate facilities for leisure activities, he observed, had prompted the $3 million renovation and expansion of Squires Student Center, about to get under way. As for fraternity/sorority policy, Dr. Hahn wrote, it seemed desirable to concentrate resources and personnel on developing expanded on-campus opportunities for many students, rather than on a Greek system for a smaller number. Moreover, if on-campus fraternity houses were constructed, they would be subject to all state regulations, including the ban against the serving of alcohol on state property, wrote Hahn. "This," therefore, "would mean programs much like those now being planned."[15]

But the matter did not go away, and eventually the administration adopted a new policy. First, various constituencies on campus worked through the implications and procedures of changing the old policy, and in May 1972 the Board of Visitors agreed that the traditional policy of non-recognition would no longer hold. As of July 1, 1972, a new era began, and fraternities and sororities were recognized as a legitimate, integral part of university life. First to gain recognition were Phi Delta Kappa and Pi Kappa Alpha, and many more soon followed.[16]

Gender, Equal Opportunity, and the Corps of Cadets

In at least two ways, it became clear that the 1964 decision to make participation in the Corps of Cadets voluntary for men left big questions unresolved. The 1964 compromise left the Highty-Tighties, the historical marching band, a monopoly of Corps members. And, while participation by men became voluntary, there was nothing voluntary about participation by women. They continued to be excluded, as they always had been. In the early 1970s, the administration revisited both of those issues.

In November 1972, President Hahn brought to the attention of the Board of Visitors an inquiry from the Department of Defense regarding a possible ROTC unit for women at VPI. The BOV agreed that, if women were admitted into ROTC, they would have to be members of the Corps of Cadets. Hahn went on to say that, in that event, they would have to live under the same twenty-four-hour-a-day military discipline as the men, separate housing would have to be made available, and they would have the right to join the Highty-Tighties marching band. In the end, the BOV approved the concept of women in the Corps, with the proviso that they be subject to the same round-the-clock regulations.

Toward the end of the 1972–1973 year, an announcement of a change in policy led two female students to decide to join the Corps. Both came from Air Force families, so both had some idea of military life, including, they said, the travel and the camaraderie. One was Deborah J. Noss, a junior in management, housing, and family development. The other was

Cheryl A. Butler, a freshman math major. One was white, the other black. Various details remained to be worked out—the design of their uniforms, for example—but they expected that incoming fall students would join them. In the meantime, they would spend six weeks that summer training at Tindale Air Force Base in Florida.[17]

Fall quarter 1973 brought a new look to the campus, as twenty-five women members of the Corps of Cadets—L Squadron—drilled in uniform. They lived together in a section of Monteith Hall, one of the Corps residence halls on the Upper Quad. One among them had chosen to be in the Corps without also being in ROTC; two were in Army ROTC; and twenty-two were in the Air Force ROTC. As the senior members of the new unit, Deborah Noss was the commander; a junior, Shirley Burnett, executive officer; and sophomore Cheryl Butler the administrative officer.[18]

The call for a new marching band came from both the administration and the students. The number of civilian students rapidly rose, and the number in the Corps kept slipping. The restriction of membership in the Highty-Tighties to members of the Corps of Cadets meant that an ever-increasing fraction—by the 1970s, the vast majority—of students found themselves excluded from participating in a marching band.

When the Virginia Tech football team played at Alabama in 1973, President Marshall Hahn and Vice-president Leslie Malpass watched two half-time shows—the Highty-Tighties and Alabama's far larger "Million Dollar Band." On the return trip, the story goes, Malpass said to Hahn, "If you want a big time football team, you're going to need a big time band." Hahn agreed, and, back in Blacksburg, Malpass told Tony Distler (department head of performing arts and communications) to start a new marching band. In September 1974, at a game against the University of Houston, the Marching Virginians, under the direction of Roger Heath, stepped onto the field at Lane Stadium. Tony Distler's voice boomed over the loudspeakers, "Ladies and gentlemen, we are happy to present the world's youngest university band, the Marching Virginians!" Civilians in the crowd greeted the new band and its performance that day with great enthusiasm—though the members of the Corps, the Highty-Tighties, and even many Corps alumni were said to have sat in "stone-faced silence."[19]

As early as fall 1971, the Highty-Tighties regimental band brought a women's drill team onto the football field. In spring 1975, near the end of the school year, the Highty-Tighties decided to admit women to the band itself. The Corps of Cadets included women, and those women could join the Highty-Tighties. As had been the case when the Corps itself began to admit women, two main considerations were at work. Women placed a claim on membership, and the Highty-Tighties needed reinforcements. The first two female members, it was reported, would be a freshman in engineering, H. Elizabeth Thompson, and a sophomore in animal science, Stephanie Hahn.[20]

Students and Student Life at the New VPI

Student life at Virginia Tech moved a great distance in the dozen years or so after Marshall Hahn returned to Blacksburg in 1962. The voyage from 1962 to 1975 was by no means always smooth, but the distance traversed was tremendous. Members of the Corps of Cadets might continue to try to lay a proprietary claim on the institution—as first inhabitants, the constituency accustomed to dominance, whose traditions ruled the domain—but, for good or ill, a set of major competing claims was also made. Female students as well as men claimed the institution; black students as well as white; graduate students as well as undergraduates; and, most of all, civilians as well as members of the Corps. Had the transformation been smoother, had it been uncontested, it would have been far less significant.

Cheryl Butler embodied the changes—and their complexity—at what, by the time she enrolled, had become Virginia Polytechnic Institute and State University. A black student on a historically white campus, and a female on what had long been an overwhelmingly male campus, she enrolled at Tech as a civilian. But then another opportunity presented itself, and after her freshman year she became a charter member of L Squadron, a full member of the Corps of Cadets. First, she participated in the river of new students that made Tech a more coeducational and multiracial institution. And then another barrier fell—the Corps of Cadets became for the first time entirely voluntary—and she left the civilian side to join the military.

A generation earlier, as a female math major, she might have attended the Radford College campus of VPI, but she could not have enrolled in Blacksburg. As a black student, however, she would have been barred from Radford, too, so she might have gone to Virginia State College, the state's other land-grant school. Dual changes that took place at VPI during her early childhood—policy changes regarding both gender and racial identity—made it possible for her to enroll at the Blacksburg school. One final policy change, late in Marshall Hahn's administration, permitted her to make yet another selection among her widening constellation of choices at the new VPI.

Students leaving Williams Hall, early in the morning of May 13, 1970, after their overnight takeover.

[1] Hill interview; *Techgram*, December 1971.

[2] SGA president William L. Coulborne Jr. letter to Hahn, 11 May 1967; Coulbourne letter to Hahn, 31 May 1967.

[3] Hahn papers, 1967; Hill interview.

[4] Kennelly interview with James D. Watkins.

[5] University archivist Tamara Kennelly's interviews with Turner, Blackwell, and Scott (like the one with Watkins) are available online at the website for Virginia Tech's Special Collections.

[6] *Techgram*, January 1972.

[7] Kennelly interviews with Scott and Watkins; letters in *Techgram*, December 1971.

[8] Hahn interview, 10 February 1990.

[9] Hahn memorandum to students, faculty, and staff, 19 May 1970.

[10] James W. Dean report about the disruption, 14 April 1970; *Techgram*, May 1970; Maurice Fliess, "Tech Injunction Lifted by Court," *Roanoke Times*, 12 May 1970: 20.

[11] The *Chronicle of Higher Education* carried a number of stories across the spring and summer of 1970 about universities' quest for a way to deal effectively with campus disturbances.

[11] Dean to Hahn, 11 January 1971.

[12] Hahn interview, 10 February 1990.

[14] Published accounts of the events of May include Ben Beagle, "Hahn's View: Dissent, Yes; Disruption, No," *Roanoke Times*, 14 May 1970, and Chad Runyon, "May 13, 1970: The Night the Students Took over Williams," *Collegiate Times*, 30 October 1992.

[15] Hahn letter, 15 March 1966. Dr. Dean routinely appeared at Alcoholic Beverage Control Board hearings in those years to oppose applications from local merchants or restaurant owners for ABC licenses, for either on- or off-premises sale of alcoholic beverages.

[16] *Context* 7 (spring 1973); Casmira-Anne Brown, "Greeks and Geeks: A Study of the Early Greek System at Virginia Tech," in Wallenstein, *Essays, Fall 1997*.

[17] *Techgram*, July 1973.

[18] *Techgram*, December 1973, July–August 1974. Special Collections has a lengthy interview (also available online) by Tamara Kennelly with Cheryl Butler McDonald that reveals much about the experiences of the first cohort of women in the Corps at Tech.

[19] Christine Staudt, "The Marching Bands of Virginia Tech," in Wallenstein, *Essays, Spring 1998*; Steven Palmer Robeson, "The Spirit of Tech: The Marching Virginians, 1974–1998," in Wallenstein, *Essays, Fall 1998*.

[20] *Techgram*, November 1971, May 1975.

17: Intercollegiate Athletics at a State University, 1967–1974

Virginia Tech athletics had any number of high points in the late 1960s and early 1970s. In 1967, for example, Frank Loria garnered All-American accolades—just as he had the year before—for a stellar season in football. The year before, future major leaguer Johnny Oates had brought a successful baseball season to a resounding conclusion when, in the bottom of the ninth inning, he hit a three-run homer that gave VPI a victory over ACC champion UNC. In the sports pages of the *Bugle* of the mid-to-late 1960s, one can see a transition in names for VPI teams. The school was often called Tech, rather than VPI, and the players were interchangeably the Gobblers, the Techmen, and the Hokies. The future, of course, lay with the Hokies.

Until well into the presidency of Hahn's predecessor, Walter Newman, athletic facilities at VPI were dismal and primitive, but that began to change before Newman stepped down, and it picked up momentum on Hahn's watch. By the mid-1960s, Tech had fine facilities in the major sports—Cassell Coliseum (as it would later be named, after Stuart Cassell) and Lane Stadium. During the Hahn years, other new facilities came along—a grasstex outdoor track in 1965, a new field house, a tennis pavilion.

In the second half of his presidency, as in the first, Dr. Hahn continued to see a need for the school's athletic programs to rise along with the academic ones. Speaking to the BOV in late 1972, and thinking in particular of football, he said that this would mean VPI would have to schedule tougher opponents. Anticipating larger crowds at home games, he urged adding 5,000 bleacher seats at Lane Stadium—where seating capacity at that time stood at 35,000—and eventually increasing the stadium's permanent seats to 50,000, together with an expansion of the Golden Hokie box. The BOV approved the concept.[1]

Athletics at Virginia Tech began to reflect the changing student population. Jerry Gaines, the first African American ever to compete for Virginia Tech, came to Blacksburg as a freshman in 1967. Before he graduated in 1971, he set a number of records for his performances on the track team. Only for a brief time was he Tech's sole black intercollegiate athlete, as black players soon changed the complexion of the men's basketball and football teams. Moreover, Tech began to field female teams as well, though such sports as women's basketball were club sports at first, without scholarships or significant other institutional support.

Football

In the 1970s, President Hahn played an active role in determining who coached the football team. He wanted a dominant team, and it was not happening fast enough. After six straight winning seasons, the team went 4–5–1 in 1969 and 5–6 in 1970. So, in December 1970, Jerry Claiborne—the winningest coach in school history, but whose last two years had been disappointing—was pressured to resign. Charlie Coffey was named the new football head coach, but Coffey ran into problems of his own. After going 4–7 in 1971, the team improved to 6–4–1 in 1972, but then came a disastrous season, 2–9, in 1973. Another change at the top made Jimmy Sharpe the head coach. Although 1974 was an improvement, with a 4–7 record, the next winning season did not come until 1975, when Tech went 8–3.[2]

Players wanted to win, coaches wanted to win, the school president wanted to see victories, and so did large numbers of alumni. If we forget the overall record, there's nonetheless much to see. The team obtained major contributions from many players, and for the first time in school history those players were likely to be black as well as white.

The first black football player to play for VPI was John Dobbins, recruited in early 1969 from nearby Radford High School. Also the first black athlete to be given a scholarship, he played on the freshman team in 1969 and then in 1970 joined the varsity. Leading the team in rushing offense in 1971 and 1972 was James "J.B." Barber—and in 1973 and 1974, Phil Rogers. Barber also led the team in scoring in 1971 and 1972 (he rushed for thirteen touchdowns in 1972). James Barber accumulated 2,052 career yards between 1971 and 1973, and Phil Rogers, who was switched to quarterback his senior year, accumulated 3,025 total yards between 1973 and 1975 (he rushed for 1,036 yards in 1973).[3]

17.2   Jerry Gaines, Tech's first black athlete—Jeremiah "Jerry" Gaines enrolled at VPI as a freshman in 1967—the first freshman to get a full scholarship in track, the first black student to be awarded an athletic scholarship at VPI, indeed Tech's first black athlete. For four years, he proved a strong student and an outstanding athlete, and he went on to become a prize-winning teacher of foreign language at the high school level.

In his freshman season, in spring 1968, Gaines broke the school record in the long jump. In the winter of his sophomore year, he led the Tech team to an upset championship in the state indoor meet—the first in the team's history—with second place in the 60-yard high hurdles, second in the triple jump, first in the 60-yard low hurdles, and a first-place finish (a school-record indoor performance) in the long jump. On it went though his four stellar years. (Craig Swift, "Toeing the Line: Jerry Gaines and Virginia Tech," in Wallenstein, *Essays, Fall 1998*)

At quarterback, Don Strock was the man in 1971 and 1972. The team had not gone to the air much his first year on the varsity, but Coach Coffey turned Strock loose, and Strock was the nation's number two passer in 1971. (The other half of Virginia Tech's throw-and-catch threat that year, Mike Burnop, set a Virginia Tech single season record with 46 catches; the next three years, it would be Ricky Scales, who rang up 2,272 career yards with 18 touchdowns on 113 receptions between 1972 and 1974.) The 1972 season again featured quarterback Don Strock, the nation's number one passer that year. The fifth man in intercollegiate football to amass 3,000 yards, he completed 228 of 427 pass attempts for a total of 3,243 yards. Against the University of Houston in 1972, Strock completed 34 of 53 pass attempts for a total of 527 yards, although the game ended in a tie, 27–27. Between 1970 and 1972, Strock's contributions on offense totaled 5,871 total yards. He subsequently had a long career in the NFL with the Miami Dolphins.[4] As for the team in 1972, one high point came at Homecoming, when Tech defeated Big Eight leader Oklahoma State in a wild finish, 34–32, and another came in the final game of a 6–4–1 season, when Tech trounced Wake Forest, 44–9.

Virginia Polytechnic Institute had a long and intense rivalry with Virginia Military Institute, with the annual Thanksgiving Day game—held in Roanoke, midway between Lexington and Blacksburg—the highlight of many a season. President Hahn wanted to change all that, however, and had the VMI game changed to a Saturday. Eventually the two teams stopped playing at all. Meanwhile, a once-upon-a-time in-state rivalry with the University of Virginia emerged again.

VPI and Virginia had played often early in the twentieth century, but then Virginia refused to play VPI. The interruption is sometimes ascribed to Virginia's unhappiness over a loss to VPI in 1905, when one of VPI's all-time great players, Hunter Carpenter—after five (!) years of frustration—led his team to a 9–1 record, including an 11–0 victory in Charlottesville. The two teams never played after 1905 until 1922, but then play resumed. In 1966, after VPI had pretty routinely thrashed its opponent, including a 24–7 win in Charlottesville that year, Virginia again suspended play. In 1970, however, the series picked up where it had left off. Tech lost that first year, 7–0, in Blacksburg; but then it won 6–0 in Charlottesville in 1971; lost 24–20 in Charlottesville in 1972; won 27–15 in Blacksburg in 1973; and lost 28–27 on a controversial call in 1974. The series would continue, and it would continue to be spirited and competitive.[5]

Men's Basketball

During Jerry Gaines's spring track season his freshman year, VPI announced having signed the school's second black athlete, Charles Lipscomb, a basketball player who enrolled fall 1968. Virginia Tech was entering a new era in intercollegiate athletics. At stake was the matter of whether the school would continue to reflect only white Virginians in its recruiting and its competing.

At stake, too, was President Hahn's declaration that the school could reasonably be expected to play in the NCAA tournament. In the 1965–1966 season, the VPI team had gone to the National Invitational Tournament (NIT) in New York City—the school's first appearance in post-season play. Temple University ended the Tech season in the first round, 88–73.

The next year, 1967, Tech went farther. After opening the season by defeating fourth-ranked Duke, 85–71, the Gobblers beat Purdue 79–63 in

17.4 Highlights of Hokie football after the Hahn years—In a 21–10 defeat of Vanderbilt University in 1983, defensive back Ashley Lee made two interceptions and ran both back for touchdowns—one run of 88 yards, the other of 94, for a total of 182 yards and an average of 91. No collegiate player had ever totaled or averaged such yardage on interceptions.

Lee, however, was overshadowed by #78 Bruce Smith's exploits on defense. A junior that year, Smith led the nation with twenty-two sacks and was named to a number of All-American teams. Mike Johnson was another of the great players on defense in 1983, and the Hokies led the nation in rushing defense (69.4 yards per game) and scoring defense (8.3 points per game). Tech won nine games (the most since 1905), four of them shutouts (the most since 1938), including a 48–0 walloping of the University of Virginia to close out the season at nine wins, two defeats. The only serious blemish to the season was the lack of a bowl bid. The next year, Bruce Smith's senior year, he was awarded the Outland Trophy, Tech went to the Independence Bowl, and the Buffalo Bills made Smith the #1 pick in the NFL draft.

In March 1981, Virginia Tech ended a quarter-century as a football independent by joining the Big East Conference. Frank Beamer ('69), who had played football for VPI in the 1960s, became his alma mater's head football coach in December 1986. Those two facts set the backdrop to the emergence of Virginia Tech as a collegiate football powerhouse in the 1990s. In 1995, despite losing the first two games, Virginia Tech won the Big East championship, ended the season #1 in the nation in rushing defense (77.4 yards per game), and won ten games in a row for the first time in school history, as it defeated Texas, 28–10, in the Sugar Bowl. Cornell Brown became Tech's fourth consensus All-American football player—after Frank Loria, Bruce Smith, and Jim Pyne.

And then there was Michael Vick.

front of 11,500 fans—decades later, still the largest crowd ever to see a basketball game in Cassell Coliseum. Selected to play in the National Collegiate Athletic Association (NCAA) tournament, the Gobblers played Toledo in the first round. Toledo had handled VPI in regular season play that year, winning the season finale 90–71, but Tech won at the NCAA, 82–76. Then VPI defeated Indiana University, 79–70, to reach the Final Eight—the first team from the state of Virginia ever to go that far. In the regional final game, Tech led Dayton by as many as ten, but Dayton finished with a surge to force overtime and then went on to end Tech's season, the final score 71–66.[6] Had VPI held on to win that game, it would have gone to the Final Four. After 1967, though, Tech did not return to post-season play until 1973. In the meantime, two of the starting players in 1966–1967, junior guard Glen Combs and senior forward Ron Perry, went on to play professional ball in the American Basketball Association.

Among the notable developments in Tech basketball during the years after 1967, junior Lloyd King led the team in scoring in 1969–1970 with 19.5 points per game. Also that year, for the first time ever, an African American played varsity basketball for VPI; Charlie Lipscomb was the team's second leading scorer with at least 20 points in three different games and a 12.4 average for the season. In 1970–1971, King led again with an even more impressive 21.3 points, and Lipscomb improved his average to 14.0 points, but a new player, Allan Bristow, was the team's second leading scorer, with a 20.4 average that year. The next year, 1971–1972—Don DeVoe's first year as coach—at Morgantown, West Virginia, Tech defeated the Mountaineers in triple overtime, 105–101. Bristow set new school scoring records that year with 662 total points and a 24.5 average.[7]

In 1972–1973, Bristow's senior year, he set a VPI single-game scoring record with 52 points in a 117–89 victory in the coliseum over George Washington University. The team set a new team record that year with an average of 85.5 points per game and finished the regular season at 18–5.

As in 1966, Tech went to the NIT in 1973, where it joined fifteen other hungry teams, among them UNC and number 10 Minnesota. With 26 points from Bristow, Tech won its first-round game, 65–63, over the Lobos of New Mexico. In the quarterfinal game, Tech edged Fairfield University, 77–76. Next up was Alabama, which had taken out Minnesota in its quarterfinal game. The final score was Virginia Tech 74, the Crimson Tide 73.

By then, only one team lay in Virginia Tech's improbable path to a tournament championship—Notre Dame, coached by Digger Phelps. Earlier that week, Notre Dame player Dwight Clay had celebrated his team's semi-final victory by declaring, "It doesn't matter who we play [for the championship—Alabama or Virginia Tech], we'll beat either one." Fired up, Tech took an early ten-point lead. Notre Dame charged back, and Tech still led at the half, but by only 44–40. After the break, Notre Dame continued to pour it on, took the lead, and went out to 70–58 with seven minutes to play. Then it was Tech's turn to surge. Just before the buzzer ended play in regulation, Craig Lieder hit a bucket to tie the score and force overtime.[8]

Notre Dame went out in front again and, with one minute to play, led 91–87. Bobby Stevens completed a three-point play to close the deficit to one. Tech had the ball with twelve seconds left in overtime. Time out. Bobby Stevens handled the ball. He looked for Craig Lieder, but Lieder couldn't shake free of the defense. Stevens took the shot himself. It bounced off the rim, but Allen Bristow was able to tip it back out toward the free-throw line. Stevens grabbed it, threw it up again, and this time scored.

The Gobblers of Virginia Tech had won, 92–91, in overtime. They had made their way through four games, and won every one of them, by a total margin of five points and an ever-diminishing spread—two points, one point, one point, and, finally, one point in overtime. That Sunday night, 8,000 fans greeted the team at Woodrum Airport in Roanoke. On Main Street in Blacksburg, another 3,000 welcomed the Gobblers back from the Big Apple. Earlier that evening, Dan Rather had said on the CBS Sunday News, "Some coaches call the NIT the tournament of losers. The game of no names. But the turkeys from Tech are somebody. They're winners."[9]

Women's Basketball

Women students were playing basketball at VPI as early as 1923–1924, the third year of coeducation. For some years, the "Turkey Hens"—a platoon among the small numbers of female students at VPI—continued to play, sometimes traveling to such schools as Roanoke College and Radford. When coeducation began in earnest after the split with Radford in 1964, the numbers of female students rapidly rose. Moreover, Title IX, enacted by Congress as part of the Educational Amendments of 1972, made it improbable that Tech could long continue to neglect intercollegiate sports for female students—though it did for a time.

During the 1971–1972 year, Tech women played basketball as a club sport. That meant basketball was like any other student organization, recognized as a school group but located in the Department of Physical Education, not the Athletic Department, dependent on a volunteer coach and ineligible for athletic scholarships. The first year, the games were all played at other schools, but on January 23, 1973, the "Hokie Honeys" played Emory and Henry at the coliseum. At the close of the season, the

17.5 Highlights of Hokie hoops after the Hahn years—After the VPI Gobblers' NIT championship in 1973, the next time the school went to post-season play in men's basketball, it was the Hokies of Virginia Tech playing in the NCAA in 1976, though they lost in the first round that year. In 1977, they returned to the NIT, beating Georgetown but then losing to Alabama. In 1978, Tech joined the Metro Conference and won the Metro Tournament that first year.

The 1980s featured highlight performances by several Tech players. On January 21, 1980, Les Henson hit a shot from the length of the court—89 feet, 3 inches—to defeat Florida State 79–77. In 1982, Dale Solomon became the first Virginia Tech player to score 2,000 points. Dell Curry, who finished at Tech in 1985–1986, set a new school career scoring record—2,388 points—before becoming one of the original members of the NBA Charlotte Hornets.

Bimbo Coles played under new rules—four years, for example, unlike Allen Bristow; and (beginning his freshman year) with a three-point shot, unlike any of his predecessors—but, by any measure, he was a great scorer. On February 6, 1988, he stole the ball with time running out in regulation and scored a lay-up to force overtime. By the time the game was over, he had scored a total of 51 points in a come-from-far-behind, double-overtime, 141–133 victory over the University of Southern Mississippi in Cassell Coliseum. That summer, after his sophomore year, he played in Korea on the 1988 Olympic squad, which won the bronze medal.

In 1995, in something of a replay of 1973, Tech played in the NIT and went to overtime in the championship game—and when Shawn Smith hit two free throws with less than a second on the clock, Tech defeated Marquette, 65–64. The next year, with Ace Custis and his soft jumper leading the way, Tech rose to as high as a #8 national ranking.

team played in the state tournament, sanctioned by the Virginia affiliate of the Association of Intercollegiate Athletics for Women (AIAW). There the Hokie Honeys lost their first game but then rebounded to defeat the College of William and Mary and then Hollins College.

Professor Joe Sgro of the Department of Psychology often took the elevator to his office on the fifth floor of Derring Hall. One day, he was accosted in the elevator by a psychology major named Deanne Starbird, a member of the basketball club who knew that Sgro had some experience coaching basketball. By the time they got off the elevator at the fifth floor, the story goes, Starbird had recruited Sgro as the club's new coach. Sgro coached the team for the next three seasons (1973–1974 through 1975–1976). He has been described as the team's "scheduler, travel planner, chauffeur, accountant, lobbyist, and occasional trainer."[10]

Sgro worked hard and well, as did his team. That first season, 1973–1974, his star player was perhaps Cindy White, a freshman who led the team in scoring—she had 22 points in a 55–37 victory over Lynchburg

17.6 Women's basketball at Tech since the Hahn era—After the 1975–1976 season, Coach Sgro relinquished his many roles. He had been unable to obtain athletic scholarships for his players, though other teams were beginning to recruit players with the promise of support—Roanoke College his first year, Madison College his second, and Old Dominion his third year. He had been unable to so much as get institutional funding to support travel to the Virginia Invitational tournament in February 1976. In his view, Athletic Director Frank Moseley was hostile to the development of women's sports at Tech, even getting in the way of the team's operations as a club sport. Moreover, taking on the task of heading up a Ph.D. program that his department was inaugurating, Sgro could no longer volunteer the time it took to coach the team.

Sgro's lobbying, backed up by looming pressure from Title IX, may have helped, and in any case the Virginia Tech Board of Visitors voted in 1976 to upgrade women's sports. Swimming, tennis, and basketball would become varsity sports. The school hired a women's basketball coach, John Wetzel, who had played men's basketball at Tech early in the Hahn years and had subsequently played and coached in the NBA before returning to Tech as a graduate assistant to Charlie Moir, the coach of the men's freshman team. In Wetzel's first season (1976–1977), Helena Flannagan became Tech's first woman basketball player with a partial athletic scholarship. The team's first varsity game was in Blacksburg against Virginia State College, which the Fighting Gobblers lost 46–42.

When play began the next year (1977–1978), the coach was Carolyn Owens. Two players were on full scholarship—Kim Albany and Sis Spriggs—and Sandy Berry, Donna Cooper, and Pauline Landis had partial grants. For Tech's third year of varsity women's basketball, the coach was Carol Alfano, and she stayed on all the way through 1996–1997. During her career at Tech, the NCAA, finally recognizing the importance of women's collegiate athletics, elbowed the AIAW aside and created a parallel universe of women's sports, including a national tournament at the end of each season. One of Tech's all-time great players, Renee Dennis, scored 1,791 career points in the 1980s and had her number retired.

College. In her sophomore year, she scored 33 points in a season-opening 73–60 victory at East Tennessee State. At the close of the Hahn era, women's basketball remained a club sport, but the players and their volunteer coaches had established the basis for a varsity sports program, which soon followed.

Wins and Losses

Varsity football provides a window on a number of changes that took place at Virginia Tech in the third quarter of the twentieth century. Like a host of colleges across the nation, the school had had a football team since the 1890s. Sometimes it was competitive, sometimes not, but it always provided opportunities to develop athletic, leadership, and teamwork skills, and it garnered support from many alumni for whom it provided a connection to their alma mater.

From 1945 through 1953, the VPI football squad never had a winning season, and twice it won no games at all, but—midway through those years—the modern era in intercollegiate sports at VPI began. The school inaugurated a fund-raising program that funded athletic scholarships, recruited a new head coach and athletic director, and began to plan for greatly improved athletic facilities.

President Hahn voiced a hope and an expectation that national prominence in intercollegiate athletics—in the major sports—would accompany a rise in academic prominence and, in fact, would facilitate that rise. For good or ill, Virginia Tech launched a sustained effort to take the programs in men's basketball and football to new heights. Those efforts met with uneven results, but a number of post-season appearances for both teams bespoke a measure of substantial if episodic success. Regardless of outcomes, whether by game or by season, citizens played games that had importance to them and to their fans.

And, at a people's university, by the time Marshall Hahn left his post, black men were competing and representing the school on what had, since the beginning of the programs, absolutely excluded all black players. In that respect, school teams were beginning to look more like the society from which they were drawn. Moreover, taking root was a small but growing collection of programs for female athletes. In yet another way, athletics, the Virginia Polytechnic Institute and State University of 1975 was not the same institution as the Virginia Polytechnic Institute of 1962.

Several seasons in the 1990s saw the Tech team, the Lady Hokies, generate twenty-game winning seasons. In 1994, the Lady Hokies beat #19 Southern Mississippi, 60–59, to win the Metro Conference tournament championship and thus, for the first time, went to the NCAA, though they lost their opening-round game to Clemson. In 1995, Tech won the regular season Metro championship, returned to the NCAA tournament, and won their first match-up, over St. Joseph's, but then lost to the eventual national champion, Connecticut. The Lady Hokies achieved their first-ever national ranking after defeating archrival Virginia, ranked #9 at the time, 69–62 at Cassell Coliseum.

After Tech joined the Atlantic 10 Conference, the Lady Hokies experienced rough sledding for a couple of seasons, and the Athletic Department pressured Coach Alfano into leaving. The new coach, Bonnie Henrickson, brought "Bonnie Ball" to Blacksburg. In her first season (1997–1998), the team returned to its winning ways with a 20–9 record. In the Atlantic 10 tournament, Tech breezed past Fordham, 79–40; took St. Joseph's, 67–62; edged George Washington, 73–72; and defeated Massachusetts in overtime, 66–64. In the NCAA tournament, Tech beat Wisconsin but then lost to Florida.

Virginia Tech joined the Big East in women's basketball. In 2001–2002, the Lady Hokies won often but not often enough. Along the way, they gave the University of Connecticut a scare at the Cassell, losing by nine points, on powerhouse UConn's way to a perfect 39–0 season and a national championship. The Tech players missed out on the NCAA, but they went to the NIT, where they made it to the Final Four before losing in overtime to the University of Houston.

1 BOV minutes, 11 November 1972.

2 *Hokies Handbook*, 34–35, 40; Doughty and Lazenby, *'Hoos 'n' Hokies*, 102–103.

3 *Hokies Handbook*, 146–47, 149–50; Doughty and Lazenby, *'Hoos 'n' Hokies*, 103–12; *Techgram*, September 1972; 1972 *Bugle*.

4 *Hokies Handbook*, 37–39, 151; *Techgram*, December 1972.

5 Jonathan Fisher, "Carpenter's Team: Champions of the South," in Wallenstein, *Essays, Fall 1997*; Doughty and Lazenby, *'Hoos 'n' Hokies*, 77–88, 95–119.

6 Mark Berman, "1967: The 1 That Got Away," *Roanoke Times*, 20 March 2002: B6, B9.

7 Whitehead and Whitehead, *Under the Hoop*, 102–107.

8 Jason Niemczyk, "Hokie Hoops: The History of Virginia Tech Men's Basketball," in Wallenstein, *Essays, Spring 1998*.

9 Ibid., 28.

10 Deanne Starbird, "Basketball Over," *Collegiate Times*, 7 February 1973; Brendan P. Sherry, "A Decade of Transition and Turmoil: A History of Women's Basketball at Virginia Tech, 1970–1979," in Wallenstein, *Essays, Spring 1998*.

Dr. and Mrs. Hahn, on the occasion of Homecoming late in his presidency. Courtesy of T. Marshall Hahn Jr.

Governor's Day football (which originated in 1965) at Lane Stadium, October 1974. The Hokie Bird mascot towers over Marshall Hahn (in his final football season as VPI president) and Mills Godwin (early in his second term as Virginia governor).

With this basket shot in overtime at the buzzer, underdog Virginia Tech captured the 1973 NIT basketball title against Notre Dame in Madison Square Garden

In overtime, with this shot at the buzzer by Bobby Stevens, underdog Virginia Tech won the 1973 NIT championship in Madison Square Garden.

18: Boundaries and Connections
—VPI and Community Development

Building a university involved many things, and far from least among them was community development, strengthening the community and the local institutions so essential to the continued growth and development of VPI. Located as it was in Blacksburg—in rural Montgomery County, forty-plus miles from Roanoke—one of VPI's handicaps in faculty recruiting was the lack of a modern hospital in the area to meet the more serious medical needs of its faculty and staff and their families. Similarly, the public school system was in need of improvement—especially, from a VPI perspective, for the benefit of the families of people already on the faculty and staff and also to make it easier to attract outstanding new people.

Blacksburg and VPI did not always work together in harmony. In 1957, when negotiations were under way to bring VPI into the town of Blacksburg, students held an animated rally that put an end to such talk.[1] On many matters, however, the town and the school worked together, often in opposition to other parts of Montgomery County. The school, the town, and the county had a great interest—not, however, always perceived as an identical interest—on various issues that required VPI to deal with local matters that reached beyond the campus.

Especially in view of VPI's tremendous growth—whether already accomplished or clearly in prospect—President Hahn worked to address such problems, as did many other people at VPI, in Blacksburg, and throughout Montgomery County. Growing as it did through the 1960s, the school inevitably had a tremendous impact on the community. Gains entailed losses. Tussles ensued.

Regarding relations between the school and the town, one of the first things to which President Hahn turned his attention had to do with race relations—said another way, black access—in a town that was still segregated. Not for another two years did the Civil Rights Act of 1964 gain passage in Congress, and much remained to be done in Blacksburg. VPI would be hosting conferences—whether in Blacksburg or, if necessary, elsewhere—that would have black as well as white participants, and all participants, Hahn insisted, would have to have the same access to public facilities. He made his case, and, as he was able to report, barriers to equal access came down.

The Old High School

After Marshall Hahn became president in 1962, he became aware of nearby property that VPI did not own but needed. He soon began a quiet campaign to acquire it.

One lot, 5.6 acres in downtown Blacksburg, was the site of the former Blacksburg High School, the former Blacksburg Elementary School, and a one-time vocational education building. The public school property was squeezed into a block separating part of the eastern edge of the campus from the commercial establishments in the downtown area. The old, red brick school buildings, in typical public school architecture, were across Otey Street from the Faculty Center (later the continuing education center, now the Donaldson Brown Hotel and Conference Center), along with an adjacent parking lot. The same block contained the Blacksburg Armory, then owned jointly by VPI and the town of Blacksburg.

The buildings were no longer used by the Montgomery County school system—a replacement for the old high school building had opened in 1954, and two new elementary schools opened early in the years of the Hahn administration, the Margaret J. Beeks Elementary School in 1963 and, later, the Gilbert F. Linkous Elementary School. County school officials therefore planned to dispose of the property. Dr. Hahn alerted state officials in Richmond—Governor Albertis S. Harrison Jr.; budget director L. M. Kuhn—in February 1963, and in April he characterized VPI's acquisition of the property as essential.[2]

The property was appraised at $415,000. An attempt to negotiate a purchase failed, but the County School Board did not sell it until late summer 1965. By that time, word was out that VPI was going to buy the property at whatever price it took, and it would be futile for local investors to bid the price up. All that would do was increase the cost to taxpayers, and few bidders showed up at the public auction. Marshall Hahn and Stuart Cassell attended the auction and bought the property for $310,000.

18.2 The Huckleberry rail line—A rail line connected Blacksburg with the old Virginia and Tennessee line at Christiansburg (Cambria Depot) from 1904 into the 1960s. One of President Hahn's early construction priorities, however, called for a longer runway at the VPI airport (see chapter 11). Such an airport runway meant closing down the Huckleberry (Blacksburg) spur of the Norfolk & Western rail line from Christiansburg—the 4,600-foot runway would cut it in two—as well as hauling coal for the VPI power plant a bit farther. Hahn, Cassell & Co. worked most of the complications out with the help of Harry Wyatt at Norfolk & Western. The railroad gave the spur railroad right-of-way and other property to the town and county—on part of which Blacksburg later built its town hall and a bike path.

(Actually, President Hahn did have a limit; he had been authorized to pay up to $350,000, he later acknowledged.)

After extension of utility lines and some renovation, VPI put the land and buildings to good use—quite aside from preventing what might have been inappropriate commercial development of the property. The old parking lot provides parking—lots of it, though rarely enough—for Donaldson Brown Hotel and Conference Center and other facilities. The old buildings still stand largely as they were in the 1960s, but they now provide urgently needed space for University activities. The former high school building has been used ever since by the College of Architecture and Urban Studies. The former elementary school building has been principally used for information units—University Publications, photo labs, radio studios, and a publications art group. Virginia Tech in recent years has leased the Blacksburg Armory, now owned entirely by the town, and converted it to offices, galleries, and studios for the Department of Art and Art History.

18.3 Ambler Johnston, Marshall Hahn, and Smithfield Plantation—The redoubtable J. Ambler Johnston, whose life had so long been intertwined with VPI, made sure early on that his old friend Brockenbrough Lamb and the new president of VPI would come to know each other. Dr. Hahn, for his part, cultivated the acquaintance with Brockenbrough, his wife, and their son and his wife. The younger Brockenbrough Lamb, known to family and close friends as Brockie, was a prominent lawyer, a member of the Richmond firm of Christian, Barton, Parker, Epps & Brent. The elder Lamb was, for many years, judge of the Chancery Court of the City of Richmond. Judge Lamb's wife owned Smithfield. Acquiring property from the Lambs for VPI would be a family affair.

The friends enjoyed each other's company, and it is in the little matters of the texture of personal relationships that big changes at Tech were sometimes arranged. In 1965, Ambler Johnston dug up an old telegram, dated 15 July 1935, that he had sent to Dr. Julian Burruss, then president of VPI, relating to Judge Lamb and Smithfield. The Smithfield property had been a matter of some concern to VPI for at least thirty years, he observed. At least once, Judge Lamb saw fit to explain to Dr. Hahn that Ambler Johnston was "a slide rule addict" who lived by approximations, some of which had to be changed to be within "what you characterize (to my delight) as 'the limits of flexible veracity.'" (Johnston letter to Hahn and Lamb, 17 May 1965; Lamb to Hahn, 31 May 1965)

Smithfield

Another, larger nearby property was the Smithfield tract, farmland west of campus between VPI and the Henry Heth farm. The 400-acre tract, largely surrounded by University-owned land, was important to VPI's development for several reasons. At the time, it was leased by VPI and was used intensively in VPI agricultural research and farm operations. The land would be essential for VPI's future growth.

Perhaps equally important, the State Highway Commission's long-range plans included a Blacksburg by-pass for US 460, a primary east-west route that connected eastern Virginia—via Lynchburg, Bedford, Roanoke, and Christiansburg—with Blacksburg, where it ran along Main Street before it headed over Brush Mountain, through Giles County, across the New River, and into West Virginia. The open farmland immediately west of the VPI campus would be a desirable location for such a four-lane, divided highway.

When Dr. Hahn and Mr. Cassell first began thinking seriously about the matter, neither the physical location nor the construction priority for the by-pass had been fixed. But if the highway were to traverse Smithfield, and adjacent property remained in private hands, commercial development—whether gas stations and motels or taverns and music stores—could generate serious problems for the institution. A university must have room to grow. Hahn and Cassell agreed from the outset that there was no choice but somehow to obtain Smithfield.[3]

Smithfield was owned by Mrs. Janie B. Lamb of Richmond. Her husband, Judge Brockenbrough Lamb Sr., was a close friend of J. Ambler Johnston. Johnston, knowing how potentially valuable Smithfield might be to VPI, did not take long to bring Dr. Hahn and Judge Lamb together.

The Smithfield effort by the VPI people involved Judge and Mrs. Lamb, together with their son and daughter-in-law, Mr. and Mrs. Brockenbrough Norveil Lamb Jr. In autumn 1964, while a guest in the home of the younger Lambs, Dr. Hahn initiated serious discussion of the purchase of the Smithfield property. All agreed that the discussion should continue.[4]

The elder Mrs. Lamb died in early spring 1965—Dr. Hahn sent flowers and messages of condolence, personally and on behalf of VPI—but the negotiations with the other Lambs went on. In summer 1966, Brockie Lamb and his family visited Blacksburg and VPI as guests of the Hahns, and they toured the campus and the Smithfield properties. By late summer, Dr. Hahn declared himself "very pleased" with progress.[5] Moreover, Mills Godwin had become governor the previous January, so Hahn felt confident that he would find support in Richmond.

Shortly before Christmas 1966, the parties reached a lease-purchase agreement—a ten-year lease, expiring December 31, 1976, of $115,789.20, plus taxes. The purchase option permitted purchase of ten 40-acre parcels

18.4 Smithfield Plantation—The Smithfield property, full of history, was part of a 120,000-acre grant by the Crown of England to James Patton in 1745. William Preston, Patton's nephew, was an Irish-born Indian fighter, Revolutionary War hero, and frontier political leader. Smithfield Plantation was the home Preston built on the Allegheny frontier in the 1770s.

William Preston's family produced a long line of state governors, congressmen, and other leaders in public life, as well as people directly connected to the early history of VPI. One of William Preston's sons, later Governor James Patton Preston, was born at Smithfield, as was John Buchanan Floyd, another pre-Civil War governor of Virginia and the son of William Preston's daughter Letitia.

James Patton Preston's children were vitally connected with the beginnings of VPI. The school originated in the 1850s as a white boys' Methodist school, the Olin and Preston Institute—named in part after William Ballard Preston, a state legislator, member of the US House of Representatives, secretary of the Navy, and, finally, a member of the Confederate Senate. Solitude House stands on a section of the old Smithfield estate that belonged to another son, Robert T. Preston, and came into the possession of Virginia Agricultural and Mechanical College in its first year of operation, 1872. Yet a third son of James Patton Preston, James Francis Preston, had a third portion of the original estate and left two sons—Hugh Caperton Preston, who attended VAMC in the 1870s, and another William Ballard Preston, who was commandant of cadets at VAMC, professor of English literature there, and, beginning in 1888, professor of agriculture and director of the Agricultural Experiment Station. (Dorman, *The Prestons*)

In 1959, Mrs. Lamb gave the Smithfield plantation house to the Association for the Preservation of Virginia Antiquities (APVA). Since then, the structure has been restored, and it is periodically open to the public as a historic landmark. The *Smithfield Review*, a journal that focuses on the history of the area west of the Blue Ridge (a good description of the original Patton grant), is edited and published by current or retired members of the Tech faculty and staff, among them Lon Savage and math professor Hugh G. Campbell.

over ten years for $68,000 each. The arrangement gave VPI control over the land during the ten years, satisfied the Lambs' preferences in view of tax considerations, and also reflected the insufficiency of funds to acquire the tract all at once. As things turned out, the purchase was completed rather quickly. Funds from the sale of rights of way to the State Highway Department for the by-pass construction paid for six of the ten parcels, and Governor Godwin's office made available funds for the purchase of two additional parcels. To make possible the acquisition of all of the property during Godwin's administration (the governor had to approve the overall agreement for it to be legal), the VPI Educational Foundation advanced the money for purchase of the two remaining parcels, with a state commitment for repurchase.[6]

Once the deal was approved, President Hahn wrote notes to several key players in the lengthy process to thank them: Carter Lowance, the governor's right-hand man; controller Sidney Day; Doug Hamner Jr., director of engineering and buildings. On a similar note that went to state budget director L. M. Kuhn, Hahn added, "I know you did the job, and again I am deeply indebted to you.... I thanked everyone [listed] above, but all [of us here at VPI] know where most of the credit is due." Hahn observed at another time that, "If the land had not been acquired prior to the construction of the by-pass [which occurred in the 1970s], both the value of the land and the likelihood of real estate development would have increased greatly." Years later, Kuhn would say that the Smithfield situation leading to the purchase "was the nearest thing to a real emergency that Marshall Hahn ever had."

Cement Plant Fight

In late autumn 1964, it became apparent that something was afoot in the Ellett Valley, east of Blacksburg. An unidentified company was buying options on large tracts of land for unannounced purposes, and rumors were rife. Early in the spring, it all became clear. The Louisville (Kentucky) Cement Company planned a big cement plant to use the abundant limestone in the valley and had already purchased options on more than 1,500 acres. Announcement of the company's plans came at a meeting of the Christiansburg Chamber of Commerce in Christiansburg. No one from Blacksburg was invited, except the chairman of the County Board of Supervisors, who happened to live in Blacksburg.

All of which perhaps unwittingly intensified some latent ill feeling that had long prevailed between the two towns. Some folks from Christiansburg—as well as a good many rural citizens of Montgomery County—resented what they perceived as Blacksburg's snobbishness. There undoubtedly were elements of town-gown friction, the causes of which were rooted in community history. VPI was the dominant employer and by far the most important economic engine in the area, and some administrators and faculty across the generations had demonstrated considerable insensitivity to the concerns of neighboring communities. The cement plant issue brought community conflict into the open for many months. Blacksburg and VPI were adamantly in opposition; Christiansburg and the county generally were supportive.

The big concern was the serious air pollution generated in cement manufacturing. The proposed plant location was a beautiful valley only a few miles from the VPI campus. Tops of the tall smokestacks would be nearly level with the Blacksburg plateau. The negative impact of dust-laden air on normal domestic and business activities was not hard to imagine. Beyond that, for the scientists working in VPI's laboratories, greenhouses, and horticultural research plots, short of atomic warfare there could hardly have been a worse threat.

The prospect of attracting other research and development facilities to University Research Park or elsewhere in the community would evaporate. Blacksburg's two small high-tech industries, Poly-Scientific (which had become a division of Litton Industries) and Electro-Tec, would have to close. Together they employed about 300 workers. By contrast, the cement plant would provide jobs for about 80 employees at full operation.

All of this generated serious problems for Marshall Hahn. The rector of the Board, Harry C. Wyatt of Roanoke, was senior vice president of the Norfolk & Western Railroad. For a railroad, a new cement plant is good news indeed because of the prospect of high-volume freight. President Hahn no doubt felt he had to speak with care in opposition. Moreover, Hahn also was closely aligned with Governor Harrison and his industrial development director, Joe Hamrick, in stressing Virginia's continuing need to attract new industry to the state and otherwise strengthen the Old Dominion's business and industry. Joe Hamerick strongly supported the cement plant development.

The redoubtable Byron Cooper, the geologist who headed VPI's Department of Geological Sciences, had personally been investigating the limestone deposits in the Ellett Valley for decades. He was quick to realize the implications, and in early March 1965 he wrote the president a long, technical letter on the subject, with calculations documenting the sulfur content of the limestone. Daily production of 4,000 barrels of cement, Dr. Cooper pointed out, would mean 16.3 tons of sulfur dioxide. In the peculiar atmospheric inversion common in the Ellett Valley, he calculated, the sulfur dioxide could be dissolved in water vapor and oxidized into 22 tons of sulfuric acid.

In March, Dr. Hahn wrote to Harry Wyatt summarizing a discussion of the proposed plant location that he, Wyatt, and Louisville Cement president Boyce F. Martin had had earlier. Hahn had told Martin he wanted to see Louisville Cement locate in Virginia, and he proposed making available VPI's services in helping locate a suitable site. The Ellett location, however, would pose serious problems for both VPI and the community. Also, Hahn observed, "the intensity of opposition and resentment from the citizens…is at such a level it could very well be a disservice to the company if it were located here." The president passed along Byron Cooper's technical analysis of the sulfur problem, which he said had been verified by independent professionals.

Blacksburg and VPI urged the County Board to enact an effective air pollution control ordinance, along with a basic zoning ordinance. President Hahn testified on behalf of the air pollution control measure, but prefaced his remarks with strong support for industrial development generally. Industrial growth was essential for Virginia to broaden its economic base and raise the standard of living, he said. Hahn urged both the passage of a sound and workable air pollution control measure and the land-use ordinance, for he said Virginia Tech's stake in the matter was vital: "I am certain we can expect in the next decade the development of a major complex of desirable industries and research facilities throughout the areas accessible to the university." The new Corning Glass plant near Blacksburg, already under construction, was a harbinger of things to come, he suggested. But with the kind of air pollution problem the plant would generate, said Hahn, neither VPI nor Blacksburg could reach their potential. The president sent copies of his statement to the local Board of

Supervisors, to his own Board of Visitors, and to Boyce Martin at Louisville Cement Company.

Meanwhile, James J. Pandapas, president of Poly-Scientific Co., bought a full-page advertisement in the *Montgomery News-Messenger*, the local newspaper, to oppose the cement plant. Pandapas also wrote to Boyce Martin, sent along a petition signed by most of Poly-Scientific's employees, and offered personal and corporate assistance in identifying more suitable locations for the plant. Another citizens' petition opposing the cement plant—citing "irreparable harm" to the community and signed by some 1,250 people, among them scores of VPI engineering professors and scientists—also was sent to Martin. It pledged "the professional scientific and engineering talents" of its signers, without charge, in finding a suitable location for such a plant elsewhere in Virginia.

In October 1965, a delegation from Blacksburg went to Richmond to talk to Governor Harrison about the problem. The group agreed not to make public statements, although Cecil Akers of Electro-Tech sent Dr. Hahn a summary of the arguments used with the governor, essentially

18.5 Acquiring a facility for the German Club—Charles O. Gordon ('42) was a leader in the German Club while in school, and the experience was valuable to him. In the 1970s, he bought the property across Southgate Drive from Lane Stadium and led an effort to establish a fitting clubhouse for German Club members.

Charlie Gordon (see box 14.7) tells the story of his purchase of the property on which German Club Manor was later developed. He says he purchased the property in 1973 from a couple named Wade living in Christiansburg. He had heard the property was for sale by the Wades and went to ask them about it. A friendly older couple invited him in, and they sat around the kitchen table with a cup of coffee talking about it. He explained what he wanted to do with the property—develop a facility for the German Club. They asked if he would be willing to give them time to think about it further. Gordon readily agreed, and they all agreed that he would return the next day to get their decision.

Next day he went back and asked what they had decided. They had talked it over, they said, had decided that Gordon's proposed use of the property seemed most appropriate, and had decided to sell it to him. He asked if he might write out an option on the property and get them to sign it. They

that the proposed plant would seriously damage VPI and the community and that the cement company had demonstrated "less than good faith." Joe Hamrick later issued a long statement to the effect that there was no basis for the governor to become involved and that Louisville Cement Company had assured him that air pollution would not be a problem. Dr. Hahn and others repeatedly asked why, if the company could control the air pollution, it opposed the enactment of the county's proposed air pollution control ordinance.

About a year later, in autumn 1967, the *Wall Street Journal* published a brief story from Louisville, Kentucky, regarding an announcement by Boyce F. Martin, the company president, that Louisville Cement had dropped plans to build a cement plant near Blacksburg, Virginia. The property acquired for the proposed cement operation, approximately 1,350 acres, had been sold to Indian Hills, Inc., a land development company. According to the *Journal*, Martin said the proposed cement plant was so bitterly opposed because people associated with VPI "consider themselves a technical center and weren't happy about a cement plant

> said, "Yes, but you haven't even asked how much we wanted for it." Gordon said, "Yes, that's right," and they told him. He said he paid about $125,000 for the 11 or so acres. Then he went back to Blacksburg and asked Marshall Hahn about the property. Hahn said VPI was interested in buying it and was hopeful it could soon be purchased. Gordon astonished him by replying, "I have some news for you; I have already bought it." He asked Hahn's help in implementing his plans for developing the German Club facilities on the site, for he expected that it would be a long, difficult process, though he had no idea it would take as long as it did. Neighborhood residents expressed considerable concern about traffic and noise, and a fight over zoning the area to suit the German Club's plans persisted through the 1970s.
>
> Charles Gordon and other alumni members set up the German Club Alumni Foundations to help fund the project. Over the years, they raised funds to pay for the clubhouse and provide an endowment. The facility was opened and dedicated in 1981. Not only does the German Club make use of the facility, but various University groups schedule special luncheons, dinners, and other meetings there. (Gordon interview, at the German Club Manor guesthouse, 18 November 1994; Justin D. Taylor, "105 Years of the German Club at Virginia Tech," in Wallenstein, *Essays, Spring 1998*)

operating there." Marshall Hahn observed that Boyce Martin's words were considerably less harmful than the cement plant would have been.[7]

Public School Improvements

The Blacksburg schools were and are part of the county system, and educational priorities in rural Montgomery County, Virginia, in the mid-1960s were different from those in Blacksburg. So were a good many other priorities, for the political and community leaders who represented the dominant rural interests in the county, and in Christiansburg, the county seat, tended to view VPI and Blacksburg with decided mistrust. If the university community took a strong stand on any issue, large numbers of county-oriented citizens were likely to take the other side. The intensity of the political divide between Blacksburg and the surrounding county had shown up clearly in the cement plant squabble in 1965.

The public school problems had simmered for a while, and the issue was not entirely one of VPI and Blacksburg versus the rest of the county. Struggling to modernize and strengthen the county schools, the County School Board and Superintendent Evans L. King had come up with a plan to build new high schools in Blacksburg and Christiansburg and to consolidate two small rural high schools into those two new high schools. The rural high schools would be converted for elementary and secondary education, along with extensive other school improvements to ease overcrowded conditions. The rural communities involved were bitterly opposed to the idea; the local high schools were too important to community life to let go. Busing pupils to a consolidated high school was simply unacceptable.

A referendum on a $4.5 million bond issue to finance the plan was scheduled for April 19, 1967. The faculty and staff of VPI and a large majority of Blacksburg citizens strongly supported the bond proposal. Citizen leaders organized public meetings in Blacksburg, Christiansburg, and elsewhere to try to generate support for the bond issue. The *Montgomery News Messenger* was full of the controversy about the school plan and the coming referendum. (Bob McNeil, who had retired on disability from VPI, was then on the newspaper's staff and wrote most of its editorials.) The *News Messenger* strongly supported the bond issue and the consolidation plan. So did the Roanoke newspapers, which devoted a good deal of attention to the matter.

The proposal was narrowly defeated by a margin of 66 votes out of the total 4,457. Proponents of the bond issue were a little unsettled; surely, they said, it all must have been a misunderstanding. The School Board promptly set about to try again, and a little later presented the Board of Supervisors with a petition of some 3,300 citizens, mostly business and professional people from Blacksburg and Christiansburg, to have another referendum. The Board approved one and scheduled it for June 9, 1967, less than two months after the first one.

Proponents worked even harder to make sure everyone understood the importance of approving the bond issue. Dean Malpass, chairman of a volunteer group called "Citizens for Community Development," helped organize a number of discussion programs on the pending referendum. President Hahn sent the faculty and staff a reminder of the importance of the referendum and urged them to register and vote.[8]

The results were even worse than before; voters turned out in record numbers to defeat the proposal almost two to one. Nearly 5,000 votes were cast, a heavy majority of them from rural Montgomery County and the two easternmost precincts in Christiansburg.[9] In the months following, there was much talk about Blacksburg annexing large chunks of county territory and becoming an independent city (and thereby operating its own school system). The difficulties in such a course were daunting, however, and nothing came of it.

It took two years to bring a school funding and improvement program to referendum again. By that time, the school plan had been changed—new high schools would be built in Blacksburg and Christiansburg, but the two smaller rural community high schools were to be retained. Funds would be borrowed from the State Literary Fund and other sources for construction of new facilities at Allegheny High School and Auburn High School and for other school improvements. This time, the VPI and Blacksburg school supporters attempted to stay out of the headlines and off the TV tubes, although President Hahn and his lieutenants worked hard behind the scenes. Voters this time—April 8, 1969—approved the bond issue.[10]

Blacksburg High School on Main Street was converted into Blacksburg Middle School, and a new Blacksburg High School was built on Patrick Henry Drive, farther from the center of town. Over the years, the new high school became one of the best in the state. New faculty at

Virginia Tech, recruited from across the United States and indeed from around the world, sent their children there, and some of the teachers, too, were drawn from the families of VPI faculty.

A Modern Hospital

VPI and the surrounding community also worked for some years to obtain a modern hospital for the area. In the mid-1960s, the Blacksburg and Christiansburg Chambers of Commerce initiated a survey of their communities to determine interest in organizing a non-profit hospital. A small private hospital had been operated at Christiansburg for many years, certainly beneficial over the years but increasingly inadequate for the growing county. Radford Hospital, in the city of Radford, did not provide a satisfactory alternative; it, too, needed major improvements, and it was some distance away, not easily accessible on the roads of that era.

In 1966, land was acquired—between Blacksburg and Christiansburg, on Route 460—as a site for a new hospital, and the community made application for federal Hill-Burton funds to help finance its construction. The Hill-Burton program could fund up to 55 percent of construction costs if matched with local funds. A local fund drive was organized to generate the matching funds; the facility was to be called the "A. M. Showalter Memorial Hospital" in honor of the physician who had been instrumental in founding and operating the little hospital in Christiansburg. By early September, about $610,000 had been pledged, and President Hahn wrote to Henry Thouron, president of Hercules Power Company, at Wilmington, Delaware, seeking a major gift for the campaign. Hercules, one of the largest employers in the area, operated the munitions plant near Radford for the US Army. The proposed hospital, Hahn stated, was "essential to the continued development" of the university.[11]

Les Malpass and Harry Swink were co-chairmen of the campus campaign for the hospital, conducted without fanfare. By June 1967, they reported that VPI faculty and staff had contributed something more than $142,000; the overall fund drive had reported gifts and pledges of about $950,000.[12]

But there were difficulties with obtaining the federal money. The community's Hill-Burton application was rejected in 1966 and again in 1967 and 1968. Federal officials made it clear that the project would not be approved unless it was consolidated with Radford Community

Hospital. That brought the fund drive to a halt, and the community had to change course.

After a time, local leaders began negotiating with the Hospital Corporation of America (HCA) at Nashville, Tennessee, where Dr. Tom Frist Jr. and his colleagues were putting together a group of for-profit hospitals. An announcement came in February 1969 that HCA had purchased the property originally acquired for a hospital and would build a 100- to 150-bed hospital there. There was discussion, too, of a training center for nurses' aids, lab technicians, and other paramedical personnel.[13]

The hospital was completed in 1970 and dedicated in August 1971. Dr. Frist called it "one of the prettiest and best equipped hospitals that I have ever seen anywhere in the country," and Marshall Hahn called it "a long-needed asset to the entire community." Hahn was able to get Mills

18.6 Housing a growing town and school—As Tech grew, so did Blacksburg. The school ran out of space to house students—President Hahn built as much on-campus housing as possible, but he also planned for an overflow that could not be accommodated on campus—and the community became home to the surplus. Not that students tended to mind much, for after a year or two on campus, many of them welcomed the freedom and responsibility of fending more for themselves and finding their own places. For that to happen, there had to be places. In the 1960s and in succeeding decades, supply did not always keep up with demand.

The history of Tech became also a history of the surrounding community, even more than had been the case before, and Harry H. Hunt III and Peter Snyder helped transform the community. Hunt was a mortgage underwriter operating out of Virginia Beach, and Snyder had been a student at Virginia Tech, when they met in 1965 and formed a partnership. That winter, they began putting up a constellation of apartment buildings, Terrace View. By 1973, in eight phases, they had built a total of 808 apartments.

A rapidly growing college community needs homes for faculty and graduate students as well as for undergraduates. West on Price's Fork Road, beginning in 1968, the Snyder Hunt partnership built Oak Manor, a community of 120 townhouses. On what had been a farm a little farther out on Price's Fork, between 1973 and 1984 Snyder Hunt built Hethwood, a planned urban development of 300 single-family houses, 300 townhouses, and the Foxridge complex of more than 1,600 apartments, together with a shopping center, basketball and tennis courts, and jogging trails and swimming pools. Tech continued to grow, and Foxridge added more apartments.

Godwin, who by then had finished his (first) term in the governor's office, to participate as well in the dedication ceremony. Along with several local physicians and other leading citizens, President Hahn was invited to join the new hospital's board of trustees, and he did so.[14]

VPI and Its Neighborhood

VPI grew prodigiously during the 1960s. As it did, it had a growing impact on its surroundings. And it continued to grow. As an engine of economic growth, the school generated huge numbers of jobs—some went to local people, great numbers to people drawn in from other places. Considerations like the nature of high-tech jobs—and the environment they required—could lead to successful efforts to prevent the growth of dirtier economic activities like the cement factory. Continued growth would require vigilance in the decades to come—not always maintained—regarding other properties nearby for the university's use.

The emergence of VPI as a university inevitably meant the area around it would develop in a manner differing from what would have otherwise been the case. There would be squabbles over land use and friction over various matters. The growth of on-campus eating and other facilities could mean that the school's presence did not generate as many off-campus economic opportunities as might otherwise have developed. Certainly, the population would be larger. The community would be more diverse. The public elementary schools and Blacksburg High School would—by many measures—be far better. As a college town, Blacksburg would bring a wide range of cultural amenities as well as economic opportunities to the area.

[1] Kinnear, *The First 100 Years*, 399–400.

[2] Cox, *Special Place*, 91–96; Hahn papers, 1963.

[3] Hahn interview, 5 August 1989.

[4] Hahn letters to the Lambs, the elder and younger, 26 October 1964.

[5] Hahn letter, 5 September 1966.

[6] Details about the arrangement and the rationale are given in a Hahn letter to W. Ernest Norcross, president of the Alumni Association, 6 May 1971. One piece of the land, 13.37 acres, was retained by the Foundation for hotel or motel development, and there, after the by-pass was constructed, so was the Red Lion Inn.

[7] Most of the material in this account of the cement plant conflict is from papers in President Hahn's files, principally from 1965. Some elements came from Warren Strother's personal memories. A brief article appeared in *Techgram*, 1 May 1965.

[8] Malpass letter, 13 June 1967; Hahn memo, 30 May 1967.

[9] *Roanoke Times*, 10 June 1967.

[10] *Roanoke Times*, 9 April 1969.

[11] Hahn letter, 12 September 1966.

[12] Malpass/Swink letter, 9 June 1967.

[13] *News Messenger*, 3 April 1969.

[14] Hahn letters, 10 May, 17 August, 30 August 1971; Frist letter, 6 May 1971. As for contributions to the original Hill-Burton campaign, arrangements were made to return them to the donors or, alternatively, to leave the money in a special fund for specified uses.

19: Marshall Hahn, Virginia Tech, and a Wider World

VPI and its president alike knew that the world extended far beyond Blacksburg, but the degree to which it did had the capacity to surprise. Not only did President Hahn work to obtain his legislative priorities in Richmond, recruit new deans and faculty members from far and wide, and seek alumni and corporate support for his growing enterprise, but he was tapped to chair a statewide commission that had, it seemed, nothing to do with either his experience or the institution's needs. Not only did academic life get reorganized, but new schools of education and veterinary medicine began to take shape on the Blacksburg campus, and Tech began to develop graduate programs across the state, particularly in Northern Virginia. Not only did the members of a research university—especially one of the public land-grant variety—expect to work on social and economic problems and hope to see their work have a positive impact, but the school's faculty and alumni went out into the world and sometimes found themselves in places like the Philippines or on the cover of *Time* magazine, and even undergraduates gained extraordinary research experience both on campus and far from it.

The Metropolitan Areas Study Commission

Among the matters to which Governor Mills E. Godwin Jr. called the attention of the 1966 legislature were the problems of Virginia's central cities and the urbanizing counties that surrounded them. (Virginia's six standard metropolitan areas at that time were the cities and urban communities near Washington, DC, the Richmond area, the Norfolk-Portsmouth area, the Newport News-Hampton area, the Roanoke area, and the Lynchburg area, and others were emerging.) Urging "a fresh look" at city-county relationships amid rapid urban growth, Godwin proposed a special commission to examine the sufficiency of existing statutes governing the relationships of local governments in major urban areas. The governor's brief reference to urban concerns in his opening address to the General Assembly stressed a growing problem in Virginia, where cities were not a part of the counties within which they were located. Marshall Hahn, in his wildest imagination, could hardly have anticipated in January 1966 what Governor Godwin's reference to such concerns would mean for him, personally, in the years immediately ahead.

In spring 1966, Governor Godwin decided that, if anybody in Virginia could help resolve the tangled issues involved in Virginia's city-county conflicts and frequent annexation cases, it was VPI's vigorous young president, Marshall Hahn. On the governor's recommendation, the 1966 General Assembly had mandated a formal study of the governmental problems of the state's metropolitan areas. The authorizing statute declared it "the policy of this Commonwealth" and necessary in "the public interest" that the expansion and development of the metropolitan areas proceed on a sound and orderly basis "within a governmental framework and economic environment which will foster constructive growth and efficient administration." The legislation provided for a fifteen-member commission to be appointed by the governor to recommend how that best could be done. The study group, officially the Metropolitan Areas Study Commission, was directed to report its findings and recommendations no later than October 1, 1967.

President Hahn knew a political hot potato when he saw one, and when the governor approached him about accepting the chairmanship, he demurred. Hahn recalled, years later, "I told him, one, I'm covered up with alligators; I've got more to do than I can really do justice to, and, two, I don't really know anything about urban area problems, problems of annexation." But the governor would not take "no" for an answer. As Hahn put it later, "When the governor, who also has in his hands many of the factors that controlled the destiny of the university, says he just had to have me do it, well, I did it." But it was not a task he had sought, nor was it one he "embraced enthusiastically." It was "an interesting experience, but terribly, terribly time consuming."[1] Hahn had to keep the Commission chairmanship among his top priorities from June 1966 to November 1967.

19.1 A busy college president, 1966-1967—The eighteen months in 1966 and 1967 when Marshall Hahn chaired the Metropolitan Areas Study Commission were likely the busiest of any in the twelve and a half years of his presidency. Hahn worked hard and traveled extensively in that connection, but his VPI responsibilities remained. When he could be in Blacksburg, he worked most evenings and weekends, catching up; Lon Savage, his executive assistant, made sure that Hahn was aware of everything he needed to know. Hahn spent lots of time on airplanes and in automobiles those days, but he was in his Burruss Hall office or in meetings on campus much more than one might have expected. Regular administrative staff meetings had been instituted by that time, and Hahn didn't miss many. Yet he did other traveling, too, aside from that related to the Metropolitan Areas Study Commission. His daily calendar from those years recorded countless meetings and functions, near and far, for corporate board meetings, meetings of national and regional education associations, the Ferrum College board (of which he was a member), alumni groups, and other commitments. He rarely missed regular University Council sessions; when he did, Warren Brandt filled in for him. Sometimes, important meetings in which it was essential that the president participate had to be delayed until Dr. Hahn's calendar could accommodate them.

The ebb and flow of campus concerns remained, however, perhaps intensified by the president's frequent absences. The problems in the Alumni office during Bruce Ross's brief tenure in 1966-1967 required attention, and the vacancy in the development office resulting from Craig Fabian's departure remained open for most of 1967. The state budget requests for VPI for 1968-1970 were being formulated. The fraternity-sorority question became insistent, and Dr. Hahn appointed a committee chaired by Dean Malpass to look into it. A new on-campus corporation to operate a bookstore, snack bars, and other on-campus businesses was organized. Moreover, Hahn somehow found time to invite Clement French from Washington State University to the campus for a week in March 1967 as a consultant (see chapter 13).

In late 1967, time was running out to turn in the Commission's report. Dr. Hahn, anxious that the report be clear and easily readable, called on many people for help in the final weeks of its preparation. Weldon Cooper and his staff at Charlottesville edited the working draft to include eleventh-hour changes. Hahn himself edited it for clarity, then Warren Strother edited or rewrote parts of it for readability, and Dr. Wilson Snipes, head of the VPI English department, double-checked the grammar. The publications art staff at VPI came up with the cover design. For the participants in those hurry-up efforts in Dr. Hahn's personal office in the president's home to complete the manuscript, memories remain vivid to this day.

The members whom he and Godwin selected turned out to be a diverse group of widely respected and able people, and Hahn was able to bring them along toward a report to which all but one member could eventually agree. The members included Delegate Willis M. "Wick" Anderson, a former mayor of Roanoke; Senator FitzGerald Bemiss of Richmond, who a few years earlier had chaired a study commission on the need for parks and recreational facilities in Virginia; George Long of Charlottesville, the executive secretary of the Virginia Association of Counties; Harold I. Baumes of Richmond, the executive secretary of the Virginia Municipal League; and Dr. Weldon Cooper of Charlottesville, director of the University of Virginia's Institute of Government. They also included Senator William F. Parkerson Jr., who was a leading anti-annexation attorney, having not long earlier represented Henrico County in a bitter court case against the city of Richmond.

President Hahn wrote to each member on June 6 to say it was an honor and privilege to serve as chairman and to work with them on so challenging an assignment, and he wrote again on June 9 to call the first meeting, for June 22, at the capitol in Richmond. At that first meeting, Governor Godwin stopped by to stress the importance of the study and the urgency of coming up with new approaches. "Time is pressing for realistic and far-reaching solutions, for a fresh look, for a hard look, a penetrating look, from the perspective of a metropolis, and not just a city with its corona of suburbs," Godwin told the group.

A list of resource people in cities and metropolitan areas throughout the state was developed, and selected individuals were invited to meet with the Commission. The Commission also set up a series of public hearings—one in each of the metropolitan areas—which were held in May and June 1967 and generated media attention and public discussion. The report of Weldon Cooper's Committee on Governmental Structures was published by the Commission in April 1967 as *Governing the Virginia*

Metropolitan Areas: An Assessment. It was designed, Hahn reported, "to identify the scope and document in detail the problems facing Virginia's metropolitan areas."[2] A summary was published as an interim report, *Metropolitan Virginia, 1967: A Brief Assessment.*

In late summer 1967—after all the talk, the committee reports, the testimony of expert witnesses, and the opinions expressed at the public hearings—the Commission had to come to some decisions, and Marshall Hahn turned up the pressure. Little by little, in ever more frequent meetings, the Commission worked toward a collection of recommendations. Not until late October—beyond the October 1 deadline—was a general agreement among Commission members even in sight, and it was November 17 by the time Hahn could submit the Commission report to Governor Godwin.

19.2 The Hahn Commission report—The recommendations of the Hahn Commission (as the study commission was frequently called in those days), encompassing "a program of action" for the Commonwealth, included (1) creation of a state commission on local government to focus the state's concern for orderly growth and development of its metropolitan areas; (2) a new unit of government, the service district, encompassing an entire metropolitan area, to provide certain area-wide services, but with built-in safeguards to insure existing local governments would persist; (3) division of the state into planning districts, operated by new planning district commissions, a majority of whose members would be elected officials from the governing bodies of the local governments in the planning district; and (4) expansion of the State Division of Planning into a division of state planning and community affairs, to facilitate area-wide planning, assist the localities, and provide technical assistance to the proposed commission on local government.

The Hahn Commission recommended that the proposed commission on local government—rather than special annexation courts—decide annexation cases in metropolitan areas that had not created service districts. To encourage development of service districts, the Commission urged, the state should relieve the localities in such districts of the costs and administration of public welfare programs as soon as possible after January 1, 1970. Similarly, the state should, as soon as possible after July 1, 1975, take responsibility for expressways and arterial and primary roads in the cities and counties participating in service districts. An "urban assistance incentive fund" also would be set up in the governor's office to encourage innovation in solving urban problems. Submitted with the report were draft bills to implement the various recommendations.

President Hahn achieved a small miracle in obtaining anything like the agreement he did among the commission members. Only one—Senator Parkerson, the lawyer-legislator who had made a career out of representing Virginia counties in annexation cases—objected to the majority recommendations. Parkerson insisted upon publishing a vigorous, detailed dissent in the final report, and it proved to be a red flag for local officials in suburban counties. The proposed state commission could add a whole new element to city-county relationships—even requiring an area-wide referendum in which a majority could force consolidation—and strong opposition rapidly developed. Even the governor failed to support that element of the Commission proposals. Separate from Hahn Commission considerations, Governor Godwin was proposing a blue ribbon commission to recommend changes in the Virginia state constitution, to include the Hahn Commission proposals for a commission on local government and the use of an area-wide referendum to force the organization of service districts or even consolidation.

The draft legislation initially prepared by the Hahn Commission was held up, rewritten, and not introduced in the House and Senate until February 1. Much had been dropped from the package of proposals. Any new framework for local government had been made "permissive" or "optional," for example, and the proposed commission on local government had been eliminated. A *Richmond Times-Dispatch* editorial (8 February 1968), summing up the situation, observed that the "basic thrust" of the Hahn Commission's recommendations had been eliminated. The "totally voluntary action" by cities and counties in metropolitan areas, as permitted under the pending legislation, meant that nothing at all would be changed, said the paper. Several members of the commission were dismayed. Weldon Cooper, in a memo to the legislators who had served with him in the study (12 February 1968), warned, "Now that many of the key elements of the original package have been abandoned, I do not want to be regarded as necessarily favoring all that remain." (For contemporary accounts of the General Assembly's treatment of the Hahn Commission's proposals, see *Times-Dispatch*, 25 January and 2, 16, 17, and 21 February 1968.)

The volatile politics of the Richmond area in the late 1960s—a factor that compounded the problems in the General Assembly with the Hahn Commission recommendations—was related to the steadily increasing African American proportion of Richmond's population. As George Long later recalled, Henrico and Chesterfield counties were apprehensive about the possibility of forced consolidation with Richmond city. Former Senator FitzGerald Bemiss recalled concerns arising out of pressures to bus pupils between districts to achieve school desegregation: "When the busing thing came along, this really threw a monkey wrench in the works."

As matters turned out, Governor Godwin was right that a new policy was needed, and his Metropolitan Areas Study Commission came up with a report that could have addressed the needs, but the Hahn Commission proposals themselves were greatly diluted before any gained enactment. Commission members, years later, nonetheless remembered Marshall Hahn as an extraordinarily effective chairman.

George Long, for one, doubted that—in the beginning—anyone on the Commission agreed with any other member on anything about metropolitan area problems. "I'm not sure we all agreed on all the points at the end," he said, "but I think some progress was made." What most impressed him about Hahn's leadership of the Commission, Long remembered, was his ability to lead a discussion, to summarize what had been said in a few words, and to move the participants along in their thinking. "Everybody got a chance to talk," Long said, and explained: "As they progressed he would say, do you mean so and so, and so and so, and that agrees with somebody else.... The consequence was that in the end he was able to bring forth that statement we had been talking about. Everybody agreed more than they thought they would."[3]

Weldon Cooper expressed similar respect for the VPI president who worked so long and hard to come up with the Commission's recommendations. "In terms of keeping abreast of the work of the commission, in terms of leading the discussion, but not dominating it (there's a big difference)...he had fifteen of us...represent[ing] every point of view known to man, and yet he was able to guide it. He did his homework, he read the reports, he had his own ideas, but he tolerated other people's ideas," said Cooper. "Looking back on it, he was one of the most effective, if not the most effective chairman of a legislative study commission I have ever had anything to do with."[4]

Harold Baumes, long since retired, said that without Hahn's leadership the Commission would not have come out with the report it did. It likely would have said "yes, we recognize the problems and we should work further on them," he said. Hahn "had a brilliant mind and knew he could go into any field where there was division, and his forte was getting people together and inspiring them to greater heights in their solutions to these problems," as Baumes put it. "He was a great leader. Even if you differed with him, and some of the arguments became pretty heated, nobody got mad at him. You couldn't get mad at Marshall Hahn. He kept our feet to the fire until a seemingly insurmountable problem became surmountable, and that's what happened in this report."[5]

Bill Parkerson, who, more than anyone else, disagreed with the direction in which Hahn led the group, was similarly impressed. "Surely," he said, "Marshall Hahn was a leader.... For one thing, he...always seemed to totally comprehend the subject matter...the way he picked it up was amazing." And then, Parkerson commented, "there's the force of his personality."[6]

Taking a People's University to the People, via a College of Education

In the final years of President Hahn's administration, the university put together a College of Education and also laid the groundwork for what became the Virginia-Maryland Regional College of Veterinary Medicine. A number of considerations pointed toward establishing a College of Education that would pull together various undergraduate programs at VPI and also develop new graduate programs. Not only would this mean consolidating the VPI programs, it would also raise the level of public school teaching and administration across the Commonwealth. In

19.3 Marshall Hahn, governor of Virginia, 1970-1974?—The media people took notice of the Commission and its chairman. On July 6, 1967, for example, Helen Dewar published an article in the *Washington Post* about Hahn's rapid development of VPI, his work with the study commission, and his finely honed political instincts. Already there was "growing speculation" about a possible Hahn candidacy for the governorship, she wrote. Earlier, on May 10, Guy Fridell had profiled Hahn in the *Norfolk Virginian-Pilot*. The continuing media exposure resulting from the Commission's work—and also Hahn's public speeches, for he spoke frequently throughout the state as part of an effort to make Virginians more aware of some of the local governmental problems with which his commission wrestled—put him in the limelight.

The public attention and intensifying speculation as to a possible bid for the governorship undoubtedly had its effect, although Hahn said repeatedly that he was not at all interested in political office. Privately, he was writing friends that, even if he were interested, the last thing he would do was acknowledge the fact and thus politicize the commission study (e.g., letter to Mrs. Virginia Warren of Alexandria, 27 August 1967).

Indeed, by 1968, the young college president had been badly bitten by the political bug. In March 1968, shortly after the General Assembly

1969, moreover, VPI established in Reston the beginnings of what became the Northern Virginia Graduate Center—and, even later, the Northern Virginia Center in Falls Church—and in the 1970s Reston quickly became a major venue where VPI offered coursework in the new graduate programs in education.

The self-study back in 1966 had pointed the school toward developing a graduate program in education, but what was in place was a scattered collection of undergraduate curricula. In the late 1960s, various VPI faculty were professional education people who taught in the Department of Health and Physical Education and elsewhere. The Department of Education offered bachelor's degrees in agricultural education, business education, distributive education, elementary education, and vocational industrial education. A cooperative program with the math department offered a degree in math education, inaugurated in 1968. Beginning in 1970, VPI offered a bachelor's degree in science education and a master's degree in health and physical education. Doctoral programs, too, were under discussion.

approved what remained of the Hahn Commission recommendations, the first of Hahn's trial balloons concerning his possible candidacy for the governorship was lofted. Jim Latimer, the highly regarded political writer for the *Times-Dispatch*, published a big, front-page story under the headline "Hahn May Seek Governorship in 1969" (6 March 1968). Hahn was considering the possibility of entering the 1969 Democratic primary "if he were convinced a Democratic Party majority wants him to run," Latimer wrote. In the end, Hahn concluded that his chances were not good, and he stayed on at VPI.

As he himself explained many years later, "I felt that there was a very good chance of winning in the primaries, but with a runoff with the four candidates. I was concerned that with the runoff, there would be a bruising battle, and a good prospect of not winning in the general election then. What I didn't want to do was be a defeated gubernatorial candidate. So, while I thought there was a good chance, I didn't think that it was a sure enough prospect that I was willing to take the risk." In sum, said Hahn, "It was a reach and...you know, I am never one to back away from a challenge, but I don't tackle something to lose, and the odds just didn't look good enough." And finally, "I have no regrets, either that I took a look at it, or that I didn't run." (Hahn interview, 10 February 1990)

By February 1970, President Hahn recommended to the Board of Visitors that a dean-designate be appointed, effective July 1 that year, to plan a new College of Education, with the college to be officially created as of July 1, 1971. He was able to report that VPI's various colleges, SCHEV, and the state Department of Public Instruction all supported the proposal, and the BOV signed on. Appointed that summer to head VPI's seventh college was Karl T. Hereford, who since 1967 had served as a high administrator in the US Department of Education. Hereford had an Ed.D. from the University of Kentucky (1954), and he brought four years' experience as a public school teacher and administrator in Kentucky, followed by a decade as a professor of education at Michigan State University, where he developed considerable experience with international programs.

VPI encountered serious reservations about its initiative in graduate education programs. State budget director John McCutcheon, for example, wrote President Hahn in August 1971 raising questions about the new College of Education and the need for additional programs for training school teachers and for graduate work in education.

Responding at length to McCutcheon, Hahn traced the historical background to education courses and graduate programs at VPI, spoke in terms of efficiency regarding the consolidation of education programs at the Blacksburg campus, and then went to work arguing the case for the Commonwealth's compelling need for what VPI was attempting to do. The need for graduate programs in education, Hahn insisted, was real. True, Virginia had two other public universities that awarded doctorates in education, but their combined output averaged a mere sixteen per year—less than one-third of the need just to replace annual turnover; not even one-tenth of what was needed to bring Virginia to nationally accepted standards. Data from the state Department of Education indicated a need for 1,580 new people with master's degrees in education each year; the state was producing less than a quarter of that number. Finally, Hahn cited the Community College system's projected need by the year 1980 for 2,700 instructional, supervisory, and administrative personnel—triple the number currently available.[7]

Dean Hereford set about creating a College of Education. He worked from the premise that what was wanted was "a strong graduate program," one "with an off-campus emphasis," and "as much or as little undergraduate education" as seemed "appropriate." Rather than focus on training new teachers, "We really needed to grab hold of teachers in service and, through the device of a master's degree or a sixth year, really upgrade…not just their qualifications but their function." Astonished to find an "enormous enrollment in undergraduate education" (he used terms like "inundated" and "suffocated"), he tried to cap enrollments so he could concentrate his resources on what he saw as the central mission. After all, that mission was, as he characterized it, "to develop a really first-rate graduate school," both in Blacksburg and off-campus.[8]

Carl O. McDaniels—one of the young stars recruited to Virginia Tech (in 1969) at the time it was preparing to launch the college—related his sense of what President Hahn was attempting to build. Hahn's "vision" was that it was "not enough," McDaniels said, to give the new college "structure" and "life": "You had to bring in the best of faculty and administration. You had to attract then the top students at the undergraduate and graduate levels." And, he continued, Hahn "saw that, once you had those pieces together," you were ready to go to Northern Virginia, the state's fastest growing region, and be a part of the action there. "He did not want to have another University of Virginia," where everyone had to come to the central campus. "The Commonwealth was our campus, and we are going to be attracting people from all over Virginia. We'll come to them with some programs, and for some programs they will have to come to us."[9]

McDaniels also developed two key points regarding diversity and excellence. McDaniels recalled Hahn as committed to developing "a diverse faculty." You must, said McDaniels, have "a good faculty that is diverse to attract students who are diverse. So we attracted women, we attracted African Americans, we attracted students who had excellent public school and community college credentials. And those students were attracted by the quality of the faculty, and the care of the faculty." Regarding the college faculty's diversity in gender and in racial identity, McDaniels observed, "It was not a reflection of…the faculty that existed in the university at that time; it was really a much more diverse faculty than any other college on campus was able to attract. Of course we set out to do that in the beginning." McDaniels tied Hahn to this multifaceted agenda. "I think he understood from his experience" at Kansas State "how to set up the conditions to attract the best people. I think he had a vision of our College of Education leading the way with graduate programs in off-campus locations."

The College of Education had great support from the entire Hahn administration. Hereford spoke of how "the university really went to the mat to support the development of this little college. It never wanted for resources." McDaniels expressed much the same thought. In his view, Hereford had accepted the deanship precisely because of the great opportunities to build something excellent and innovative "under the direction of an outstanding and supportive president."[10]

Planning for a College of Veterinary Medicine

In the 1980s, the Virginia-Maryland College of Veterinary Medicine began enrolling students and granting degrees. The school began operations in 1980, on the watch of Marshall Hahn's successor, President William E. Lavery, and to Lavery must be given much of the credit for obtaining such a school.

The preliminary planning, though, was begun by 1974. VPI had long offered courses in veterinary medicine—it could hardly have done otherwise, given the historic importance of the agricultural curriculum at the A&M school. From undergraduate courses to a doctoral program was a far cry, but proponents, among them President Hahn, argued the urgent need to train more people who were highly qualified to oversee the health of the animal half of the nation's food supply. (At the time, Virginia had a small number of places reserved each year at other schools, including the University of Georgia, and the Southern Regional Education Board opposed the establishment of a school in Virginia.)

The General Assembly appointed a commission to study the question of a vet medical school in Virginia. In late 1973, the commission turned in its report, approving such a school and saying it should be located at Virginia Tech. At a BOV meeting in November 1973, Hahn spoke approvingly of the prospects—certainly the need—for establishing the program. In February 1974, though, Warren Strother spoke with regret of the failure of the outgoing governor, A. Linwood Holton, to include funds in his budget proposal, and the BOV recommended that the legislature add funds for planning costs in the 1974-1976 state budget for the university.

The legislature did, in fact, appropriate $225,000 to develop plans for a new college, though it did not commit itself to funding eventual construction, no matter how the planning developed. The new governor, Mills Godwin—back for a second term (he could not succeed himself, but he could return after a term away)—approved the appointment of a dean to begin planning for the college. But, in light of worsening economic and fiscal conditions, he held back the money and advised Tech to go ahead if it wished but with private funds. In May 1974, the BOV authorized such an appointment, and indeed a dean was appointed, to begin his duties September 1—recruited, as his widow, Jane, later recalled, with the assistance of President Hahn's customary energy, together with the *Hokie* plane.

The new dean of the projected school was Richard B. Talbot, who had served since 1968 as dean of the College of Veterinary Medicine at the University of Georgia. Talbot's degrees were from Midwestern land-grant schools (DVM, Kansas State; and Ph.D., Iowa State), and his teaching experience was at two land-grant schools (Iowa State and Georgia). He had been a member of the Virginia legislature's commission on the matter of a veterinary college the previous year, so he had ample opportunity to become acquainted with the situation in Virginia before he was offered the opportunity to lead the quest at Virginia Tech. Though there were delays beyond the anticipated opening of the school in 1978, it did open in 1980 as a joint venture with Maryland.[11]

VPI and NASA

Virginia Tech left fingerprints all over the National Aeronautics and Space Administration. Christopher C. Kraft Jr., class of 1944, worked in the space program from the 1950s into the 1980s. He directed flight operations for the Mercury, Gemini, and Apollo programs; worked on the space shuttle; and, from 1972 to 1982, directed the Lyndon B. Johnson Manned Space Center in Houston. As early as 1962, *Life* magazine included Kraft in its list of the most important young men in America.

19.5 Chris Kraft returns to VPI—In view of Kraft's national popularity as well as his distinguished career, Craig Fabian proposed an elaborate program—and took charge of the planning—involving the award of the Alumni Association's Distinguished Alumnus Citation to Kraft during a weekend convocation. In previous years, with Board approval, the citation had been awarded to various alumni for exceptional service and significant achievement. Kraft's would be the first such award in the Hahn administration. The Chris Kraft program, described as a "testimonial of honor," was set for November 11-13, 1965. It all fell into place beautifully. Chris, Betty, and their children, Kristi-Anne and Gordon, came in on Thursday from Hampton in time for a news conference and a luncheon. Ambler Johnston gave Kraft a copy of *The Air Arm of the Confederacy*, and the civilian students presented an engraved tankard. The members of the Cadet Corps welcomed one of their own with a mounted replica of the Corps' ceremonial cannon, "Skipper."

At a formal convocation, Kraft was presented the original painting for the *Time* cover, by Pittsburgh artist Henry Koerner; Robert D. Sweeney, the magazine's public affairs director, came down from New York to make the presentation. President Hahn gave Kraft a Steuben crystal piece as well as the Distinguished Alumnus Citation itself. The convocation speaker—Dr. Ray Bisplinghoff, special assistant to NASA administrator James Webb—talked about the special importance of creativity.

The Krafts were the houseguests of the Hahns for a busy weekend—a Friday morning television appearance in Roanoke; induction into the Virginia

As flight director of the Manned Spacecraft Center, Kraft attracted national attention with his relaxed and levelheaded direction of the Gemini space flights. Millions of Americans watched their television screens in awe as the astronauts rode tiny space capsules into the unknown void of space, in preparation for the trip to the moon itself. In the August 27, 1965, issue—following Kraft's Space Center performance during the Gemini-5 flight—*Time* magazine ran a cover story on him.

VPI itself was playing an important role in the national space program, involving sophisticated technology transfer. During summer 1965, the University hosted another in a series of summer space conferences; this one focused on unmanned space flights to other planets. Earlier conferences had examined the technology NASA was using in the dramatic exploratory manned spacecraft ventures then attracting so much attention. The first major engineering conference on the campus was back in

Tech chapter of Omicron Delta Kappa, national leadership fraternity; a student-faculty convocation; and a taped radio program. Fabian also organized a dinner for Kraft and many of his VPI classmates, which they all enjoyed immensely. Saturday's agenda was full, too, with a meeting with the VPI Board, a special luncheon, and the Tech-Villanova football game. A dozen bands, participating in Band Day, serenaded the Krafts at halftime. Media people turned out in force to cover the festivities.

Afterward, Harry Wyatt and the N&W Railway provided a private railway car back to Washington, where the Krafts took a plane to Houston. Kraft wrote Hahn to expressed his sincere appreciation for it all. Dr. Hahn's guidance and enthusiasm, Kraft wrote, had "caused the campus to show a quality never before present," and he looked forward, he said, to VPI's emergence as "one of the greatest universities in the country." Hahn wrote back to say "everyone thoroughly enjoyed and were honored by your visit." It was quite a weekend. (Hahn papers, 1965; VPI *Bulletin* 59/1, January 1966)

Chris Kraft returned to Virginia Tech to give the Founders Day address in 1974 on "Space in the 1970s." Declaring that the space program had "evolved from a decade of exploration to a decade of exploitation," he celebrated the returns on investment during the 1960s. Those benefits, he said—byproducts of the space program—included medical monitoring systems; improved blood analyzers; and electronic controls that could be used by paralyzed people. (*Techgram*, May 1974; Christopher C. Kraft, "Commitment for Tomorrow," *Context* 8 [autumn 1974]: 16-19)

1950, organized by Dr. Dan Pletta, then the energetic head of engineering mechanics (now engineering science and mechanics). Others were held during the 1950s, after NASA was organized, growing out of VPI's work with the Langley Air Force Base Research Center. The national space program was at full blast by 1961, when the summer conference focused on the physics of the solar system and reentry dynamics. Funded primarily by a $49,250 grant from the National Science Foundation, it was sponsored jointly by VPI, the NSF, and NASA. About 100 invited Canadian and American scientists participated. Dr. John Stack, NASA's assistant director, found it productive and urged that another such conference be put together in the following year. Such intensive examination of the problems of space travel was terribly important, he said.

The second space conference—in August 1962, weeks after Marshall Hahn became president of VPI—attracted even more attention. D. Brainerd Homes, director of NASA's manned space program, was among the speakers. So were Dr. Wernher von Braun, the German rocket expert, and Dr. Harold C. Urey, a Nobel laureate in physics, who joined a couple of dozen other widely known scientists and rocket experts. Similar conferences were held in 1963, 1964, and 1965, with the chairmanship rotating among faculty leaders. By 1965, the conference was examining unmanned space flights to other planets; Mariner IV but recently had sent back data from Mars.[12]

19.6 Summer Study Abroad begins for VPI students—Summer 1967 brought a new opportunity for VPI students. Dr. Joachim Bruhn, head of foreign languages, arranged for groups to spend time that summer in Germany, Russia, or Mexico, where they would live with a local family, develop their proficiency in the language, and be exposed to the culture and politics of the host nation. The program was designed for any student, in any curriculum, so long as he or she already had a working knowledge of the German, Russian, or Spanish language. This was only a beginning, for it was expected that the program would develop in two ways in the next few years. Bruhn hoped to arrange for additional groups to go to France in summer 1968 and Italy and Scandinavia in 1969. Moreover, plans were in the works to facilitate longer visits for students who wished them. (*Techgram*, May 1967; see also April 1972)

VPI in the Philippines

Dr. Ruben W. "Charlie" Engel (Ph.D., Wisconsin, 1939) came to VPI from Auburn in 1952 to build a strong Department of Biochemistry and Nutrition, primarily for graduate level work. In 1966, he was appointed associate dean for research and graduate studies in the College of Agriculture. Dr. Kendall W. King, one of Dr. Engel's former students who, like Engel, had gone to Wisconsin for his Ph.D., succeeded him as department head. King's work in Haiti had previously attracted considerable attention, for he had had extraordinary results with malnourished infants and young children in Haiti with a low-cost, high-protein cereal blend that Haitian mothers were taught how to prepare and use.

In such ways, VPI in the Hahn years built on the premises of the Smith-Lever Act of 1914. Tech extended the benefits of its research activities through off-campus programs that took the results not only across the state but around the world.

In June 1967, VPI entered into a contract with the US Agency for International Development (AID) to assist in planning a nutrition program for the Philippines. The next month, Charlie Engel went to Manila on an assignment as special assistant to W. C. Haroldson, mission director for AID there, to develop a comprehensive program to combat malnutrition in the Philippines, especially among children.

Later in 1967, several other VPI people also traveled to Manila and other areas in the Philippines to work with Dr. Engel, AID, and Philippine officials on the planning project. They included Dr. Kendall King, who joined Engel in Manila for two months in September. Dr. Thomas C. Campbell, assistant professor of biochemistry and nutrition, also spent about six weeks in Manila, and Dean Wilson Bell went over for ten days in November to review the project activities and plans. Finally, President Hahn went to Manila for five days in December to participate with officials from AID and the Philippines in the official opening of a comprehensive national nutrition program.[13]

The five-year comprehensive nutrition program Engel put together with Haroldson in Manila involved the development of "mothercraft" centers to reach more than 92,000 infants and preschool children with specially prepared foods to improve nutrition levels. High-nutrition, low-cost foods—carefully tested to insure acceptability and wholesomeness—would be developed to supplement locally available corn and rice. Food for Peace commodities were to be used initially but then phased out as newly developed foods became available. Much of the research work would be done on the VPI campus, and VPI would provide special training for Philippine government and educational laboratory personnel, both in Blacksburg and in the Philippines. It envisioned funding by US AID/Philippines and other international agencies such as the World Health Organization of approximately $305,000 annually.

Herbert J. Waters, assistant administrator in Washington for the US AID "war on hunger" program, wrote to President Hahn in January 1968 that he was "most delighted" with the way the project was developing and with VPI's role in it. It was the first "multi-faceted program to combat malnutrition," Waters wrote, and "we are keenly interested in following its progress and helping in any way possible to ensure its success." The initial VPI two-year contract in support of the National Nutrition Program in the Philippines was budgeted at about $163,000 for the first year and $183,000 for the second.[14]

19.7 Undergraduate research—in Antarctica—The benefits to undergraduate students of studying at a research university are not necessarily self-evident. The cartoon has it that the faculty members are all off researching somewhere and the students are left with teaching assistants. In the early 1970s, another image came into focus. In fall quarter 1973, for example, the second installment of a five-year research project took Virginia Tech faculty and students—graduate students and undergraduates, male and female—to Antarctica for eight weeks. Directing the project, which the National Science Foundation was funding (with $95,000 that second year), were botany professor Bruce Parker, the principal investigator; biology department head Robert A. Paterson; and Robert C. Hoehn, an assistant professor in civil engineering.

The students—all of them with backgrounds in chemistry, microbiology, geology, or engineering—had trained the previous summer at Mountain Lake, west of Blacksburg, to bond as an efficient group, prepared to live and work under challenging weather conditions. The news story carried the headline "Unique Antarctic Research Resumes" and opened with the sentence: "The first and only research program in Antarctica to employ undergraduate students, including women, will begin its second field operations this fall" (*Techgram*, November 1973).

Later in 1968, Dr. Engel and his wife, Florence, went to Manila, where he headed up VPI's participation and served as nutrition advisor for the program. Engel found himself immersed in a new career that lasted until his retirement from Virginia Tech in 1977.

In the meantime, President Richard Nixon appointed President Hahn in 1972 to a six-year term on the National Science Board, the governing board of the National Science Foundation. In that capacity, Hahn helped formulate the nation's science policy. In late 1973, Hahn and five other NSF people went to Antarctica for two weeks to visit research stations there and review the programs the United States had under way. From the South Pole, he wrote on December 4: "This is both the most demanding and the most fascinating experience of my life." He spoke of the region's indescribable beauty and its dangers, cold, and dryness; of traveling by everything from jet to sled; of working with scientists from Italy, Russia, Japan, and New Zealand; and reported: "I have been on glaciers, salt lakes, fresh lakes, the sea ice, and an active volcano. The seals and penguins have seen so few men that they are fearless, and I have petted and played with both."[15]

The Stone Commission

President Hahn could never assume that what he had accomplished was nailed down and would prove permanent. The best evidence of the contingency of it all came in 1972 when the General Assembly established a Commission on Higher Education. In Senate Joint Resolution 21's original language, the commission was to explore the feasibility of creating a "Board of Higher Education" to replace the State Council of Higher Education, the State Board of Community Colleges, and the governing boards of the various state colleges and universities. Such a move would curtail the autonomy of a university president to pursue institutional transformation of the sort Marshall Hahn had achieved at Virginia Tech. Beyond that, by threatening a number of the specific achievements of the Hahn years, the commission—first through its mere establishment, then through some of its actions—called into question much of what he had done during the 1960s.

The entire episode, which unfolded over the next two years and consumed enormous administrative energy at Tech, exemplified the continuing challenges to President Hahn's efforts and also his continued leadership—his continued involvement in state politics, whether to secure further institutional change or to forestall what he saw as serious threats to public higher education in Virginia. Hahn understood that he had to work in the realm of state politics as much as he had to work on campus or with alumni. Some of Hahn's involvement in the wider world was more on his own terms, some less, but never, as president of a large and growing public institution, could he work as though the campus was his universe.

19.8 Countering the Shaner Report to the Stone Commission—The Stone Commission, named for its chair (until he died in August 1973), Senator William F. Stone, put the actual work into the hands of a management consultant firm, Donald Shaner and Associates of Chicago, Illinois. Late in the proceedings, what were purported to be fragments of the report—perceived at Tech as misleading and damaging—were leaked to the press. A story by Charles Cox, "Cuts, Controls on College May Be Recommended," appeared in the *Richmond Times-Dispatch*, September 19, 1973, several weeks before that year's gubernatorial and legislative elections. Cox, the paper's education writer, stated as what seemed to be fact that Virginia's system of higher education was "overbuilt"—especially, it seemed, at Radford, Longwood, and William and Mary, though perhaps new money might have to go into three urban campuses: VCU, Old Dominion, and George Mason. A similar story— "College Building Criticized," by Carl Shires—appeared in the *Richmond News Leader* the same day.

President Hahn's staff went to work to fight the latest fire. Two days later, a memo to him outlined Virginia Tech's criticism of the Shaner Report, or what had been leaked of the report. The memo characterized the leaks to the press as appearing "calculated to begin clouding the public institutions' chances during the 1974 session, especially for capital outlay funds, and also aimed toward building the climate for greater appropriations for private institutions for enrollment of larger numbers of students." Hahn was urged to "start lighting some backfires promptly." Such efforts might include "an outright attack on the validity of the study, based on the experience at VPI and U.Va., if Mr. Shannon's University will join us." Moreover, "the entire report should be made public before the election, to avoid the whispering campaign, and to get it out in the open where we can intelligently attack" it. The Shaner studies of Virginia's public institutions of higher education, he observed, at least so far as the "VPI model" was concerned, "appear to be so entirely wide of the mark, and so superficial, that they are eerie," and the public should be apprised that the report "could have been written without spending a dollar or visiting a school." Because so much was at stake, "the higher educational community must attack, and with reasonable dispatch. It would appear essential that you take the leadership in this area, because I don't see anyone else among the colleges and universities doing it."

In the days ahead, Hahn was a whirlwind of activity. On behalf of the Council of Presidents of State-Aided Institutions of Higher Learning in Virginia, Hahn wrote on September 25 to the Commission's new chair, Senator Edward E. Willey, requesting that the full report on each institution be made available to that institution "as soon as possible"; that sufficient time be given for review; that meetings be held with the Commission to go over those reports; and that "after such meeting and any necessary analysis and correction," the reports be released to the public.

On October 5, in another letter to Willey, Hahn sought to correct what he saw as serious misrepresentations of his own words in the Richmond press that day. Stating his support of the Commission's work, he explained, "My concern was expressed about the widespread rumors generated by newspaper accounts, which are spreading across the State and feeding on one another, to the effect that there are system-wide problems of mismanagement and overbuilding in the State-supported colleges and universities." Insisting that he had "consistently...declined to discuss the consultant's reports," and in fact had seen only the preliminary report about his own school, he went on: "When asked directly if there are charges of mismanagement, overbuilding, and overspending at this University, I deny that there are such allegations because I know of no such charges."

In the weeks ahead, news leaks included one recommendation that Christopher Newport College be abolished and another that Radford College be once again merged with Virginia Tech. Despite apparent success in getting an opportunity to address the preliminary report before a final report was issued, President Hahn had to address the Radford question again, together with many others, in a statement issued January 28, 1974. Though such a merger had not been mentioned in the report to which Tech had earlier responded, the final Shaner report to the Commission included such a recommendation, and Hahn took strong exception as to both the improper process and the dubious merit. After pointing out various "questionable or even erroneous conclusions set forth in the consultant's report," Hahn took direct aim at the issue of Radford's separate existence: "None of the conditions which made it desirable to separate" the two schools ten years earlier "have changed," he insisted. In the end, Radford and Tech remained separate institutions, but the episode revealed how little it could be assumed that the great policy initiatives of the 1960s were all locked in.

Marshall Hahn, Virginia Tech, and a Wider World

In the interests of maximizing what he could get done, President Hahn worked hard, made administrative changes, and collapsed the time to travel by acquiring the *Hokie* and flying places. He extended his workdays by getting started at four and five in the morning. He had so much to do, "both off campus and on campus," as he later explained, that he "compensated for it by working so hard and working so long" that he "still spent a lot of time on the campus."[16]

The relationship between VPI and the nation's space program offers something of a metaphor for a president's travels and his institution's reach. Not only did President T. Marshall Hahn preside at the Blacksburg campus, exhort the alumni, and lobby the legislature. As a consequence of the close relationship he developed with Governor Godwin, he was asked to chair a statewide commission on the governance of metropolitan areas—and his experience on that commission sparked an interest for a while in running for the Virginia governorship himself. Back in Blacksburg, he laid the groundwork for an innovative college of education and a regional college of veterinary medicine. And, not only did he get away with his family to the Caribbean from time to time to recharge his batteries, but he even followed his school's and the nation's researchers to the South Pole and the western Pacific.

[1] Hahn interview, 7 October 1989.

[2] American Red Cross speech, Portsmouth, 11 January 1967.

[3] George Long interview.

[4] Weldon Cooper interview.

[5] Harold Baumes interview.

[6] William Parkerson interview.

[7] Hahn letter, 10 September 1971.

[8] Franklin interview with Hereford, 7, 10, 16, 31. The success at the core mission was itself a source of some concern on campus, Hereford recalled, since by the mid-1970s the College of Education was producing close to half of the university's doctorates (actually, more like a quarter or so, but still a lot).

[9] Carl McDaniels interview.

[10] Franklin interview with Hereford, 31; McDaniels interview.

[11] The section on Vet Med is drawn from *Techgram*, February 1974, March 1974, June 1974, October 1974; Warren Strother, "The View from Here," *Context* 8 (autumn 1974); and files in College of Veterinary Medicine, RG 20, Special Collections.

[12] The material on NASA and the VPI conferences is drawn from the *Techgram*, 15 July 1961, 2 September 1962, 1 August 1963, 1 August 1964, and 1 September 1964, as well as an interview with Dan Pletta.

[13] Dr. Engel returned to the US in early December 1967 and spent a good part of January 1968 reviewing the program plan with AID officials in Washington and planning VPI participation in it (*Techgram*, December 1967; Engel memo, 25 January 1968). For more on the program, see Engel interview.

[14] Waters warned, however, that budget reductions in the AID program necessitated further review of possible funding levels (Waters letter, 22 January 1968; memo, 3 December 1968).

[15] Hahn interview, 10 February 1970; letters to James J. Pandapas, 2 October 1972, and Gene Rowe, 20 November 1973; handwritten note, 4 December 1973.

[16] Hahn interview, 7 October 1989.

Always involved in activities beyond the campus, in 1972 President Hahn served as president of the Virginia chapter of the American Cancer Society. Courtesy of T. Marshall Hahn Jr.

Dr. Ruben W. Engel, professor and department head of biochemistry and nutrition. Engel Hall is named in his honor.

20: Centennial

T. Marshall Hahn Jr.'s first day at the office as president of VPI—July 2, 1962—had marked the centennial of President Abraham Lincoln's signing the Morrill Land-Grant College Act, the act of Congress that later led to the establishment of what was known until 1896 as Virginia Agricultural and Mechanical College. Also in 1962, Virginia Polytechnic Institute celebrated its ninetieth birthday.

During the year 1972—actually, the entire academic year 1971-1972—Virginia Polytechnic Institute and State University celebrated its own centennial, and Marshall Hahn completed his tenth year as the school's president. The extraordinary changes of President Hahn's early years had had time to take hold. Much of the dust had settled, and it was becoming clear what kind of institution the school had become—and what kind of school it was becoming, for further changes were either under way or in prospect.

Centennial Celebration, 1972

A campus publication, the *Techgram*, observed in September 1971 that Virginia Polytechnic Institute and State University was beginning its hundredth academic year and also kicking off a yearlong centennial celebration. Enrollment approached 13,000—appropriately enough, writers might have noted, one hundred times the figure from Virginia Agricultural and Mechanical College's first year.

Three major new buildings approached completion. One was Whittemore Hall, named for John W. Whittemore, faculty member for thirty-five years and dean of engineering from 1952 to 1963. Another was Cheatham Hall, designed to house programs in forestry and wildlife and named after Julian N. Cheatham, class of 1933 and executive vice-president of the Georgia-Pacific Corporation. The third was McBryde Hall, built on the site of the former McBryde Building, named for Tech's fifth president and home of several departments in the College of Arts and Sciences: mathematics, history, political science, and sociology.

Other kinds of monuments to Tech's growth also emerged in the centennial year. Scheduled for publication at the beginning of March 1972 was a 500-page book, a heroic undertaking, *The First 100 Years: A History of Virginia Polytechnic Institute and State University*.[1] Its author was Duncan Lyle Kinnear, widely known as Lyle or "Deacon."

Kinnear brought impressive credentials to his task. Having earned his bachelor's and master's degrees at Tech, he had taught psychology and education at his alma mater since 1936, so he had an intimate acquaintance with the school's more recent history. His dissertation (completed at Ohio State University in 1952) explored "A History of Agricultural Education in Virginia," so he also brought training in history and knowledge of his topic's early years. With the inducement of "one year of reduced teaching responsibilities and one year of no teaching" (as he reported)—so he could focus on the assignment at hand—he agreed to take it on. Over the frenetic months ahead, working through huge piles of materials on the dining room table at his Price's Fork home—a young records administrator, Douglas D. Martin ('64), kept finding yet another box of materials—Kinnear filled one after another yellow legal pad in longhand narrative. A team of other people converted longhand to typewriting, edited the results, and brought the book down to manageable size, still a hefty volume.[2]

Kinnear rued about his task that he had to proceed with little previous written work on which to draw. Regarding Tech's faculty and staff of the first hundred years, he observed as he finished his book, "Everyone was so busy getting the job done that nobody worried about putting it down on paper." "Beyond a shadow of doubt," Kinnear wrote, "VPI in its first century was more concerned with making history by rendering service on all fronts than it was with recording this history." Yet he was committed to recounting "the contributions of its programs, faculty, and alumni to the state and the nation." And he had reason to be gratified with the response to his book. One reviewer, Guy Fridell, spoke in glowing terms about how well Kinnear had gone about "light[ing] the candles" on Tech's "100th birthday."[3]

20.1 Duncan Lyle Kinnear (1904-2001)—In 1969, a longtime professor at VPI was asked to take on the task of writing a centennial history of the school, and, with some reluctance but much encouragement, he did so. Kinnear was himself an institution. From his home in Rockbridge County, he had arrived at VPI as a freshman in 1923, intent on studying agricultural engineering. Serious illness three years later forced him to return to his home in the Shenandoah Valley for rest and recuperation.

He did not soon get back to Blacksburg. For six years, he "taught school, helped operate the family farm, was appointed deputy commissioner of revenue, served as a bank appraiser, became president of the local telephone company," and gained a maturity and a breadth of experience that served him well after he returned to VPI in 1932 for his senior year. Looking to prepare to teach science, he abandoned his former program of study—he later said that his "greatest contribution to engineering was to get out of the field" (Kinnear, *The First 100 Years*, viii). Free to return as a civilian student (given the 1924 policy change ending the requirement that juniors and seniors remain in the Corps of Cadets), he lived off campus in a boarding house, where he picked up the sobriquet "Deacon," a name that stuck throughout the rest of his long life.

After graduation in 1933, he returned for three years to Rockbridge County, where he taught science and served as high school principal. But in 1936 he returned permanently to Blacksburg. He earned a doctorate; married Florence Price, a Latin teacher at Blacksburg High School; and taught—for a number of years at both Radford and Blacksburg—courses that included math, vocational education, and applied psychology.

Kinnear pursued an interest in history, becoming, as he liked to say, an amateur historian, something that he defined as a person "who remembers events whether they happened or not" (*The First 100 Years*, ix). Between 1969 and 1971 he wrote a big book on VPI's first hundred years. Then he retired from teaching, though he still lived at Price's Fork when the school celebrated its 125th birthday in 1997. As one of the authors of this book said to the other at the Deacon's funeral, "he was a grand old man." As his widow replied emphatically, "He sure was."

During four days in May 1922, Virginia Polytechnic Institute cele-brated its Golden Jubilee. Fifty years later, Tech planned what was called a "Centennial Founders Day Program." March 19 marked the precise day the school turned a hundred, but the Board of Visitors, recognizing that March 19 that year fell on a Sunday and during spring break, opted to schedule the observance five days later.

The Founders Day festivities harked back to the Golden Jubilee in lin-ing up participants. These included direct descendants of the first student, the first Board of Visitors, and Tech presidents from Charles L. C. Minor to Walter S. Newman. Speakers included John W. Hancock Jr., class of 1925 and president of the VPI Educational Foundation, which had spon-sored Kinnear's book. President T. Marshall Hahn noted that Tech had begun as a "people's university" and vowed that it would remain one. Wilson B. Bell, the director of university development, expressed the wish that Founders Day "become an annual event" on campus, a wish that came true.[4]

Governor Linwood Holton, who came to campus for the celebration, had invited President Richard Nixon to Blacksburg and then, when the president sent his regrets, Elliott Richardson, US Secretary of Heath, Education, and Welfare. When Richardson, too, proved unable to attend, HEW undersecretary John G. Veneman rushed to Tech to represent the federal government's office in charge of education.

Various events followed during the year of celebration. The evening after Founders Day, three women from Tech's first coeducational class, who enrolled in 1921—Mary Brumfield Garnett, Lucy Lee Lancaster, and Carrie Sibold—were feted at a dinner at the Donaldson Brown Center for Continuing Education.

At a "rededication ceremony" for McBryde Hall in April, faculty gath-ered and took their places in students' seats. Told they should prepare for class by reading about President McBryde, they took notes while Kinnear recited McBryde's accomplishments. William C. Havard Jr., dean of the College of Arts and Sciences, also spoke. During the same ceremony, President Hahn, alumnus and architect J. Ambler Johnston, and history department head and Civil War historian James I. Robertson Jr. celebrat-ed a bequest from Frank L. Curtis to the history department in support of research in Virginia history and the history of the Civil War (a fund that continued to support such research into the twenty-first century).[5]

Centennial Montgomery County Day took place on May 23 to recall the county's support of the school at that crucial moment a hundred years before, when the offer of $20,000 to help launch a land-grant institution swung legislative votes to the support of a little Methodist school at Blacksburg. The 1972 Tech Board of Visitors, together with descendants of the 1872 county Board of Supervisors, attended a luncheon that ended with a huge cake that had 100 candles. Tech and the county's public schools alike dismissed afternoon classes, and thousands of people turned out to watch or march in a parade around campus and through downtown Blacksburg.

After the Centennial commencement in June, one major event remained, and it took place in October, intended to coincide with the time of year that Virginia Agricultural and Mechanical College opened its doors in 1872. Termed the University's "Second Century Emphasis Week," the two-day program—which took place at the Donaldson Brown Center for Continuing Education—brought a hundred state leaders from education and the private sector to campus to consider what the role of higher education ought to be. What should be a university's priorities? How should higher education be financed? These and other questions framed the discussion, as Virginia Tech looked to its own role in the future.[6]

The Board of Visitors took various actions during the centennial year that set the stage for developments across the next quarter-century and more. The Board approved a system of fraternities and sororities. It established an Academy of Teaching Excellence. It also created the position of Alumni Distinguished Professor and named geology professor F. Donald Bloss the first ADP. And it inaugurated Alumni Scholarships, the first five of which went to entering freshmen in 1972. The Alumni professorships and scholarships reflected initiatives of the Alumni Association, which wished to offer men and women who had once studied at Tech opportunities to observe the centennial celebration in tangible, continuing ways. The Alumni Association acted in accordance with President Hahn's observation that no better uses could be made of private contributions to the University.

Commencement took place as a centennial activity, and television newsman David Brinkley spoke at the graduation ceremony at Lane Stadium. Graduates—President Hahn designated them the "centennial graduation class"—numbered 2,182 who received bachelor's degrees, 385 who completed master's programs, and 114 who earned doctorates.

As it celebrated its hundredth anniversary, the University was operating on a whole new scale, in total enrollment and in graduate programs. Nearly as many people completed doctoral programs in the centennial year as had attended Tech in its first year; almost as many doctorates were awarded in 1972 as in all the commencements combined that ever took place before Hahn's appointment as president.

20.2 Adopting a new name for President Hahn's university—Within the first few years after Marshall Hahn became president, people with connections to VPI—especially among the alumni—began seriously considering a new name for the place. The Higher Education Study Commission Report, released in December 1965, urged that a new name be adopted, one that better described the rapidly growing institution than did "Virginia Polytechnic Institute." The old name, said the Commission, did "not convey to the average citizen in the United States an accurate conception of the role and scope of the program maintained at Blacksburg." Accordingly, a better designation should be chosen, "one that will indicate its historic importance as the land-grant university of Virginia," and the word "University" should be included.

The president's office did what it could to make the ground rules clear. In January 1967, Lon Savage wrote a letter—accompanied by the appropriate pages of the Commission Report—to Bruce Ross, the director of alumni affairs. "If a decision is made to consider the question of a name change," the letter advised, "such consideration would be done by means of a lengthy study, involving the full university community and most assuredly the alumni." No such study was under way, the note continued, so "the administration has not solicited comments or opinion on a name change." If any alumni wished to make unsolicited suggestions, that was fine, but the question was not up for serious discussion.

It was not so much that Hahn was against a change of name. After all, he had, from the beginning of his presidency, referred to the institution as "the University," and he had moved multiple mountains to convert a polytechnic institute into a research university. Yet a change of name invited trouble. The decision regarding a voluntary Corps of Cadets had badly split the alumni in 1964, and the breach was not yet healed. There were other fires to fight before taking on the matter of name change. No need to invite a conflagration.

Over the next few years, the question kept coming up, and eventually the time seemed right to take it on. But what should the new name be, if the school were to adopt one? "Virginia State University" sounded promising. It would echo such institutions as North Carolina State, Mississippi State, Montana State, and Kansas State. Virginia's other land-grant school, though, had already adopted the name Virginia State College, and before long it became Virginia State University.

In 1970, the legislature rolled out the Blacksburg school's new name. In much the way that the school's first name had been retained in 1896 when VAMC became VPI—Virginia Agricultural and Mechanical College and Polytechnic Institute (the shorter name, VPI, though used unofficially as early as 1896, was formally adopted only in 1944)—its third name was retained when it became Virginia Polytechnic Institute and State University. Marshall Hahn celebrated his tenth anniversary as president of a school that had a new institutional identity from the place to which he first returned in 1962.

The name did not obtain universal approval. Some people from Tech remember that, in a student-run naming context in the 1970s, one nomination—intended to be long; faithful to the school's agricultural past; and yet indicative of the recent changes—was something like the "Eastern Institute of Enlightenment and Intellectual Outgrowth," to be abbreviated as EIEIO (see *Virginia Tech Magazine* 26/2 [winter 2004]: 2). In any case, the 1970 moniker proved unwieldy, and more and more—especially in the sports pages—the school became known as Virginia Tech, though the old name lived on too. In distant cities, fellow conference goers might see a name tag and ask its wearer about Virginia Tech: "Is that anywhere near VPI?" Too often the full name gets corrupted by media people into forms like "Virginia Technical College." People in Europe and Asia often understand a "polytechic institute" as not at all a "state university." Even some Virginia Tech faculty—seeking an upgrade, perhaps, or greater formality without giving the full name—have been known to present themselves as associated with an institution, "Virginia Tech University," that has nonetheless never existed. Among other possibilities, the time for "Virginia A&M University" would seem to have passed. In view of the shelf life of every previous name (never less than twenty-four years, but never longer than forty-eight), another name could be said to be due by 2018, and perhaps the twenty-first century would see Virginia Tech University after all.

The Student Population at Virginia Tech

The University as it stood at the centennial had changed markedly since the time Marshall Hahn took the helm a decade earlier, in 1962. Overall size offered one measure of change. Student enrollment, which had stood at an all-time high of 5,827 in 1961-1962, Walter Newman's last year, doubled by 1970. Beginning in 1966, it rose a thousand each year—exceeding 10,000 in fall 1968; 12,000 fall 1970; 14,000 fall 1972; and 17,000 fall 1974 (see appendix 1).

Within those numbers, too, the student population showed tremendous change. In 1962, most VPI freshmen and sophomores—as well as large numbers of juniors and seniors—were in the Corps of Cadets. A decade later, not one in ten Tech students was in the Corps. At the beginning of Hahn's administration, women had routinely numbered no more than one in twenty among VPI's students. In the 1970s, the fraction surged past one in four. In other ways as well, the numbers alone charted at least a partial transformation of one Southern, historically white, landgrant school. The numbers of African Americans enrolled at VPI jumped from single digits into low triple digits. The number of graduate students was far higher than ever before.

Graduation figures reveal some of the changes. Through 1962, the largest number of degrees ever awarded to Tech students had come in 1950, in the aftermath of World War II, at the height of the GI Bill's impact on the school. The 1950 total was 1,443, of which 93 percent were bachelor's degrees. In 1962, at President Newman's last commencement, the total was 1,165. By the middle of the decade, all the numbers began to surge. Hahn's first several commencements awarded just over 1,000 bachelor's degrees. That number began a rapid growth in 1968 and, beginning in 1970, always exceeded 2,000. The number of master's degrees awarded reached a new high, 186, in Newman's final year. The figure reached 385 at the centennial commencement of 1972 and then, beginning in 1975, always exceeded 800. The number of doctoral degrees awarded also reached a new high, 25, in Newman's final year. Beginning in 1970, the number always exceeded 100 (see appendix 2).

The growth continued through the years that followed. In 1997, for example, when Tech celebrated its 125th year, enrollment was approximately 25,000. The school awarded 5,701 degrees in 1996-1997—9 percent to doctoral candidates, 24 percent to master's students, and 67 percent to undergraduates. In the thirty-five years since President Newman stepped down, enrollment had more than quadrupled, the total number of degrees awarded had roughly quintupled, and the number of graduate degrees had multiplied by nearly eight.

The College of Arts and Sciences

When Leslie Malpass succeeded Burke Johnston as dean of the College of Arts and Sciences in summer 1965 (see chapter 4), the College consisted of thirteen departments (these included air science and military science, the two ROTC departments under direction of active military officers who commanded the Air Force and Army ROTC units at VPI). The regular academic departments were biology, chemistry, English and foreign languages, geological sciences, health and physical education, history and political science, mathematics, philosophy and religion, physics, statistics, and vocational education. Most offered major programs; one exception was philosophy and religion; the other, health and physical education. In addition, arts and sciences students could elect to major in economics, in cooperation with the economics department (at that time in the College of Business). Byron Cooper's geological sciences department offered majors in both geology and geophysics, and the biology department offered options in botany and zoology. Vocational education students could opt to major in distributive education, industrial arts, or vocational-industrial.

20.3 The Department of Psychology and Sociology—The Department of Psychology and Sociology supplies a good example of how the disciplines in the College of Arts and Sciences grew in size and independence during the Hahn years. In 1965, Dr. Brandt, working through appropriate channels, pulled "rural sociology" out of the College of Agriculture, where it was a separate curriculum in agricultural education, and put it in a new psychology/sociology department, with a new curriculum, in the College of Arts and Sciences. Dr. Randolph S. Thrush came to VPI from Ohio State University that year as an untenured associate professor of psychology and headed the combined department. At that time, psychology did not yet have a baccalaureate program, although B.S. and M.S. degree programs were inaugurated in sociology.

As the department was being organized, Dr. Leland B. Tate Jr., who in 1937 had been the first sociologist appointed at VPI outside the Agricultural Experiment Station, moved to the new psychology/sociology department. His colleagues who held appointments in the Agricultural Experiment Station and in the Agricultural Extension Service did not move to the new Arts and Sciences department, although those with Extension appointments, Dr. George Blume and Dr. Donald Fessler, had nominal ties. Two assistant professors—Dr. Daniel F. Johnson (Ph.D., Columbia, 1965) and Dr. Joseph Germana (Ph.D., Rutgers, 1965)—were also recruited in 1965, and two others, Dr. Raymond Bowman and Mr. Willard Bradfield, were transferred from vocational and technical education.

The combined undergraduate curricula included nine psychology courses, eleven sociology courses, and two jointly listed offerings, plus half a dozen graduate-level sociology courses. But sociology and psychology were split into two sections in fall 1967 and soon reorganized as separate departments. Leland Tate was designated acting co-chair for sociology; Dr. John Wright (who had joined the faculty the year before) was his counterpart for psychology. Three additional faculty members were hired in sociology—John A. Ballweg and Charles A. Ibsen in sociology and Joseph Benthal in anthropology. As for Dr. Thrush—who had chaired the combined department, headed Upward Bound, and written the proposal that secured a Rockefeller Foundation grant to fund scholarships for black and Appalachian students— he left for the University of Wisconsin to direct the counseling center there (*Techgram*, October 1967).

After a year, Dr. Gordon Erickson was recruited from Tennessee to head the sociology department, and Dr. William Pavlik came from another land-grant school, Rutgers University, as the first full professor and department head in psychology. Both departments grew rapidly in the years ahead; enrollments grew, and so did the number of faculty and the range of course offerings. By 1972-1973, the psychology department included seventeen faculty members—two clinical psychologists and fifteen general experimental psychologists. The first baccalaureate degree in psychology was awarded in 1968. A master's program in experimental psychology was initiated in 1970, and the first graduate students arrived in fall 1971. By 1974, a Ph.D. program in psychology was approved, with three areas of concentration—clinical psychology, applied behavioral science, and general experimental psychology.

The arts and sciences programs were the heart of the general education resources of the institution. Budding engineers, or architects, or research scientists, whoever, turned to the College of Arts and Sciences for their basic courses in such foundation areas as English, math, physics, biology, chemistry, political science, and history. Arts and sciences faculty carried more than half of VPI's entire instructional load. Marshall Hahn had argued vigorously before the State Council of Higher Education that, to attract top-flight faculty for such courses, VPI had to have major programs in those fields. The key to strengthening the entire institution, Hahn and Brandt insisted, was to build, as rapidly as possible, a strong arts and sciences college. This was at the bottom of their efforts to get strong new leadership for the college.

The University's rapid growth in the 1960s had the greatest impact upon the College of Arts and Sciences. Separate departments were soon established for English, foreign languages, history, and political science. By the mid-1960s, the curriculum had been organized into three divisions. The Humanities included English, foreign languages, and philosophy/religion. The Social Sciences consisted of economics, history, political science, and psychology/sociology. And Mathematics and the Natural Sciences included physics, chemistry, biological sciences, geological sciences, mathematics, and statistics. A baccalaureate program in health and physical education had been organized (along with a greatly expanded intramural athletic program). A philosophy major was initiated in the late 1960s by the department of philosophy and religion. All of the departments were dramatically strengthened academically as they increased in size, and graduate programs multiplied rapidly, spurred along by the new emphasis on research.

With a much more cooperative attitude on the part of the State Council director and in the Council itself, and with all VPI courses open to women students, enrollment in the College of Arts and Sciences began a swift climb. Already by fall quarter 1965, more than 1,500 students enrolled as arts and sciences majors; a year later, the total approached 2,000. Dean Malpass and his department heads had been busy recruiting the additional faculty needed to teach them.[7] In June 1966, the reinstated bachelor of arts degree was conferred on some fifty candidates. New master of arts programs were approved for English and history, and new undergraduate majors were authorized in French, German, and Spanish. A series of courses in such fields as art, music, and theater were approved as a new general arts and sciences program for fall 1966.

20.4 The Department of History at a state university—There had been no department of history before the 1960s, though Weldon Brown, for one, had taught history since 1939, and George Shackelford, Leslie Ray Mellichamp Jr., Wilford H. Lane, and William E. Mackie had been among those who joined the faculty by the 1960s. The Department of History and Political Science was organized early in the Hahn presidency, and before long the two disciplines each went their own way.

Archer Jones chaired the combined department, but he left to become dean of arts and sciences at the University of South Carolina, and, beginning in 1964, Dr. Mackie (who had earned his Ph.D. at the University of North Carolina that year) was acting chair for a time. Like departments across the University—whether new ones or those that had been around forever—history recruited swiftly in the growth years of the late 1960s and early 1970s. Joining the department in 1966, for example, were associate professor G. G. Williamson (Ph.D., Johns Hopkins, 1954) and assistant professors David D. Burr (Ph.D., Duke, 1967) and Thomas C. Howard (Ph.D., Florida State, 1965). Following in 1967 were full professor James I. Robertson Jr. (Ph.D., Emory, 1959); associate professor Robert G. Landen (Ph.D., Princeton, 1961); and assistant professor Michael A. Alexander (Ph.D., North Carolina, 1969). Beginning in 1967, Dr. Landen served as department head in history. (*Techgram*, October 1964, June 1967)

Before the 1960s were out, a department that had not existed when Dr. Hahn arrived as president was awarding not only the B.A. but also master's degrees. Between 1968 and 1972, many new appointments were made, typically assistant professors who had just received the Ph.D.—among them Joseph L. Wieczynski (Ph.D., Georgetown, 1966) in Russian and Soviet history; Thomas J. Adriance (Ph.D., Columbia, 1968) and J. Dean O'Donnell Jr. (Ph.D., Rutgers, 1970) in French history; Young-tsu Wong (Ph.D., Washington, 1971) in the history of China; William L. Ochsenwald (Ph.D., Chicago, 1971) in the history of the Middle East; Ronald J. Nurse (Ph.D., Michigan State, 1971) in American foreign relations; and Neil Larry Shumsky (Ph.D., California-Berkeley, 1972) in American urban history. This entire cohort—all of them appointed during President Hahn's second five years—remained in the department into the 1990s.

Performing and Studio Arts

With traditional restrictions on VPI's curriculum removed, the arts began to flourish, especially after 1967. A program in art had its roots in architecture, where four or five art faculty members had held appointments for some years, primarily to teach elective courses to architecture students. In 1967, VPI initiated a bachelor's program in art, with courses in drawing, watercolor, printmaking, design, painting, sculpture, art appreciation, and art history. The program's faculty and budget continued for a time to be lodged in the College of Architecture, and after the new architecture building was opened, the art studios, offices, and Art Gallery were all located there. Later, administration of the program was moved into Arts and Sciences.

Theater had long existed at VPI as an extra-curricular club program, at first the Thespian Club or Dramatic Society and later the Tech Players or Maroon Mask. Beginning during World War II, various men filled the position of director of dramatics, a part-time position at VPI: J. Philip Milhous into the 1960s; Robert Mardis from 1961 to 1965 (he produced a mixture of classical and avant-garde plays in Burruss Hall); and then Don Alldredge. Until 1967, when the Department of English established two full-time positions in theater, it offered only one survey course in drama. The people who filled the new positions were P. A. "Tony" Distler—who was recruited from Tulane University, where he had resigned after the administration there made it clear that no new funds or facilities would be made available for theater—and Don Drapeau, who played the roles of designer and technical director. Together with Don Alldredge, they set about to establish curricular offerings in theater and a coordinated production program.

In summer 1968, theater was moved from English to the new fine arts program, with Distler as its coordinator. A baccalaureate program in theater arts was instituted in the fall of 1970. By then, Distler had convinced the VPI administration that the school needed another theater venue than the Burruss stage, and, after a brief stay at the Wesley Foundation, the newly renovated Squires Hall included a new theater with state-of-the-art lighting and sound systems as well as other advanced features. When introducing the new theater, President Hahn said: "This outstanding facility will add a new dimension to the cultural life of the university."[8]

Music at VPI had roots that reached back into the 1880s, when the predecessor to the Corps of Cadets' regimental band, the Highty-Tighties, originated, and a VPI glee club also had existed for many years, but, as in art, the 1960s inaugurated a new era in music. One of the young faculty members whom Dr. Brandt personally recruited was Stanley G. Kingma, a 1959 graduate of Purdue University, where he had been a member of the nationally famous Purdue Glee Club. When Brandt recruited him in 1964, Kingma was working as a mechanical engineer for General Motors. Brandt brought him in as a mathematics instructor and, in addition, arranged for Kingma to take over direction of the VPI Glee Club. Kingma, not exactly sure what he was getting into, took a year's leave from GM to explore the possibilities at VPI.

Kingma did not return to General Motors when the year was up, but neither did he stay in math. He began building a wide ranging extra-curricular choral music program, one that evolved into the New Virginians, a collegiate entertainment group that still exists today. Kingma was moved in 1967 to the English department, which was the institutional home of music courses at that time, and in 1968 to Jim Dean's student personnel organization. In the years that followed, he made a considerable impact on choral music as well as other musical activities on and off campus. Brandt years later recalled of Kingma that "he was just super."

When the first faculty position in music as such was created in 1967, violinist Donald W. Grisier was appointed to it. Grisier was the founder of the University Orchestra. A second music faculty member, instructor Julieta Sykora, was added a year later, and the music program, which—like theater—was moved in 1968 into a new fine arts program, offered course in orchestra, chamber music, jazz ensemble, and general music literature.

As the university attracted a larger and increasingly diverse student population, the demand for music courses and performing groups intensified. In 1970, a Department of Performing Arts and Communications was organized under the leadership of Dr. Tony Distler. The Highty-Tighties and Stan Kingma's Glee Club and University Choir were assigned administratively to the new department. The University Orchestra became the New River Valley Symphony, and such ensembles as the Meistersingers and the Chamber Choir were formed, as well as Tech Men and Tech Mates, male and female glee clubs. In summer 1974 the University initiated a baccalaureate program in music.[9]

By the mid-1970s, Virginia Tech was offering undergraduates the opportunity to major in art, music, or theater. Extracurricular activities of the club variety, like theater, had been assimilated in part into degree programs. Meanwhile, such activities themselves had been greatly expanded, and Tech had an impact on the wider community through music in particular. No longer was it true that a Tech student could earn a degree in any field he or she wished—as long as it was science, engineering, business, education, agriculture, or home economics.

A People's University

In a myriad of ways, Virginia Polytechnic Institute had become a state university. The curriculum included a near universe of academic subjects.[10] The school offered at least a baccalaureate degree in music, art, and theater. In short order it offered a bachelor's degree and, by soon afterward, at least a master's degree in history, sociology, and psychology. Moreover, no social group in the state's population was any longer categorically excluded from enrollment, as white women had been until 1921 and as black Virginians had been into the 1950s.[11] And none faced restrictions as to what programs they could pursue, as non-black women had from 1944 to 1964 and as black men had in the 1950s. White men, too, escaped one of the institution's chief restrictions, the one that required most male freshmen and sophomores to be in the Corps of Cadets.

Individual students, one after another, put a face on these changes. As for the mandatory Corps of Cadets, the class of 1969—the class admitted one year after the 1964 change in policy—included thousands of students who would not have enrolled at Tech (or at least would have been less likely to) had the old requirement still been in place—among them, Raymond D. Smoot Jr., who became the University's vice president for administration and treasurer; Thomas C. Tillar Jr., who became the University's vice president for alumni relations; Frank M. Beamer, who became head coach of the Virginia Tech football team, which played its home games at Lane Stadium and, after each regular season, went to bowl after bowl[12]; and Charles W. Steger Jr., who earned an architecture degree and went on to become dean of the College of Architecture for many years and then, in 2000, president of Virginia Polytechnic Institute and State University.

Countless other students put faces on the changes of the Hahn years. One black female, Marguerite Harper, earned a history degree in 1970, and another, Jackie Butler, earned a sociology degree the same year. And if the civilian male underclassmen, like Ray Smoot, revealed the end of the old rule of mandatory participation in the Corps, Deborah Noss and Cheryl Butler revealed the companion (though later) move to an all-voluntary Corps, when women were at last permitted to join if they wished.

President Hahn had envisioned a people's university, and by the 1970s all kinds of evidence demonstrated the magnitude of change since he took over in 1962. Virginia Polytechnic Institute and State University ended its first century and began its second, an institution radically different from Virginia Agricultural and Mechanical College of 1872 and radically different, too, from the Virginia Polytechnic Institute of 1922 or even 1962.

Another Ten Years, Another Hundred

The yearlong centennial celebration was nearing an end as President Hahn contemplated what he wanted to say at the second annual Founders Day convocation in April 1973. A month beforehand, he wrote to rector Gene Rowe that, "with the very fine help of Lon Savage and Warren Strother," he was working on the address he would give. They had agreed, he said, that it should be "a major Address," one that would "attempt to focus the attention of the University community on the challenges of the next decade, just as my inaugural address a decade ago sought to do."[13]

The moment came. Speaking in Burruss Hall auditorium, Hahn looked back a decade to his words, on inauguration day in 1963, about the "challenges and opportunities facing VPI in the decade ahead." That decade was now history, he said, retrospect rather than prospect: "The projections for the Commonwealth's economic, industrial, and urban growth did indeed come to pass. And with that growth came the necessity for dramatic increases in the quality and capacity of the instructional, research, and extension programs of this University. The University's enrollment did indeed more than double in a decade, and this institution was forced to add as much physical plant as had been developed in all of its previous history."

20.5 Achievements of the 1960s, challenges of the 1970s—In his Founders Day address in 1973, President Hahn reviewed some of the major developments of the decade between 1962 and 1972:

Forty new degree programs have been developed and ten new academic departments established. Our teacher preparation programs have been consolidated into the new College of Education. The School of Science and General Studies, organized primarily to offer service courses for the professional schools, evolved into the College of Arts and Sciences. With the new College came further strengthening of the degree programs in the sciences, and the addition of undergraduate and graduate degree programs in the humanities and social sciences. The College of Arts and Sciences, of course, has developed into the University's largest College. At the same time[,] the traditionally strong programs in Agriculture, Architecture, Business, Engineering, and Home Economics, all have acquired strengthened national reputations.

Having surveyed the recent past, Hahn stood for a moment in the present and stated the questions that all institutions of higher education, particularly public land-grant institutions, must periodically ask:

But it is time to take stock. Have we achieved the level of excellence which should be possible with the resources which have been made available? Are we, in fact, effectively meeting the educational needs of today's young people? Are the resources of the University being used effectively to provide continuing educational opportunities for citizens across the Commonwealth? Can the yield in the investment of public funds for the benefit of the Commonwealth and its citizens be increased? Can we improve the traditional approaches and organization in fulfilling most effectively our missions? These and other questions deserve the thoughtful consideration of everyone in the University community as this institution enters its second century.

And he moved to the near-term future. Economic growth and development would continue, he noted, and would continue to be vital, but environmental concerns had to be addressed as well. Higher education had various roles to play, too, in improving the "quality of life" for all the state's citizens—"the disadvantaged, the returning veterans [from the Vietnam War], the elderly, all must be brought into the mainstream of our economy and our society." The University must direct greater attention to extension activities—making its instructional strengths available to people across the state, especially "as higher education becomes a lifelong process."

As for campus activities, Hahn spoke of enhanced programs of academic advising and career counseling, and he urged periodic recalibration of academic offerings—"continuing analysis of both proposed new degree programs and existing programs in relationship to the need and opportunities for graduates of such programs." Referring to a recently completed Report of the Task Force for Innovation in Instruction, Hahn endorsed many of its recommendations and added his own. Much good work was being done toward creating and sustaining "that special academic environment said to be necessary for instructional programs of the highest distinction"; to create it, much remained to be done.

Finally, there was the matter of public support and institutional resources. "Much of the mystique of higher education, stemming in large part from the dedication of a largely non-college generation to the assuring of higher education for its progeny, has disappeared as opportunities for higher education have become more available. Much of the reservoir of goodwill toward institutions of higher learning has been depleted. There have been questions of campus disorder, the youth culture, and the often self-serving posture of the educational establishment." The state and federal governments could not be counted on, as he put it, to throw dollars "without questions over the ivied walls of academe." The academic world had to assume an increasing "competition for the public dollar." At the same time, he noted, "the distinction between public and private institutions is blurring." Private funds would be increasingly vital to the University's well-being. "Public institutions must attract increased private support if they are to serve effectively. This University has little choice but to expand its development efforts, and identify major sources of non-public funds in a comprehensive development program."

Then Hahn set out what he called "The Challenge of the 1970s." In particular, he outlined the contours of an optimal "learning environment" on campus, but he warned that achieving it "will not simply happen. Indeed, the dedicated and sustained efforts of all of us, faculty, students, and staff working together, will be required if the environment we seek is not to remain an elusive goal. Despite the very real and rapid strengthening of the academic programs in recent years, there has persisted a view that The University has not yet quite arrived."

All the resources in the world would not be available to Virginia Tech, he noted, and, regardless, all the resources in the world would not suffice absent one vital factor—"the personal commitment and determination of every faculty member and every student, indeed of every member of the University community. Each of us must devote our individual efforts at the maximum level of our ability toward achieving real excellence in the educational programs of this University."

After surveying the range of challenges Virginia Tech would face in the decade ahead, Hahn concluded in characteristic fashion—forceful, energetic, optimistic:

> I hope these observations have not been interpreted in a negative context, for they have not been so intended. Indeed the challenges before us offer extraordinary opportunities. I am convinced that working effectively together, we can sustain an excitement, an enthusiasm, and an optimism that will generate a bright future for this institution. The strong foundations on which we build, the momentum that we have achieved, and the strong support that the University now enjoys, are assets of very great importance. With the full cooperation of us all, and with the sustained and dedicated efforts of students, faculty, and staff, I am confident that we cannot but achieve our goals. Let us be determined that it will be so. Thank you.

The Board of Visitors, 1973-1974. Pictured are John T. Faircloth Jr., James L. Whitehurst Jr., Dr. Roy R. Smith, R. B. Pamplin Sr., President Hahn, and C. Eugene Rowe (rector). Photo from the 1974 *Bugle*.

1 *Techgram*, November 1971, March 1972.

2 Kinnear, *The First 100 Years*, xiii. Doug Martin later earned graduate degrees at Tech and became senior human resources manager, looking after benefits for the University's countless employees.

3 *Techgram*, November 1971; Kinnear, *The First 100 Years*, xi; *Techgram*, October 1972.

4 *Techgram*, April 1972. Warren Strother recounts the spring events in "The View from Here," *Context* 6 (summer 1972).

5 *Techgram*, June 1972.

6 The speeches are published in *Context* 7 (winter 1973).

7 Malpass also had to find new department heads. Four of his departmental chiefs turned in their resignations within six months of his arrival (Malpass interview, 12 October 1989).

8 Dennis Price, "Theater at a Technical School? A Brief History of Theater at Virginia Tech," Wallenstein, *Essays, Fall 1998.*

9 Regarding the developments in music, see the insert in *Techgram*, September 1974.

10 At the beginning of the twenty-first century, Tech had no law school and (though it has the College of Veterinary Medicine) no human medical school. It did not offer a degree program in anthropology. As for foreign languages, those that were not focused on Europe had spotty offerings, even in the 1990s, and fiscal considerations jeopardized even some of the European languages that had previously been offered.

11 Though desegregation had clearly begun—the formal obstacles to enrollment had been banished—the proportion of black students remained small in the mid-1970s and, indeed, a quarter-century and more later. As was observed in the context of a university self-study in 1975-1976, "The percentage of minority students enrolled at VPI&SU falls far short of the total percentage of the minority population in the state. In 1970, the black population in Virginia represented 18.5 percent of the state's total population. In the fall of 1975, however, only 1.5 percent of the University's total enrollment was black, while other minorities represented 1.0 percent of total enrollment. Some members of the University community believe that VPI&SU needs to increase its efforts to enroll minority students" (*The University Self-Study, 1975-76*, Report of the Steering Committee to the Commission on Colleges, Southern Association of Colleges and Schools [Blacksburg VA: Virginia Polytechnic Institute and State University, 1977], 75-76).

12 Nicholas Watson, "Frank Beamer: Virginia Tech Player, Virginia Tech Coach," in Wallenstein, *Essays, Fall 1998.*

13 Hahn to Rowe, 19 March 1972.

Epilogue

During the excitement of the centennial celebration during the academic year 1972-1973, Marshall Hahn got carried away with enthusiasm and made what sounded like a pledge to stay a second ten years. He went public about it in his Founders Day address, in April 1973, when he reported that the Board of Visitors had asked him to stay on as president for another ten years and that he had agreed to do so.[1]

Staying on that long was perhaps not entirely out of the question, but it was far from a sure thing. In fact, any number of considerations already had Hahn looking toward alternative futures, futures into which he might well move much sooner than ten more years.

Looking Back, Looking Forward

For one thing, Hahn often explained later, the challenge was gone—or was considerably diminished. That was true in that he had overcome the greatest obstacles and launched the greatest changes. Early on, Marshall Hahn had brought his Board of Visitors around, neutralized the State Council for Higher Education, and politicked with enormous effectiveness at the General Assembly. From the legislature, he had managed to extract tremendous levels of cooperation in bringing to fruition his major goals for higher education, not just at the Blacksburg campus, which itself was rapidly growing, but across the entire Commonwealth.

Tremendous change—change of all sorts—was readily visible all over the Blacksburg campus. During the decade after 1962, the school had grown prodigiously—in the size of its student population, in the range of its undergraduate majors, in its graduate programs, and in its physical infrastructure. Already by 1964, Tech had split from Radford College and dropped the requirement that male freshmen and sophomores participate in the Corps of Cadets. By the 1970s, the school was clearly coeducational and multiracial. Members of the faculty were—far more of them than ever before—holders of doctoral degrees and engaged in significant research. New deans, most of them recruited by the team of Marshall Hahn and Warren Brandt, had entered upon their duties in recent years. The bulk of the faculty had come out of graduate school and begun their teaching careers after Hahn assumed the presidency of VPI. Extraordinary energy, with a strong sense of direction, pervaded the faculty and the administration.

In 1962, VPI was an overwhelmingly white, male, military school. Although the largest school in the state, it was in 1962 still a small school, largely a teaching college, an undergraduate institution, one that, having started out as an "agricultural and mechanical" school, continued to concentrate on technical subjects. By 1972, Virginia Polytechnic Institute and State University had doubled in size; it was drawing women as well as men and black students as well as white ones from across the state; and it had become—as Hahn had referred to it from the beginning of his time at the helm—a university, a comprehensive research university.

Yet significant challenges remained, old ones had a way of reappearing, and by 1974 new ones loomed. After Hahn's early successes in neutralizing SCHEV, the State Council had surfaced again as an obstacle to developing the University in Blacksburg. An economic downturn after 1973 made it far more difficult than in the mid-1960s to obtain significantly enhanced state funding for higher education. In various ways, the tailwind that had boosted Hahn's efforts—and complemented his enormous energy—must have seemed to be turning into a headwind. In that sense, too, in other words, the thrill was diminished.

Through the 1960s, many members of the Tech community had felt, and expressed, concerns that Marshall Hahn might leave the Virginia Tech presidency for a similar position at some other university. But he had already done that, been a university president. The major enticements to leave Tech emanated from other kinds of sources. In 1969, he had fancied a run for the Virginia governorship. In the early 1970s, he was thinking of other kinds of challenges. Heading up a major foundation interested him briefly, but no such situation seemed, in his words, "dynamic" enough.[2]

During the late 1960s and into the 1970s, Hahn spent more and more time dealing in various ways with leaders in business and industry, and there he could see ways to make more money for his family than higher education could provide. At the Georgia-Pacific Corporation, the chairman of the board and president, Robert B. Pamplin Sr., tried to lure Hahn away from his duties at Tech. Even a man like Marshall Hahn would need time to get up to speed in the corporation before he could take it over, and no time, to Pamplin's way of thinking, was too soon to get started. Hahn was not ready to go, though. Beginning in January 1973, Hahn served on the board of Georgia-Pacific—he first sought and obtained approval by the Virginia Tech Board of Visitors—but for a time that was as far as it went.

A Change at the Top

It could be said that President Hahn's pledge to stay ten more years was a consequence of his warnings from time to time that no person should stay in such an office for too long. Hahn's observations to the effect that "it is not in the best interest of a university for one person to serve as president for too long a time" had occasioned an unsettled feeling among various constituents, and it was to assuage that uncertainty, one could say, that Hahn had made his pledge.

In August 1974—in addition to alerting Governor Mills Godwin and a few other people—T. Marshall Hahn told rector C. Eugene Rowe that he had made up his mind. The time had come. Rowe advised his colleagues on the Board of Visitors, at a regular meeting on August 9, that Hahn would be leaving the Virginia Tech presidency by the end of the 1974-1975 academic year. Rather than set a specific time during the months ahead, Hahn made a new pledge to stay until "such time as a successor is appointed and begins serving."[3]

In various messages, the president explained his motivations: "It is essential for an individual to develop a program and to establish a pattern of progress along a charted course. But it is also important that there be periodic infusion of new ideas and new approaches resulting from change in the presidency. Thus during the past several years, from time to time I have suggested to the University's Board of Visitors that the time for a change was approaching. While it is flattering that the board has continued to disagree with that suggestion, my own view is that it will be in the best interest of the University that such a change occur in the near future."

Walter Newman, Hahn's predecessor, summed up the response to it all as well as anyone: "He has done a wonderful job—he had been most effective as president—and we'll miss him."

---

1. The December 1974 *Techgram*: Looking back, looking ahead—The December 1974 issue of *Techgram* looked back on the recently concluded football season (and the rushing exploits of Phil Rogers); and it looked as well ahead at the varsity basketball season (just getting under way with Coach Don DeVoe). At the recent Homecoming, the Gobblers had defeated the University of Richmond Spiders 41–7; Deborah Dowdy, a junior biology major, had been named Homecoming Queen; and the class of 1924, celebrating its fiftieth anniversary, had established a scholarship fund for future Virginia Tech students.

In other ways, too, the newspaper looked ahead as well as back as it reported the news. Enrollment that fall quarter had reached 17,470 (nearly 6,000 of them women), including 2,394 graduate students—figures that, contrasting with the much smaller numbers a decade earlier, suggested still more growth to come. Also that fall, Lee C. Tait ('41) had been reelected president of the Alumni Association Board of Directors. The National Institutes of Health had awarded another $378,529 to the Anaerobe Lab for continuing research by W. E. C. Moore, Lillian V. Holdeman, and Tracy D. Wilkins. Irene Spieker, a sophomore on the women's running club (women's varsity teams were on—or just over—the horizon), had set a course record in winning the Tennessee Cross-Country Championship for Women, hosted by the University of Tennessee.

And the *Techgram* reported a collection of decisions by the Board of Visitors. The BOV had approved a master's degree in public affairs and administration (forerunner of the Center for Public Administration and Policy—CPAP—and its doctoral program). It was backing a prospective vet school, for which the state legislature had earlier that year approved planning. It had approved a new award—each of the seven colleges would, each spring, be recognizing an Outstanding Senior. And it had appointed William Lavery to be Marshall Hahn's successor as president of Virginia Polytechnic Institute and State University.

The End of the Hahn Era at Virginia Tech

At the same time as the announcement went out, Hahn also explained his timing. Ever the political being, he understood the implications that the legislature's biennial clock had for a change at the top at Tech. Had he announced a year earlier, it would have been on the eve of the General Assembly's 1974 session. At such a time, had he still been in office when the legislature met, his lame-duck status would have weakened him in his advocacy regarding funding requests and any policy initiatives. Were he to wait another year, too little time would remain for his successor to have gained a handle on the institution, its budgetary needs, and the workings of the legislature. The timing of his announcement would permit the Board of Visitors to appoint someone, in the words of Warren Strother at the time, "well in advance of the 1976 session of the General Assembly—so that the new president will have become familiar with the University's financial concerns and with the state government."

During the next three months, more than a hundred candidates emerged from across the nation, but, in November, the Board of Visitors appointed an inside candidate, Dr. William E. Lavery, to take office on January 1, 1975. Lavery had first come to VPI in 1965, when he left the Federal Extension Service in Washington, DC, to join Dr. W. E. "Bill" Skelton's Cooperative Extension staff as state leader for administration, and he had filled other posts and carried other responsibilities at Tech since that time. Upon two recommendations by President Hahn—that a new position be created and that Lavery fill it—Lavery had been appointed in August 1973 as executive vice president. In that capacity, Lavery had been the person through whom the other four vice presidents reported to the president, and he had acted for the president when Hahn had to be away. In addition, he chaired certain University committees, assisted in negotiations with state and federal agencies, and heard students' appeals from decisions made by the vice president for student affairs. For a year and more, in short, Lavery had been learning a great deal about the University and the office of its president, the responsibilities for which he would now take on.[4]

Meantime, it was announced that Marshall Hahn, when he left the Tech presidency on December 31, 1974, would become an executive vice president at the Georgia-Pacific Corporation. Major changes in management were on the horizon at a major university and at a major corporation. Dr. Thomas Marshall Hahn Jr. left academe and moved on to new challenges. Virginia Polytechnic Institute and State University continued more or less to move along the path that President Hahn had charted for it.

In the years after Hahn left academe, he was commemorated for his accomplishments. At the University of Kentucky, a banner in front of the Administration Building honored Hahn as a "Distinguished Alumnus" and identified him as having earned his B.S. there in 1945 and having served as "President, Virginia Tech University." Virginia Tech awarded him the Ruffner Medal—seen as the highest recognition the University can bestow—in 1982 for his outstanding work on behalf of the University and in 1991 named a new campus building in his honor.[5] A plaque outside Hahn Hall carries the following inscription:

> T. Marshall Hahn, Jr. Hall
> Named in honor of T. Marshall Hahn, Jr.
> Distinguished Scholar, Educator, Corporate Leader
> Head, Department of Physics 1954-1959
> President 1962-1974
>
> His leadership and vision immeasurably strengthened
> Virginia higher education and transformed
> this institution into a widely recognized,
> comprehensive university.
>
> April 6, 1991

There were other honors, too. The class of 2003 recognized Dr. Hahn with its class ring and Mrs. Hahn with a commemorative ring. At one school or the other, Kentucky or Tech, could be found various Marshall Hahn scholarships, fellowships, and professorships.

Virginia Tech after T. Marshall Hahn

Virginia Tech continued, in large part, along the course President Hahn had set for it. In size, the greatest growth took place on his watch, but in the quarter century after he left, enrollment continued to climb. It first crested 6,000 his first year at the helm; was above 17,000 when he stepped down; and by the end of the century was pushing through a "firm cap" of 25,000. The enhanced emphasis in the Hahn years on faculty research persisted and if anything grew in the years ahead. The female proportion of students edged ever closer to parity; but the number of African American undergraduates topped out at about one-quarter the 20 percent that would reflect the statewide population.

Particular institutional developments from the Hahn years had varied futures. The Vet School thrived, but the College of Education lost its separate identity in the 1990s when it was merged into a College of Human Resources and Education. Then, in a spate of "restructuring," the College of Arts and Sciences, the largest college at Tech, vanished in 2003. First, it was divided, as a new College of Science broke off that year. Then the college containing Education was merged into what remained of old Arts and Sciences to produce a new College of Liberal Arts and Human Sciences.

Other latter-day developments included Virginia Tech's acceptance of an invitation in 2003 to join the ACC. Spurned in the 1950s and again during Hahn's presidency in the 1960s, Tech followed a strange and entirely unpredictable path out of the Big East Conference, which it had joined only a few years before, into the Atlantic Coast Conference. Whatever the conference Tech played in, the football program had grown in the direction Hahn had looked for, as the school's considerable visibility grew in part because of the success Coach Frank Beamer's teams had in Lane Stadium and on the road. Also in 2003, Tech broke ground at last on a new home for the Alumni Association.

As for state politics and fiscal matters, approaching four decades after 1966 there was scant evidence of the likes of Governor Mills E. Godwin Jr. or the 1966 Sales Tax legislature in Richmond. A combination of cyclical downturns in the economy, limited areas of discretionary state spending, and fiscal priorities in state politics led to periodic sharp cuts in state funding of higher education. As the proportion of college costs supported by the state went down, tuition payments took up much of the slack. After the 1980s—especially in the early 1990s and again a decade later, and in sharp contrast to the mid-1960s—public higher education in Virginia revealed a tendency of increasing privatization.

This was true at Tech, and it was true at the community colleges. The community colleges had been designed for two constituencies, those seeking vocational training and those preparing to transfer into four-year institutions like Tech, and either way, as Marshall Hahn observed in 2003, the goal was "to really bring higher education within the reach of as many young people in the commonwealth as possible." Hahn had reason to feel gloomy when he observed about students at community colleges in particular, "So many are there because it's the only affordable way for them to receive a higher education." He predicted: "Raising tuition significantly is going to eliminate a tier of students at community colleges, and the commonwealth will be the loser."[6]

T. Marshall Hahn after Virginia Tech

Marshall and Peggy Hahn had bonded with Blacksburg in the 1950s during their first tour at VPI. When they returned to Virginia from Kansas in 1962, they moved into the Grove, the home for the VPI president. But Hahn knew he would not always be president at Tech, and in the late 1960s student unrest fostered an additional consideration for moving the family away from campus. In early 1970 he began building a new home on what was then the outskirts of Blacksburg, and the family moved into it in 1971. As President Hahn and the Board of Visitors had agreed, the home was large enough for University entertaining. On his departure for Georgia-Pacific, the company purchased the home and gave it to the Virginia Tech Foundation. Soon after his leaving Tech, the Hahns began acquiring the farmland for Hickory Hill Farm, where they subsequently spent a good part of each year. The Hahn family has given to the Virginia Outdoors Foundation a conservation easement of the 900-acre farm, ensuring that it will remain open farmland and forest.[7]

As early as 1966 and increasingly in the following eight years—confident that he had inaugurated the essential changes at VPI—Hahn occasionally considered his professional options. Fading into the distant past were the days that young Marshall went hungry during the Great Depression in the 1930s. Nor were Marshall and Peggy any longer "both poor as church mice," in her words, as they had been when they courted long distance by means of three-cent postage stamps in the late 1940s. But serving in academic administration did not bring in a lot of money in the 1960s, and Hahn wanted to do right by himself and right by his family. There seems little doubt he wanted another big challenge. Going into industry would bring an opportunity to make real money and, at the same time, present a different kind of challenge than he had taken on before.[8]

During the years of his presidency, Marshall Hahn had played a key role in recruiting many of the faculty and administrators who came to Tech. But he himself had been recruited—certainly he had been approached—by a number of other universities and by a variety of corporations. In particular, Robert B. Pamplin Sr. was looking for someone he could groom as his successor as CEO of the Georgia-Pacific Corporation, a company that had, from its beginnings in the 1920s, been run by former Tech people, chief among them Pamplin himself, VPI class of 1933. Pamplin—he later explained that he had particularly appreciated the hard-nosed way he thought Hahn handled the Williams Hall takeover at Tech in May 1970—had his eye on the VPI president.[9] In a sense, Hahn left one Tech institution, the University, for another, the Georgia-Pacific Corporation, when he brought his presidency to an end at the start of 1975.

Hahn left the presidency of Virginia Tech to become an executive vice president of Georgia-Pacific, initially heading the company's chemicals division. Before he made the switch, he knew he needed to know more than he did about the forestry industry and, in particular, its chemical division. In characteristic fashion, he put together a pile of books that would help him prepare and polished them off: "I got a bunch of chemical engineering books, and I got all the books that they used for the MBA…at Harvard, and I got some books on forestry and read them all."[10]

2. Folk art at the High Museum —During his time at Kansas State, before becoming president at VPI, Marshall Hahn developed a keen interest in American practitioners of folk art. At first, he emphasized Kansas painter Streeter Blair (see box 5.2) but, over the years, his interests expanded and his collection grew. In 1996 he donated 130 pieces to create the T. Marshall Hahn, Jr., Collection at the High Museum of Art in Atlanta, Georgia. The artists represented in the collection include painter Mattie Lou O'Kelley from Georgia and sculptor Edgar Tolson from Kentucky.

After an apprenticeship of a year with the chemicals division, he was given the added responsibility of heading the pulp and paper division. A year later he was named president, and from 1983 to 1993 he served as chairman and CEO of Georgia-Pacific (which moved its corporate head-quarters from Portland, Oregon, to Atlanta, Georgia). The CEO of Georgia-Pacific operated much as had the CEO of Virginia Tech, except that GP was in dire straits when Hahn took it over. A heavy debt load threatened the firm on both sides, as a sharp rise in interest rates drove up costs at the same time as depressed sales tore into revenues. Through a number of strategic changes in corporate direction, Hahn saved the company and then watched it flourish. Sales almost doubled between the first and last of his ten years at the helm, from $6.5 billion to $12.3 billion. Someone from the forest products industry said of him in 1990, three years before he stepped down at GP: "He's got steel in his spine. He works like the dickens. And besides that, he's the smartest man I've ever met."[11]

No institutional challenge—no matter how great, no matter how well met—could entirely satisfy Hahn the man. His adventures out on the Chesapeake Bay and later on the open seas offered evidence of his need to try himself out in new, sometimes dangerous, venues. His trips to equatorial Africa, his safari adventures, and his display of the trophies he brought back to his spacious home in Blacksburg offered better evidence. So his retirement to Blacksburg was no quiet affair. The man had always been bigger than life. He continued to be.

[1] *Techgram*, May 1973.

[2] Hahn interview, 31 August 1989.

[3] *Techgram*, September 1974.

[4] *Techgram*, September 1973.

[5] The Ruffner Medal is named after William H. Ruffner, a figure vital to the establishment of VPI in the 1870s. Other winners from that period constitute a who's who of people in this book. In 1977, the award's first year, it went to president-emeritus Walter S. Newman and also (posthumously) to Stuart K. Cassell. C. Eugene Rowe was recognized with the Ruffner Medal in 1978; Lucy Lee Lancaster in 1979 (a member of VPI's first coeducational class, the class of '25, she had spent her entire professional life as a librarian at VPI); John W. Hancock Jr. in 1980; and W. Thomas Rice and Robert B. Pamplin Sr. in 1981.

[6] Beth Macy, "Cuts Put Community College Beyond Some Students' Reach," *Roanoke Times*, 6 January 2003: A1, A4.

[7] Mike Gangloff, "900-acre Ellett Valley Viewshed Preserved," *Roanoke Times*, 3 January 2004, New River Current 1.

[8] Hahn interview, 31 August 1989; Mrs. Hahn interview.

[9] Erik Calonius, "America's Toughest Papermaker," *Fortune*, 26 February 1990: 82.

[10] Hahn interview, 10 February 1990.

[11] Monroe, *Maverick Spirit*, 144-83; Calonius, "America's Toughest Papermaker," 80, 82.

The Board of Visitors, 1974-1975. Pictured are John T. Faircloth Jr., Christopher C. Kraft Jr., Mrs. E. H. (Helen) Lane, Dr. James F. Tucker, Dr. Roy R. Smith, President William E. Lavery, and C. Eugene Rowe (rector). Photo from the 1975 *Bugle*.

The University of Kentucky honored Marshall Hahn as a distinguished alumnus. Photo taken in 2001 by historian James C. Albisetti of the University of Kentucky.

Hahn Hall, chemistry building, dedicated on the Virginia Tech campus in 1991. Photo by Dixie D. Galyean (December 1991).

Dr. Hahn at the Georgia-Pacific Corporation. Courtesy of T. Marshall Hahn Jr.

Appendix 1
Enrollment at Virginia Tech, 1951-1952 through Fall 1985

Year	Enrollment
1951-1952	3,259
1952-1953	3,215
1953-1954	3,322
1954-1955	3,747
1955-1956	4,420
1956-1957	4,786
1957-1958	5,138
1958-1959	5,318
1959-1960	5,496
1960-1961	5,747
1961-1962	5,827
1962-1963	6,358
1963-1964	6,555
1964-1965	7,305
1965-1966	7,711
1966-1967	9,064
1967-1968	10,254
Fall 1968	10,289
Fall 1969	11,028
Fall 1970	12,043
Fall 1971	13,282
Fall 1972	14,471
Fall 1973	16,367
Fall 1974	17,470
Fall 1975	18,477
Fall 1976	18,238
Fall 1977	19,648
Fall 1978	20,261
Fall 1979	20,780
Fall 1980	21,069
Fall 1981	21,584

Fall 1982	21,510		
Fall 1983	21,357		
Fall 1984	21,454		
Fall 1985	22,044		

Note: Through academic year 1967-1968, figures include all students enrolled during the year. Beginning in 1968, figures are for fall term only.

Appendix 2
Undergraduate and Graduate Degrees Conferred at Virginia Tech, 1953-1985

Year	Bachelor's	Master's	Doctorates
1953	620	120	7
1954	504	90	5
1955	470	113	7
1956	549	90	13
1957	710	99	10
1958	911	127	16
1959	858	131	12
1960	896	122	18
1961	881	162	20
1962	954	186	25
1963	1,032	205	22
1964	1,008	194	24
1965	1,087	173	52
1966	1,064	208	64
1967	1,170	247	128
1968	1,348	250	86
1969	1,766	241	90
1970	2,068	234	107
1971	2,117	295	128
1972	2,182	385	114
1973	2,297	634	102
1974	2,660	767	132
1975	2,999	870	156
1976	3,034	861	186

1977	3,211	1,027	167
1978	3,250	834	178
1979	3,373	866	193
1980	3,521	898	194
1981	3,436	938	211
1982	3,639	963	227
1983	3,680	914	246
1984	3,851	1,003	333
1985	3,757	812	332

Note: The doctoral figures beginning with 1984 include the graduates from the new College of Veterinary Medicine.

Appendix 3
Appointed Members of the Virginia Tech Board of Visitors, 1962-1974

Furr, Guy L. Sr. ('16), 1954-1962; rector
Smith, Oscar F. III ('26), 1954-1962
Read, Granville M. ('14), 1955-1962 (died December 1962)
Sanders, Paul D., 1955-1963
Yates, Mrs. E. Floyd (Mary), 1955-1963
Lane, Edward H. Sr. ('12), 1956-1966
Will, Erwin H. ('22), 1958-1966
Showalter, Mrs. English (Jean), 1959-1967
Cochran, George M., 1960-1968
Erwin, William J. Sr., 1960-1968
Graham, Mrs. Henderson P. (Jouette), 1961-1964
Rice, W. Thomas ('34), 1961-1968; rector, 1962-1964
Wilhelm, Mrs. Donald Jr. (Jane Gilmer), 1961-1968
Williams, Wyatt A. ('36), 1962-1970
Wyatt, Harry C. ('24), 1962-1970; rector, 1964-1970
Hancock, John W. Jr. ('25), 1962-1971
Blewett, William E. Jr., 1963-1965 (died October 1965)
Gibbs, Mrs. Mavis M., 1963-1971
Johnson, Adger S. ('28), 1964-1973
Cutchins, Clifford A. III ('45), 1965-1976 (and again later; rector)

Landis, John W., 1966-1970
Miles, Waldo G., 1966-1970
Bolling Mrs. A. Stuart Jr., 1967-1971
Givens, J. Edwin ('31), 1968-1976
Goodykoontz, Robert O. ('30), 1968-1976
Rowe, C. Eugene ('33), 1968-1976; rector, 1970-1975
Lane, Mrs. E. H. Jr. (Helen), 1968-1977
Casto, Harold J. ('45), 1970-1974
Whitehurst, James L. Jr. ('63), 1970-1974
Kraft, Christopher C. Jr. ('45), 1970-1978
Smith, Roy R. ('43), 1971-1978
Clement, G. Frank, 1971-1979; rector, 1975-1978
Pamplin, Robert B. Sr. ('33), 1971-1979
Robinson, Mrs. J. Kenneth (Katherine), 1971-1979
Faircloth, John T. Jr. ('41), 1973-1981
Russell, Robert E. ('64), 1973-1981
Brinkley, Parke C. ('37), 1974-1982; rector
Tucker, James F., 1974-1982

Bibliography

For the most part, this book is based on primary sources, the raw materials of history—interviews, newspaper articles, university archives, college catalogs, and yearbooks (the *Bugle*). Most of these items—including such Virginia Tech publications as *Techgram* and *Context*—are available in Special Collections in Newman Library on the Tech campus.

Aside from the papers of Marshall Hahn, interviews supplied the bulk of the material for the book. Some of these—part of the "Oral History of the Virginia Tech College of Education"—were conducted by Nancy Franklin with Karl T. Hereford, 2 November and 6 December 1989, and by Linda Dunn with Duncan Lyle Kinnear, 26 July 1990. Others were conducted by Virginia Tech archivist Tamara J. Kennelly with a number of black students from the Hahn years—among them Cheryl Butler McDonald, Marguerite Harper Scott, and James Darnell Watkins—and are available in Special Collections and online.

Most of the interviews, more than one hundred (he considers them conversations), were conducted by Warren H. Strother. Tapes of most of these, and in many cases transcripts, are available in Special Collections in Newman Library. All shaped the authors' understanding of the Hahn years, though not all are quoted or cited (and an occasional quote is from a conversation with Hahn not taped). Those cited in the notes (whether to each chapter or to boxes in the text) are as follows:

Baumes, Harold. 22 March 1989.

Beck, James R. "Jimmy" (Carneal & Johnston architect). 17 October 1990; 19 December 1990.

Bell, Wilson. 6 February 1989.

Bemiss, FitzGerald (state senator). 20 March 1989.

Blackburn, Joseph E. "Joe." 21 March 1989.

Brandt, Warren W. 26 July 1989.

Brown, Gordon. 28 June 1989.

Burchard, Charles. 19 June 1989.

Byrne, William H. "Billy" (airport manager). 20 June 1991; 3 Aug. 1994.

Cato, W. H. "Bill." 13 June 1992.

Cook, Thomas E. 30 October 1989.

Cooper, Weldon. 23 May 1989.

Cutchins, Clifford A. III. 17 March 1989.

Dean, James W. 21 June 1989.

Engel, Ruben W. "Charlie." 10 April 1989.

Evans, Edward B. 29 May 1991.

Godwin, Mills E. Jr. 14 March 1989.

Gordon, Charles O. "Charlie." 16 October 1988; 18 November 1994.

Gray, George. 15 May 1989; 16 May 1989.

Hahn, T. Marshall Jr. 1 July 1989; 8 July 1989; 10 July 1989; 5 August 1989; 31 August 1989; 7 October 1989; 10 February 1990; 24 March 1990.

Hahn, Margaret Louise "Peggy." 14 November 1989.

Hamel, Dana B. 20 March 1989; 19 March 1990.

Hancock, John W. "Jack." 10 February 1989.

Harrison, William B. 14 April 1992.

Heterick, Robert C. 22 June 1989.

Hill, David E. 13 April 1990.

Johnston, G. Burke. 12 December 1990; 23 August 1990.

Jones, James Beverly "J.B." 24 May 1989.

Kroontje, Wybe. 17 March 1989.

Kuhn, L. M. (state budget director). 22 March 1989.

Long, George. 23 May 1989.

Lucas, J. Richard. 27 January 1993.

McDaniels, Carl. 21 June 2001.

McEver, H. Macauley "Mac." 16 November 1989.

Malpass, Leslie F. 31 March 1989; 12 October 1989.

Martin, James E. 25 July 1989.

Matthews, William B. "Bill." 8 February 1989.

Meade, Harold F. 28 May 1991.

Moore, W. E. C. 28 April 1989.

Nichols, James E. 8 June 1990.

Parkerson, William F. Jr. "Bill" (state senator). 22 March 1989.

Paterson, Robert A. 24 April 1992.

Paschall, Davis Y. "Pat." 15 March 1989.

Pletta, Dan. 24 July 1991.

Price, Howard. 20 Dec. 1990.

Rawls, Sol Jr. 21 Aug. 1991.

Rice, W. Thomas. 10 July 1989.

Robeson, Andrew. 15 February 1989.

Rutland, Leon W. "Lee." 8 May 1991.

Savage, Lon K., and James R. Montgomery. 4 September 2001.

Skelton, W. E. "Bill." 4 December 1989.

Smith, Alfred W. 2 February 1993.

Smith, W. Roy (state legislator). 15 September 1989.

Warner, Mrs. Jeane. 5 June 1991.

Weisend, Wendell H. "Wendy." 12 October 1990.

Wilhelm, Jane Gilmer. 2 November 1990.

Will, Erwin H. 23 March 1989.

Willey, Robert F. 30 January 1991.

Williams, Wyatt A. 13 March 1989.

Wilson, Coyt. 17 May 1989.

What follows is a list of sources—published books and essays and unpublished theses and dissertations—that are cited in this book or that supply further context for the history of higher education across the nation in general and in Virginia in particular. When these works are cited in our notes, only brief titles and authors' last names are used.

Allison, Clinton B. *Teachers for the South: Pedagogy and Educationists in the University of Tennessee, 1844-1995.* New York: Peter Lang, 1998.

Alvey, Edward Jr. *History of Mary Washington College, 1908-1972.* Charlottesville: University Press of Virginia, 1974.

Andrews, M. Carl. *No Higher Honor: The Story of Mills E. Godwin, Jr.* Richmond: Dietz Press, 1970.

Atkinson, Frank B. *The Dynamic Dominion: Realignment and the Rise of Virginia's Republican Party since 1945.* Fairfax VA: George Mason University Press, 1992.

Bartley, Numan V. *The New South, 1945-1980.* Baton Rouge: Louisiana State University Press, 1995.

Bettersworth, John K. *People's University: The Centennial History of Mississippi State.* Jackson: University Press of Mississippi, 1980.

Bishop, Morris. *A History of Cornell.* Ithaca: Cornell University Press, 1962.

Bounds, Stuart Murray. "Environmental and Political Correlates of Appropriations for Higher Education in Virginia, 1950-1972." Ed.D. dissertation, College of William and Mary, 1974.

Brickman, William W., and Stanley Lehrer, editors. *A Century of Higher Education: Classical Citadel to Collegiate Colossus.* Westport CT: Greenwood Press, 1962.

Brinkley, John Luster. *On This Hill: A Narrative History of Hampden-Sydney College, 1774-1994.* N.p., 1994.

Brint, Steven, and Jerome Karabel. *The Diverted Dream: Community Colleges and the Promise of Educational Opportunity in America, 1900-1985.* New York: Oxford University Press, 1989.

Brooks, Lyman Beecher. *Upward: A History of Norfolk State University, 1935-1975.* Washington DC: Howard University Press, 1983.

Calcott, George H. *A History of the University of Maryland.* Baltimore: Maryland Historical Society, 1966.

Carey, James C. *Kansas State University: The Quest for Identity.* Lawrence: Regents Press of Kansas, 1977.

Cato, William Hall. "The Development of Higher Education for Women in Virginia." Ph.D. dissertation, University of Virginia, 1941.

Chait, Richard Paul. "The Desegregation of Higher Education: A Legal History." Ph.D. dissertation, University of Wisconsin, 1972.

Clark, E. Culpepper. *The Schoolhouse Door: Segregation's Last Stand at the University of Alabama.* New York: Oxford University Press, 1993.

Cochran, John Perry. "The Virginia Agricultural and Mechanical College: The Formative Half Century, 1872-1919, of the Virginia Polytechnic Institute." Ph.D. dissertation, University of Alabama, 1961.

Cohill, Andrew Michael, and Andrea L. Kavanaugh, editors. *Community Networks: Lessons from Blacksburg, Virginia.* Boston: Artech House, 1997.

Cohodas, Nadine. *The Band Played Dixie: Race and the Liberal Conscience at Ole Miss.* New York: Free Press, 1997.

Colston, Chris. *Hokies Handbook: Stories, Stats and Stuff about Virginia Tech Football.* Wichita KS: Wichita Eagle and Beacon Publishing Co., 1996.

Cottrol, Robert J., Raymond T. Diamond, and Leland B. Ware. *Brown v. Board of Education: Caste, Culture, and the Constitution.* Lawrence: University Press of Kansas, 2003.

Couper, William. *One Hundred Years at V.M.I.* 4 volumes. Richmond: Garrett and Massie, 1939.

Cox, Clara B. *Generations of Women Leaders at Virginia Tech, 1921-1996.* Blacksburg VA: Virginia Polytechnic Institute and State University, 1996.

————. *Images and Reflections: Virginia Tech, 1872-1997.* Louisville: Harmony House, 1997.

————, editor. *A Special Place for 200 Years: A History of Blacksburg, Virginia.* Blacksburg VA: Town of Blacksburg, 1998.

Cremin, Lawrence A. *American Education: The Metropolitan Experience, 1876-1980.* New York: Harper and Row, 1988.

Cristo, Anthony Bandeira. "The Development of the Community College System in Virginia to 1972." Ph.D. dissertation, Duke University, 1973.

Cronin, David E., and John W. Jenkins. *The University of Wisconsin: Renewal to Revolution.* Madison: University of Wisconsin Press, 1999.

Cross, Coy F. II. *Justin Smith Morrill: Father of the Land-Grant Colleges.* East Lansing: Michigan State University Press, 1999.

Cummins, Cedric. *The University of South Dakota, 1862-1966.* Vermillion SD: Dakota Press, 1975.

Curry, Leonard P. *Blueprint for Modern America: Nonmilitary Legislation of the First Civil War Congress.* Nashville: Vanderbilt University Press, 1968.

Curti, Merle, and Vernon Carstensen. *The University of Wisconsin: A History, 1848-1925.* 2 volumes. Madison: University of Wisconsin Press, 1949.

Dabney, Virginius. *Mr. Jefferson's University*. Charlottesville: University Press of Virginia, 1981.

———. *Virginia Commonwealth University: A Sesquicentennial History*. Charlottesville: University Press of Virginia, 1987.

Deel, Anthony Blaine. "Virginia's Minimal Resistance: The Desegregation of Public Graduate and Professional Education, 1935-1955." M.A. thesis, Virginia Polytechnic Institute and State University, 1990.

Dennis, Michael. *Lessons in Progress: State Universities and Progressivism in the New South, 1880-1920*. Urbana: University of Illinois Press, 2001.

———. *Luther P. Jackson and a Life for Civil Rights*. Gainesville: University Press of Florida, 2004.

Dethloff, Henry C. *A Centennial History of Texas A&M University, 1876-1976*. 2 volumes. College Station: Texas A&M University Press, 1975.

Dingledine, Raymond C. Jr. *Madison College: The First Fifty Years, 1908-1958*. Harrisonburg VA: Madison College, 1959.

Doherty, William T. Jr., and Festus P. Summers. *West Virginia University: Symbol of Unity in a Sectionalized State*. Morgantown: West Virginia University Press, 1982.

Dober, Richard P. *Campus Architecture: Building in the Groves of Academe*. New York: McGraw-Hill, 1996.

Dorman, John Frederick. *The Prestons of Smithfield and Greenfield in Virginia*. Louisville: The Filson Club, 1982.

Doughty, Doug, and Roland Lazenby. *'Hoos 'n' Hokies—The Rivalry: 100 Years of Virginia/Virginia Tech Football*. Dallas: Taylor Publishing Company, 1995.

Doyle, William. *An American Insurrection: The Battle of Oxford, Mississippi, 1962*. New York: Doubleday, 2001.

Dunnavant, Keith. *Coach: The Life of Paul "Bear" Bryant*. New York: Simon and Schuster, 1996.

Dyer, Thomas G. *The University of Georgia: A Bicentennial History, 1785-1985*. Athens: University of Georgia Press, 1985.

Ehrlich, Thomas, with Juliet Frey. *The Courage to Inquire: Ideals and Realities in Higher Education*. Bloomington: Indiana University Press, 1995.

Ely, James W. Jr. *The Crisis of Conservative Virginia: The Byrd Organization and the Politics of Massive Resistance*. Knoxville: University of Tennessee Press, 1976.

Emerson, Bruce. "A History of the Relationships between the State of Virginia and Its Public Normal Schools, 1869-1930." Ed.D. dissertation, College of William and Mary, 1973.

Eschenbacher, Herman F. *The University of Rhode Island: A History of Land-Grant Education in Rhode Island.* New York: Appleton-Century-Crofts, 1967.

Faragher, John Mack, and Florence Howe, editors. *Women and Higher Education in American History.* New York: W. W. Norton, 1988.

Ferrell, Henry C. Jr. *Claude A. Swanson of Virginia: A Political Biography.* Lexington: University Press of Kentucky, 1985.

Fisher, Regina Bowles. "Coeducation at the University of Virginia, 1920-1940." M.A. thesis, University of Virginia, 1942.

Fite, Robert C. *A History of Oklahoma State University Extension and Outreach.* Stillwater: Oklahoma State University, 1988.

Fitzpatrick, Frank. *And the Walls Came Tumbling Down: Kentucky, Texas Western, and the Game That Changed American Sports.* New York: Simon and Schuster, 1999.

Freeland, Richard M. *Academia's Golden Age: Universities in Massachusetts, 1945-1970.* New York: Oxford University Press, 1992.

Geiger, Roger L. *Research and Relevant Knowledge: American Research Universities since World War II.* New York: Oxford University Press, 1993.

———. *To Advance Knowledge: The Growth of American Research Universities, 1900-1940.* New York: Oxford University Press, 1986.

———, David W. Potts, and W. Bruce Leslie. "Exploring Our Professional Backyards: Toward Writing Recent History of American Colleges and Universities." *History of Higher Education Annual* 20 (2000): 79-91.

Godson, Susan H., et al. *The College of William and Mary: A History.* 2 volumes. Williamsburg VA: King and Queen Press, 1993.

Godwin, Mills E. Jr. *Selected Speeches of the Honorable Mills E. Godwin, Jr., Governor of Virginia.* N.p., n.d.

Gordon, Lynn D. *Gender and Higher Education in the Progressive Era.* New Haven: Yale University Press, 1990.

Goree, Cathryn T. "Steps toward Redefinition: Coeducation at Mississippi State College, 1930-1945." Ph.D. dissertation, Mississippi State University, 1993.

Graham, Hugh Davis. *The Uncertain Triumph: Federal Education Policy in the Kennedy and Johnson Years.* Chapel Hill: University of North Carolina Press, 1984.

Gulley, F. Stuart. *The Academic President as Moral Leader: James T. Laney at Emory University, 1977-1993.* Macon GA: Mercer University Press, 2001.

Harlan, Louis R. *Separate and ·Unequal: Public School Campaigns and Racism in the Southern Seaboard States, 1901-1915.* Chapel Hill: University of North Carolina Press, 1958.

Harper, Laura Jane, and W. Carlene Howery. "History of Home Economics at V.P.I." Unpublished manuscript, 1985.

Heinemann, Ronald L. *Harry Byrd of Virginia.* Charlottesville: University Press of Virginia, 1996.

Hofstadter, Richard, and C. DeWitt Hardy. *The Development and Scope of Higher Education in the United States.* New York: Columbia University Press, 1952.

Hollis, Daniel Walker. *University of South Carolina.* 2 volumes. Columbia: University of South Carolina Press, 1951-1956.

Hopkins, James F. *The University of Kentucky: Origins and Early Years.* Lexington: University of Kentucky Press, 1951.

Horowitz, Helen Lefkowitz. *Campus Life: Undergraduate Cultures from the End of the Eighteenth Century to the Present.* New York: Alfred A. Knopf, 1987.

Hulse, James W. *The University of Nevada: A Centennial History.* Reno: University of Nevada Press, 1974.

Hyman, Harold M. *American Singularity: The 1787 Northwest Ordinance, the 1862 Homestead and Morrill Acts, and the 1944 G.I. Bill.* Athens: University of Georgia Press, 1986.

Jones, Nancy Bondurant. *Rooted on Blue Stone Hill: A History of James Madison University.* Charlottesville: University of Virginia Press, 2004.

Karman, Thomas A. *A History of the Oklahoma State University College of Education.* Stillwater: Oklahoma State University, 1989.

Kean, Melissa Fitzsimmons. "'At a Most Uncomfortable Speed': The Desegregation of the South's Private Universities, 1945-1964." Ph.D. dissertation, Rice University, 2000.

Kinnear, Duncan Lyle. *The First 100 Years: A History of Virginia Polytechnic Institute and State University*. Blacksburg VA: Virginia Polytechnic Institute Educational Foundation, 1972.

——. "A History of Agricultural Education in Virginia with Special Emphasis on the Secondary School Level." Ph.D. dissertation, Ohio State University, 1952.

Kluger, Richard. *Simple Justice: The History of Brown v. Board of Education and Black America's Struggle for Equality*. New York: Alfred A. Knopf, 1976.

Knoll, Robert E. *Prairie University: A History of the University of Nebraska*. Lincoln: University of Nebraska Press, 1995.

Kraft, Christopher C., with James L. Schefter. *Flight: My Life in Mission Control*. New York: Dutton, 2001.

Kuhn, Madison. *Michigan State: The First Hundred Years, 1855-1955*. East Lansing: Michigan State University Press, 1955.

Lassiter, Matthew D., and Andrew B. Lewis, editors. *The Moderates' Dilemma: Massive Resistance to School Desegregation in Virginia*. Charlottesville: University Press of Virginia, 1998.

Lesesne, Henry H. *A History of the University of South Carolina, 1940-2000*. Columbia: University of South Carolina Press, 2001.

Levine, Arthur, editor. *Higher Learning in America, 1980-2000*. Baltimore: Johns Hopkins University Press, 1993.

Lewis-Smith, Lanora Geissler. *Radford College: A Sentimental Chronicle through Its First Half-Century*. Radford VA, 1971.

Link, William A. *William Friday: Power, Purpose, and American Higher Education*. Chapel Hill: University of North Carolina Press, 1995.

Lockmiller, David A. *History of the North Carolina State College of Agriculture and Engineering of the University of North Carolina, 1889-1939*. Raleigh NC, 1939.

Lucas, Christopher J. *American Higher Education: A History*. New York: St. Martin's Press, 1994.

McCandless, Amy Thompson. *The Past in the Present: Women's Higher Education in the Twentieth-Century American South*. Tuscaloosa: University of Alabama Press, 1999.

McCaughey, Robert A. *Stand, Columbia: A History of Columbia University*. New York: Columbia University Press, 2003.

McCormick, Richard P. *Rutgers: A Bicentennial History.* New Brunswick NJ: Rutgers University Press, 1966.

McMath, Robert C. Jr., et al. *Engineering the New South: Georgia Tech, 1885-1985.* Athens: University of Georgia Press, 1985.

Manley, Robert N. *Centennial History of the University of Nebraska.* 2 volumes. Lincoln: University of Nebraska Press, 1969.

Martin, Tracy. "Black Education in Montgomery County, Virginia, 1939-1966." M.A. thesis, Virginia Polytechnic Institute and State University, 1996.

Miles, Saranette Denise. "A Fighter to the End: The Remarkable Life and Career of Laura Jane Harper." M.A. thesis, Virginia Polytechnic Institute and State University, 1999.

Miller, Mark F. *"Dear Old Roanoke": A Sesquicentennial Portrait, 1842-1992.* Macon GA: Mercer University Press, 1992.

Mohr, Clarence L., and Joseph E. Gordon. *Tulane: The Emergence of a Modern University, 1945-1980.* Baton Rouge: Louisiana State University Press, 2000.

Monroe, Doug. *The Maverick Spirit: Georgia-Pacific at 75.* Lyme CT: Greenwich Publishing Group, 2001.

Montgomery, James Riley, Stanley J. Folmsbee, and Lee Seifert Greene. *To Foster Knowledge: A History of the University of Tennessee, 1794-1970.* Knoxville: University of Tennessee Press, 1984.

National Association of State Universities and Land-Grant Colleges, *Serving the World: The People and Ideas of America's State and Land-Grant Universities.* Washington DC: National Association of State Universities and Land-Grant Colleges, 1987.

Nevins, Allan. *The State Universities and Democracy.* Urbana: University of Illinois Press, 1962.

Neyland, Leedell W. *Historically Black Land-Grant Institutions and the Development of Agriculture and Home Economics, 1890-1990.* Tallahassee: Florida A&M University Foundation, 1990.

————, and John W. Riley. *The History of Florida Agricultural and Mechanical University.* Gainesville: University of Florida Press, 1963.

Nieman, Donald G. *Promises to Keep: African-Americans and the Constitutional Order, 1776 to the Present.* New York: Oxford University Press, 1991.

Parker, William Belmont. *The Life and Public Services of Justin Smith Morrill.* Boston: Houghton Mifflin Company, 1924.

Patterson, James T. *Brown v. Board of Education: A Civil Rights Milestone and Its Troubled Legacy.* New York: Oxford University Press, 2001.

Patterson, Zella J. Black, with Lynette L. Wert. *Langston University: A History.* 2 volumes. Norman: University of Oklahoma Press, 1979.

Pezzoni, J. Daniel. "Our Native Stone: Architecture and Identity at Virginia Polytechnic Institute, 1872-1922." *Smithfield Review* 1 (1997): 37-52.

Pollard, James E. *History of the Ohio State University: The Story of the First Seventy-five Years, 1873-1948.* Columbus: Ohio State University Press, 1952.

Poulton, Bruce R. *North Carolina State University: The Quest for Excellence.* New York: Newcomen Society of the United States, 1987.

Pratt, Robert A. *We Shall Not Be Moved: The Desegregation of the University of Georgia.* Athens: University of Georgia Press, 2002.

Proctor, Samuel, and Wright Langley. *Gator History: A Pictorial History of the University of Florida.* Gainesville: South Star Publishing Co., 1986.

Rainsford, George N. *Congress and Higher Education in the Nineteenth Century.* Knoxville: University of Tennessee Press, 1972.

Robertson, Jenkins Mikell, compiler. *Historical Data Book: Centennial Edition.* Blacksburg VA: Virginia Polytechnic Institute and State University, 1972.

Roebuck, Julian B., and Komanduri S. Murty. *Historically Black Colleges and Universities: Their Place in American Higher Education.* Westport CT: Praeger, 1993.

Rosenblatt, Roger. *Coming Apart: A Memoir of the Harvard Wars of 1969.* Boston: Little, Brown, 1997.

Ross, Earle D. *Democracy's College: The Land-Grant Movement in the Formative Stage.* Ames: Iowa State College Press, 1942.

Rudolph, Frederick. *The American College and University: A History.* New York: Alfred A. Knopf, 1962.

Rulon, Philip Reed. *Oklahoma State University—since 1890.* Stillwater: Oklahoma State University Press, 1975.

Salmon, Emily J., and Edward D. C. Campbell Jr., editors. *The Hornbook of Virginia History.* 4th edition. Richmond: Library of Virginia, 1994.

Samuels, Albert L. *Is Separate Unequal? Black Colleges and the Challenge to Desegregation.* Lawrence: University Press of Kansas, 2004.

Sansing, David G. *Making Haste Slowly: The Troubled History of Higher Education in Mississippi*. Jackson: University Press of Mississippi, 1990.

Sawyer, William E. "The Evolution of the Morrill Act of 1862." Ph.D. dissertation, Boston University, 1948.

Scanlon, Edward James. *Randolph-Macon College: A Southern History, 1825-1967*. Charlottesville: University Press of Virginia, 1983.

Schrecker, Ellen W. *No Ivory Tower: McCarthyism and the Universities*. New York: Oxford University Press, 1986.

Shabazz, Amilcar. *Advancing Democracy: African Americans and the Struggle for Access and Equity in Higher Education in Texas*. Chapel Hill: University of North Carolina Press, 2004.

Smith, David C. *The First Century: A History of the University of Maine, 1865-1965*. Orono: University of Maine at Orono Press, 1979.

Smyth. Ellison A. *RetroSpect, or Growing up in Blacksburg and Other Tales through a Long Life*. Blacksburg VA: Pocahontas Press, 1993.

Sonner, Ray Vincent. "Madison College: The Miller Years, 1949-1970." Ed.D. dissertation, University of Virginia, 1974.

Stadtman, Verne A. *The University of California, 1868-1968*. New York: McGraw-Hill, 1970.

Stephens, Frank F. *A History of the University of Missouri*. Columbia: University of Missouri Press, 1962.

Sweeney, James R. *Old Dominion University: A Half Century of Service*. Norfolk VA: Old Dominion University, 1980.

Synnott, Marcia Graham. *The Half-Opened Door: Discrimination and Admissions at Harvard, Yale, and Princeton, 1900-1970*. Westport CT: Greenwood Press, 1979.

Temple, Harry Downing. *The Bugle's Echo: A Chronicle of Cadet Life, vol. 1, 1872-1900*. Blacksburg VA: Virginia Tech Corps of Cadets, 1996.

Tillar, Thomas C. Jr., editor. *Tech Triumph: A Pictorial History of Virginia Tech*. Blacksburg VA: Virginia Tech Alumni Association, 1984.

Toppin, Edgar. *Loyal Sons and Daughters: Virginia State University, 1882 to 1992*. Norfolk: Pictorial Heritage Publishing Company, 1992.

Topping, Robert W. *A Century and Beyond: The History of Purdue University*. West Lafayette IN: Purdue University Press, 1988.

Tushnet, Mark V. *The NAACP's Legal Strategy against Segregated Education, 1925-1950.* Chapel Hill: University of North Carolina Press, 1987.

Vaughan, George B. *The Community College in America: A Short History.* Washington DC: American Association of Community and Junior Colleges National Center for Higher Education, revised 1985.

———. *Pursuing the American Dream: A History of the Virginia Community College System.* Richmond: Virginia Community College System, 1987.

Veysey, Laurence R. *The Emergence of the American University.* Chicago: University of Chicago Press, 1965.

Wallenstein, Peter. "Black Southerners and Non-Black Universities: Desegregating Higher Education, 1935-1967." *History of Higher Education Annual* 19 (1999): 121-48.

———. *Blue Laws and Black Codes: Conflict, Courts, and Change in Twentieth-Century Virginia.* Charlottesville: University of Virginia Press, 2004.

———, compiler. *Essays on the History of Virginia Tech: Fall 1998.* Blacksburg VA: Virginia Tech, 1998.

———, compiler. *Essays on the History of Virginia Tech: The 125th Anniversary, Fall 1997.* Blacksburg VA: Virginia Tech, 1997.

———, compiler. *Essays on the History of Virginia Tech: The 125th Anniversary, Honors Colloquium, Spring 1998.* Blacksburg VA: Virginia Tech, 1998.

———. *From Slave South to New South: Public Policy in Nineteenth-Century Georgia.* Chapel Hill: University of North Carolina Press, 1987.

———. *Virginia Tech, Land-Grant University, 1872-1997: History of a School, a State, a Nation.* Blacksburg VA: Pocahontas Press, 1997.

Walsh, Mary Roth. *Doctors Wanted, No Women Need Apply: Sexual Barriers in the Medical Profession, 1835-1975.* New Haven: Yale University Press, 1977.

Webster, Sandy, editor. *I Remember Paul: A Collection of Letters from Alumni of Virginia Tech and Friends of Paul Derring.* Blacksburg VA: Young Men's Christian Association of Virginia Tech, 1993.

Wells, Thomas Learned. "The Legislative Consequences of Urban Growth: The Case of Virginia, 1966." Ph.D. dissertation, University of Virginia, 1968.

Whitehead, Kyle, and Brenda Whitehead. *Under the Hoop: 78 Years with the Hustlin' Hokies.* Blacksburg VA: K. Whitehead, 1986.

Wildes, Karl L., and Nilo A. Lindgren. *A Century of Electrical Engineering and Computer Science at MIT, 1882-1982.* Cambridge MA: MIT Press, 1985.

Wilkinson, J. Harvie III. *Harry Byrd and the Changing Face of Virginia Politics, 1945-1966.* Charlottesville: University Press of Virginia, 1968.

Wills, Brian Steel. *"A Greater Story": The History of the University of Virginia's College at Wise.* Charlottesville: University of Virginia Press, 2004.

Wise, Henry A. *Drawing out the Man: The VMI Story.* Charlottesville: University Press of Virginia, 1978.

Wynkoop, Mary Ann. *Dissent in the Heartland: The Sixties at Indiana University.* Bloomington: Indiana University Press, 2002.

Young, Harold N. *The Virginia Agricultural Experiment Station, 1886-1966.* Charlottesville: University Press of Virginia, 1975.

Index

Atomic Energy Commission, 12
Auburn University, 77, 245, 363

Babb, Winston C., 141
Babcock & Wilcox Inc., 50
baby boom, 9, 169
Bahamas, 212–214
Baldwin Piano Company, 104
Ballweg, John A., 380
Bank of Virginia, 201
Barber, James "J.B.," 315
Barnes, Edwin L., 296
Barringer Hall, 220, 222
Barringer, Paul B., 220, 223
baseball, 141, 313
basketball, 136–139, 147–148,
    317–324, 394
Bass, Marvin, 142
Bassett, J. Douglas, 141
Bates, John W. Jr., 277
Baumes, Harold I., 350, 353–354
Beagle, Ben, 31
Beamer, Frank M., 318, 385, 397
Beamer, Rufus, 75, 358
Bell, Wilson B.: and Hahn's inau-
    guration, 25; as dean of
    Agriculture, 75, 78, 157, 286,
    363; and athletics, 141, 142; as
    director of development, 266,
    272, 374
Bemiss, FitzGerald, 352
Bendheim, Leroy, 195
Benthal, Joseph, 380
Berry, Sandy, 323
Bethlehem Steel, 264
Betts, Ping, 277
Beyer, Gerhard, 92
Big East Conference, 318, 324, 397
Bird, Lloyd C., 121, 123, 124, 125
Bisplinghoff, Ray, 360

Black Alumni Reunion, 293
black athletes, pioneer, at VPI,
    147, 319, 314, 315, 317
Blackburn, Joseph E., 61, 121, 253
Blacksburg High School, 330–331,
    341–342, 373
black students, 129, 147, 292–296,
    378, 390, 397
Blackwell, Eli Whitney, 294
Blair, Streeter, 107, 399
Blake, Octave, 210
Blazer, Roy, 176
Blewett, William E., Jr., 47, 50,
    155, 158, 159
Bloss, F. Donald, 375
Bluefield College, 54
Blume, George, 380
Board of Visitors. *See* VPI Board
    of Visitors
Boatwright, John, 115
Bodell, Donald N., 245
Bollinger, Gilbert A., 91
Bonsack, Samuel E., 164
Boon, James F., 243
Boston, Mary Smedley (grand-
    mother), 6
Boushall, Thomas C., 201–202
Bowman, Raymond, 380
Boynton, Henry B., 227
Bradfield, Willard, 380
Bradley, Bill, 146
Bradley University, 85
branch colleges, 1, 17, 54, 66,
    124–127, 192, 196–198, 199,
    233, 294. *See also* community
    college system
Brandt, Esther, 28

Hahn, Thomas Marshall Jr., 42
(photo), 325 (photo), 326
(photo), 390 (photo), 404
(photo); and his family, 5–7,
19–20, 21 (photo), 28, 122, 149
(photo), 211–214; before VPI,
1–8; as physics department
head, 5, 8–14, 49; recruited to
the presidency of VPI, 14–16;
introduces VPI as a "university,"
23, 27; inauguration of, 25–28;
as art collector, 107, 399; travels
overseas, 212–214, 363, 365,
400; considers a run for the
governorship, 354–355; leaves
VPI for Georgia-Pacific, 393,
395–396
Hahn, Thomas Marshall Sr.
(father), 5, 6, 8, 122, 211–212
Hahn, William (son), 7, 21
(photo), 131 (photo)
Hahn Hall, 69 (photo), 396, 403
(photo)
Hairston, LaVerne "Freddie," 294
Haiti, 363
Hall, L. A., 102
Hall, Ogden H., 168
Hall, Otis, 286
Hall, Thomas H., III, 268, 272
Hall Report, 268–272, 274
Hamel, Dana B., 198, 205, 243
Hamrick, Joseph C., 115–116,
336–337, 339
Hammon, Charles G., Jr., 32
Hammond, Guy, 32, 178
Hamner, Doug, Jr., 335
Hampton University, 11, 129, 294
Hancock, John W., 47, 69 (photo),
106, 141, 374, 400; and the
BOV, 31, 41, 68 (photo); and

the 1964 Corps decision,
155–156, 158, 160, 163, 168;
and Hahn's getaways, 209–210,
213, 214
Hardcastle, Jane, 208
Harder, Martha, 181
Haroldson, W. C., 363
Harper Hall, 55
Harper, Laura Jane, 29, 54–55,
176, 210, 227, 233
Harper, Marguerite, 294–296, 385
Harrar, George J., 30, 122
Harris, Charles, 102, 277
Harrison, Albertis S., Jr., 17, 18,
19, 32, 34, 46–47, 60, 61–62,
115, 156, 158, 161, 189, 211,
331, 336, 338; becomes gover-
nor, 16; at VPI, 26, 28, 145–146;
and VPI finances, 64–65, 82,
115–116, 119, 190–191,
194–196
Harrison, William B., 245, 257
Hatch Act of 1887, 11
Hatcher, T. W. "Inky," 77
Harvard University, 19, 81, 104
Havard, William C., Jr., 374
Hawkins, G. B. "Bill," 99
Hawkins, J. G., 277
Hawthorne, Sandy, 299
Hayes, Brooke, 176
Hazelgrove, W. P., 141
Heath, Roger, 309
Heckel, Maynard C., 286
Henrickson, Bonnie, 324
Henson, Les, 321
Hercules Power Corporation, 342
Hereford, Karl T., 356, 358, 368
Heterick, Robert C., 247–248
Heth, Henry, 333
Hethwood, 334

Rich, John B., 209
Richard Bland College, 205
Richardson, Elliot, 374
Richmond, John D., 123
Richmond, Fredericksburg, and
    Potomac (RF&P) Railroad, 47,
    157, 165
Richmond Kiwanis Club, 32
Richmond Professional Institute,
    26, 127–128, 188
Richmond Times-Dispatch, 32,
    302, 352
Rider College, 109
Rigney, M. Garland, 163, 184, 290
Ritchie, R. R., 142
Roanoke Electric Steel, 47, 106
Roanoke Junior League, 32
Roanoke Memorial Hospital, 24
Roanoke Technical Institute, 47,
    66, 67, 123–124, 127
Roanoke Times, 31, 162
Robertson, A. Willis, 24
Robertson, James I., Jr., 35, 89,
    374, 382
Robertson, Jenkins Mikell, 98,
    240, 263
Robeson Hall, 12, 37, 221
Robeson, Frank L. "Scribe," 5, 37,
    221
Robinson, Edwin S., 91
Rockefeller Foundation, 30, 122,
    295–296, 380
Rogers, Phil, 315, 394
Roosevelt, Theodore, 37
Ross, Bruce, 241–242, 257, 266,
    349, 376
ROTC, 30, 152, 156, 159, 160, 162,
    164, 165, 308, 379
Row, Stuart, 257

Rowe, C. Eugene, 110 (photo),
    400; biography of, 104; and the
    Alumni Association, 26, 100,
    103, 104, 108, 159, 174, 241,
    262–266; and the YMCA, 104,
    178; as BOV rector, 386, 390
    (photo), 393, 401 (photo)
Rowe, Mary Lewis, 104, 264–265
Rudder, James Earl, 171
Ruffner, William H., 400
Ruffner Medal, 157, 275, 396, 400
Russell, George E. "Buddy," 246
Russell, John Dale, 123–124, 125,
    202
Russell, Robert E., 122
Rutgers University, 380
Rutland, Leon W., 77–78, 79, 90
Ryland, Walter, 300

sales tax, 34, 123, 188–190, 198,
    202, 397
Sanders, Paul D., 46, 114
Saunders, Stuart, 105, 141
Saunders Hall, 218
Saunier, Paul, Jr., 194
Savage, Lon K., 32, 89, 123, 178,
    206, 210, 266, 334, 349, 376, 386
Scales, Ricky, 316
Schewe, M. W., 162, 164, 165, 168,
    170–171, 178286
School of Architecture, 55
School of Home Economics, 55
Schriver & Holland, 227
Schuck, Carol, 115
Schweickert, Bob, 136, 139–140,
    143
Scott, John E., Jr., 102
Scott, Marguerite Harper,
    294–296, 385
Sebo, Steve, 142

Umbarger, Joseph H., 59
University Choir, 384
University Council, 166, 182, 281–282, 298, 299, 349
university development, 95–109, 261–277
University Honors, 219
University of Alabama, 181
University of Arkansas, 77
University of California, 85, 91, 297
University of Chicago, 5, 123
University of Colorado, 78, 82
University of Connecticut, 291
University of Georgia, 293, 359
University of Illinois, 29, 55
University of Kansas, 96
University of Kentucky, 2, 3, 5, 6, 8, 123, 134, 356, 396, 402 (photo)
University of Maryland, 74–75
University of Michigan, 96
University of Missouri, 92, 180
University of Montana, 89
University of Nebraska, 179, 180, 284
University of New Hampshire, 86
University of North Carolina, 85
University of Pittsburgh, 175
University of South Carolina, 15, 16, 20, 36, 137, 382
University of South Florida, 85, 88
University of Tennessee, 1, 55, 75, 181, 380, 394
University of Utah, 91
University of Virginia, 10, 11, 102, 111, 129, 194, 277, 350, 366; and VARC, 17, 18, 61–62; and SCHEV, 51–52, 61–62; and

branch or community colleges, 51–52, 124–125, 196–198, 202; and student unrest, 297, 301; and football rivalry with VPI, 317
University of Wisconsin, 86, 363, 380
University Orchestra, 384
Upper Quad, 36, 162, 172, 173
Urban College of Boston, 294
Urey, Harold C., 362
US Agency for International Development (USAID, 284, 363–364
US Army, 122, 156, 165, 275
US Census Bureau, 294
US Coast Guard, 211
US Communicable Disease Control Center, 86
US Department of Agriculture, 53
US Department of Defense, 308
US Department of Health Education and Welfare, 356, 374
US Naval Academy, 6
US Navy, 6, 7, 29, 109, 209
US Steel, 267
US Supreme Court, 189
Utz, Silas Alex "Sonny," 139–140

Vandenberg, H. P. C., 243
Vanderbilt University, 104
Van Doren, Mark, 107
Vawter, Charles E., 220, 222, 223
Vawter Hall, 220, 222
Venegas, Carmen, 208
Veneman, John G., 374
Vick, Michael, 318
Vietnam War, 122, 162–163, 297–299
Virginia Academy of Science, 32

Virginia Agricultural and
Mechanical College, 11, 377
Virginia Associated Research
Center (VARC), 17, 18, 61–62
Virginia Association of
Broadcasters, 199
Virginia Association of Colleges,
26
Virginia Association of Soil
Conservation Districts, 32
Virginia Commonwealth
University, 77, 128, 188, 257,
366
Virginia Electric and Power
Company, 46, 50
Virginia Farm Bureau Federation,
301
Virginia General Assembly. *See*
General Assembly
Virginia Higher Education Study
Commission, 121, 126–130, 131
Virginia-Maryland Regional
College of Veterinary Medicine,
87, 358–360, 397
Virginia Military Institute, 11,
129, 162; and basketball games
with VPI, 138; and
Thanksgiving Day football
games with VPI, 136, 139, 144,
316–317
Virginian Railroad, 64
Virginia Outdoors Foundation,
398
Virginia Polytechnic Institute:
name of, 377; reorganization of,
in 1944, 113
Virginia Polytechnic Institute and
State University: name of,
376–377; centennial, 95,
371–376, 386–389, 391

Virginia Poultry Federation, 32
Virginia State University, 123, 128,
129, 205, 292, 311, 377
Virginia Tech Alumni Association,
26, 33, 35, 46, 47, 96, 97–99,
101, 108, 157, 159, 261–277,
375; women's chapter, 268, 271
Virginia Tech Athletic Association,
134, 135, 147
Virginia Tech Foundation, 9, 47,
82, 95, 100, 104, 106, 207–209,
335, 374, 398
Visiting Scholars Program, 107
VPI Airport, 105, 207–209
VPI Board of Visitors, 9, 25,
56–57, 95, 193, 282, 359, 375,
393–395; selects Hahn as president, 14–15, 22; Hahn's
relations with, 45–51; membership on, 31, 46–47, 66–67, 68
(photo), 275, 390 (photo), 401
(photo), 407–408 (list); and the
Corps of Cadets, 153–162
VPI Development Council,
263–264, 266
VPI Educational Foundation. *See*
Virginia Tech Foundation
VPI Historical Data Book, 263
VPI Self-Study (1965–1966), 204,
244, 246, 279, 282

Wake Forest University, 142
Wall Street Journal, 339–340
Wallace, Maude E., 229
Wallace Hall, 119, 224, 228–229
Wampler, Charles W. Jr., 68
(photo), 155, 159
War Memorial, 157, 178, 252, 275,
297
Ware, Ted, 147

Warm Hearth Retirement
Community, 284
Warner, Spurgeon "Pop," 123, 142,
209, 210
Warriner, Dortch, 195–196
Washington State University, 246
Waters, Herbert J., 364, 369
Watkins, James D., 292–294
Weaver, Edgar N., 212
Weaver, H. A. "Hobie," 267
Weaver, James H., 142
Webb, James, 360
Weeks, Joe, 120
Wesley Foundation, 177, 383
Westermann, Harland, 287
Western Electric, 267
Westinghouse, 180, 241
West Virginia University, 30
Wetzel, John, 147, 323
White, Cindy, 322
Whitehurst, James L., Jr., 390
(photo)
Whittemore, John W., 54, 81,
82–83, 228, 372
Whittemore Hall, 228
Wieczynski, Joseph L., 382
Wilhelm, Jane, 22, 46, 50, 68
(photo), 114, 155, 168
Wilkerson, Woodrow W., 46–47,
123, 155, 197
Wilkins, Tracy D., 86
Will, Erwin H., 46, 50, 51, 68
(photo), 116, 155, 159, 163, 164
Willey, Edward E., 365
Willey, Robert F., 263, 264, 266
Williams, John E., 36, 221
Williams, Lloyd W., 221
Williams, Wyatt A., 34; on the
BOV, 31, 46, 49, 68 (photo),
113–114, 155–156, 168; and the

1964 Corps decision, 155–156,
163, 164, 166, 168
William Preston Society, 51
Williams Hall, 36, 221; 1970 student takeover of, 299–306, 311
(photo), 399
Williamson, G. G., 382
Willis, Gordon, 141
Wilson, Coyt T., 245, 257, 279
Wilson, John D., 257
Wine, William E., 37, 223
Wine Awards, 37
Wingard, S. A., 26, 92
Winter, Tex, 139
women students: at VPI, 59,
66–67, 112–115, 169, 183–184,
289, 292–196, 364, 374, 378,
397; and the Corps of Cadets,
308–311; and intercollegiate
athletics, 314, 320–324, 394; at
other Virginia institutions, 129;
at other southern white land-
grant schools, 171. *See also*
Radford University
Women's Student Union, 184
Wong, Young-tsu, 382
Woods Hole Institute, 91
Worcester, Willis G., 82, 168, 286
Works Progress Administration
(WPA), 208
World War I, 173, 221
World War II, 6, 9, 109, 151, 156,
167, 175, 208, 221
Worthington, Hugh, 36
Wright, John, 380
WUVT, 290, 300